Viticulture

VOLUME 1 RESOURCES

Viticulture

VOLUME I RESOURCES

edited by

B.G. Coombe and P.R. Dry

contributing authors

A.J. Antcliff, R.M. Cirami, B.G. Coombe, P.R. Dry, G.R. Gregory,

W.J. Hardie, D.I. Jackson, M.G. McCarthy, K.H. Northcote,

R.E. Smart, M.B. Spurling

WINETITLES

ADELAIDE

First published in 1988
Reprinted 1990 with corrections
Reprinted 1992 with alterations
Reprinted 1995
Reprinted 1997
Reprinted 1998

Winetitles
2 Wilford Avenue, Underdale SA 5032

National Library of Australia
Cataloguing-in-Publication data

Viticulture. Volume 1, Resources

Bibliography.
Includes index.
ISBN 1 875130 00 4.
ISBN 1 875130 02 2 (set).

1. Viticulture — Australia. 2. Grapes — Australia.
I. Coombe, B.G. (Bryan George). II. Dry, P.R.
III. Title: Resources in Australia.

635 .8 0994

Volume 2 — Practices
ISBN 1 875 130 01 2

Wholly produced in Adelaide, South Australia
Designed by Michael Deves
Typeset in Perpetua
Printed and bound by Finsbury Press, Adelaide

Contents

This book is dedicated to the memory of
ALLAN JAMES ANTCLIFF
viticulturist and progenitor of grape breeding in Australia

ACKNOWLEDGEMENTS

Many people have made important contributions to the writing of this book. The authors and publishers would like to gratefully acknowledge those who have helped in writing, reading and advising on the early drafts of chapters; their advice has helped to make this text more accurate and relevant.

Many people have contributed to individual chapters and the authors of these chapters would like to acknowledge these specific contributions:

Brenton Baker, Clarrie Beckingham, Wally Boehm, David Bruer, Greg Buchanan, K.R. Burrows, Phil Cole, Leona Coleman, Tony Devitt, Graham Due, John Elliot, J. Flehr, Brian Freeman, Jim Furkaliev, Andrew Geyle, Peter Gherardi, John Gladstones, Geoff Godden, Olga Goss, Richard Hamilton, G. Hardie, Professor Jerry Hatfield, Peter Hayes, Peter Hedberg, S. Henshell, Albert Heslop, David Hodge, George Kerridge, Professor Lloyd Lider, Peter May, Graham McIntyre, Geoff McLean, David Moss, Phillip Nicholas, Vic Patrick, Fred Peacock, Andrew Pirie, Professor J.A. Prescott, Ivan Roberts, Max Sauer, Peter Scholefield, Ken Semmler, Russell Soderland, Mike Stannard, Graham Stirling, David Symon, Ron Webber, John Whiting, C. Winks, Ross Wishart, Doris Zuur.

Thanks are also due to those authors of this present volume who, in addition to the writing of their own chapters, have served in the refereeing of other chapters.

The publishers also would like to acknowledge the financial support provided for the publication of this book by the following bodies:

The Australian Wine Board
The Australian Grape and Wine Research Council
The Australian Wine and Brandy Corporation
The Australian Society of Viticulture and Oenology

AUTHORS' AFFILIATIONS

The late Dr A.J. Antcliff, CSIRO Division of Horticulture, Merbein Vic. 3505
R.M. Cirami, SA Dept of Agric., Nuriootpa Research Centre, Nuriootpa SA 5355
Dr B.G. Coombe, Waite Agric. Res. Institute, University of Adelaide, Glen Osmond SA 5064
P.R. Dry, Roseworthy Agricultural College, Roseworthy SA 5371
G.R. Gregory, NSW Dept of Agriculture, McKell Building, Haymarket NSW 2000
W.J. Hardie, Milawa Vineyards Pty Ltd, Milawa Vic. 3678
D.I. Jackson, Lincoln College, Canterbury, New Zealand
M.G. McCarthy, SA Dept of Agric., Nuriootpa Research Centre, Nuriootpa SA 5355
Dr K.H. Northcote, CSIRO Division of Soils, Waite Road, Urrbrae SA 5064
Dr R.E. Smart, MAFTech Ruakura Agriculture Centre, Hamilton, New Zealand
M.B. Spurling, Roseworthy Agricultural College, Roseworthy SA 5371

FOREWORD

This book had its genesis in the mid-1970s with a proposal to the Australian Wine Board by Mr Colin Gramp. A publication committee was appointed and editors and authors were selected to write a comprehensive reference book on Australian viticulture. The Wine Board bore the cost of typing and preliminary production details. The original authors invested considerable time and effort in their task and are to be thanked for their contributions. However, the project as originally envisaged proved to be too large and unwieldy, and eventually came to a halt. As a consequence some of the material originally planned for the book has not been used and much of it has now been rewritten.

The project was renewed by the newly-formed Australian Society of Viticulture and Oenology, leading to a grant to T.H. Lee and B.G. Coombe from the Australian Grape and Wine Research Council made in June 1987 to see that the book was published. A new format was developed: the sections on grapevine biology were deleted, due to the recent publication of works on these topics, and the remaining material was divided into two volumes, the first on Resources dealing with those matters that concern pre-planting decisions, and the second on Practices, concerning all aspects of establishing and operating a vineyard. Related aspects that are the province of specialists away from the vineyard — grape breeding, tissue culture propagation and economic surveying — are excluded, as is post-harvest handling, which is not normally the concern of the independent grapegrower; these exclusions embrace such matters as must and raisin handling, although tablegrape preparation for the market is included because the grower usually does the work.

The two volumes are intended to help those who are seeking information on the how and the why as well as the what. Despite the large volume of literature that has been published during the last two decades, there are many subjects that have not been collated before, and these have been heavily referenced. In addition, considerable attention has been given to the choice and spelling of words in the hope of providing a unifying influence. This applies particularly to the naming of varieties, which has become considerably confused during the two centuries of grapegrowing in this country; the decisions are seen in Table 6.2 (pages 122-3). The word 'variety' has been chosen rather than the more correct word 'cultivar' because of its significance to this industry. The common usage of the phrase 'red varieties', meaning those that make red wine, has been accepted; on this basis 'red varieties' may have black berries.

Viticulture in Australia is innovative and largely unconstrained by legislative controls. Many new methods have been developed and adopted, most of them motivated towards the lowering of the cost of production to cope with low grape prices, by the reduction of the costs of specific operations and by the cost-benefit effects of increased yield; this latter trend has focussed attention on the vexed question of balance between yield and grape quality. Another significant recent change is the large planting of winegrapes in scattered regions in the cooler areas of Australia. These changes are bringing with them many new problems that require solutions based on principles. It is our hope that these volumes will help people to find answers.

We thank Dr Terry Lee for his enthusiastic encouragement and help in the production of these volumes.

BRYAN COOMBE and PETER DRY
Adelaide

CHAPTER ONE

Development and Status of Australian Viticulture

G. R. GREGORY

1.1 The beginnings

1.1.1 The first vines

The genesis of Australian viticulture coincided with settlement in 1788, grape cuttings and seeds collected at Rio de Janiero and the Cape of Good Hope having been brought in with the First Fleet and successfully established at Farm Cove, the site of the present Sydney Royal Botanic Gardens. By 1791 Governor Phillip had established three acres [1.2 ha] of grapes 19 km to the west of Sydney on the Parramatta River under more favourable conditions; a settler named Phillip Schaeffer became Australia's first private vigneron, having planted one acre [0.4 ha] of vines by that time (Laffer 1949).

However, up until the early 1800s, the importation and cultivation of the vine was largely an affair of the Government, which attempted to encourage the establishment of vines despite frequent references to the debilitating effects of 'blight' in the early records. In all probability this was caused by the disease known as 'anthracnose' or 'black spot' caused by the fungus, *Elsinoe ampelina*. In an attempt to foster the fledgling industry, the Duke of Norfolk in 1801 sent out two Frenchmen who appeared 'to have a perfect knowledge of the cultivation of a vineyard and the whole process of winemaking'. They were Antoine Landrier and Francois de Riveau, who were originally prisoners of war held at Portsmouth. Their attempts to establish vineyards were thwarted by 'blight' and in 1804 Governor King reported that 'the Frenchmen knew but little of the business, and that he was sending one home' (Maiden 1917).

Two leading pioneers of vine culture in the new colony also became famous in other spheres. The first was Gregory Blaxland, who with Wentworth and Lawson first crossed the Blue Mountains to the west of Sydney in 1813, thereby providing the gateway to vast areas of rich agricultural land on the slopes and plains beyond. The second was Captain John Macarthur, the accepted founder of the Australian wool industry. Macarthur, along with the Reverend Samuel Marsden, purchased, on their arrival in 1879, the first Spanish Merino sheep brought to Australia by a Captain Waterhouse who had acquired them in South Africa.

Gregory Blaxland planted a vineyard on his 'Brush Farm' property in the Parramatta Valley (near the present suburb of Eastwood) with vines he had introduced from the Cape of Good Hope between 1816 and 1818. He made history by shipping a quarter of a pipe of fortified red wine to London in 1822, for which he gained a Silver Medal from the Society for the Encouragement of Arts, Manufactures and Commerce which had originally offered a gold medal 'for the finest wine, not less than 20 gallons [90 litres], of good marketable quality, made from the produce of vineyards in New South Wales'. Awards were also received for subsequent shipments, notably a gold medal for a pipe of wine produced on his vineyard in 1827.

John Macarthur, coming to Australia in 1790, was amongst the earliest settlers. One of the first references to grapes in the official records came from his wife, Mrs Elizabeth Macarthur, when on 18 March 1791 she wrote from Sydney:

The grape thrives remarkably well. The Governor sent me some bunches this season, as fine as any I ever tasted, and there is little doubt but in a very few years there will be plenty. (Maiden 1917)

Because of a dispute with Governor William Bligh, Macarthur went back to Britain in 1809 but returned with his sons James and William in 1817, after spending 18 months in France and Switzerland collecting vines and information on viticulture.

In a lecture on 'Colonial Vine Culture' by Alan H. Burgoyne, M.P., a well-known merchant in Australian wines, published in the *Journal of the Royal Society of Arts,* of 24 May 1912, he says:

It would seem that in the years 1815-16, at the termination of the Napoleonic campaign, subsequent to the battle of Waterloo, one Captain John Macarthur with his two sons, journeyed on foot from district to district of those parts of Europe whence vines had already come, and where the culture of the vine was the chief feature

of the countryside. This journey must have been indeed adventurous, since every high road was infested with footpads and camp followers—those bad characters and human outcasts always so common during and after a long international war.

The result of this extended tramp was a bundle of vine cuttings representative of each district visited. These were taken with not a little jubilation back to the Antipodes, and at once efforts were made to propagate them. These cuttings were found, however, after cultivation until fruit-bearing, to the great dismay of those who had collected them with so much trouble, to be in almost every case worthless. (Maiden 1917)

The Macarthurs planted their first vineyard at Camden Park in 1820 and became Australia's first commercial winemakers. Some texts record that later they planted another near Penrith, but it seems more likely that this was also located at Camden Park on the flats adjoining the Nepean River. By 1827 it is recorded that the Macarthur's vintage amounted to 90,000 litres (Ilbery 1984).

By 1830, interest in grape production began to gather momentum. It was in this year that James Busby, published *A Manual of Plain Directions for Planting and Cultivating Vineyards, and For Making Wine in New South Wales,* his second book on viticulture but the first that incorporated first-hand experience with grape culture in Australia. Busby, at the age of 24 years, came to the Colony from Scotland with his father in 1824. Soon after his arrival he was employed by the Government to teach viticulture at a male orphanage at Cabramatta, with a view to the general cultivation of the vine in the colony. His father, John Busby, a mineral surveyor and civil engineer, was appointed to supervise coal mining at Newcastle, thus establishing the Hunter Valley connection with the grape.

In 1831 Busby returned to Europe when he travelled to Spain and France to study viticulture and collect grape cuttings. In a letter to Mr C. Fraser, the Colonial Botanist for New South Wales, of 24 January 1832 he writes:

After having been only seven weeks in London I embarked for Cadiz, spent some time at the Xeres-de-la-Frontera, where I learned the whole art and mystery of making sherry wine, and thence across the country to Malaga, where they make the fine muscatelle raisins. If the particular kind of grape from which these are made succeeds in New South Wales, it will certainly be one of the most important things that has yet been tried in the colony.

— a prophetic statement taking into account the

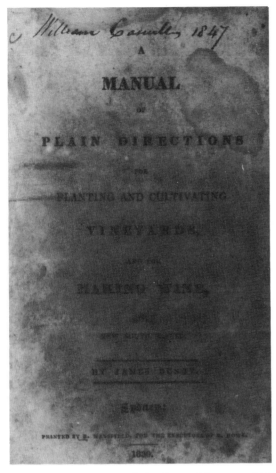

Figure 1.1. The cover of the first publication which incorporated first-hand experience with grape cultivars in Australia; James Busby's 1830 Manual.

present significance of the Australian dried vine fruit industry. In the same letter Busby goes on to relate:

From Malaga I proceeded by sea to the north of Spain, after having engaged two cases of vines cultivated at Xeres, and two of those cultivated at Malaga, to be sent to London as soon as the season would allow of their being sent. I commenced my researches in France at the foot of the Pyrenees, and proceeded by Perpignan. Montpellier, Marceilles (sic), and to the district where they make the French raisins, thence through the Hermitage, Burgundy, and Champaigne (sic) districts to Paris, where I remained only eight days. I was altogether about four months absent, and I can now say that including my journey to the Bordeaux in 1822, I have visited almost every wine district of any celebrity in France.

I have been careful to collect cuttings of every variety which I found cultivated, and have got to the number of from sixty to seventy. But independently of these I have also made what I call a nursery collection, viz,: Two cuttings each of 550 varieties (437 of them are the gift of Mr Delile, of Montpellier, the remainder I purchased from the Royal Nursery of the Luxemburg at Paris).

I have tendered this collection to the Secretary of State, for the purpose of founding an experimental garden under your direction. The offer has been accepted, and I believe the Governor will receive a despatch upon the subject by the same ship which conveys this letter. (Maiden 1917)

The Mr Delile referred to in this letter was the Director of the Botanic Gardens of Montpellier.

Ilbery (1984) records that 'his collection (of which there are various estimates of the number) comprised 433 from the Botanic Gardens, Montpellier, 110 from the Luxemburg Gardens, 44 from Sion House near Kew Gardens in England and 91 from other parts of Spain and France.'

The majority of the cuttings collected by Busby were duly shipped to Sydney by the convict ship *Lady Harewood* in early 1832. This lot was packed in closed cases of damp moss, lined round the sides with damp-proof paper, under the supervision of Richard Cunningham who later in that year was appointed as Colonial Botanist for New South Wales to replace Mr Fraser, who died in December 1831.

Some of the Spanish varieties, together with some duplicates from the French collections, did not reach London in time for the first shipment. They were established in soil in open cases and shipped later by the *Camden* (Laffer 1949).

The cuttings arrived 'in a good state of preservation' and were planted at the Sydney Botanic Gardens. Official records state that of the 650 varieties received '362 varieties were alive and for the most part healthy' as at January 1833.

A James Backhouse reported in 1836 that he was a member of a committee, which included William Macarthur, that was appointed to test Busby's vines. The best were distributed at various times, many to Camden and the 'Kirkton' property in the Hunter Valley which was an 800 hectare land grant made to Busby's father in 1824. Cuttings were also sent to establish a representative collection in the Adelaide Botanic Gardens whence thousands of cuttings were spread throughout South Australia.

The original collection was ultimately lost through neglect. J.H. Maiden, a former Government Botanist and Director, Botanic Gardens, Sydney relates that a gardener there, Mr L. Wooff, told him in 1898 that 'one of the first jobs he did was to pull down the wooden trellises and root out the Busby grape vines'. This was in August 1857.

Busby returned to New South Wales briefly

Rowland Flat (SA), c.1890, showing G. Gramp & Sons' Orlando winery and surrounding vineyards.

before departing to New Zealand in 1833 to take up the position of British Resident. It has been stated that Busby's role in the development of Australian viticulture may have been overstated. It is clear, however, that his influence was profound in that he secured for the infant industry a diverse genetic base which remained substantially unaltered for the next 130 years.

The first commercial vineyards in the Hunter Valley began to emerge in 1830 with vines planted in that year by George Wyndham at 'Dalwood' near Branxton and at 'Kirkton' near Belford, between Branxton and Singleton by William Kelman, Busby's brother-in-law, at that time manager of the property.

In Victoria, Edward Henty took cuttings to Portland in 1834 (the year that State became a separate entity), but there is no further record of Henty or the fate of the cuttings. The initial planting in the Yarra Valley was made in 1838 by William Ryrie at Yering, and by 1848 the area of grapes in the district had increased to 40 hectares (Laffer 1949).

In South Australia grapes were planted soon after settlement of the colony in 1836, much of the early development taking place close to the centre of

Adelaide, at Reynella and in the Southern Vales district. The first vines were planted by John Barton Hack in North Adelaide in 1837 with material obtained from Launceston. However, credit for the first to make wine in South Australia remains disputed, the claimants being John Reynell, Richard Hamilton and a Walter Duffield who shipped a case of 1844 white wine made in the Mount Lofty Ranges to Queen Victoria in 1845 (Ilbery 1984).

Although the Barossa Valley was explored in 1837 by Colonel William Light and German immigrants began to settle there in 1842, it took until 1847 for the first vines to be planted in the district by Johann Gramp at Jacobs Creek, 2 km from the present Orlando winery. A little further to the north in the Clare-Watervale district, the Sevenhills vineyard was planted by Austrian Jesuit fathers in 1848 (Ilbery 1984). It is interesting to recall that the German connection with Australian viticulture was first established by William Macarthur, who brought out several German vignerons as colonists in 1839, and there is evidence of several German 'vinedressers' at Camden Park as early as 1832.

In Western Australia it seems that credit for the first vine plantings there should go to Thomas Waters

Figure 1.3. Panorama of the Hunter Valley district, February 1923, with Lindeman's 'Ben Ean' vineyard and winery in the foreground; a scene not too different from the way it appears today.

of 'Olive Farm' who arrived in September 1829, soon after the colony came into being on 18 June of that year. Waters was a botanist who brought with him a collection of plants and seeds from South Africa, together with a knowledge of winemaking that he had acquired from the Boers. He was granted a property on the Swan River soon after arrival. Records indicate that by 1834 he had one-fifth of a hectare of vines planted and in a letter of 1842 he noted that he used wine made at 'Olive Farm' to barter for other goods. Captain John S. Roe came to Western Australia in June 1829 and became the colony's first Surveyor General. He was granted in 1840 the 'Sandalford' property, also in the Swan Valley, where he planted table grapes and currants (Ilbery 1984).

Although attempts to establish a viticultural industry in Tasmania were thwarted by the cool climate and disease, it is interesting to note that grapes for wine were grown successfully there by Bartholomew Broughton at his 'Prospect Farm' as early as the 1820s. Also in the 1840s Dr Matthias Gaunt of Windermere, East Tamar, was making wine from grapes grown on his property (Ilbery 1984).

In Queensland there has been a small viticultural industry since the state's separation from New South Wales in the 1850s. The first vines in the Stanthorpe area were recorded near Ballandean in 1859. Further to the north at Roma, grapes were planted by the Cornishman, Samuel S. Basset, in 1863. The vineyard is still in existence and remained in the ownership of the Basset family until the 1970s.

From the outset vineyard expansion was most rapid in South Australia, no doubt reflecting the compatibility of *Vitis vinifera* to the Mediterranean climate which prevails there. In 1860-61, 1287 hectares had been established in this State as against 641 in NSW and 460 in Victoria (Table 1.1). However, it was as late as 1890 that the renowned table wine region of Coonawarra in the South-east of South Australia was established, when John Riddoch made land available for closer settlement through his Penola Fruit Colony scheme.

1.1.2 Expansion in Victoria, then phylloxera

From the mid-1870s viticultural progress in South Australia, which is the main wine-producing State, was for a period overshadowed by development at

Table 1.1. Growth of vineyards in Australia (hectares)

Year	NSW	Vic.	Qld	SA	WA	Tas	Total
1860-61	641	461	NA	1,286	136	NA	2,524
1880-81	1,942	2,015	299	1,755	267	NA	6,279
1900-01	3,416	12,397	817	8,158	1,346	NA	26,133
1920-21	4,364	11,839	508	14,836	1,299	NA	32,846
1940-41	6,668	17,498	1,175	23,640	3,577	NA	52,560
1960-61	6,875	18,069	1,259	23,025	3,587	NA	52,815
1970-71	11,247	20,612	1,556	27,653	2,715	NA	63,783
1980-81	14,257	20,756	NA	30,417	2,446	NA	69,518[a]
*1985-86	12,621	19,651	1,205	24,523	1,743	91	59,839[b]
*1986-87	12,169	18,955	1,153	23,103	1,705	96	57,273[b]

NA   Not available.
(a)   Total includes Queensland, Tasmania and the Territories.
(b)   Total includes the Territories.

* For the first time in 1986/87, the scope of the census is agricultural establishments undertaking agricultural activity having an estimated value of agricultural operations (EVAO) of $20,000 or more. Figures for 1985-86 shown in the Table have been retabulated to this new census scope. Previously the EVAO was $2,500. Comparisons in 1985-86 between the two EVAO levels show that for total grape area the EVAO of $20,000 represented 93.9% of area for EVAO of $2,500.

Source: Australian Bureau of Statistics

Rutherglen in north-eastern Victoria, where vines were first planted in 1851 by Lindsay Brown, one year after the discovery of gold in the district.

Natural growth in Victoria was boosted in 1889 by a Government bonus of £2 for every acre of vines planted and by the time of Federation in 1901 the State could boast a total of 12,397 hectares. The dominant position of Rutherglen in a viticultural sense was terminated following the severe economic depression of the 1890s and an outbreak there in 1899 of grape phylloxera, *Daktulosphaira vitifolii,* the 'vine louse', an aphid-like insect which infests the roots of grapes, causing the severe debilitation or death of European varieties. Incidence of the pest necessitates the costly process of replanting with grafted vines, using resistant American species as the rootstocks (Chapter 8).

Phylloxera was first recorded in Australia in 1875 at Fyansford, near Geelong. Soon it infested vineyards throughout large areas of Victoria, spreading to Bendigo and up the Goulburn River to Rutherglen. Outbreaks also occurred in table and wine grape holdings near Sydney, where it was first detected at Camden in 1884. In Queensland the pest first appeared in vineyards at Enoggera, a suburb of Brisbane, in 1910.

The Parliament of South Australia passed legislation in 1894 imposing rigid quarantine restrictions—which are still in force—in a successful attempt to keep phylloxera out of the State. These

Figure 1.4. Root galls on grape vines caused by phylloxera, Daktulosphaira vitifolii.

Figure 1.5. Phylloxera also causes leaf galls on American grape species, the roots of which have varying levels of resistance to the pest.

Figure 1.6. Planting cuttings of phylloxera-resistant rootstocks at the NSW Viticultural Station, Howlong, near Rutherglen in Victoria in the early 1900s.

Figure 1.7. 'Heeling-in' cuttings of phylloxera-resistant rootstocks at Howlong in the early 1900s. The cuttings are being covered with moist sandy soil for storage and callus development, prior to planting.

restrictions involved a total prohibition on the introduction of grape cuttings or any part of the grapevine; they were relaxed only in 1964 to permit the introduction, under close Government quarantine supervision, of new varieties and selected clones.

Although grape phylloxera can still be found in north-eastern Victoria, Corowa and in the Sydney area, quarantine regulations imposed by the various state Governments halted its spread to the extent that no other viticultural regions have become infested. In non-phylloxera areas, resistant rootstocks are not essential and, generally, are used only in replant situations, and then for nematode resistance.

If it were not for phylloxera, Victoria could well have retained its position as the leading grape-producing state, but the effects of the pest were lasting and by 1915-16 plantings in South Australia again surpassed those in all other States, which is still the case today.

Figure 1.8. Furrow irrigation of a new vineyard at Mildura, December 1890.

1.1.3 Downy mildew

Another factor which favoured South Australia was the introduction of the fungus disease downy mildew, *Plasmopara viticola,* the first outbreak of which was recorded in Victoria in 1916. In NSW downy mildew was first detected in Glenfield near Sydney and at Albury in 1918. The initial appearance of downy mildew in the Hunter Valley was in November 1921, where its incidence was severe throughout the remainder of that season. The disease is most prevalent in NSW, where the summer rainfall is significantly higher than in South Australia. In fact, there are few regions in the world in which *Vitis vinifera* varieties are grown where the combination of relatively high summer temperatures and precipitation favour downy mildew more than in the Hunter Valley of NSW. Yet another noteworthy feature of Australian viticulture is the absence of downy mildew from Western Australia (along with phylloxera, codling moth of pome fruit, apple black spot and starlings), an advantage jealously guarded through quarantine.

1.1.4 Irrigated viticulture

Until the 1880s commercial viticulture was confined to areas where natural rainfall was sufficient for the production of profitable crops. In 1884 a Victorian Royal Commission was set up to investigate irrigation techniques. As a result, the then Premier of Victoria,

Alfred Deakin, who subsequently became the Prime Minister of Australia in 1903, persuaded the Canadian-born George and William B. (Ben) Chaffey to come to Australia from California.

George, the engineer and William, the horticulturist, brought with them a unique combination of skills and experience they had acquired in founding successful irrigation projects in California. They arrived in 1886 and commenced a survey along the Murray River Valley. Land was selected around Mildura, and an agreement was negotiated under which the Victorian 'Government would set aside 250,000 acres [100,000 ha] at Mildura for occupation under licence for 20 years by the Chaffey Brothers, for irrigation purposes, Chaffey Brothers to have right to construct works on any part of the area for conserving and distributing water'. Over the 20 years, the Chaffeys were to spend £300,000 on permanent improvements. As money was spent, the Chaffeys were to receive titles to the land (Fogarty 1967).

This prompted a political controversy based on charges of 'cute Yankee land grabbers' and the Opposition achieved an amendment to the enabling Bill requiring the concession to be thrown open to public tender for two months.

The South Australian Government was less apprehensive and in February 1887 legislation was enacted which secured to the Chaffeys 250,000 acres near the Victorian border; this became the Renmark

Figure 1.9. A Chaffey pumping engine driving Tangye pumps to lift irrigation water from the Murray River near Mildura; installed at the turn of the century.

Irrigation Settlement. They were to receive an acre of freehold land for every £4 spent by them or property owners on development. By the end of the year Chaffey pumps were operating at Renmark and blocks were being sold at £20 per acre with 10 years to pay.

This prompted Victoria to review its stance and a few months later the original proposals for that state were put into effect under an agreement signed in May 1887. By the end of the year subdivision of the first 25,000 acres had been planned and pumping machinery to lift water 30 m from the Murray had been designed. Early in 1888 the first settlers began to arrive (Fogarty 1967).

Thus grapegrowing in arid and semi-arid regions of Australia began, marking a major turning point in the course of viticultural development. Permanently irrigated vineyards in dry inland districts now comprise 62% of the total area and are responsible for around 80% of Australia's fresh grape production.

Following settlement along the Murray Valley, completion of the Burrinjuck Dam and Berembed Weir on the Murrumbidgee River in New South Wales enabled development of the Murrumbidgee Irrigation Areas, where the first farms were made

available in 1912 and water supplied for irrigation in July of that year.

Expansion of irrigated grape plantings was fostered by Government-sponsored soldier settlement schemes following both World Wars. Loxton in South Australia and Robinvale in Victoria were the last two major irrigation districts of viticultural significance; they came into being in this manner after World War II.

Apart from the inland districts, since the early 1970s there has been a significant upsurge in the installation of trickle and overhead and undervine spray systems to supplement natural precipitation in the higher rainfall areas, where irrigation was not previously practised. This has had a dramatic effect in realizing bigger and more reliable crops by avoiding moisture stress during dry spells and by providing frost protection in the cooler districts. There is now general acceptance that some form of irrigation is essential in the current economic environment and that the practice need not compromise fruit or wine quality.

1.1.5 Importance of Australian viticulture
Early predictions of Australia becoming Britain's vineyard have not materialized, despite the vast areas

Figure 1.10. Aerial view of irrigated vineyards near Red Cliffs, Victoria, in the Sunraysia Region. The mosaic of plantings results from the required directions of furrow irrigation runs.

of land where the combination of climate and soil is eminently suitable for grape culture. Of the 9,413,000 hectares of grape vines in the world quoted by FAO for 1985, Australian plantings amounted only to 64,000 hectares, a mere 0.7% of the total. Nevertheless, grapes represent one of Australia's major fruit crops and should maintain this position, at least in the medium term, due to: continuing high levels of domestic consumption of wine; a doubling of exports in 1986-87 compared to the previous year; improved world prices for dried vine fruit since 1984; and a significant growth in fresh grape exports during the 1980s (Table 1.2).

The value of grapes for wine, drying and other purposes was $270 m in 1985-86. This represented only 1.8% of the combined value of agricultural and pastoral production of Australia (Table 1.3). However, as with all horticultural industries, viticulture has a much greater social impact. Being an intensive form of agriculture, the grape industries provide concentrated, high levels of employment to the extent that numerous townships have developed around centres of grape production. The city of

Mildura in Victoria and the townships of Renmark and Loxton in South Australia, for example, owe their existence and continuing prosperity largely to viticulture (Table 1.4).

Increasing mechanization, particularly of the harvest operations, is reducing labour requirements. Nonetheless, it is generally reckoned that one permanent hand is required for every 15 ha of grapevines, with additional inputs during the establishment period and the two seasonal labour peaks for pruning and harvesting.

1.1.6 Size of holdings
The majority of viticultural holdings in Australia are relatively small family units of less than 25 ha, operated by the owner with the assistance of a permanent employee, if the area is sufficient. This is largely a reflection on the longstanding closer settlement policies of the various State and Commonwealth Governments. In the sample farm survey conducted annually by the Australian Bureau of Agricultural and Resource Economics (ABARE), the total average orchard and vineyard area per farm

Table 1.2. Growth in area and production, Australia

Year	Area (ha)	Production		
		Wine (kL)	Dried Vine Fruit (dried tonnes)	Table (tonnes)
1900-01	26,133	NA	NA	NA
1901-02	–	23,924	2,074	13,447
1910-11	23,923	26,668	9,181	13,034
1920-21	32,846	50,072	15,477	8,965
1930-31	45,718	59,455	51,617	13,485
1940-41	52,560	72,724	82,367	16,002
1950-51	55,242	118,362	57,027	NA
1960-61	52,815	153,487	82,982	19,616
1970-71	63,783	250,284	60,424	25,331
1980-81	69,518	374,273	61,100	22,239
1985-86	59,839[a]	389,190[b]	83,000[a]	36,710[a]
1986-87	57,273[a]	371,678[b]	59,500[a]	43,439[a]

NA Not available.
(a) EVAO $20,000, previously $2,500; see explanatory note to Table 1.1. Comparisons in 1985-86 between the two EVAO levels show that for total grape production the EVAO of $20,000 represented 97.3% of the production for EVAO of $2,500.
(b) Establishments crushing more than 400 tonnes
Source: Australian Bureau of Statistics.

for 1985-86 and 1986-87 was 17.4 ha and 17.7 ha, respectively, for the wine grape industry and for the multipurpose grape industry (primarily growers of Sultana and Muscat Gordo Blanco) 12.0 ha and 12.3 ha (ABARE 1988). These figures include only farms operated independently of commercial wineries. Grapes are commonly grown on mixed horticultural farms, particularly in the irrigation areas where citrus and grapes are the most common combination, but canning peaches, apricots, prunes and other fruit and vegetable crops also may form part of the enterprise mix.

The objective of most Government-sponsored irrigation schemes was to locate as many settlers as economically possible on the available land, and the concept of the family farm in the highly regulated, Government-controlled irrigation areas became firmly entrenched. While Victoria and South Australia no longer place restraints on subsequent aggregation or subdivision of holdings in irrigation areas, the contrary is the case in NSW where holdings cannot be in excess of 140% of the assessed home maintenance area. Currently 140% of the home maintenance area is 45.3 ha. Furthermore, companies and corporations are prohibited from owning land. Restraints are also placed on subdivision of holdings in NSW irrigation areas to maintain viable farm sizes. In Victoria and South Australia there are now no restrictions on property amalgamation or corporate ownership in the irrigation areas. Nonetheless in Victoria, as with NSW, water entitlements are tied to specific parcels of land and cannot be sold or purchased on a permanent basis. Only in South Australia is permanent transfer of water allocation permitted between farmers in the same irrigation area.

Many grape and fruit growers strongly defend water and land use regulations, because they are perceived as effective production controls, protecting them against the entry of new producers who might generate surplus production and bring down prices. However, such restrictions do not sit well with current policies to promote adjustment of rural industries to more efficient and competitive structures. They also limit scope for effecting economies of scale and the introduction of improved management systems. In recognition of the latter considerations, the controls that remain are now

Table 1.3. Utilization and gross value of grapes, Australia

		Wine	Drying	Other purposes	Total
Volume[a] (tonnes fresh weight)	1985-86	491,200	355,200	36,700	883,100
	1986-87	478,800	263,600	43,400	785,800
Gross value ('000 $)	1985-86	111,600	121,100	37,400	270,000
	1986-87	115,700[p]	105,300[p]	49,000[p]	270,000[p]

(a) EVAO $20,000, previously $2,500; see explanatory notes to Table 1.1 and 1.2.
(p) Preliminary.

Source: Australian Bureau of Statistics.

Table 1.4. Establishments with selected agricultural activity, Australia, 1985-86

	NSW	Vic	Qld	SA	WA	Tas	NT	ACT	Australia
Grapes	763	1,792	111	1,577	201	13	2	—	4,459
Plantation fruit	934	—	891	—	126	—	4	—	1,955
Orchard & other fruit	2,133	1,199	1,223	1,486	645	10	4	—	6,980
Potatoes	176	576	229	108	176	291	—	—	1,556
Vegetables (except potatoes)	912	687	1,282	692	528	210	16	2	4,329
Total — all agricultural industries	52,042	44,317	33,936	18,971	16,298	5,283	269	104	171,180

Source: Australian Bureau of Statistics

under review and seem likely to be changed.

In all three States, area controls have been removed on permanent grape and fruit plantings irrigated by private diversion from streams (and bores) and water entitlements can be sold or transferred on an annual or permanent basis. Also, there are no limitations on corporate ownership. However, as late as 1987 restrictions were applied to private diverters in NSW, where the normal maximum was 40 hectares. Nonetheless, much larger areas were approved in special circumstances to establish a new industry in a region and where large irrigation projects would not jeopardize the livelihood of traditional producers on small holdings.

Despite the foregoing impediments, many large irrigated vineyards were established in some irrigation areas from the 1960s onwards by virtue of special approvals by the administering authorities, notably in South Australia. Also, because no controls are exercised over the size of non-irrigated vineyards or those watered by private diversion, there are many large viticultural holdings in the higher rainfall areas of all States, most of which are owned by proprietary companies.

Small farm size in the irrigation areas is a continuing problem in that many of the original allocations, while mostly satisfactory at the time, became inadequate to maintain a family unit in view of rising costs and expected levels of affluence. This problem has been most troublesome in the traditional dried fruits areas of the Murray Valley. Over the years considerable aggregation has taken place to recreate viable holdings. However, the physical and economic constraints to aggregation are appreciable and to overcome them Government financial assistance usually has been required.

1.1.7 Financial performance of grapegrowers

Because of the cyclical pattern in the level of profitability of most rural enterprises, any commentary on the financial performance of grapegrowers stands the risk of soon becoming outdated. Nonetheless, annual surveys conducted by the ABARE provide reliable data on farm incomes and costs and allow comparisons to be made with other industries.

The estimates of farm characteristics and performance provided by ABARE are based on data obtained from a sample of farms, stratified on the basis of geographical area, industry and estimated value of agricultural operations. In 1986-87, the number of farms sampled for multipurpose grapes was 144 out of a population of 3,262 and for wine grapes 128 out of a population of 2,148. Vineyards operated by commercial wineries are excluded from the sample.

The farm cash operating surplus, in 1985-86, in which the cost of operator and family labour is not taken into account, was $19,577 for the multipurpose grape industry and $19,836 for the wine grape industry. These results were lower than the other horticultural industries surveyed and for most other rural industries. For example, the corresponding figures for wheat and other crops was $27,619, mixed livestock and crops $27,802, dairy $27,054 and beef $36,681. Surprisingly, the farm cash operating surplus for the sheep industry for 1985-86 of $19,910 was less than the two grape industries, but rising wool prices have altered this, with the provisional figures for sheep in 1986-87 at $31,720 as against $18,380 for the multipurpose grape and $15,100 for wine grape industries (Table 1.5).

Table 1.5. Average farm financial performance — selected industries[a], Australia — 1985-86

Industry	Total cash receipts ($)	Total cash costs[b] ($)	Farm cash operating surplus ($)
Multipurpose Grape	63,274	43,697	19,577
Wine Grape	69,309	49,472	19,836
Citrus	80,587	59,131	21,456
Deciduous canning fruit	105,371	78,474	26,897

(a)   Estimates based on farms with an estimated value of agricultural operations of $10,000 or more.

(b)   Does not include operator or family labour, only hired labour.

Source:
Australian Bureau of Agricultural & Resource Economics.

When depreciation, operator and family labour and other cost factors are taken into account, all industries surveyed in 1985-86 showed an average negative real rate of return, including capital appreciation, with the multipurpose grape industry at −5.4% and wine grape at −15.0%. However, across-the-board improvement in commodity prices gave improved projections for 1987-88, with most farm enterprises operating on the positive side of the line, but the grape industries still languishing slightly below.

1.1.8 The individual industries

Originally, wine, drying and table grape production in Australia were largely discreet and independent enterprises. Such segregation still predominates despite the large quantities of Sultana grapes that were formerly used solely for drying and are now either processed for wine or sold as table grapes. Also the principal dried raisin variety, Muscat Gordo Blanco, has been used extensively as a wine grape for many years. These two so-called multipurpose varieties account for about 50% of Australia's fresh grape production. As a result, the fortunes of the three viticultural industries are somewhat interrelated. Nonetheless, individual growers tend to opt for one outlet or another, at least on a semi-permanent basis. Accordingly, it is convenient to consider each industry separately, particularly in view of the differences in their structure and in the factors that shaped their development.

1.2 Winegrapes

Wine production in Australia has been mostly geared to cater for the needs of the domestic market. Although export sales have been a major stabilizing factor in the industry, they have never exceeded 22% of annual production (1927-28), and they represented less than 3% of the vintage in 1985-86 and less than 6% of production in 1986-87, despite the doubling of exports in that year.

Progressive development of the industry has been far from steady and has largely reflected the general economic conditions prevailing at the time. From 1900 to 1915 growth was virtually non-existent with wine production remaining around the 27,000 kilolitres mark. However, during the giddy twenties the industry picked up and was aided by the introduction of export bounty payments in 1924, plus application in 1925 of preferential tariffs in respect to Empire wines imported into the United Kingdom. These developments fostered expansion and by 1929 the vintage reached 84,560 kL.

The depression of the 1930s saw an end to this and production slipped back until the outbreak of the Second World War, when a shortage of beer and the presence of large numbers of defence personnel fostered wine sales. By the end of the 1940s the vintage had doubled from 73,000 kL in 1940-41 to 145,000 kL in both 1948 and 1950. Pre-war consumption of wine per head of population was only about 2.7 L but this increased to 4.5 L during the war.

The war-time and post-war shortage of alcoholic beverages other than wine continued until 1951-52 when clearances of fortified wine for the domestic market reached a peak of 61,067 kL. At that time, Australian consumption of table wines was less than 10,000 kL. In 1952-53 clearances of fortified wine slumped to 42,605 kL and in the following year to 40,009 kL. To meet the resultant economic downturn in the industry, the Commonwealth Government introduced in 1954 a preferential excise rate on brandy in relation to other Australian spirits. This had the dramatic effect of doubling brandy sales, thereby enabling grape growers to retain an outlet for their crops. From then until the mid-1960s there was no significant recovery, with wine grape production remaining much the same and the vintage fluctuating between 104,000 and 190,000 kL depending on seasonal conditions. It was indeed a decade of the doldrums when most vignerons struggled for survival.

By the late 1960s several factors had combined

Figure 1.11. Harvesting winegrapes in the Hunter Valley, late nineteenth century.

to recreate buoyant conditions within the industry. These included more intensive promotion, the influx of European migrants, a general improvement in wine quality through adoption of modern winemaking techniques and relaxation of licensing laws, particularly with respect to single bottle sales. Consumption of wine increased from 5.0 L per head of population in the early 1960s to 9.1 L in 1970, when the vintage reached 288,000 kL. Advances in merchandizing methods, notably greater use of 2-litre flagons and 2- and 4- litre soft packs ('wine casks' or 'bag-in-box'), continued to stimulate sales during the 1970s and by 1980 per capita consumption had jumped to 17.2 L. Glass flagon and soft pack sales in both 1981 and 1987 accounted for 67% of the market. However, over this six-year period flagons (glass containers over 1 litre) ceased to be significant, losing ground from 21% to 4% while soft packs, on the other hand, increased from 46% to 63% of the market.

Throughout the 1980s domestic wine consumption continued to increase, though at a steadier rate, to 21.6 L per head of population in 1985-86 when the total Australian vintage amounted to 389,000 kL. Thus in the space of 25 years there was a four-fold increase in per capita consumption which was accompanied by a corresponding increase in the level of investment in the industry. Nonetheless, it is generally accepted that sales growth in recent years has been largely maintained through keen competitive pricing which has tended to erode both wholesale and retail margins.

Growth in total wine sales since 1960 has been almost entirely due to greater popularity of unfortified table wines, which in 1986-87 represented 87% of the Australian market compared with 79% in 1980-81, 52% in 1970-71 and 25% in 1960-61. For the first time in about 50 years, table wine production surpassed that for all other types of beverage wine in 1968 and by 1970 wholesale sales of table wine had exceeded fortified wine sales.

When sales of table wine commenced to surge forward in the late 1960s consumption of dry red wine (including rosé) was greater than whites. However, this soon changed, with whites heading reds for the first time in 1969-70. Indeed, between 1970-71 and 1986-87, unfortified red sales rose by 69% from 27,983 to 47,347 kL whereas those for unfortified whites, including sparkling and sweet table wines, jumped from 29,278 to 239,657 kL, a massive 719% increase. This major shift in the consumption pattern was not predicted, creating an imbalance between supply and demand and leading to surplus red grape production in the late 1970s and early 1980s. It also forced increasing diversion of multipurpose grapes from drying to winemaking and the utilization for white table wine of varieties which, from a quality viewpoint, were not ideally suited for the purpose.

With regard to fortified wine, two categories improved their position during the 1970-71 to 1986-87 period. They were dessert wine, principally port types but including muscat, and cocktails and vermouth. Although the available statistics are not strictly comparable, dessert wine increased by about 15% to 19,454 kL and cocktails and vermouth by 40% to 6,703 kL. On the other hand, sales of sherry types declined by 40% to 16,791 kL (Table 1.6).

Important technological achievements involving almost all aspects of grapegrowing and winemaking accompanied growth in the industry over the last two decades. Not the least of these was the greater utilization of premium quality grape varieties which has enhanced the quality image of Australian wines and further fostered sales. Mechanical harvesting has become well established and now accounts for about two thirds of the annual crush in less than 20 years since the first machine was imported for testing. Mechanical pruning followed soon after and has been widely adopted as an additional measure to contain costs. Further advances in technology will be assisted by the establishment in 1986 of the Grape and Wine Research Council, which allocates funds derived from industry levies and matching Commonwealth Government grants for research and development activities.

Australia possesses vast areas of land where the combination of climate and soils is suitable for commercial wine grape culture. In a practical sense, therefore, the availability of natural resources provides immense scope for expansion. In recent viticultural developments, there has been a tendency to select cool climates in both tried and untried

Figure 1.12. Mechanical harvesting of winegrapes now accounts for about two-thirds of the annual Australian grape crush.

Figure 1.13. Government viticultural experts — such as Francois de Castella, Dr A.C. Kelly, Professor A.J. Perkins and M. Blunno (pictured above in his Sydney laboratory in 1911) — contributed to the early development of Australian viticultural knowledge.

regions for production of high quality table wine to emulate the conditions which prevail in Europe. This has been to the benefit of the industry in augmenting the range of wine styles that are made. Nonetheless, the tradition of 200 years of successful viticulture has provided ample evidence that neither cool nor

Table 1.6. Wholesale sales of Australian wine and brandy in Australia

	Table (kL)	Fortified (kL)	Total wine (kL)	Brandy[c] (kL alcohol)
1960-61[a]	14,334	43,315	57,649	2,101
1965-66[a]	26,644	44,177	70,831	2,479
1970-71[a]	57,261	53,228	110,489	3,064
1975-76[b]	111,983	61,857	173,840	2,674
1980-81[b]	208,847	54,027	262,874	2,449
1985-86[b]	283,460	41,722	325,182	1,997
1986-87[b]	287,004*	42,948**	329,952	1,783

* Comprised of: dry red 40,192; rose 7,155; dry white 176,227; sweet white 34,657; sparkling (inc. carbonated) 28,773.
** Comprised of: dry sherry 3,145; medium sherry 4,006; sweet sherry 9,640; dessert (port, muscat, etc.) 19,454; cocktails & vermouth 6,703.
Discrepancies in totals are due to rounding off.
(a) Wholesale sales of wine include imported wine.
(b) Sales by those wineries covering approximately 97% of grape crushings and exclude sales of imported wine and exports.
(c) Clearances of Australian brandy from bond for home consumption. In 1986-87 this represented 73.3% of the market share for brandy.

Source: Australian Bureau of Statistics.

Table 1.7. Leading world wine producers[a] (kilolitres)

Country	1984-85	1985-86
Italy	7,090,000	6,257,700
France	6,436,000	7,014,900
Spain	3,624,900	3,277,000
USSR	3,410,000	3,500,000
USA	1,670,000	1,810,000
Argentina	1,574,100	1,846,300
Romania	1,003,800	860,000
South Africa	828,200	890,000
F.R. Germany	888,700	539,500
Portugal	850,700	855,000
Yugoslavia	692,000	366,300
Greece	502,500	478,200
Bulgaria	515,500	430,000
Hungary	507,300	289,000
Australia	451,200[b]	480,000[b]
Chile	450,000	350,000
Brazil	350,000	350,000

(a) In order of importance, based on performance since 1981-82.
(b) The figure quoted for 1984-85 is consistent with that of the Australian Bureau of Statistics (A.B.S.) but there is a discrepancy for 1985-86 in that the A.B.S. figure for Australia is 389,190 kilolitres.
Source: Office International de la Vigne et du Vin (OIV)

warm regions have a mortgage on premium quality wine production.

In quality terms, Australia has demonstrated that it can match the rest of the world. Yet, despite this and the potential for further growth, it has still a long way to go in displacing its competitors with respect to quantity of production, being responsible in 1985-86 for only 1.5% of the world's vintage (Table 1.7).

1.2.1 Changes in grape plantings and usage

In keeping with demand, total Australian grape plantings have increased, though at a slower rate and not in parallel with the growth in the size of the vintage. This is because of three factors: less grapes are required to make a litre of table wine than fortified wine; increased diversion of multi-purpose grapes from drying to winemaking; and declining brandy production. Plantings expanded from 53,000 ha in 1960-61 to 64,000 ha in 1970-71 and peaked at close to 70,000 ha in the late 1970s. During this expansionary phase, many vineyards were established on soils of poor to doubtful fertility and there has since been a period of rationalization which saw the total area of grapes stabilize around the 60,000 ha mark in the mid 1980s.

The rationalization process was fostered by introduction in 1985 of a 'vine pull' scheme, under which subsidies were paid to encourage growers to remove uneconomic plantings and unwanted varieties, such as Grenache, Palomino and Doradillo. The scheme was financed on a basis of $2 from the Commonwealth matched by $1 from the participating States, which included all on the mainland, other than NSW. The scheme, which operated until 1987, was largely a social rescue program and resulted in the removal of 2,694 ha of wine varieties and 527 ha of multipurpose grapes at a cost to Governments of $6.9 m and $1.9 m, respectively.

Up until the early 1970s the quantity of the two principal multipurpose grapes, Sultana and Muscat Gordo Blanco (Gordo), crushed for wine fluctuated mostly in the range of 50,000 to 90,000 tonnes but since then has been consistently well in excess of 100,000 tonnes. The peak year was 1985 when Sultana and Gordo accounted for 167,000 tonnes of Australia's record crush of 559,000 tonnes (Table 1.8).

Diversion of Sultana grapes from drying to wine has been most pronounced in South Australia where over 50% of the crop is now crushed. Although there has been a similar trend in Victoria and New South Wales, the principal use continues to be drying.

Use of Gordo for wine has maintained a remarkably steady growth, in pace with the total vintage. Conversely, the crush of Sultana, while showing an upward trend, has fluctuated widely, reflecting its variability in cropping and, to some extent, the economic circumstances in the dried

Table 1.8. Winery intake of Sultana & Muscat Gordo Blanco (tonnes)

Year	Sultana	Muscat Gordo Blanco	Total Sultana & Gordo	Total all grapes
1960	21,803	33,184	54,987	152,704
1970	83,445	51,159	134,604	359,578
1980	66,361	62,530	128,891	502,470
1987[a]	40,407	76,654	117,061	478,776

(a) EVAO $20,000, previously $2,500; see explanatory notes to Tables 1.1 and 1.2.

Source: Australian Bureau of Statistics.

fruits industry. These two varieties represent an enormous pool of raw material with a combined fresh weight production in 1987 of 378,000 tonnes or 48% of the total crop. Of this amount Sultana accounted for 283,000 tonnes.

The price prevailing for dried vine fruit is a factor influencing the availability of Sultana for wine. Even so, it seems that winemakers will always be able to obtain their requirements of the variety as many growers prefer to forego the possibility of ultimately higher returns for dried fruit to avoid the effort and risk in drying and to benefit from the earlier finalization of payments. In the short to medium term, growers tend to specialize in one outlet or the other because of differing cultural practices and ancillary equipment requirements coupled with term financial commitments or contractual arrangements made with wineries or dried fruit packing houses, as the case may be. But in the end, everything has its price.

It is important to note that while the quantity has increased, the proportion of the vintage made up by multiputpose grapes has declined, being mostly well over 30% up to 1970 but consistently around the 25% since, except for 1984 and 1985 when it again approached 30%. The most significant change has been in the type of wine for which the multipurpose grapes are used. Originally, Gordo was used primarily for sweet and 'cream' sherry types and Sultana for distillation wine because, being early maturing, it provided fortifying spirit for the current vintage and avoided the need to carry over large spirit stocks from the previous year. Now, both are mostly used for white table wines in the lower price bracket.

The varietal composition of vineyard plantings has also altered to reflect changes in wine consumption patterns with an overall downward trend in the area of red grapes but an upward movement in superior quality table wine types, both red and white, at the expense of those less highly regarded for this purpose.

Over the period from 1977 to 1987, the vintage crush of Grenache declined from 57,000 to 31,000 tonnes, Shiraz from 75,000 to 49,000 tonnes and Mataro from 17,000 to 10,000 tonnes. Similarly the distillation/sherry varieties lost ground, though not to the extent that would have been expected, with Doradillo dropping from 37,000 to 29,000 tonnes and the combined production of Palomino and Pedro Ximenes from 31,000 to 26,000 tonnes. The biggest gain was with Riesling from 14,000 to 40,000 tonnes. Semillon increased from 27,000 to 37,000 tonnes, Cabernet Sauvignon from 23,000 to 25,000 tonnes and, most significantly, Chardonnay from virtually nothing to over 19,000 tonnes. With 30% of the area planted to Chardonnay in the 'not yet bearing' category and the demand for planting material well ahead of all other varieties, it is clear that production of this quality grape will at least double by 1990.

Although still relatively insignificant in the total vintage context, other varieties which are gaining ground are Pinot Noir (3,000 tonnes in 1986), Merlot and Cabernet Franc amongst the reds and Sauvignon Blanc and Verdelho amongst the whites.

Overall, the varietal mix of vineyards is becoming geared to a quality table wine market, providing a strong base to further enhance the reputation of Australian wines and to capture new markets. The challenge will be in gauging growth of the various market segments to achieve a balance between production and demand (Table 1.9).

1.2.2 Changes in industry structure

While the majority of winegrapes continue to be produced on small family farms, particularly in the irrigation areas, the structure of the processing sector has undergone major change. Formerly, most winemakers were private individuals, family companies or co-operatives. Through amalgamation and takeovers only one large co-operative remains, although it possesses several plants in South Australia. Many family companies have become public or have been taken over by local and multinational corporations with diverse interests.

The great upsurge in wine production since the mid 1960s caught the attention of large overseas corporations who bought into Australian wine-making mainly by purchasing well-established local companies. They brought with them expertise in consumer commodity marketing and had the capacity to inject large amounts of capital into the industry. However, for the most part, local

Table 1.9. Area and production of grapes by principal variety[a], Australia[b] 1986-87

Red varieties	Area[c] (hectares)	Production[d] (tonnes)	White varieties	Area[c] (hectares)	Production[d] (tonnes)
Cabernet Sauvignon	3,466	24,676	Calmeria	104	957
Cardinal	278	1,680	Chardonnay	2,625	18,594
Currant (incl. Carina)	1,467	18,097	Chenin Blanc	480	6,312
Grenache	2,330	30,747	Colombard	556	11,367
Mataro	730	9,968	Crouchen	621	9,746
Merlot	260	1,174	Doradillo	1,156	29,230
Muscat Hamburgh	717	3,586	Muscadelle	394	4,349
Pinot Noir	669	3,162	Muscat Blanc	514	5,642
Purple Cornichon	314	1,893	Muscat Gordo		
Red Emperor	307	2,242	Blanco	4,179	94,094
Shiraz	5,003	48,907	Ohanez	247	1,904
			Palomino & Pedro		
			Ximenes	1,492	25,606
			Rhine Riesling	3,769	40,025
			Sauvignon Blanc	643	3,883
			Semillon	2,623	36,636
			Sultana	16,343	283,412
			Traminer	736	7,249
			Trebbiano	1,486	23,187
			Verdelho	101	983
			Waltham Cross	1,311	15,171
Other Red	1,400	11,363	Other White	886	9,920
Total	16,915	157,496		40,266	628,271

(a)   Varieties with a total area of 100 ha, or more.
(b)   Excludes Northern Territory.

(c)   Total area, bearing and non-bearing.
(d)   Total production for all purposes.

Source: Australian Bureau of Statistics.

winemaking skills were retained. In like fashion, several Australian-based conglomerates and brewers bought into winemaking.

The wine boom has also attracted a large number of small grower/winemakers who comprise the 'boutique' segment of the industry. In 1987 there were 252 wineries which crushed less than 200 tonnes and of these 92 crushed less than 20 tonnes. In aggregate, they accounted for only 2.4% of the total vintage. Some are in effect the expensive hobby of professional and business people and provide for them an interesting means of tax minimization during the lengthy development phase. Some have failed and doubtless others will follow suit, while the more successful will be targets for takeover. Nonetheless, new entrants are likely to ensure that the 'boutique' winery will remain a feature of the industry.

Wineries crushing from 200 to 10,000 tonnes number 67 and account for 29.1% of the vintage. There are 13 that crush more than 10,000 tonnes and they account for the balance of 68.5% (Table 1.10).

1.2.3 Pricing of winegrapes

Except for the Murrumbidgee Irrigation Areas (MIA) of NSW and the Sunraysia district of NSW and Victoria, prices paid for grapes are determined by negotiation between individual growers and winemakers or may be simply announced by the winemaker without any formal prior discussion. In most cases it has been normal for a standard price to apply to a particular variety in any one district.

In the MIA, the Wine Grapes Marketing Board, established by a poll of growers in 1933 under the Marketing of Primary Products Act of NSW, operated for many years solely as a negotiating body in reaching agreement with the MIA Winemakers' Association upon minimum prices to apply for each variety, each vintage. However, the Board has powers of acquisition by way of vesting the crop in the Board, thereby enabling it to unilaterally fix minimum prices for grapes produced within its area of jurisdiction. The Board did not elect to utilize those powers until the 1977 vintage, when surplus production of red grapes created problems. However, the crop was divested back to growers when price agreement was reached. This arrangement prevailed for most vintages up till 1982, but from 1983 onwards the crop has remained vested and, in effect, the property of the Board, which arranges payment to growers, in some cases direct from the purchaser and in

Table 1.10. Size of wineries by tonnage crushed — 1987 Vintage (fresh grape equivalent)

Range (tonnes)	Total crushed (tonnes)	Proportion of total crush (%)	Number of wineries
0-20	1,002	0.2	92
20-50	2,435	0.5	73
50-100	3,748	0.7	52
100-200	5,023	1.0	35
200-500	6,055	1.2	18
500-1,000	12,143	2.4	18
1,000-2,000	11,705	2.2	10
2,000-5,000	24,466	4.7	7
5,000-10,000	95,669	18.6	14
10,000-20,000	97,434	18.9	7
20,000+	255,719	49.6	6
Total	515,399	100.0	332

Notes:
(i) Figures in Table 1.10 are indicative only, in that the number of wineries are as reported by levy payers. Some companies have lodged only one return per legal entity but have more than one winery.
(ii) No account has been taken of known changes to ownership of wineries since 30.6.87.

Source: Commonwealth Department of Primary Industries based on levy returns for the 1987 vintage under the Wine Grapes Levy Act, 1979 (pers. comm.).

others through the Board. Attempts, however, are always made to reach price agreement through negotiation.

In Sunraysia complementary legislation has been in force since 1980 under which a joint negotiating committee of equal numbers of growers and winemakers appointed by the Victorian and NSW Governments determines statutory minimum prices and conditions of payment for the two principal multipurpose grapes, Sultana and Muscat Gordo Blanco, only. The committee is chaired by a Government representative with no voting rights and in the event of failure to reach agreement, as applied from 1986 to 1988 inclusive, the matter is referred to an independent arbiter for determination. Although winemakers are pressing for the legislation to be repealed, grower proponents of the scheme are cognisant of the very large production of these two varieties which makes them particularly vulnerable to price cutting in the absence of controls.

The setting of statutory minimum prices for wine grapes in South Australia was terminated after the 1987 vintage, although the enabling legislation remains in place. For 1987, the only determination was an across-the-board minimum base price for all varieties of $175 per tonne. In 1986 the minimum base price for all varieties was $175 per tonne in irrigation districts and $190 per tonne elsewhere. However, from 1966 to 1985 prices for individual varieties were set annually by the Prices Commissioner under authority of the South Australian Prices Act. It was an offence to pay or offer to pay prices lower than those which were gazetted each year by the Commissioner. Price fixing of wine grapes in South Australia was introduced upon the recommendation of a Royal Commission appointed to enquire into the grapegrowing industry in that State and followed a period from 1960 to 1964 when both parties accepted price recommendations issued by the Commissioner. However, this voluntary arrangement broke down when winemakers refused to pay the recommended prices in 1965.

In making annual determinations of prices, the South Australian Prices Commissioner conducted interviews and received submissions from winemakers and growers and took into account variations in costs of producing grapes and the ability of winemakers to pay higher prices. For each variety a price was determined for irrigated and non-irrigated areas. A perceived weakness in the scheme was that co-operative wineries were not bound by the legislation, but almost invariably, their returns to grower members were higher than the fixed price, although it usually took much longer to finalize payments.

For the 1988 vintage minimum prices in the Murrumbidgee Irrigation Areas ranged from $160 per tonne for Doradillo to $400 for Cabernet Sauvignon and $800 for Chardonnay, although higher prices especially for the latter variety were received. The minimum price for both Sultana and Gordo in the Murray River districts of New South Wales and Victoria was set at $195 per tonne, but in this year of strong demand, the ruling price was from $220 to $225.

In 1988 there was considerable price variability in the non-irrigated districts where there are no statutory pricing arrangements. Chardonnay was usually sold for between $1400 and $1600 per tonne with some lots as high as $2000; Cabernet Sauvignon at around $850; Shiraz and Semillon between $500 and $650; Riesling from $450 to $500; and Grenache $220 to $300.

The desirability of statutory control over prices remains a controversial issue, opposed by winemakers and economic theorists. On the other hand, most growers see it as a necessary safeguard and point to several instances in the past when returns for grapes fell short of the level of profitability in the industry.

1.2.4 Wine industry taxation

Prior to 1970, Australian wine as such did not attract an excise duty. However, excise was raised on spirit used for fortification from 1901 to 1970, when it was abolished in favour of general excise on wine. During this period the excise ranged from $0.01925 to $0.4325 per litre of alcohol (Anon. 1985a).

In 1970 the Commonwealth Government introduced an excise duty of 50c a gallon on all Australian wine produced for sale in Australia, which in the case of fortified wine included the spirit added. This had the predictable effect of temporarily arresting growth in sales of table wine and following representations by the industry to the Government the excise was halved in May 1972 and completely removed in December of the same year.

Fortified wine, along with table wine, was then free from excise until August 1983 when excise was re-introduced on fortifying spirit at the rate of $2.61 per litre of alcohol, but reduced to $1.50 in the following month and removed entirely in June 1984, with the proceeds being refunded to producers.

Brandy remains the only fermented beverage of the grape that continues to attract an excise, which since 1983 has been adjusted in line with increases in the consumer price index. In 1988 the excise on brandy stood at $22.48 per litre of alcohol as against $26.34 for other Australian spirits. All spirits, including brandy, are also subject to a sales tax of 20% of wholesale value.

When sales tax was first introduced in Australia in 1930, all wine and brandy sales attracted the general rate of 2.5%. However, sales tax on Australian wine was removed in the following year and not reapplied until 1984 when the rate was set at 10%. At the same time, sales tax on imported wine was reduced from 20% to 10% but customs duties increased proportionately to maintain wholesale prices. In 1986, the sales tax on all wine was increased to 20%.

It will be apparent, from the frequency of changes in its form and rates, that taxation of wine is a sensitive issue, being closely linked with the economic well-being of grapegrowers. There are anti-alcohol groups within the community who are targeting wine for a higher level of taxation, presumably because, of the principal alcoholic beverages, it has been unique in registering sustained per capita consumption growth. Such views fly in the face of history and fail to recognize that even in Australia's foundling years, the administrators of the day positively encouraged grape production for wine as a measure of moderation and the preferred alternative to spirits.

1.2.5 Exports of Australian wine

Until recent years exports were mainly directed towards the United Kingdom, where the first entry of Australian wine into bond, recorded by the UK Department of Customs and Excise, was made in 1854, although small unrecorded shipments took place well before this.

Originally, practically all exports to the UK were dry, unfortified wines, because Australian fortified wines could not compete against those from Spain and Portugal due to higher costs of production, shipping charges and duties. In 1924, however, the Commonwealth Government passed the *Wine Export Bounty Act* which provided an opportunity to export sweet fortified wines to the UK. Under this legislation all wine exported overseas from Australia containing not less than 34° proof spirit received a bounty payment of two shillings and nine pence per gallon plus a refund of excise on the fortifying spirit used in its manufacture, which was roughly equivalent to one shilling and three pence a gallon. This was a measure to provide additional outlets for increasing production emanating from soldier settlement plantings after the first World War.

Coupled with the bounty payments, preferential tariffs in respect of Empire wines were introduced in the UK in 1925. Under this system Empire wines not exceeding 27° proof spirit attracted a duty of only two shillings per gallon, as against three shillings per gallon for foreign wines not exceeding 25° proof spirit, while Empire wines not exceeding 42° proof spirit attracted a duty of four shillings per gallon as against duty for foreign wines of the same strength of eight shillings per gallon (Laffer 1949).

The combination of preferential duties and bounty payments made Australian wines an attractive proposition and exports to the UK increased quickly. Total shipments to all markets increased from 4,007 kL in 1924-25 to 17,151 kL in 1927-28 which has since been exceeded only in 1986-87.

The bounty payment was progressively reduced

to one shilling per gallon in 1940 and terminated in 1947 after a Tariff Board enquiry concluded that the bounty was unnecessary in view of the improvement in local consumption.

Exports remained at a fairly high level throughout the 1930s, but slumped sharply with the onset of World War II when the British Government was forced to restrict imports of wines and spirits by a system of licensing. In 1942-43 exports fell to 3,700 kL. There was a recovery following World War II but the pre-War level was not achieved until 1986-87 (Table 1.11).

As a reflection of Britain's entry to the European Economic Community, shipments to that country, after remaining steady at around 5,000 kL from 1955 to 1970, dropped to 1,350 kL in 1973-74, when Canada became Australia's biggest overseas buyer for both wine and brandy.

Total exports during the early 1970s remained fairly steady, fluctuating mostly between 6,000 and 8,000 kL, but then declined to the lowest level since the War of 4,629 kL in 1977-78. There was a subsequent steady recovery, culminating in a quantum leap in 1986-87 to the all time record of 21,150 kL, valued at $44.5 m. This reflected not only a favourable exchange rate for exports, but also international recognition of the high quality and good value for money of Australian wine. In terms of volume, Sweden was in this year the principal importer of Australian wine (5200 kL) followed by the USA (2700 kL), United Kingdom (2300 kL), Canada (2000 kL), Japan (1800 kL) and New Zealand (1700 kL). However in terms of value of exports the USA was by far the most important market, followed by the UK and then Sweden. Total exports are estimated to have risen by at least a further 60% in 1987-88 and ongoing though more modest increases are anticipated in subsequent years.

By way of comparison, imports of wine to

Table 1.11. Exports of Australian wine (kL)

1905-06	3,274
1915-16	3,318
1925-26	7,831
1935-36	16,864
1945-46	8,112
1955-56	5,473
1965-66	8,943
1975-76	5,975
1985-86	10,828
1986-87	21,150

Source: Australian Bureau of Statistics.

Australia commenced a steady and substantial growth from around 2000 kL in 1970, peaking at 13119 kL in 1984-85 and dropping back to 7588 kL in 1986-87. Indeed, imports of wine exceeded exports for the first time in 1975-76 and remained that way for all but one year, until 1986-87.

1.2.6 Industry organization

Various statutory and voluntary bodies are involved in the regulation and organization of the winegrape and wine industries.

The Australian Wine and Brandy Corporation
The Corporation had its genesis in the Australian Wine Board which was established in 1929 under the authority of the *Wine Overseas Marketing Act* to provide overall supervision of the export trade in wine and brandy. The Corporation, which possesses similar powers, came into being by virtue of the *Australian Wine and Brandy Corporation Act 1980* which was amended in 1986 to effect several structural changes and provide for greater accountability and flexibility in operations.

The functions of the Corporation are to control the export of grape products, primarily wine and brandy; promote the consumption of these products both in Australia and overseas; improve production; and conduct or arrange research relating to marketing. Formerly, the Corporation was involved in sponsoring and funding oenological research mostly undertaken by The Australian Wine Research Institute based in Adelaide, but this function was transferred to the Grape and Wine Research Council in 1986.

Exporters of wine and brandy are required to be licensed with the Corporation and to submit samples of products intended for export for appraisal by expert Wine Inspectors to ensure they are sound and of merchantable quality.

The Corporation consists of a chairman and one Commonwealth Government member appointed by the Minister for Primary Industries and Energy, and six other members selected by an independent committee from nominations received from the industry. The Corporation's major source of income is a statutory levy on grapes used in wine production, which in 1987-88 was set at $3.00 per tonne for grapes crushed in the previous year, subject to a maximum payment of $10,000 by any one producer. As from the 1989 vintage the levy will be increased to $4.00 per tonne with maximum payment to $20,000. Income is also derived by exporter payments towards joint promotional activities and

from government grants for export promotion, provided through Austrade.

The Wine and Grape Industry Advisory Council
This body, established by the Commonwealth Government in 1987, provides a formal interface between the industry and Governments. The Council comprises an independent chairman, the presidents of national wine and grape industry organizations and the chairmen of the Corporation and the Grape and Wine Research Council. It is charged with the responsibility of advising Governments on industry issues and recommending courses of action towards effecting their resolution.

The Grape and Wine Research Council
The Council was set up in 1986 under the *Rural Industries Research Act 1985,* which provided the statutory basis for the funding and administration of grape and wine research on a long-term secure footing. Prior to establishment of the Council, the wine industry and Commonwealth Government jointly financed wine research at The Australian Wine Research institute under a series of short term arrangements. There was no statutory scheme for joint funding of grape research.

The Act provides for annual allocation of funds, derived from industry levies and matched equally by the Commonwealth, for research and development initiatives of appropriate organizations. In 1988, grapegrowers contributed $0.30 per tonne of grapes delivered for processing and winemakers $1.50 per tonne of grapes used in the manufacture of wine. The matching Commonwealth contribution is limited to a maximum of 0.5% of the gross value of production. The Council comprises a Government-appointed chairman, a Government member and seven selected members who possess relevant industry and/or research backgrounds.

The Winegrape Growers' Council of Australia Incorporated
The Winegrape Growers' Council is the vehicle by which voluntary organization of wine grapegrowers is effected at the national level. It comprises representatives of various State and regional associations of growers, namely:

(i)   United Farmers and Stockowners of South Australia Incorporated (Winegrapes Section);
(ii) Wine Grapes Marketing Board for Shires of Leeton, Griffith, Carrathool and Murrumbidgee (basically, the Murrumbidgee Irrigation Areas) of New South Wales;

(iii) Victorian and Murray Valley Winegrape Growers' Council Incorporated;

(iv) Grape Growers' Association of Western Australia Incorporated;

(v) Committee of Direction of Fruit Marketing, Queensland, a statutory authority representing most growers of fruit and vegetables in that state.

There are several other well-established, regional associations which are not directly affiliated with the Winegrape Growers' Council, particularly in districts where production is mostly in the hands of grower/winemakers.

Australian Wine and Brandy Producers' Association Incorporated

The Australian Wine and Brandy Producers' Association represents the majority of the larger winemakers and its members are responsible for over 50% of the annual crush.

Wine and Brandy Co-operative Producers' Association of Australia Incorporated

The Co-operative Association operates as a discreet national body even though, because of amalgamations, there is only one remaining major co-operative winemaker.

Australian Winemakers' Forum

Yet another separate processor group is the Australian Winemakers' Forum which was set up to cater for the interests of 'boutique' winemakers. Moves are in train to combine the three winemaker organisations into a single national body.

1.3 Drying Grapes

To a very large extent, dried vine fruit production in Australia is reliant on the Murray Valley irrigation systems. Indeed, 97.5% of Sultana and Currant plantings are located on irrigation developments of the Murray Valley (Table 1.12). Vineyards growing grapes for drying extend east along the river from Cadell in South Australia to Woorinen near Swan Hill in Victoria. Plantings of the principal raisin variety, Muscat Gordo Blanco, are more widely distributed because of its better adaptability to higher rainfall areas and its extensive use for wine. Only small quantities of grapes are dried in areas dependent on natural rainfall, namely the Swan Valley and Bindoon in Western Australia where the summer rainfall is sufficiently low to permit sun-drying of currants.

Following establishment of the Mildura and Renmark irrigation settlements in 1887 under the guidance of the Chaffey brothers, growth of the industry was fairly rapid and was fostered by Government sponsored soldier settlement schemes after both World Wars. From the 1950s onwards, however, there has been no substantive change in the planted areas of drying varieties, and production has only varied with seasonal conditions, the extent to which grapes have been diverted away from drying for winemaking and higher yields through the adoption of improved technology.

Initial plantings were Zante Currant and the raisin varieties Muscat Gordo Blanco and Waltham Cross. The first five tonnes of dried vine fruits were sent to market in 1891. Commercial Sultana vines, synonymous with the American Thompson Seedless, were first planted in 1895 and soon became Australia's principal drying variety. By the time of Federation in 1901, production of dried vine fruit had reached 2074 tonnes, after the fledgling industry had weathered the severe economic problems of the 1890s. During this time the lack of efficient transport meant that growers had to hold fruit for long periods, and being without an industry organization were often forced to sell by auction for as little as one penny per pound.

An attempt to introduce better-organized selling arrangements in 1894 was unsuccessful and Mildura's population began to decline as settlers walked off their properties. By 1895, the fortunes of the industry reached their lowest ebb. This year saw the formation of the Mildura Raisin Trust and the Renmark Raisin Trust which jointly set a minimum price of 4½ pence per pound but few

Table 1.12. Location of Sultana & Currant plantings, Australia 1986-87 (hectares)

	Sultana	Currant
Sunraysia, NSW	2,493	111
Sunraysia, Vic.	9,415	575
Kerang-Swan Hill, Vic.	2,245	26
Waikerie & Lower Murray, SA	181	31
Northern Murray, SA	1,455	355
Southern Murray, SA	402	78
Swan Shire, WA	20	117
Rest of State, WA	14	143
All others (Aust.)	118	31
Total	**16,343**	**1,467**

Source: Australian Bureau of Statistics.

Figure 1.14. Drying grapes on trays and hessian, Mildura, about 1904.

growers, if any, realised this price at the time. Nonetheless by 1896 Renmark and Mildura were able to achieve some success in a scheme of orderly marketing.

With the turn of the century, conditions began to improve. Federation saw the removal of State Customs barriers, thereby opening up new markets through interstate trade. Soon after, the transport obstacle was overcome by completion of the railway from Melbourne to Mildura in 1903.

In 1904 the Renmark Raisin Trust and Mildura Dried Fruits' Association (formerly the Mildura Raisin Trust) held their first federal meeting; by 1907 the two organizations combined to form the Australian Dried Fruits Association (ADFA) which has remained a dominant force in the industry to the present time. W.B. Chaffey was the first Chairman of the Association (Anon. 1985b).

Expansion was moderate up until the First World War. Even so, the year in which Merbein was settled, 1909, saw the first exportable surplus and by the 1910-11 season, production rose to 9181 tonnes, which in turn doubled to 19,695 tonnes by 1915-16.

In the years following the Armistice there was extensive planting through soldier settlement. The area under vines was extended at Nyah, Woorinen, Berri and Curlwaa, while new settlements appeared at Red Cliffs, Barmera, Chaffey, Bungunyah and Goodnight. Problems of disposal began to appear,

but generally the ADFA was able to maintain stable prices despite the fact that some growers and packers abandoned the scheme of orderly marketing to sell more of their allocation of production on the higher-priced domestic market. Fortunately, the years from 1920 to 1922 were boom years, but in 1923 export prices collapsed, giving producers operating independently of the ADFA a very distinct advantage.

The marketing problem eased with the introduction of Empire preference by the UK in 1925 and by Canada in the following year. This was timely as production increased to 37,594 tonnes by 1925-26. The difficulties of the mid-twenties forced a reorganization of the ADFA, and in 1923 packing companies and selling agents were formally incorporated into the Association as affiliates. This was soon followed by the formation of the Australian Dried Fruits Control Board and the Dried Fruits Boards in producing States, thereby providing statutory powers to control export and domestic marketing.

1.3.1 Production of dried grapes

The Australian dried fruits industry is characterized by marked seasonal variation in production. This is partly due to differences in the fruitfulness of Sultana buds between years, but more importantly to weather conditions during the harvest and drying seasons. Sultanas and Currants are very susceptible to rain damage when near maturity, while rain and

Figure 1.15. Muscat Gordo Blanco grapes in dip tins, about to be submerged in a fire-heated sodium hydroxide solution as a pre-drying treatment. This practice has now been replaced by rack spraying (see Figure 1.19).

Figure 1.16. Conventional, roofed drying racks now used for drying grapes in Australia.

humid weather after harvest can result in significant losses to all varieties during the course of drying. The varying quantities of drying varieties diverted to winemaking is a further factor influencing dried fruit production.

Sultanas comprise 85% to 90% of the Australian production in most seasons, currants about 7% with raisins fluctuating more widely from between 2% and 9%. Victoria is responsible for the bulk of the Australian dried vine fruit crop with 74,757 tonnes produced in 1986 compared with 14,861 tonnes in South Australia and 10,543 tonnes in New South Wales.

In the majority of seasons Australia ranks fourth to the USA, Greece and Turkey, in that order, as a world producer of dried vine fruits (Table 1.13). Greece is by far the largest supplier of currants, which account for about half of its crop, followed by Australia, the USA and South Africa. Elsewhere currants assume little significance, production being confined to sultanas and raisins.

1.3.2 Development of drying techniques

Originally Muscat Gordo Blanco was dried for raisins without pre-drying treatment, being spread on wooden trays and exposed to the sun. This produced dark, blue-brown clusters known as muscatels which, to a small extent, continue to be produced (though mostly using dehydrators) for specialty dried fruit packs. However, the practice of dipping grapes in a boiling caustic soda solution before drying was soon adopted as this greatly accelerated the rate of drying, mainly by causing fine cracks in the skins. The method was also used for Sultana.

By 1911 the use of trays for drying had been largely replaced by the locally developed system of tiered racks of wire netting which were less laborious and safer in poor drying weather. The perforated dip tin was also an early innovation, first used for dipping and then also as a harvesting container.

As exports became more important, it was necessary to compete with the light golden Turkish sultana to which buyers in England were accustomed

Table 1.13. World production of currants & raisins (sultanas & raisins) (tonnes)

	Seven year average 1976-1982	1983	1984	1985	1986(est.)
USA	193,059	317,985	247,270	248,404	196,990
Greece, incl. Crete	140,665	178,000	154,000	166,000	167,150
Turkey	91,913	100,000	75,000	125,000	110,000
Australia	74,325	84,470	86,710	76,961	100,921
Iran	59,214	72,000	72,000	76,000	80,000
South Africa	18,029	33,875	27,566	29,168	36,356
Spain	3,028	3,000	NA	NA	NA
Others	85,571	116,200	107,000	102,000	107,000
Total	665,804	905,530	769,546	823,533	798,917

NA: Not available.

Source: Australian Dried Fruits Corporation.

Figure 1.17. Spreading Sultana grapes onto a drying rack.

Figure 1.18. Almost completely dried Sultana grapes being spread on hessian undersheets for the finish drying by direct exposure to the sun.

Figure 1.19. Rack spraying of Sultana grapes with a cold dip solution to accelerate the drying rate.

rather than the amber-brown, hot-dipped fruit then produced in Australia. The Turkish method of drying sultanas was introduced in the early 1920s. It involved dipping the bunches in an emulsion of olive oil in a potassium carbonate solution at ambient temperature before spreading on the drying racks. In the 1940s a shortage of olive oil resulted in its replacement with special dipping oils which are mixtures of ethyl esters of fatty acids and oleic acid plus emulsifiers. Australian cold-dipped sultanas have

the required light golden colour similar to the Turkish product and are generally superior in quality. The cold dip does not damage the skin but alters the structure of the wax bloom, thereby accelerating water loss and consequently the drying time to 8-14 days compared with 4-5 weeks for untreated fruit.

Drying racks are mostly roofed, either 45 or 92 m long and have eight to 12 horizontal tiers of 5 cm mesh galvanized wire. The fruit is spread on the racks and after drying is shaken, originally by hand but now by tractor mounted rack shakers, onto a bottom undersheet of jute hessian or polypropylene fabric. After shaking-down, both sultanas and raisins are given a finish drying by one of three methods. The traditional method is to move the undersheets to provide direct exposure of the fruit to the sun for one to two days. Alternatives, more recently developed, are the bin dryer in which hot air is forced through the fruit or rack dehydration in which fruit is artificially dried after enclosing the rack in heavy duty plastic curtains. The latter method may be used for salvage purposes in the event of bad weather but is often used solely for finishing-off as a routine part of drying management.

In the 1970s dipping of sultanas gave way to the practice of rack spraying with the cold dip solution to the extent that only about 5% of the crop is now dipped. Two sprays are mostly applied, the second four days after the initial application. Coupled with this, the use of perforated dip tins as picking containers is being phased out in favour of plastic buckets, thereby reducing grit contamination.

Trellis-drying of sultanas was yet a further development of the late 1960s that was refined during the 1970s. The method has been found useful in bad weather, when around 50% of growers use the technique for drying at least part of their crops as a salvage operation. However, in normal seasons only about 2 to 5% of the crop is trellis-dried. It involves severing of the fruit bearing canes with secateurs at maturity and then spraying the grapes with the drying emulsion within about two days when the leaves have wilted. The fruit is left to dry on the trellis, harvested mechanically in 2-3 weeks and then given a finish-drying as for rack dried fruit. There are several variations to the method, which has the advantages of being quick and labour effective. On the other hand, even wetting of the fruit with the dip emulsion is a problem and is not always achieved, resulting in variations in colour and quality.

Only small quantities of so-called 'natural'

sultanas are dried in Australia by use of tunnel dehydrators. This fruit is not dipped and by retaining its bloom has a dark bluish brown colour similar to the Californian Thompson Seedless, which are simply dried on paper trays in the vineyard by direct exposure to the sun without pre-treatment.

Currants are placed directly on the drying racks and because of their small berry size, neither pre-drying treatment of finish-drying are required.

Until around 1973, the larger berried Muscat Gordo Blanco and Waltham Cross continued to receive the hot dip predrying treatment in fire-heated tanks containing a sodium hydroxide solution. While the fine cracks in the grape skins produced by this treatment hastened drying in good weather, they attracted vinegar fly and led to moisture uptake and mould under poor conditions. Hot dips have now been replaced with treatments based on the Sultana cold dip emulsion applied either through dipping or rack spraying. Cold-dipped raisins have a lighter colour than hot-dipped fruit, and despite the slower drying rate are less prone to mould and stickiness (Dried Fruits Processing Committee 1982).

1.3.3 Quality classification and control

Following the finish-drying, fruit is 'boxed' for delivery to packing houses, operated by either co-operatives or proprietary companies. The traditional box, holding 55-65 kg, is known as 'sweat box' as the moisture content of the fruit equalizes whilst awaiting delivery. Sweat boxes have now been replaced by bulk bins designed for fork lift handling; these contain about 500 kg of dried fruit.

Reference samples of the grade standards for Australian dried fruit are prepared each year by the Grade Fixing Committee of ADFA, following specifications laid down in the *Commonwealth Export (Dried Fruits) Regulations*. These official samples of both unprocessed and packed sultanas, currants and raisins are issued to all packing companies as soon as suitable fruit becomes available at the beginning of the season.

A representative sample of each grade and type of fruit is taken at the time of delivery and graded by visual comparison with the official samples under standardized lighting. Grades range from one to seven 'crown'; the higher number of crown, the better the quality and uniformity in colour of the fruit.

Laboratory tests may be undertaken to check moisture content and grit contamination. Appropriate charges are placed against fruit which does not meet specified standards to cover subsequent treatment costs. Hand-picking charges also may be levied on fruit damaged by mould or vinegar fly or in which there is unacceptable foreign matter (Dried Fruits Processing Committee 1982).

1.3.4 Development of orderly marketing

From its inception, the dried fruits industry has been beset with marketing problems, primarily brought about through its heavy dependence on exports for crop disposal (Table 1.14). While domestic consumption has grown steadily from around 20,000 tonnes in the 1940s to the present level of 33,000 tonnes, the quantity available for export normally ranges between 60% and 70% of production.

A steady expansion of sales on the Australian market is likely in line with population growth and increasing consumption. After a period of decline in per capita consumption of dried vine fruits from over 2.0 kg in the early 1950s to around 1.7 kg in the late 1970s, it has since steadily increased to 2.2 kg in 1987-88, a relatively high figure by world standards.

In contrast, the export market is extremely volatile due to seasonal fluctuation in world supplies. Generally, though not invariably, export prices are significantly lower than those which apply in Australia. For example, returns to packers from sales of sultanas on the domestic market increased progressively from $386 per tonne for 1966 season's fruit to $1,648 per tonne in 1985 and an estimated $1,933 per tonne in 1987. Corresponding figures for average export returns from all overseas markets for sultanas were $256 per tonne in 1966, $1,081 per tonne in 1985 and an estimated $1,511 per tonne in 1987. During this 22-year period, there were only four years, 1973, 1977, 1979 and 1980, when crop failures throughout the world lifted export prices above those on the domestic market.

The objective of the system of orderly marketing, which was developed in the 1920s and continues to operate today, is to share equitably amongst all growers the realizations from all outlets.

Originally, it relied on an arrangement whereby it was illegal to sell dried fruits unless they had been processed in a packing house registered by statutory boards in each producing State. The State Dried Fruits Boards collectively specified the proportion of each season's production that could be sold within the State and thereby on the Australian market. The balance had to be exported. This arrangement enabled reasonable prices to be maintained for domestic sales by avoiding excessive competition and provided the basis for the equalization of returns to producers.

Throughout its history the marketing system has been the subject of numerous legal challenges, the most notable of which culminated in the historic case James v. the Commonwealth in 1935-36, the first occasion in which the Privy Council was called upon to interpret Section 92 of the Constitution. Section 92 provides that trade, commerce and intercourse among the States shall be absolutely free. Up until the James case this had been wrongly interpreted as meaning no more than free of customs duties and the like. The sequence of events was that the South Australian Dried Fruits Board acquired a quantity of dried fruits from a Mr James, a packer, who was endeavouring to sell more than his domestic quota in another State to take advantage of the higher Australian price. The matter was referred to the High Court who declared the acquisition illegal and the South Australian Dried Fruits Act invalid insofar as it interferred with interstate trade. In its judgement, however, the High Court said that the Commonwealth was not bound by Section 92.

Accordingly, Commonwealth legislation was passed to support the quota system previously operated by the States. The transfer of fruit from one State to another was prohibited except under a licence granted by prescribed authorities acting on behalf of the Commonwealth. The State Boards were made the prescribed authorities. A condition of a licence to transport fruit to another State was that the specified proportion of production that could be sold in Australia must be observed.

James took the matter to the High Court which ruled that the Commonwealth legislation was valid. However, he appealed to the Privy Council which found that the Commonwealth was as much bound by Section 92 as were the States.

Faced with the collapse of orderly marketing, the ADFA in 1938 formed a company, Murray Industries Development Association Ltd (MIDA Ltd), which was able to purchase all but one packing company that was not a member of the ADFA. The assets of these companies were either sold and the registration transferred to ADFA member packers or they were closed down and the registrations relinquished. One company wholly owned by MIDA Ltd was retained to act as a competitor against non-ADFA interests. The cost of these transactions came to $269,530.

The success of these arrangements to provide a scheme of orderly marketing relied on the voluntary observance of uniform quotas for domestic sales determined by the Dried Fruits Boards for producing States, as applying to the entire Commonwealth market. This was possible by virtue of membership

Table 1.14. Dried fruits exported and retained in Australia

Season	Production (tonnes)	Sales in overseas markets		Australian consumption	
		(tonnes)	%	(tonnes)	%
7 year average					
1925-31	51,349	37,814	73.6	13,535	26.4
1932-38	72,383	56,418	77.9	15,965	22.1
1939-45	87,664	63,945	72.9	23,719	27.1
1946-52	65,005	42,320	65.1	22,685	34.9
1953-59	83,784	65,359	78.0	18,425	22.0
1960-66	88,328	67,288	76.2	21,040	23.8
1967-73	79,068	56,914	72.0	22,154	28.0
1974-80	69,685	43,236	64.1	25,314	36.9
Actual					
1981	60,190	33.872	55.9	26,770	44.1
1982	96,160	57,885	65.1	31,018	34.9
1983	84,470	57,242	65.2	30,503	34.8
1984	86,710	60,011	68.7	27,349	31.3
1985	76,961	53,163	62.0	32,574	38.0
1986	100,921	55,552	62.4	33,511	37.6

Note: For the periods 1974-80 and 1981 to 1986, inclusive, total sales differ from production due to incidence of carry over stocks.
Source: Australian Dried Fruits Corporation.

of the ADFA of all but one packer and the policy of the State Boards to restrict registration of packing companies to the minimum necessary for efficient handling of the crop. This had the consequential effect of deterring prospective packers, who were not prepared to join the ADFA and observe its rules, from entering the industry. Quotas were set by the State Boards with the advice of the ADFA and varied considerably between years depending on the size of the crop.

It was possible to maintain high domestic prices without inducing import competition through the natural advantage of the local industry particularly in respect to freight costs and through tariff protection. Also there was an understanding between the industry in Australia and in the USA not to encroach each other's home market.

These arrangements proved effective over many years but, nonetheless, remained vulnerable to the provisions of Section 92, a matter of continuing concern within the industry. This, coupled with the destabilizing activities of an independent packer, prompted the introduction in 1978 of a new marketing scheme based solely on Commonwealth legislation and therefore no longer reliant on the 'voluntary' observance of quotas set by State Boards.

The present scheme is designed to achieve the same objectives as the previous arrangements, namely to equalize the returns from both export and domestic sales of all dried vine fruits produced in Australia, in those years when the return from export sales is less than from domestic sales. It operates under the *Dried Vine Fruits Equalization Act 1979* and *Dried Vine Fruits Equalization Levy Act 1979* by imposing an equalization levy on the production of each variety in a season. However, fruit that is exported is exempt from the levy, with the effect that levy is paid only on fruit destined for the Australian market.

Originally the rate of levy was determined as the amount by which the estimated average return on the domestic market for each variety exceeded the estimated average export return. However, as from the 1986 season, the Commonwealth Government decided that assistance will be reduced at a uniform rate so that the equalized returns at the ex-packer level in 1990 will be no more than 15 per cent above average export returns, as opposed to 35 per cent for sultanas in 1984. This was done to make the industry more responsive to market signals and less vulnerable to overseas competition on the domestic market (Table 1.15).

Equalization levies are collected by the Commonwealth Department of Primary Industries and Energy and paid into a trust fund administered by the Australian Dried Fruits Corporation. The fund moneys are distributed to exporters, and through them to the packers and then growers, in the form of equalization payments on the total production, irrespective of whether sales were made on the domestic or export market. The scheme provides for advances on account of equalization and allows for adjustments to ensure that all exporters receive the same assessed average export return for the variety, despite differing actual realization from various markets (Anon. 1987).

1.3.5 Stabilization and underwriting schemes

The first stabilization scheme for the dried vine fruits industry was introduced for a five-year term in 1964, its purpose being to act as a buffer against variations in growers' incomes. A second and essentially similar scheme was introduced in 1971 (again for a five-year period) and was subsequently extended to cover most seasons until 1980 when it was terminated, at industry request. Under the schemes an annual base price was established for each variety calculated each season according to movements in grower cash costs. There were separate stabilization funds for the

Table 1.15. Dried vine fruit equalization levy, 1984 to 1987

	Currants $ per tonne	Sultanas $ per tonne	Raisins $ per tonne
1984 season production	Exempt from levy	860	Exempt from levy
1985 season production	866	530	Exempt from levy
1986 season production	546	536	Exempt from levy
1987 season production	434	400	543

Source: Australian Dried Fruits Corporation.

three varieties which received Commonwealth Government and industry contributions and from which payments to growers were made.

When the average return to the grower was within the range of $10 per tonne above or below the base price, no payment was made into or out of the fund. If the average return was more than $10 per tonne above the base price, all of the excess over the $10 per tonne, with a limitation of $20 per tonne, was paid by growers into the fund, subject to the crop exceeding a minimum tonnage. Conversely, when the average return was more than $10 per tonne below the base price, payments from the fund were made to growers. Commonwealth Government contributions to the fund were subject to a limit of $23 per tonne on specified maximum quantities of fruit.

A ceiling was placed on each fund and money collected in excess of these amounts was first used to repay any Government contributions within the plan period and then to refund growers proportionately to their contributions. At the conclusion of each plan, moneys remaining in the fund were disbursed in the same way.

Following termination of stabilization in 1980, an underwriting scheme for sultanas was commenced in 1982 under the provisions of the *Commonwealth Dried Sultana Production Underwriting Act, 1982*. It is administered by the Australian Dried Fruits Corporation. The arrangement was based on the Government guaranteeing minimum returns per tonne equal to 90 per cent of average of net returns to packers in the preceding two seasons and the estimated net return for the current season.

This operated until the 1985 season when the method of calculating the guaranteed price was altered. As from the 1986 season, underwriting is based on 80% of average of export returns at FOB level for the preceding three seasons. The scheme will operate until the 1990 season. So far underwriting has been necessary only in 1982 with payments of $16.38 per tonne. In subsequent years average returns exceeded the guaranteed minimum and the same is expected to apply for 1986 and 1987 (Anon. 1987).

There is a possibility of further changes to the equalization and underwriting schemes following a reference to the Industries Assistance Commission by the Commonwealth Government for another inquiry into the industry in 1988. The inquiry will include an examination of equalization, export control and underwriting arrangements currently in place.

1.3.6 Returns to growers

Returns to growers obviously fluctuate in line with seasonal levels in production, but the variations in income are normally dampened by the larger proportion of the crop sold on the higher priced domestic market in low crop years and vice versa.

Nevertheless, world availability of dried vine fruit has a dramatic effect. For example, net returns to growers for four-crown sultanas, while showing a general trend of progressive increases, dropped from $1,117 per tonne in 1980 to $779 per tonne in 1982 then recovered to $1,137 per tonne in 1986 (Table 1.16).

Table 1.16. Comparative returns to growers for dried vine fruits ($ per tonne)

	Sultanas 4 crown	Currants 3 crown	Raisins 4 crown
1974	493	580	520
1975	431	601	589
1976	390	657	545
1977	734	728	683
1978	683	767	708
1979	891	794	699
1980	1,117	1,008	806
1981	1,003	1,064	818
1982	779	987	669
1983	877	1,199	1,006
1984	679	1,122	1,017
1985	1,045	986	1,422
1986	1,137	1,156	1,307

Source: Australian Dried Fruits Association.

Data on average yields of dried vine fruit in Australia are not available, because with varying degrees of diversion of grapes to wineries the area devoted to drying is not accurately known. Yields of four tonnes per hectare would be expected from a well-managed vineyard in a good season, although crops of half this size are common and when weather conditions are not favourable may be as low as one tonne per hectare.

1.3.7 Marketing procedures

The prime objective of the ADFA is to provide an orderly marketing system which minimizes selling costs and maximizes returns in an equitable manner to all growers. Packing companies are not permitted to buy and sell fruit, their function being that of processors and mercantile agents. Sale, both on domestic and export markets, is effected through three major agents, two of which are members of the ADFA. Growers retain equity in the fruit until it is sold by the agents, of which the largest is Australian Dried Fruits Sales (ADFS), handling about 75% of the total production. ADFS is wholly owned by the industry, the shareholders being the Irymple Packing Company and the grower-owned and controlled co-operative packing houses of Mildura, Rivergrowers and Waikerie Products. The other ADFA member agent is Australian Fruitgrowers Marketing Company Pty Ltd (AFCO) which in 1987 took over the ADFA agency previously operated by G. Wood Son & Company. AFCO is wholly owned by the packers for which it operates as agent, namely Robinvale Producers, Berrico and Barmera Co-operatives.

The sequence of events is that upon delivery to a packing house, the dried fruit is weighed and classified into quality grades by a classer employed by the packer. Disputes between packers and growers on grade classifications are resolved by graders employed by the State Boards.

After classification, the fruit from individual growers is pooled and then destemmed, cleaned and packed in a condition ready for sale. Commonwealth inspectors are located in each packing house to ensure compliance with grade standards and general hygiene requirements, which are laid down under Commonwealth export regulations and by the State Boards in respect of domestic sales. These standards are uniform for fruit destined to either the export or Australian market.

Agents who operate on a commission, currently fixed at 2.5%, sell the fruit to distributors or manufacturers on the Australian market or approved buyers on export markets. At this stage ownership of the fruit passes from grower to buyer. The proceeds of sale, less various levies, are returned to packing houses who, after deducting packing charges and other direct costs, credit the proceeds to growers. Payments to growers are made according to the grade classification at delivery, the differential between grades being related to actual market realizations.

Growers receive an advance door payment at delivery and then progressive payments until the varietal pool of a particular season's crop is sold.

1.3.8 Export markets

As with wine, the importance of the UK as an outlet for dried vine fruits has declined dramatically, largely as a result of the entry of the UK into the European Economic Community and the imposition of tariffs on imports from non-member nations or those not possessing associate status. For the seven-year period from 1960 to 1966 exports to the UK and Republic of Ireland averaged 30,314 tonnes, 20,253 from 1967 to 1973 and 9,490 from 1974 to 1980. Exports to this destination have since declined progressively to 4,670 tonnes in 1986.

Nonetheless, the European Community, as such, remains Australia's largest market, accounting for 47 per cent of exports of dried vine fruit in 1986, of which the Federal Republic of Germany received the major share. The next largest market is Canada, which accounts for 27 per cent of exports of dried vine fruit (Table 1.17).

Sultanas are the major dried vine fruit exported from Australia accounting for 92 per cent of the total in 1986.

Table 1.17. Direction of exports of Australian dried vine fruits (tonnes)

	1981	1982	1983	1984	1985	1986
Federal Republic of Germany	9,186	18,022	5,360	16,224	16,171	17,624
Canada	8,476	13,955	12,554	15,983	16,064	14,828
New Zealand	5,582	4,846	6,570	5,685	6,111	6,559
United Kingdom & Ireland	3,748	7,810	7,321	6,604	4,821	4,670
Continent of Europe (excluding F.R.G.)	1,937	5,535	4,569	5,031	3,369	3,870
Japan	2,365	3,314	2,668	2,223	2,305	2,490
India	1	452	1,732	1,928	1,446	1,518
Other Export Markets	2,578	3,951	6,468	6,333	2,876	3,993

Source: Australian Dried Fruits Corporation.

1.3.9 Industry organization

There is a mix of Federal and State statutory bodies and voluntary associations set up under the umbrella of the Australian Dried Fruits Association which are involved in the organization of the dried vine fruits industry.

The Australian Dried Fruits Corporation

The Corporation was established by virtue of the *Australian Dried Fruits Corporation Act, 1978*, replacing the Australian Dried Fruits Control Board which was set up as far back as 1924 to generally direct the export of dried vine fruits. The functions of the Corporation are: to promote and control the export of dried vine fruit, together with its sale and distribution after export; to encourage and promote the consumption of Australian dried vine fruits outside Australia; and such other functions prescribed by the Act and its Regulations. Included amongst the latter are administration of the equalization and underwriting schemes.

In effect, the activities of the Corporation in respect to exports mirror those of the ADFA for domestic marketing. It approves all export agency arrangements, allocates fruit to available markets, sets prices for each export market, determines conditions of sale and negotiates freight rates.

The Corporation is composed of a chairman and Commonwealth Government member, both appointed by the Minister for Primary Industries and Energy, four selected members representing producers and two selected for their special qualifications. Its operations are financed by a statutory levy on production, currently set at $15 per tonne.

The Dried Fruits Research Council

The Dried Fruits Research Council, established in 1986 under the *Rural Industries Research Act 1985*, has functions similar to the corresponding body for grapes and wine in allocating industry levy funds, matched by the Commonwealth Government, to research and development projects of relevance to producers and processors. The Council's activities embrace dried vine fruits, dried tree fruits and prunes, which operate on separate accounts. The Council comprises a chairman and Government member appointed by the Minister for Primary Industries and Energy and seven other members representing industry and research and development organizations, appointed on the recommendation of a selection committee. The operative levy rate for dried vine fruits in 1987 was $2.50 per tonne.

State Dried Fruits Boards

Dried Fruit Boards with similar powers and functions operate in each producing State. They are composed of growers' representatives who are elected every three years and a Government-appointed chairman. Briefly, the functions of the Boards are: to register packing houses and to fix and enforce their standards of construction, maintenance and hygiene; prescribe and police quality grades for the domestic market; and generally foster the development and well-being of the industry. Joint action by the Boards is effected by liaison through the Dried Fruits Consultative Committee consisting of the chairman of each Board.

Originally, State Boards also had the important function of fixing and policing quotas for domestic sales of dried vine fruits, but under present marketing arrangements, as described previously, this is no longer relevant.

The Australian Dried Fruits Association

The ADFA effects voluntary organization of the dried fruits industry. Although the ADFA is not directly involved in trading, it sets the rules by which commercial transactions with the commodity are conducted within Australia. Briefly, its role covers: the setting of Australian prices, terms and conditions of sale for dried fruits; promotion of sales within Australia; and liaison with State and Commonwealth authorities in the exercise of orderly marketing and product quality control. Its sphere of activities embraces dried tree fruits and prunes as well as dried vine fruits.

The ADFA has an enviable record of achievement on behalf of the industry and current grower membership is 4700. It has branches in each producing district and its policy is determined by a Federal Council which meets annually and is made up of grower, selling agent and packer representatives. A Board of Management directs the day-to-day affairs of the Association.

1.4 Tablegrapes

Grape production for fresh consumption commenced soon after settlement and was Australia's first commercial viticultural enterprise. However, recorded information on early development of the industry is scarce, reflecting its past minor significance in most districts.

The Commonwealth Yearbook quotes Australian production of table grapes in 1901-02 at 13,400 tonnes. According to figures from this source there was little overall growth in production for about

Figure 1.20. Viticultural workers displaying the growth of a Muscat scion grafted on the phylloxera-resistant rootstock 41 B (V. vinifera-Chasselas × V. berlandieri) at the Narara Viticultural Station near Gosford, NSW, in June 1914.

40 years, with 16,002 tonnes being recorded in 1940-41 and then rising to 19,600 tonnes in 1960-61 and 25,300 tonnes in 1970-71.

Expansion which took place in the early 1960s was partly associated with the wide acceptance by consumers of the seedless Sultana as an attractive dessert variety which occurred at that time and has since been fostered by widespread use of gibberellic acid to increase berry size.

Current statistics on fresh grape utilization in Australia list three categories; wine, drying and other purposes. For all intents and purposes, prior to 1988, 'other purposes' can be regarded as 'tablegrapes' and on this basis, production in 1986-87 was 43,400 tonnes, which represents a substantial uplift in the significance of the industry over the last decade. Nonetheless, tablegrapes represent only 5% of fresh grape production (Table 1.18). In 1988, there was a significant quantity of grapes processed for sale as juice and other unfermented grape products. Accordingly, the 'other purpose' statistic subsequent to 1986-87 will be no longer a reliable guide to table grape production.

As distinct from the Murray Valley districts and Murrumbidgee Irrigation Areas where growing of grapes for the fresh fruit market developed as a sideline to other horticultural pursuits, specialist table grape production on a relatively small scale has been long established near cities to meet the requirements of the local market. Those which catered for the early market included Stanthorpe in the Queensland Granite Belt and the Pinkenba and Nudgee Districts on the outskirts of Brisbane; the Orchard Hills, Liverpool and Camden areas close to Sydney and the Hunter Valley near Newcastle. Mudgee and Orange in the central tablelands of New South Wales also had a significant role in supplying the late market. Muscat Hamburg (Black Muscat) was by far the most important and profitable variety in all these districts, some of which have now been lost to urban development.

Specialist tablegrape production has also been a long established enterprise in the Swan Valley of Western Australia. Apart from supplying the Perth market, growers in this district developed a steady export trade to South East Asia with Cannon Hall Muscat and the late maturing Ohanez as the original major varieties.

In South Australia tablegrapes came mainly from the Marion district on the Sturt River and Payneham on the Torrens River. Since the loss of these areas to residential subdivision in the 1950s, specialist table

Table 1.18 Production of table grapes, Australia (tonnes)

Year	NSW	Vic	Qld	SA	WA	Total
1901-02	3,531	5,192	762	2,845	1,118	13,447
1910-11	3,977	2,960	1,274	2,572	3,251	13,034
1920-21	2,703	2,511	659	970	2,122	8,965
1930-31	3,739	3,860	2,100	905	2,880	13,485
1940-41	4,947	4,324	2,536	1,624	2,569	16,002
1951-52[c]	3,183	4,773	2,264	790	1,610	12,630
1960-61	5,659	7,234	3,330	1.084	2,308	19,616
1970-71	6,991	11,000	4,329	1,059	1,952	25,331
1980-81	5,004	8,475	NA	2,545	1,290	22,239[a]
1985-86[b]	7,562	19,950	4,535	3,046	1,606	36,710
1986-87[b]	8,476	26,571	3,802	2,860	1,694	43,439

NA   Not available
(a)   Includes Queensland
(b)   Listed as 'other wine' to winemaking and drying. Also, EVAO $20,000, previously $2,500 — see explanatory note to Table 1.1.
(c)   Figures for 1950-51 are not available
Source: Australian Bureau of Statistics.

grape production relocated to the South Australian Riverland. Indeed, with the introduction of fast, refrigerated transport a shift to the inland irrigation districts became common to all eastern States. This has been aided by the commercialization of a range of varieties which cover a much broader maturity spectrum.

In the late 1970s and early 1980s the potential for expanding exports of tablegrapes were recognized, prompting a number of growers, mostly located in the Sunraysia and Mid Murray districts of Victoria and New South Wales, to establish specialist enterprises, utilizing modern technology and new varieties, aimed at capturing a greater share of these markets. This represented a new emphasis in the industry which has now broken loose from the confines of the domestic market to focus on the international trading arena. At the same time, there has been a big spin-off to the domestic trade in that the better quality fruit available has greatly expanded sales.

Another major thrust in the industry has been to extend the marketing season at the 'front end', not only through the planting of early maturing varieties, but also by planting new vineyards in northern Australia to take advantage of the warmer climate there. Substantial plantings have been made in the Northern Territory aimed initially at the pre-Christmas market in the southern States and several new areas in Queensland are being developed for the same purpose. New plantings of Sultana

and Flame Seedless at Menindee in New South Wales are intended to fill the January market gap. Also, at Murray Bridge and other former glasshouse tomato-producing districts in South Australia, many glasshouses are being utilized profitably for producing premium pre-Christmas table grapes (Heslop 1986). Likewise, commercial interest in glasshouse production of tablegrapes has recently extended to the Sunraysia district.

Despite the significance of the foregoing developments, greatest growth in the industry resulted from growers switching production away from drying grapes to table grapes in the Victorian and New South Wales districts based on Robinvale, Swan Hill and Mildura which, by far, produce the majority of the Australian crop.

1.4.1 Domestic Marketing

Tablegrapes are mostly marketed in 10 kg packs, the dimensions of which are prescribed under uniform State regulations. In this respect Australia differs from most western nations where statutory controls over package sizes for fresh fruit and vegetables on domestic markets are rare. The cases are mostly constructed of either fibreboard or expanded polystyrene foam which have replaced wooden packages that were used in the past.

The majority of sales are made through merchants or commission agents located at central markets in the principal cities. Again, Australia is somewhat unique in that the agents are required to be registered, and in most States their maximum commission is fixed by legislation, currently at 10% in New South Wales.

In most States, there are no quality grades for locally sold table grapes, but minimum maturity requirements are prescribed and enforced by State Departments of Agriculture. These vary slightly depending on the variety but require a sugar content sufficient to give a minimum brix reading of 16^0 for most varieties, 18^0 for the higher acid Sultana (Thompson Seedless) and 15^0 for several low acid varieties. Australia, as a member of the Organisation for Economic Co-operation Development (OECD), has an obligation to adopt by 1990 grade standards for both domestic and export fresh produce that comply with OECD standards. Already these have been incorporated in Commonwealth Export Control Orders for grapes and will soon be adopted by the States to cover local sales. Common use of internationally recognized standards should further facilitate the export trade in table grapes.

1.4.2 Exports of tablegrapes

Exports of tablegrapes throughout most of the 1970s fluctuated between 500 and 1000 tonnes and were mostly confined to South East Asia, with limited quantities to the United Kingdom. However, 1978 saw commencement of a steady increase to 6,000 tonnes in 1984-85 and then successive jumps to 11,500 tonnes in 1985-86 and 18,400 tonnes in 1986-87. Further expansion is expected and exports could well reach 25,000 tonnes in 1987-88. While Singapore has remained the major overseas market, the growth in exports was coupled with the emergence of new markets in Europe, New Zealand and the Middle East (Table 1.19).

Table 1.19. Direction of exports of grapes, Australia 1986-87 (tonnes)

Singapore	3,859
United Kingdom	2,498
Hong Kong	2,368
New Zealand	1,559
Netherlands	1,316
United Arab Emirates	1,240
France	914
West Germany	501
Others	4,162
Total	**18,417**

Source: Department of Primary Industries & Energy.

Development of exports has been aided by greater availability and competitiveness of air freight, but most consignments are shipped in refrigerated sea containers which are generally packed at the centres of production.

As with the domestic market, seedless grapes are the preferred varieties for export and of these Thompson Seedless constitutes well over 50% of total shipments. Thompson Seedless is the name ascribed to the so-called 'cultured' Sultana possessing a large berry size, exceeding 15 mm in diameter. This is achieved by bunch trimming and a program of treatment with the growth promotor gibberellic acid at the flowering and post-flowering stage of bunch development. Other varieties of significance are the early maturing Flame Seedless, Cardinal and Ruby Seedless, which matures a little later than Thompson, and the later maturing Red Emperor, Ohanez, Calmeria and Ribier.

Export growth has relied upon correct adoption of a package of technology covering both vineyard cultural operations and postharvest handling. The fruit is immediately cooled after harvest and packed in polyethylene bags ('poly liners') placed inside the packages. A pad impregnated with sodium metabisulphite is included. The polyethylene bag ensures that the air is saturated, thereby maintaining freshness of the fruit, and the metabisulphite pad releases sulphur dioxide gas to inhibit mould.

Grapes for Europe are now invariably shipped in shallow (one bunch deep), 5 kg fibreboard tray packages which have been returning to the grower between $7 and $10 per package. For South East Asia, 10 kg fibreboard packs are used although polystyrene cartons also are consigned by air. Most sales in Europe are on a consignment basis, while for other markets the prices are generally predetermined prior to shipment.

1.4.3 Prices of tablegrapes

Prices for tablegrapes vary considerably depending on the time of the season and variety. Muscat Hamburg and Cardinal varieties marketed during December are currently attracting prices on the Sydney wholesale produce markets as high as $27 per 10 kg pack, but later level out in a range between $10 and $20. Prices for Thompson Seedless are generally consistently high throughout the season ranging between $17 and $20 per 10 kg pack whereas the smaller-berried Sultana brings lower prices, mostly in the $9 to $15 range. Midseason Muscat Hamburg, Waltham Cross, Flame Seedless and Purple Cornichon generally bring between $10 and $15.

1.4.4 Industry organization

In contrast to the drying and wine grape industries there is little statutory or voluntary organization of the table grape industry.

At the statutory level, the Commonwealth in 1988 set up three new horticultural organizations, the *Australian Horticultural Corporation* (AHC), the *Horticultural Research and Development Corporation* (HRDC), and the *Horticultural Policy Council* (HPC), all to service particular needs of the fresh fruit and vegetable industries. The AHC is designed primarily to encourage, facilitate and co-ordinate export marketing, the HRDC to identify research and development needs and arrange for the conduct of R & D projects; and HPC to provide policy advice to Governments. Tablegrapes fall within the ambit of these organizations and the industry will largely determine the extent to which it becomes involved in their operations.

Voluntary organization of the table grape industry at the national level is currently in a formative phase but should be finalized soon. The *Victorian Grape Packers and Exporters Association* has been in existence for many years, as was the *Viticulturalists Union of Western Australia,* which in the early 1970s became the *Grape Growers Association of Western Australia Incorporated.* Both these groups cater for the interests of table grape growers.

However, it was not until the early 1980s that attempts were made to create a more representative organizational structure for the industry. At this time the *Mildura, Robinvale and Sun Centre (Swan Hill) Table Grape Growers Association* was formed, and subsequently similar organizations were set up in South Australia and at Stanthorpe in Queensland. In 1984, at the first National Table Grape Industry Technical Conference, an *Interim Australian Table Grape Growers Council* was formed, incorporating the new and previously established associations. It is expected that these interim arrangements will be formalized at the Third Technical Conference scheduled for late 1988.

1.5 Concluding remarks

The viticultural industries throughout the course of their development have experienced chequered fortunes, conforming to the normal cyclical pattern of profitability common to most agricultural pursuits. However, it is significant that their present economic strength is not dependent on any substantive, artificial circumstance such as export bounties or Empire trading preference which applied in the past. Indeed, their recent growth has been forged in a generally unfavourable international trading environment in which competitors often enjoy the advantage of favoured market access and subsidies placed on production. This augurs well for the future, and providing further growth is market driven, the long term prospects for Australian viticulture are sound.

Further reading

Busby, J.A. (1925) A treatise on the culture of the vine and the art of making wine, Sydney. (Reprinted by The David Ell Press, 1979).

Coombe, B.G. (1987) Viticultural research and technical development in Australia, Proc. Sixth Aust. Wine Industry Tech. Conf., Adelaide, July, 1986. Australian Industrial Publishers, Adelaide. pp. 20-4.

de Castella, F. (1891) Handbook on Viticulture for Victoria, Melbourne.

Kelly, A.C. (1861) The Vine in Australia, Melbourne, (Reprinted by The David Ell Press, 1980).

Laffer, H.E. (1949) The Wine Industry of Australia, Aust. Wine Board, Adelaide.

Sutherland, G. (1892) The South Australian Vinegrower's Manual; a practical guide to the art of viticulture in South Australia, Government Printer, Adelaide.

References

Anon. (1985a) Report of the Inquiry into the Grape and Wine Industries, Department of Primary Industry, 1985.

Anon. (1985b) Australia Dried Fruit News, Vol 12, No. 3, Feb. 1985.

Anon. (1987) Eighth Annual Report of the Australian Dried Fruits Corporation for the year ended 30th June, 1987.

Dried Fruits Processing Committee (1982) Grape Drying in Australia.

Fogarty, J.P., Great Australians, George Chaffey, Oxford University Press, Melbourne.

Heslop, A.J. (1986) Overview of the Australian table grape industry. Proc 2nd National Table Grape Industry Conf., 9-10 July 1986.

Ilbery, J. (1984) Vineyards and Vignerons of Australia, Len Evans Complete Book of Australian Wine, Summit Books, Sydney, pp. 39-180.

Maiden, J.H. (1917) The Grapevine. Notes on its introduction into New South Wales, Agric. Gaz. of NSW, 28, 427-33.

CHAPTER TWO

The Grapegrowing Regions of Australia

P. R. DRY and R. E. SMART

Since their introduction to Australia in 1788, grapevines have been cultivated in many parts of its southern regions. The viticultural significance of these regions has changed with time for a variety of reasons: for instance, the large impact of phylloxera in Victoria last century and more recently, the effect of urban sprawl around Adelaide and Perth, and the renewed interest in table wines from cooler regions. Vineyard development in Australia has been restricted to a relatively small number of areas and, even with the major vineyard expansion of the late 1960s associated with increases in wine consumption, most plantings were in 'traditional' areas. Plantings irrigated from the Murray and Murrumbidgee Rivers have increased since the early 1900s and now account for approximately 80% of Australia's grape production. Compared with Europe, a higher proportion of Australian grapes are grown in warmer areas. With increased demand for table wines, there has been recent interest in cooler climates for improved wine quality.

2.1 Classification of grapegrowing regions

The role of climate in determining both quantity and quality of grape production is regarded as paramount. Previous classifications of climate have been based on one climatic variable (e.g. temperature, as with degree of summation used in California; Amerine and Winkler 1944) or a combination of two parameters (e.g. the Branas heliothermic index; Branas et al. 1946).

These are considered inadequate for various reasons and a classification has been developed (Smart and Dry 1980) encompassing the major climatic variables of significance to grape production in Australia—temperature, the rainfall-evaporation difference (aridity), humidity and solar radiation. Each of these variables exhibits diurnal and seasonal variation, and the justification for characterizing the fluctuations may be found in Smart and Dry (1980) and Chapter 4. The indices are designed to be representative of a standard growing season (October to March inclusive) though it is recognized that the length of actual growing season depends on region, variety and each year's climate. As simplistic as the indices are, they do in fact provide an explanation for differences in yield, quality, disease incidence, irrigation requirements and variety suitability between regions.

2.1.1 The variables used

The climatic variables used are based on readily available, long-term climatic averages (Australian Bureau of Meteorology 1975a,b, 1977, 1981, 1985, 1987) and are as follows:

Temperature

The annual curve of mean temperature is approximately sinusoidal and hence may be essentially described by two values: we have chosen the approximate peak of the curve—the mean January temperature (MJT)—and the mean annual range (MAR) which is the difference between January and July mean temperatures. The implication of a high MAR for the same MJT is that spring and autumn temperatures will be lower, and so vine development proceeds more slowly in spring and ripening takes place under lower temperatures in autumn. Because of the nature of the temperature-time curve, MJT is well correlated with degree days (Smart and Dry 1980) and is essentially the same as the mean temperature of the warmest month, first brought to notice as a useful index by Prescott (See Chapter 4).

Aridity

Mature, well-watered and vigorous vineyards evapotranspire about half of the evaporation rate as measured by a guarded Class A pan evaporimeter (Smart and Coombe 1983). A simple index of irrigation water requirement of vineyards is therefore calculated from monthly totals by subtracting rainfall (mm) from 0.5 of Class A Pan evaporation (mm). The data are summed for the standard growing season (October to March).

Relative humidity

The 9 am per cent relative humidity for January is taken as an index of relative humidity over the growing season; the relative humidity at 9 am approximates the daily mean figure.

Sunshine hours

The average daily bright sunshine hours in the standard growing season (October to March) is used as an index of solar radiation. Estimates of global solar radiation can be derived from sunshine and cloud data, although regression coefficients vary from place to place (Black 1956).

2.1.2 Comparison of regions

Table 2.1 gives details of climatic averages for Australian viticultural regions. As well as the indices listed above, data are presented for rainfall and raindays, and length of the frost-free growing season. Problems associated with the use of climatic data from particular station(s) for a given region have been discussed in Smart and Dry (1979, 1980); also see footnotes of Table 2.1.

The order of the regions listed below is based on temperature and aridity, the two most important climatic factors determining grape production in Australia. Regions are grouped into classes as follows: MJT $\geq 25\,°C$; MJT from 23.0 to 24.9 °C; 21.0 to 22.9 °C; 19.0 to 20.9 °C and 17.0 to 18.9 °C. There are no grapegrowing regions considered where MJT is less than 17.0 °C. Within each MJT class, regions are generally arranged in order of decreasing aridity with some modification to allow for grouping of regions in close proximity.

Figure 2.1 shows the locations of regions discussed. Tables 2.2 and 2.3 give the principal varieties used in major regions and Table 2.4 shows the average yield for a range of regions. The rest of the Chapter is a description of viticultural regions in Australia. Information on the average harvest date for Shiraz in each region can be found in Table 7.4.

2.2 Regions with MJT ≥ 25°C

2.2.1 Roma (Qld)
The wine industry in Queensland is very small (1,153 ha in 1987). Roma, 500 km west of Brisbane (26°35'S, 148°47'E) at an elevation of 300 m, was the traditional centre of winemaking in the state, but has now been supplanted by the Stanthorpe region. Vines were first planted in 1863.

The area produces tablegrapes and winegrapes. This is the hottest commercial grapegrowing area in Australia at the present time. Radiation, humidity and evaporation are very high, and it has the most summer-dominant rainfall of Australian grapegrowing areas. The main soils are Hard Mottled-yellow Duplex with Hard Brown Duplex and also Siliceous Sands. Common pests are thrips, downy mildew and oidium. Most varieties are spur-pruned. Yields are moderate (about 12 tonne/ha for Shiraz). Because of high temperatures vintage is very early.

2.2.2 Other regions
There are small plantings of winegrapes at Alice Springs, NT (MJT = 29.4°C), and tablegrapes at Menindee, NSW near Broken Hill (MJT = 26.8°C), Townsville, Qld and at other places in Queensland, the Northern Territory and northern Western Australia. The harvest period varies from October to early January.

2.3 Regions with MJT from 23.0 to 24.9°C

2.3.1 Swan Valley (WA)
The vineyards of the Swan Valley are located 20 km east of the city of Perth. The first vines were planted in 1830. By the 1850s, plantings had expanded and included table and winegrapes. The first dried fruit was produced in 1912.

More recently the area of vines has declined due to low yields, unwanted varieties and competition from alternative land-uses including urbanization. The many small wineries of the region were traditionally producers of fortified wine but now make increasing amounts of table wines.

Regional resources
The viticultural area of the Swan Valley is generally a flat river plain set between coastal sands on the west and the foothills of the Darling scarp, rising to an elevation of about 60m in the east. The climate is of pronounced Mediterranean type with a hot and dry summer with very high solar radiation and evaporation and mild wet winters.

The soils of the Swan Valley are variable (see Table 3.4). Soil types not well suited to viticulture have sandy, gravelly or sandy-loam top soils overlying an impervious clay subsoil (see Yellow Duplex Soils, Chapter 3). The most desirable soils are the fertile alluvial soils (e.g. Friable Loams, Chapter 3) associated with the Swan River, having deep sand or loam topsoil (Pym 1955). Low yield and vigour are associated with drainage problems and/or summer water stress. Water resources in the region are restricted to artesian and sub-artesian bores. Water from the Swan River is saline.

Management practices
Fungal diseases are not usually problems in this climate. However, rootknot nematodes are widespread in the sandy soils. Clean cultivation during summer with covercropping in winter are normal practices. Row spacings are commonly 3 to 3.5 m with single-wire or narrow T-trellises. Vigour and yields are generally low except on deeper alluvial soils.

There are about 600 ha of vineyards in the Swan Valley producing 5,000 tonnes of grapes, 2,600 tonnes of which are for winemaking and the rest for drying and table grapes (1987). The principal varieties are Chenin Blanc, Grenache, Muscadelle and Shiraz for winemaking, Cardinal, Sultana, Italia and Emperor for table use and Zante Currant and Muscat Gordo Blanco for drying.

Summary
The Swan Valley faces pressure from alternative land uses such as urbanization and hobby farms. Expansion is limited due to water shortage. The recent trend has been towards an increased proportion of table wine production. Also a large amount of replanting of table grapes has taken place since 1979. The State Government has initiated a program to improve the viability of grapegrowing in this region.

2.3.2 Sunraysia (Vic., NSW)
This region comprises the Murray River areas near Mildura. The remarks also apply to Robinvale, 70 km to the south-east. The region lies within latitudes 34°00'S and 34°45'S and longitudes 140°55'E and 143°00'E. The Chaffey brothers commenced the irrigation settlement in the late 1880s and the First Mildura Irrigation Trust was formed in 1895. Blocks were allocated to soldier settlers after both World Wars. Dried fruit from the varieties Sultana, Zante Currant, Muscat Gordo Blanco and Waltham Cross has been the most important product of these vineyards.

Table 2.1 Climatic data for viticultural regions in Australia[a]

Region	Station	Temperature				Rainfall and Evaporation					Relative humidity %	Bright Sunshine Oct-Mar h/day
		MJT °C	MAR °C	HDD°C days[b]	Frost Free days[c]	Annual rainfall mm	Oct-Mar rainfall mm	Oct-Mar raindays	Oct-Mar evap. mm	Aridity index mm		
MJT > 25°C												
Roma	043030[d]	27.3	15.2	3136	244	602	397	36	1270	238	56	(9.0)
MJT 23-24.9°C												
Swan Valley	009067	24.3	11.4	2375	365	739	107	22	1342	564	47	9.7
Sunraysia	076026	23.9	13.7	2244	272	283	134	26	1542	637	49	9.7
MIA	075028	23.8	15.3	2201	212	409	197	32	1407	506	51	9.3
Swan Hill	077042	23.6	14.3	2155	254	347	153	25	(1300)	497	52	(9.3)
Riverland	024023[e]	23.0	13.2	2084	296	274	130	29	1280	510	51	9.6
MJT 21-22.9°C												
Mudgee	062021[f]	22.9	15.0	2055	210	668	361	36	1328	303	63	8.0
Hunter Valley	061260[g]	22.7	12.8	2075	248	743	534	67	973	-48	58	7.3
Adelaide Plains	023020	22.6	12.1	2046	275	441	153	33	1314	504	45	(9.0)
Rutherglen	082039	22.3	15.4	1775	185	590	258	38	1265	375	50	9.3
Clare	021014	21.9	13.6	1774	195	634	199	35	(1250)	426	47	(8.8)
Southern Vales	023034[h]	21.7	10.8	1913	-	656	182	39	(1200)	418	49	(8.6)
Barossa	023321[i]	21.4	12.6	1715	259	503	161	38	1249	464	47	8.8
Goulburn Valley	088053[j]	21.2	13.7	1681	201	597	248	33	1113	309	52	9.0
MJT 19-20.9°C												
Granite Belt	041175	20.5	13.1	1703	180	795	503	64	1023	9	69	(8.1)
Margaret River	009574	20.4	7.6	1693	-	1159	194	42	-	-	62	8.1
Mt Barker/ Frankland	009581[k]	20.4	9.8	1619	258	747	228	60	1162	353	61	(7.9)
Padthaway	026089[l]	20.4	11.4	1606	-	526	178	54	1305	475	65	(8.2)
Great Western	*[m]	20.2	12.2	1464	258	591	238	44	(1200)	362	59	8.3
Langhorne Creek	024545	19.9	10.3	1521	-	410	135	48	1156	443	60	8.3
Coonawarra	026045[n]	19.6	9.8	1432	-	646	218	56	1135	350	-	7.8
Yarra Valley	086050[o]	19.4	11.0	1489	-	911	404	70	911	52	63	7.4
Geelong	087025[p]	19.0	9.6	1471	-	538	249	49	1029	266	62	7.8
MJT 17-18.9°C												
Macedon	088036[q]	18.5	12.8	1035	114	753	294	43	923	168	64	(8.0)
Heywood	090048	17.7	8.4	1302	-	853	300	71	-	-	67	7.0
Launceston	091123[r]	17.2	10.3	1020	-	788	311	53	1070	224	65	7.3

N.B. See opposite page for notes to Table 2.1.

40

Table 2.2 Area (ha) of principal grape varieties in major Australian regions (MIA, Sunraysia, Riverland), 1986-1987 (Source: Australian Bureau of Statistics)

Variety	Murrumbidgee Irrigation Area (NSW)	Sunraysia[a] (NSW & Vic)	Riverland[b] (SA)	Total these Regions	% of Australian total
White					
Sultana	9	14153	2038	16200	99
Muscat Gordo Blanco	557	1177	1933	3667	88
Trebbiano	913	-	360	1273	86
Semillon	1181	11	34	1226	47
Doradillo	125	186	761	1072	93
Waltham Cross	19	876	142	1037	79
Palomino and Pedro Ximenes	162	46	546	754	51
Riesling	105	167	337	609	16
Colombard	151	213	173	537	96
Chardonnay	178	161	183	522	20
Red					
Shiraz	786	166	643	1595	32
Currant (incl Carina)	-	712	464	1176	80
Grenache	77	120	826	1023	44
Cabernet Sauvignon	212	112	393	717	21
Mataro	104	38	421	563	80

a Includes Kerang-Swan Hill
b Includes Waikerie and Lower Murray, North Murray and South Murray

Notes to Table 2.1

( ) Denotes estimate
* Mean of 079080 and 08900
a Australian Bureau of Meteorology (1975, 1977, 1981, 1985, 1987)
b HDD°C is summation of mean temperatures >10°C during Oct-Apr.
c For temperatures of 2°C within the screen (Foley 1945)
d 043020 evaporation
e Loxton used in preference to Renmark (MJT = 24.7°C) or Waikerie (024550) (MJT = 23.3°C) data because of location of recording station.
f 065035 evaporation
g 061260 data used in preference to 061242 (MJT = 23.7°C) because of location of recording station; 061242 evaporation
h 023753 rainfall and raindays
i 023307 frost-free days
j 081049 evaporation
k 009843 evaporation
l Mean of 025507 and 026023 for rainfall data
m Frost-free days data for 079080 — experience suggests actual period is much shorter for Great Western
n 026013 evaporation
o 086104 evaporation, rainfall and relative humidity
p 087065 evaporation
q 082042 evaporation
r 091104 evaporation

Wine production commenced in 1914 and recently has increased dramatically: an average of 60,000 tonnes per annum have been processed in the five years up to 1986. The majority of private holdings vary in size from 5 to 20 ha. At present, about 80 per cent of the crop is used for drying whilst a small but increasing proportion is used for table grapes.

Regional resources
The region is generally flat to gently undulating with occasional long sandy rises. Elevation is about 50m. The climate is characterized by very high levels of solar radiation, temperature and evaporation, and low humidity (see Figure 2.2). Rainfall is very low (275 mm) and of uniform incidence. Sandy loams of the Barmera and Nookamka series(see Calcareous Earths and Red Sandy Earths, Chapter 3) are preferred for vineyards, while light sands (Brownish Sands, Chapter 3) and soils heavier in texture than clay-loams (e.g. Cracking Clays, Chapter 3) are avoided.

Many soils are prone to watertable development making subsurface drainage necessary (Penman *et al.* 1939, 1940; Hubble and Crocker, 1941). Salt damage is a consequence of poor soil drainage and/or poor water quality. The level of the River Murray is maintained by a series of locks and each year about

Table 2.3 Area (ha) of principal varieties in Australian regions (others), 1986-1987 (Source: Australian Bureau of Statistics)

Variety	Hunter (NSW)	Rest of NSW[a]	Rest of Vic.[b]	Central (SA)[c]	Barossa (SA)	Northern (SA)[d]	South-East (SA)[e]	Western Australia	Total these Regions	% of Australian total
White										
Riesling	82	53	231	260	968	477	866	200	3137	83
Chardonnay	422	277	326	201	269	142	326	105	2068	79
Semillon	664	54	40	40	457	42	30	64	1391	53
Palomino & Pedro Ximenes	-	1	12	149	424	117	13	20	736	49
Traminer	139	51	51	28	85	49	117	13	533	72
Sauvignon Blanc	50	18	88	95	81	51	46	42	471	73
Crouchen	-	-	-	7	218	57	47	-	329	53
Chenin Blanc	-	-	59	50	91	16	10	99	325	68
Muscadelle	-	-	34	2	208	9	27	44	324	82
Frontignac	-	14	36	28	151	1	25	4	259	50
Red										
Shiraz	549	132	386	512	895	211	595	106	3386	68
Cabernet Sauvignon	227	161	377	417	353	239	711	230	2715	78
Grenache	1	7	7	368	705	78	41	96	1303	56
Pinot Noir	72	42	141	62	75	16	153	18	579	87
Currant (includes Carina)	-	1	1	8	6	14	-	260	290	20
Merlot	13	5	66	44	18	19	50	-	215	83

a Includes Mudgee, Corowa
b Includes Rutherglen, Goulburn Valley, Glenrowan-Milawa, Yarra Valley, Avoca, Great Western, Drumborg
c Includes Southern Vales, Adelaide Plains, Langhorne Creek
d Includes Clare, Watervale, Auburn
e Includes Coonawarra, Padthaway
f Includes Swan Valley, Margaret River, Frankland-Mt Barker

200,000 ML are pumped from it for irrigation of these horticultural areas.

Management practices
The most significant pest is rootknot nematode (*Meloidogyne* spp.) on light-textured soils. The absence of significant spring and summer rainfall ensures that the diseases downy mildew and black spot (anthracnose) appear only sporadically. Oidium is more serious from time to time. While soils are low in nitrogen and phosphorus, responses to their application are often undetectable. Vines on sandy soils respond to foliar zinc sprays applied before flowering.

Lime-induced chlorosis can also be a problem and is mainly a consequence of poor irrigation management. Frost likelihood requires appropriate soil management measures in spring. Furrow irrigation is most widespread but overhead and undervine sprinklers have been installed in many new plantings. For most of the area water is supplied increasingly by a water-on-order system and a total of about 900 mm is usually applied over the season in seven irrigations. All vines are trellised, principally with a single wire or narrow-T trellis 30 cm wide at 0.9 to 1.4 m high. Row width is usually 3.3 m and vine spacing 1.2 to 2.4 m. The method of pruning is determined largely by variety, vine vigour and trellis type. Sultana is cane-pruned because of low fruitfulness of basal nodes. Otherwise, vines on single wire or narrow T-trellises are mainly spur-pruned on bilateral cordons, and vines on the wide-T trellis are commonly cane-pruned.

This region has high vine vigour and yields are commonly over 25 tonne/ha. The main varieties are Sultana, Muscat Gordo Blanco, Zante Currant, and Waltham Cross with smaller areas of winegrapes such as Colombard, Chardonnay, Riesling and Shiraz.

Summary
The development of Sunraysia has been closely associated with the dried vine fruit industry, since this region produces about 80 per cent of Australia's sultanas, raisins and currants. Diversions of traditional drying varieties (e.g. Sultana, Muscat Gordo Blanco) to table wine production and the planting of varieties used only for wine have become important.

2.3.3 Swan Hill–Kerang (Vic.)
This region is located on the River Murray approximately 180 km south-east of Mildura. It has many similarities to the Sunraysia region but is slightly cooler and has more rain, and thus is less favourable for production of dried fruit than

Table 2.4 Yields [a] (tonne/ha) for selected grapegrowing regions for the period 1980-1986

Region	Low	Average	High
Sunraysia (Vic)	14.6	19.6	22.4
Riverland (SA)[b]	15.1	17.5	19.8
MIA (NSW)	15.0	17.0	18.4
South-East (SA)	8.5	11.4	13.8
Central (SA)[c]	5.8	7.4	9.3
Barossa (SA)	5.0	7.3	8.7
Swan (WA)	5.6	6.6	8.4
Northern (SA)[d]	3.2	6.4	8.2

a Yield (tonne/ha) = Total grape production (wine, drying, table) in tonnes per total bearing area in ha.
b North Murray District only
c Includes Southern Vales
d Clare-Auburn

Data source is Australian Bureau of Statistics

Sunraysia (Anon 1955). It is an important centre of tablegrape production, suppplying both the Sydney and Melbourne markets: the main varieties are Sultana, Waltham Cross, Ohanez and Emperor.

Winegrapes and dried fruit are also produced in this region. The main soils are Calcareous Earths, with lesser amounts of Sandy Earths, Hard Red Duplex soils, and Brownish Sands.

2.3.4 Riverland (SA)
The Riverland region comprises a number of horticultural areas adjacent to the River Murray between Nildottie to the west and Paringa to the east. The main centres are Waikerie, Barmera, Berri, Loxton and Renmark (34° S to 34°30′ S, 139°40′ E to 140°48′ E).

The first major development of irrigated agriculture in the Riverland occurred at Renmark. The Chaffey brothers from California, under an agreement with the South Australian Government, commenced an irrigation scheme in 1887. Other small irrigation settlements started along the river from the 1890s until the First World War. These early settlements produced grapes mainly for drying, but distilleries were set up from 1917 to 1919 to utilize unwanted drying grapes, particularly Muscat Gordo Blanco.

Soldier settlement schemes were established after both World Wars with private holdings initially being 8 to 12 ha in size and each typically planted with

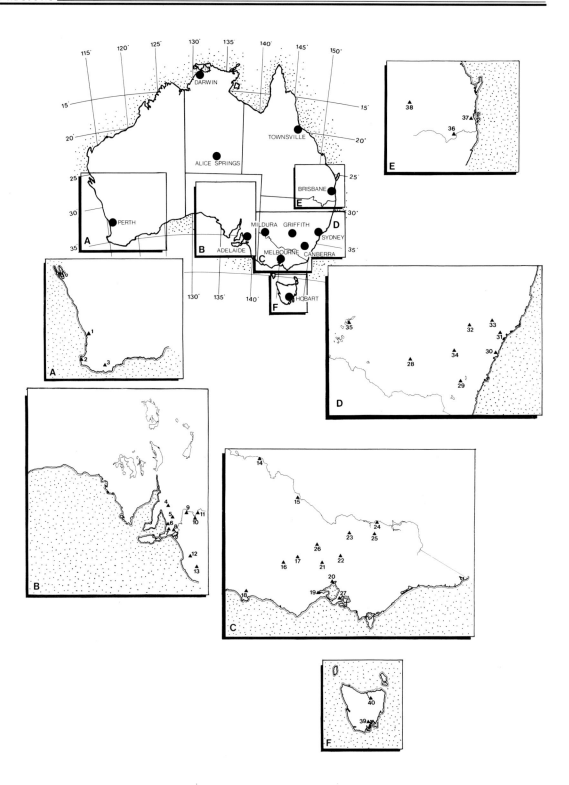

Figure 2.1. Location of Australian grapegrowing regions mentioned in Chapter 2. (For key, see page 45).

several horticultural crops—mainly vines, citrus or stonefruit. The varieties planted before 1960 were generally either the 'drying' varieties like Sultana and Muscat Gordo Blanco or varieties such as Doradillo, Pedro Ximenes and Grenache for spirit or fortified wine production. As a result of the increased demand for table wine, some vineyard plantings by proprietary wineries followed—for example, at Morgan (Penfolds); at Qualco, west of Waikerie (Yalumba, Seppelts, Penfolds, Orlando) and near Renmark (Angoves); these included many traditional table wine varieties and they now produce about a sixth of the region's winegrapes. The region produces 180,000 tonnes of winegrapes, 25,000 tonnes of drying grapes, and 3,000 tonnes of tablegrapes.

Regional resources
The climate in most respects is similar to that of the MIA with high summer temperatures, but rainfall is lower, mainly due to the drier summer and autumn.

Two dominant landforms are used for horticulture in the Riverland; the river valley terraces and the mallee highlands. The river valley contains dissected terraces of various heights, occasional sandhills and stranded sandbars. The soils (see Calcareous Earths, Chapter 3) are grey and brown clays on the terraces, often overlying coarse layers of sands on the sandhills and sandbars. Soils of these types are irrigated in Cobdogla, Renmark and Lyrup. The mallee highlands consist of a gently rolling landscape superimposed with a series of discontinued east-west parallel sand dunes. Sandhill soils (see Brownish Sands, Chapter 3) are mainly deep red sands or loamy sands with moderate calcium carbonate at depths of 0.5 to 1.0 m.

On the flatter areas and in depressions, soils are of heavier texture, to sandy clay loams or heavier; they are shallower and overlay layers of calcium carbonate at depths of 0.3 to 0.8 m. In the depressions and down-slope areas, shallow watertables frequently develop requiring the installation of tile drains; drainage effluent is collected in sumps and pumped into evaporation basins or discharged into deep limestone strata. Large areas of the highland soils are irrigated in Waikerie, Loxton and Berri.

Management practices
All vineyards are irrigated with water from the River Murray. In early years furrow irrigation was the only system available, but now newer methods, particularly overhead sprinklers and to a lesser extent

---

Key to Figure 2.1 (opposite)

A. Western Australia
1. Perth
2. Margaret River
3. Mount Barker

B. South Australia
4. Clare
5. Nuriootpa
6. Adelaide
7. McLaren Vale
8. Langhorne Creek
9. Waikerie
10. Loxton
11. Renmark
12. Padthaway
13. Coonawarra

C. Victoria
14. Mildura
15. Swan Hill
16. Great Western
17. Avoca
18. Drumborg
19. Geelong
20. Melbourne
21. Kyneton
22. Seymour
23. Shepparton
24. Rutherglen
25. Milawa
26. Bendigo
27. Mornington Peninsula

D. New South Wales
28. Griffith
29. Canberra
30. Sydney
31. Cessnock
32. Mudgee
33. Muswellbrook
34. Cowra
35. Menindee

E. Queensland
36. Stanthorpe
37. Brisbane
38. Roma

F. Tasmania
39. Hobart
40. Launceston

microsprinklers and drip irrigation, are predominantly used.

The older plantings were made with ungrafted vines but during the 1980s there was a change to the use of grafted vines and these are now generally used to overcome the problems of nematodes and to provide satisfactory vigour. Yields between 20 and 40 tonnes/ha are obtained with grafted vines. All vines are trellised. In older plantings a single-wire or narrow-T about 1.0 m high is used; some later plantings have wide-T trellises (about 1.2m wide and 1.2m high), but in most recent plantings a single wire 1.5m high has been used to facilitate mechanization of pruning and harvesting. Vines on the high single wire are either hedge or minimal pruned. Row width is usually 3.4 to 3.7 m and vine spacing 2 to 3 m, depending on the rootstock used.

The most significant diseases are downy and powdery mildews which cause serious loss in about one year in three to five: the former is often associated with overhead irrigation. Black spot (anthracnose) is seen occasionally in cool wet springs, particularly on Sultana. Rootknot (*Meloidogyne* spp.) and other nematodes reduce yields in many vineyards, sometimes seriously. Other pests include mites, light brown apple moth, mealy bug and vine scale. Phylloxera is not present in the region. The soils are normally deficient in nitrogen and this is supplied to vines by growing cover crops or by light fertiliser applications. Zinc deficiency occurs and foliar sprays are routinely applied.

Summary
The Riverland is Australia's most productive winegrape-growing region, producing approximately one-third of all grapes used for winemaking.

2.3.5 The Murrumbidgee Irrigation Area (NSW)

This viticultural region, commonly termed the MIA, is a large tract of irrigated land situated on the south-western plains of NSW (34°S, 146°E) at an elevation of 140 m.

The township of Griffith is central to the region. A large-scale public irrigation scheme was initiated in 1906. Winegrape growing commenced in 1913, and the first winery was built in 1917. Production increased slowly at first (4,500 tonnes in 1930, 22,000 tonnes in 1941), but expanded considerably in the 1960s to reach 85,000 tonnes in the 1980s. The 5,000 ha of vineyards are on small family farms where grapes are grown together with other horticultural crops.

Regional resources
The region is quite flat which allows the extensive use of water reticulation and irrigation by gravity. The climate is characterized by high solar radiation, low rainfall uniformly spread throughout the year, and high evaporation with low relative humidity in summer (Figure 2.3).

The Riverine plains were deposited by ancient streams and thus consist of highly variable alluvial soils with sands and gravel embedded in clays (see also 'Riverina' Table 3.4). Vines are commonly grown on soils with sandy loam to loam topsoils overlying clay loam or sandy clay loam to clay subsoils, many of which contain limestone rubble. Many of the soils are prone to waterlogging (Taylor and Hooper 1938). Salinity problems occur in areas of impeded drainage where salt has accumulated in the topsoil. Reclamation is achieved by leaching irrigations and tile drainage. Vines can only be grown economically with irrigation in this region. Water is taken from the Murrumbidgee River and is of low salinity.

Management practices
The MIA is relatively free of pests and diseases although, in the occasional years with summer storm, downy mildew may reduce yields. To overcome the problem of summer weeds created by furrow irrigation, the inter-row space is cultivated after each 2 to 3 irrigations. Soils were normally left undisturbed in autumn and winter, and the volunteer cover crop ploughed-under in early spring; however, winter cover crops are now being sown and herbicides are replacing under-vine cultivation. Irrigation water is available on a roster basis each fortnight and vineyards are irrigated up to twelve times each growing season, a total of 500 to 600 mm being applied. Prior to planting, new vineyards are carefully graded to ensure efficient flood irrigation.

Hand-pruning is mostly to two-node spurs; approximately one-third of the vineyard area is pruned by machine. In addition, about one-half of the crop is picked by machine. The excellent growing conditions produce large, high-yielding vines. Pruning weights in excess of 1 kg per m row length (3 tonne/ha) and commercial yields as high as 10 kg per m row length (30 tonne/ha) are not uncommon.

Summary
The Murrumbidgee Irrigation Area has developed steadily to become a major viticultural area in

Australia. The region is strategically located between the important markets of Sydney and Melbourne. Advances in grape handling and winemaking have enable the MIA wineries to produce table wines along with traditional fortified wines.

2.3.6 Other regions

These include vineyards at Wagga Wagga, Wellington and Inverell in New South Wales, near Echuca in Victoria, and on the coastal plains between Perth and Bunbury in Western Australia. Both winegrapes and tablegrapes are produced. Regional resources and management practices are similar to those in nearby regions within this classification.

2.4 Regions with MJT from 21.0 to 22.9 °C

2.4.1 Adelaide Plains (SA)

Development in the Angle Vale-Virginia area along the northern fringe of metropolitan Adelaide (34°38′S, 138°35′E) commenced in the 1940s and mainly consists of small winegrape vineyards. At present (1987) there are about 300 ha of vineyards.

Regional resources
Vineyards are planted on red-brown earths (Hard Red Duplex soils, Chapter 3) and calcareous earths of the flat, northern Adelaide plains. The climate is characterized by low, winter-dominant rainfall and very high summer evaporation. Evaporation is among the highest for commercial grapegrowing regions in Australia, due in part to the high wind-run. The majority of vineyards are irrigated from underlying aquifers; over-utilization, causing a lowering of the water level and an increase in salinity, has led to legislated restrictions on water use. One large vineyard development is irrigated with treated sewerage effluent.

Management practices
Drip irrigation is most common as salinity limits overhead sprinkler application and water supplies are limited. All vineyards are trellised with single wire or narrow-T at about 1.2 m; cane- and spur-pruning are used. Vigour and yields are generally moderate. The main varieties are Shiraz, Sauvignon Blanc, Cabernet Sauvignon and Riesling.

Summary
Expansion in the region is unlikely due to restrictions on the use of underground water. In fact, the vineyard area has halved in recent years as growers have turned to alternative crops.

2.4.2 Barossa (SA)

This region has two sub-regions: the Barossa Valley (with the towns of Nuriootpa, Tanunda and Lyndoch) and the Barossa Hills (with the towns of Eden Valley, Springton and Angaston). The area lies approximately 50 km north-east of Adelaide (34°30′S, 139°14′E). The first vineyard was planted in 1847 and further plantings followed up to the 1880s, fostered by the decline of the vineyard area in the eastern states. Development was further enhanced by Federation in 1900, since trade barriers between states were lifted and Barossa wines were shipped in large quantities to the eastern markets. Of the 800 grapegrowers in 1970, 30 per cent had less than 8 ha of vines, and only 11 per cent more than 24 ha (Smith 1970); by 1987 the number of growers had declined to 528. Winery companies own about 10 per cent of the total vineyard area of 6,000 ha (1986).

The majority of holdings are mixed farms with other enterprises such as grazing, orchards or poultry. Many of the grapegrowers are descendants of the original German settlers. Until the 1960s, the major varieties grown in the region were Grenache, Shiraz, Doradillo and Pedro Ximenes for fortified wines and spirit. Table wine is now the most important product of the region, and the pattern of varieties has changed (Table 2.3).

Since the early 1960s, most new plantings have been with varieties such as Cabernet Sauvignon and Riesling, and more recently with Chardonnay, Semillon, Pinot Noir and Merlot. Much of the new planting has taken place in the Barossa Hills.

Regional resources
The 'valley' consists of a plain running north-east/south-west at 180 to 290 m elevation. It is bounded to the west by small hills and gentle slopes and to the east by the steeper Barossa Hills that rise to more than 600 m at the southern end. The altitude near Eden Valley and Springton varies from 360 to 450 m. The climate is characterized by moderate rainfall with marked winter dominance and high summer evaporation and low relative humidity (Figure 2.4). There is a marked increase in rainfall, from 490 to 690 mm, from the northern to the southern extremities of the region. Vines suffer water stress in most parts of the region in most seasons, especially on shallow soils. The mean temperature during the growing period is up to 2 °C cooler in the Hills areas resulting in later maturity (Boehm 1970). There is occasional frost risk in low-lying vineyards. Alluvial material eroded from the

eastern ranges has formed the deepest and most productive soils for viticulture. The most important vineyard soils (see also Table 3.4), occupying about 85 per cent of the area, are:

a) Red-brown earths (Alkaline Red Duplex Soils, Chapter 3) with sandy loam to clay loam topsoil over red-brown clay sub-soil, of reasonable structure and drainage (40 per cent);

b) Alluvial soils (Friable Loams, Chapter 3) of deep, uniform profile, well drained, fertile and acid to neutral reaction (10 per cent);

c) Sand over clay and deep sands (Siliceous and Bleached Sands, Chapter 3) (33 per cent);

d) Dark cracking clays Ug5.16, Chapter 3) with self-mulching surface soils and deep uniform clay profiles of alkaline reaction and highly fertile (2 per cent).

In the hills, podsolic soils (Yellow Duplex Soils, Chapter 3) of variable depth with rocky outcrops are dominant with many sites being prone to erosion (Northcote 1959; Northcote *et al.* 1954; Northcote and de Mooy 1957). Supplies of good underground water are limited. Where soil types are suitable, dams provide storage from local run-off or from non-permanent streams.

Management practices

In general, the region is relatively untroubled by major pest and disease problems. Outbreaks of downy mildew are infrequent, only occurring in years with wet springs and summers. Oidium is a problem for susceptible varieties in most seasons. Rootknot nematode, now recognized as a serious problem of sandy soils, can be overcome by using resistant rootstocks. Deterioration of soil structure and erosion in some areas is thought to be due to excessive cultivation during the growing season. The addition of organic matter, cover crops and reduction in cultivations have slowed the decline in soil structure. Minimum tillage systems have been adopted in some vineyards. In 1978, only 12 per cent of the vineyard area was irrigated (French *et al.* 1978); today most vineyards have limited irrigation, mainly by drip. To minimize frost damage, herbage is turned in early in spring and further cultivation is delayed until after the frost danger period.

Control of water erosion on sloping land is achieved through the use of contour planting. The traditional trellis is a single wire at 50 cm height, but higher trellises are now installed in both existing and new vineyards: these are either a single wire at 1.0 m or higher, narrow-T or two-wire vertical trellis. Small areas of untrellised 'bush' vines remain in some old plantings. Row width is usually 3.6 m

and vine spacing 2.1 to 2.4 m. Traditionally, most vines were pruned to canes but spur pruning has become more popular, for economic reasons. Node numbers on hand-pruned vines are usually low.

Mechanization of pruning and harvesting is becoming more common. In comparison with the valley floor, harvest is up to three weeks later on elevated sites (see Table 7.4). Vine vigour is very low to moderate, depending on soil type and water availability; large extremes exist. For example, vines growing on sandy soils in the drier northern area are typically low in vigour while those on clay-loam soils in the southern area are typically moderate in vigour.

Summary

The Barossa is the premier winemaking centre and arguably the best-known wine-producing region in Australia. More than half of the grapes processed in the region are grown elsewhere. Recent development in the cooler hills areas has taken advantage of the greater potential for quality table wine production. Overall, however, the vineyard area in the region has decreased by about 1,500 ha since 1980 as uneconomic, low-yielding vineyards have been removed (including 615 ha under the government-sponsored Vine Pull Scheme in 1986). For the remaining vineyards, clonally-selected planting material, rootstocks, better trellises and limited irrigation are providing large improvements.

2.4.3 Clare (SA)

Vineyards are located between Clare (38°48′S, 138°39′E) and Auburn. The first vineyards were planted in the 1840s around Clare and the area developed slowly to reach 2,200 ha in the mid 1980s. Until the 1960s, the main products were raisins (mainly currants) and fortified wine, but since that time most plantings have been made for table wine. Development by large winery companies has been a feature of the last decade.

Regional resources

The terrain is undulating to hilly. The valley between low ranges to the west and east is at an elevation of 425 m (Clare), but many vineyards are found between 450 and 500 m. Among the variable soils, vineyards are planted on slopes on red and yellow podsolic soils (Red and Yellow Duplex Soils, Chapter 3) and on the valley floor on red-brown earths (Alkaline Red Duplex Soils, Chapter 3) with good water-holding capacity. The climate is similar to the more elevated parts of the Barossa.

Figure 2.10. Old cordon-trained, spur-pruned vines growing in a red duplex soil near Clare, SA.

Management practices
Birds are the major grape pest and control is difficult. Most vineyards are not irrigated, but there is some drip irrigation using water from bores and farm dams. Trellising, spacing and pruning are similar to the Barossa. Vine vigour and yield vary with soil type, from low to moderate in non-irrigated vineyards, and are comparable with those of the Barossa (Figure 2.10).

The main varieties grown in this area are Riesling, Cabernet Sauvignon, Shiraz and Chardonnay (Table 2.3).

Summary
Clare has developed as an important wine-producing region in the last twenty years, and now has a reputation for high quality table wines. Recent vineyard developments by large winery companies have not offset the declining area controlled by small growers. In 1986, 313 ha were removed in the Vine Pull Scheme and the number of growers decreased from 78 to 46.

2.4.4 Southern Vales (SA)
Situated on the southern fringe of Adelaide (35°3′S to 35°17′S, 138°30′E to 138°40′E), the region extends from Happy Valley–Reynella in the north to Willunga in the south. The main concentration of vineyards is found in the McLaren Vale–McLaren Flat area. The first vines in the region appear to have been planted within a few years of the proclamation of South Australia in 1836. Over the next 100 years or so, the vineyard area gradually increased and many wineries were established. Up until the 1950s, the area specialized in fortified wines.

New vineyards and wineries developed during the table wine boom of the 1960s, particularly on the fringes of the established areas. The urban spread of Adelaide has considerably reduced the vineyard area, especially near Reynella; the present area is about 2,200 ha. Much of the vineyard area is owned by the 40 or so winery companies. Half of the grapes produced are processed outside the region, mainly in the Barossa Valley. Vineyard size is generally small, with 60 per cent of vineyards being less than 8 ha. These small vineyards are often associated with other enterprises such as almond production or grazing, or are managed by part-time hobby farmers.

Regional resources
In the Reynella area, vineyards are found on gently undulating land at about 100 m elevation and at scattered sites in the Mt Lofty Ranges to the east, up to 320 m. The majority of vineyards in the McLaren Vale–Willunga district are found on flat to gently undulating land within 12 km of the sea. The climate is characterized by warm summers, moderate winters, winter-dominant rainfall, low relative humidity and relatively high evaporation. Since less than 30 per cent of annual rainfall occurs in the growing season (October to March) there is high likelihood of drought, especially on shallow soils. Vines are planted on a wide range of soil types (see Table 3.4) including podsolic soils (Dy3.61) of low fertility, fertile red brown earths (Dr2.23), terra rossa (Um6.24), rendzina (Um6.21), solodic (Dy3.43) and dark cracking soils (Ug5.1).

Supplies of underground water are available for irrigation but are variable in quantity and quality. Drip irrigation is by far the most common method of application.

Management practices
There have been large changes in vineyard management in the last decade. More than 60 per cent of the area is now irrigated and new plantings of superior clonal material have increased average yield. A large area of Shiraz was planted in the late 1960s to early 1970s leading to a surplus of this variety by the late 1970s. Many vineyards of unwanted varieties were top-grafted to other varieties, particularly to Riesling and more recently Chardonnay, Sauvignon Blanc and Pinot Noir.

Mechanical harvesting is widely used by at least half the growers and mechanical pruning is becoming more common. Row spacing varies from 2.7 to 4.0 m and vine spacing from 1.5 to 2.2 m. Contour planting has been used in some vineyards on the slopes of the eastern hills. With the extensive use of irrigation, soil tillage is used less with the preferred soil managment system being an undervine herbicide strip and sod in the inter-row space which is controlled by mowing. Poultry manure is used in large quantities and urea is often applied through the drip-irrigation system.

The most widely-used trellis is a single wire at 0.6 m in older plantings and a single wire or narrow-T at 1.0 to 1.2 m in those of more recent origin. Vine vigour and yield are low to moderate, but depend on soil type and water availability. The main varieties are Shiraz, Cabernet Sauvignon, Grenache, Riesling and Chardonnay (Table 2.3).

Summary
The Southern Vales has emerged as an important region from the point of view of both wine quality and tourism, but there is limited scope for expansion due to urban development.

2.4.5 Rutherglen (Vic.)

The 'North-East' grapegrowing region of Victoria comprises plantings at Corowa (NSW) and Rutherglen (Victoria) (36°03′S, 146°28′E) adjacent to the River Murray, and those near Milawa (36°26′S, 146°22′E) and Glenrowan approximately 40 km to the south. The first vines were planted in the district in 1851 and over the next thirty years rapid expansion occurred; most of the present winemaking companies were established in that period. In the late 1890s two calamities befell the industry–phylloxera and the depression. Despite the introduction of phylloxera-resistant rootstocks, many growers abandoned their vineyards. The region has subsequently enjoyed increased prosperity and the wine boom of the 1960s resulted in reconstruction and modest expansions. The present area is around 700 ha.

The Rutherglen area has an enviable reputation in Australia for the quality of its fortified wines. Most vineyards belong to wineries.

Regional resources
The countryside at Rutherglen and Milawa is largely flat at an elevation of about 150 m, though foothills of the Great Dividing Range rise immediately east of Milawa (e.g. elevation at Beechworth is 550 m). The climate of the growing season is hot, with low humidity and moderate rainfall. Evaporation and radiation levels are both moderate, but water-stress is common during the summer. Spring frosts occur occasionally throughout the area.

Soils of the Rutherglen region (see Table 3.4) are either based on alluvial deposits from the River Murray, or are derived from sandstone and shales

in the upland areas. The latter typically have loam topsoils overlying clay subsoils. Some Rutherglen vineyards use water from the River Murray for irrigation and good supplies of underground water are available in the Milawa area.

Management practices
This area has two pests that are not commonly found in other parts of Australia: phylloxera, controlled by rootstocks, and *Xiphinema index*, the nematode vector of fanleaf virus, for which there is no adequate control. Traditionally, row spacing is 3.5 m and trellises are generally low, one- or two-wire trellises or narrow-T trellis. Cane pruning is most common. Vine vigour and yields are generally low. Trellises and yields on newer vineyards are higher. Principal varieties in the area are Shiraz, Cabernet Sauvignon, Chardonnay, Riesling and Brown Frontignac. Minor varieties include Dourado and Graciano.

Summary
The Rutherglen area is acknowledged as a premium fortified wine region; there is now increasing emphasis on table wine production. Good potential exists for the production of table winegrapes in the foothills of the Great Dividing Range (36°23′ to 37°02′S, 145°10′E).

2.4.6 Goulburn Valley (Vic.)

The Goulburn Valley is 130 km north of Melbourne, with vineyards and wineries scattered around the townships of Nagambie, Seymour and Shepparton (36°23′ to 37°02′S, 145°10′E). The Goulburn River runs from south to north through the region.

Regional resources
The region is quite flat at an elevation of about 140 m. The climate is similar to Rutherglen, with slightly lower temperatures, evaporation and sunshine hours, and similar rainfall, raindays, humidity and wind run. Soils (see Table 3.4) in the area are varied and commonly alluvial in origin. There is a full range of texture classes with sandy loams predominating. Gravel subsoils are associated with the prior river course. Water resources of the region are excellent, coming from the Goulburn River and from aquifers at about 30 m.

Management practices
Management practices are generally similar to the Rutherglen area, with irrigation being more widely used. The old low single-wire trellis is being replaced with 1.2 to 1.4 m high single wire, narrow-T, or

wide-T trellises on the newer plantings. Pruning is both spur and cane. Phylloxera-resistant rootstocks are employed in most plantings. Vine vigour and yields are moderate to high, depending on irrigation and soil depth.

Summary
The area has a reputation for quality table wines. The grapegrowing resources are very good and there are opportunities for expansion in the surrounding areas.

2.4.7 Mudgee (NSW)

The Mudgee viticultural region is located on the western slopes of the Great Dividing Range, some 260 km north-west of Sydney. The vineyards are located mostly to the north of the township (32°36′S, 149°36′E) at an elevation up to 600 m. The first plantings were made in 1858 and by the 1880s 180 ha of vineyards produced grapes for thirteen wineries. The industry declined in the 1890s, with only two wineries remaining by the 1930s.

With the boom of the mid-1960s, interest in the area was revitalized and 1700 tonnes were crushed in 1987 from 450 ha of winegrape vineyards. The area is well regarded for the quality of table wines, both white and red.

Regional resources
The majority of the region's vines are planted on the slopes of gently rolling country. Summers are mild to hot and spring frosts can be a problem (Figure 2.5). Relative humidities during the growing season are moderate to high and both solar radiation and evaporation are high. Rainfall distribution is relatively uniform but shows a slight summer dominance. The soils (see Table 3.4) are generally suitable for viticulture. Slightly acidic loam or sandy loam topsoils over near neutral clay subsoils are common. Water resources of the region are limited as the Cudgegong River is some distance from the vineyards, creeks carry insufficient water and most bores have inadequate flow; farm dams and a few high-yielding bores provide some water for irrigation.

Management practices
Diseases and pests are usually adequately controlled with protective sprays. The occurrence of frosts requires careful selection of the vineyard site. Row spacings are commonly 3.3 m with vines 1.5 to 1.8 m apart. Trellis systems have evolved from low single wires to high (1 to 1.8 m) trellises or narrow- to wide-T. Vines are traditionally spur-pruned.

Most vineyards are not irrigated but the proportion is increasing. The major varieties are Shiraz, Cabernet Sauvignon, Pinot Noir, Semillon, Chardonnay and Riesling for winegrapes and Muscat Hamburg for tablegrapes. Yields are low to moderate, ranging from 2 to 10 tonnes.

Summary
The Mudgee region has many suitable characteristics for viticulture and is representative of other areas of the central-west of NSW. The main limitation to production is water availability.

2.4.8 The Hunter Valley (NSW)

The Hunter Valley extends north-west from the port of Newcastle on the Pacific coast (31°31′ to 33°15′S, 149°30′ to 152°E). There are two viticultural areas within the valley; the Upper Hunter, centred around Singleton, Denman and Muswellbrook, and the Lower Hunter, nearer the coast and adjacent to Cessnock. Settlement commenced in the Lower Hunter in 1826 and vineyards soon became part of mixed holdings, with the famous 'Kirkton' vineyard of James Busby being planted in 1830. Modest expansion continued through the 1880s but the Depression of the 1890s caused major problems for the Hunter Valley wine industry. A small recovery followed World War I, but in the years 1925 to 1927 about three-quarters of the crop was lost due successively to downy mildew, drought and hail. Following the Depression

Figure 2.11. Frequent application of foliar fungicides for control of fungal diseases is essential in the Hunter Valley, NSW. (See Colour Plate 9)

of the 1930s, expansion commenced slowly to reach a peak during the wine boom of the late 1960s and early 1970s. Production increased substantially from 1,500 tonnes to 23,500 tonnes between 1965 and 1979. Much of this expansion took place in the Upper Hunter.

In the last decade both area and production have declined as uneconomical vineyards, planted on poor sites in the 1970s, have been removed. In 1987, almost 17,000 tonnes were produced from 2,300 ha. Much of the vineyard area is owned by winery companies. About two-thirds of the vineyard area is located in the Lower Hunter.

Regional resources
The terrain is gently to markedly undulating, bordered to the north, west and south-west by the Great Dividing Range. The summer climate in the Hunter Valley is hot and humid, with high cloudiness and high rainfall (Figure 2.6). Rainfall is often highest just prior to and during harvest in February; the summer falls are often intense and much runoff results. Although the long-term average water deficit during summer is small (due to high rainfall and low evaporation) the variation in rainfall is high and in some years the vines suffer considerable water stress. High temperatures result in a vintage period which is one of the earliest and shortest in Australia (see Table 7.4).

Whereas alkaline soil profiles are common in low rainfall areas, here, with higher rainfall, the soils are more strongly leached and acidic. Soils of sandy to clay loam are mostly acid Red Duplex Soils (see Chapter 3) formed on shale and sandstone parent material and are variable in fertility. Red clay loam soils, mostly alkaline Red Duplex Soils (Chapter 3), partly of volcanic origin, are found in narrow strips on the hillsides. These soils have concentrations of free lime and are highly regarded for grapegrowing. Podsolic soils (see Yellow Duplex Soils Chapter 3) derived from sandstones, shales and conglomerates, are lacking in organic matter, have low pH and dense yellow clay subsoils often near the surface. Alluvial soils (see Friable Loams, Chapter 3) on the flood plain are fertile, of silty texture, deep and well-drained. Water resources in the Lower Hunter are limited to farm dams and occasional bores. Those properties adjacent to rivers have a regular supply of good quality water as is common in the Upper Hunter.

Management practices
Downy mildew is the most serious grape disease in the Hunter Valley due to the warm temperatures and high rainfall during the growing period. Six to eight protective sprays are routinely applied, the number increasing to 15 in wet seasons (Figure 2.11). Aerial spraying is widely used. Bunch rot, caused by high rainfall near harvest, can cause substantial losses. Whereas previously the vineyards were cultivated throughout summer it is now common to cultivate less often, e.g. three times—in autumn, winter and spring.

The proportion of vineyards with undervine herbicide and inter-row mowing is steadily increasing. The use of irrigation (mainly drip) has been extended to cover about two-thirds of the total vineyard area. Modest amounts of water are applied with the aim of minimizing the effects of the short-term droughts.

On hillsides, the vines are sometimes set to run across slopes. The traditional low single-wire trellis has given way to a higher trellis with the fruiting wire generally at 1 m and a foliage wire at 1.3 m height. Narrow T-trellises of 0.5 to 0.9 m width have also been introduced. Cane pruning is most common on low vigour vineyards, with low node numbers per vine. Many of the newer vineyards are pruned less heavily to spurs. Semillon, Shiraz, Chardonnay and Cabernet Sauvignon are the most important varieties (Table 2.3): the first two have been the mainstay of this region for many years.

Vine vigour and yield vary from very low with old vines on poor soil without irrigation, to very high on deep alluvial soils with irrigation.

Summary
From the mid-1960s the vineyards of the Hunter Valley have changed from small family-owned estates to larger commercial enterprises. Extensive capital investment has been encouraged by the proximity to the large Sydney market and a reassessment of traditional practices has led to higher levels of production and the use of such labour-saving devices as mechanical harvesting. The climate of the region, with frequent summer droughts, high temperatures and humidity, and the prevalence of vintage-time storms, creates special problems.

2.4.9 Other regions
These include vineyards near Bendigo (MJT = 21.8 °C) and Heathcote in Victoria, on the western slopes of the Great Dividing Range in NSW at Cowra, Young and elsewhere, on the Murray River at Nildottie and Murray Bridge in South Australia and between Busselton and Bunbury in Western Australia. Mainly winegrapes are produced.

2.5 Regions with MJT from 19.0 to 20.9 °C

2.5.1 Langhorne Creek (SA)
The region is bounded by the Mt Lofty Ranges to the north and Lake Alexandrina to the south, and lies 55 km south-east of Adelaide (35°25′S, 138°58′E). The first vineyard was planted in 1858

on the flats of the River Bremer. There are approximately 410 and 30 ha adjacent to the Rivers Bremer and Angas respectively (1987), owned by private growers and three wineries.

Regional resources
Vineyards are planted on a gently and slightly undulating plain. Two rivers, the Bremer and the Angas, traverse the area. The climate is characterized by low winter-dominant rainfall, high relative humidity and moderate temperatures during the growing season. A feature of this area is the limited daytime temperature rise caused by cooling sea breezes in the afternoon. The comparison of rainfall with evaporation indicates the need for irrigation. Most vines are grown on deep alluvial soils (Table 3.4) that are slightly acidic red-brown sandy loams over 1 m deep, or more shallow grey-brown clay loam topsoils over friable clay.

Vineyards in the region are normally irrigated in winter by controlled flooding from the rivers, whose water is dammed and distributed through levee banks. One flooding to a height of 1.0 to 1.5 m supplies sufficient water to satisfy most of the vine requirements during the growing season. Groundwater for vineyard irrigation is withdrawn from a confined aquifer; although water yields are good, salinity is high.

Management practices
Oidium is a serious problem in most years due to the dense vine canopies; downy mildew and bunch rot are occasional problems.

Natural soil fertility is high and application of artificial fertilizer is uncommon. Most vines are trained to 1.0 to 1.2 m single wire trellis but newer vineyards have employed more elaborate trellises for better canopy management, including three vineyards with the Geneva Double Curtain training system. Both spur- and cane-pruning are practised. Vigour and yields are high. The main varieties are Cabernet Sauvignon (25% of planted area), Shiraz, Palomino/Pedro Ximenes and Chardonnay.

Summary
This small vineyard area has a good reputation for wine quality. Lack of suitable water resources restricts further expansion.

2.5.2 Padthaway (SA)
This region is located in the south-east of South Australia (36°30′S, 140°25′E). The vineyards are located near the villages of Padthaway and Keppoch. This was one of the few new areas developed in

Australia during the 1970s. A trial planting of 20 ha was established in 1964, and by 1986 there were about 1400 ha operated mainly by large wine companies. The crop is processed in other regions, mainly Coonawarra.

Regional resources
The majority of vines are planted on a plain at the foot of a low range of hills. The main soils are red-brown earths (Alkaline Red Duplex Soils, Chapter 3) on the plain with red-brown sandy loams and loams (Uc6 and Um6 soils, Table 3.4) of usually less than 0.45 m depth over limestone on the flanks of the hills. The climate of the region is similar in many respects to Coonawarra. However, annual rainfall is lower and summer temperatures are higher. Frost can also be a problem. Good quality water underlies the area at 4 to 8 m depth. Bore yields are high—greater than 2,500 kL per day. The use of water is controlled by legislated water rights.

Management practices
These correspond in the main to those of the Coonawarra area, but as irrigation is more necessary, 90 to 95 per cent of the vineyards are watered by furrow, travelling irrigator, fixed overhead sprinkler or drip. Trellises are high (up to 1.5 m); narrow-T, wide-T or 2-wire vertical trellises are widely used. Vigour and yields are generally high, reflecting good water availability. The main varieties are Riesling, Shiraz, Cabernet Sauvignon and Chardonnay (Table 2.3).

Summary
The high land prices and limited areas of suitable soil at Coonawarra have influenced the rapid development of this region. The potential for further development appears to be limited by water entitlements.

2.5.3 Coonawarra (SA)
One of Australia's most southerly wine-producing areas, this region is located in the south-east of South Australia (37°18′S, 140°50′E). The vineyards are restricted to a narrow north-south strip of land 20 km long with an elevation of 60 m. The first viticultural development occurred in the 1890s and comprised up to 400 ha mainly of Shiraz and Cabernet Sauvignon. Due to economic problems this area declined during the next fifty years to 100 ha, producing mainly grapes for distillation.

From 1950 onwards (and particularly after the mid-1960s) winery companies expanded the vineyards to about 1800 ha by the mid-1980s. Much of the vineyard area is now owned by large winery companies with a small area owned by small wineries and independent growers. The total production from the south-east of South Australia is used almost exclusively for the production of table wine. Most of the grapes are processed within the region.

Figure 2.12. A typical vineyard at Coonawarra, SA, showing a high trellis for frost protection, mechanized pruning and no cultivation. (See Colour Plate 7)

Regional resources

The region is flat. The climate is characterized by moderate, winter-dominant rainfall, moderate temperatures during the growing season, high relative humidity, and moderate solar radiation (Figure 2.7). Rainfall is high (67 mm) during the vintage month of April and may cause problems with bunch rot. Although temperatures during the growing season are generally moderate, heat-waves may occur during January and February. Frosts have been known to occur as late as December and the risk of frost damage is further exacerbated by the flat terrain. During recent years, the large area of vineyard, kept weed-free in spring, appears to have reduced the risk except on the fringes (Figure 2.12).

All vine plantings are found on the limited areas of well-drained soil. A narrow strip of red soil commonly termed 'terra rossa' (non-cracking subplastic clays, Chapter 3) is most extensively used for grapevines (see also Table 3.4 and Figure 3.4). Aquifers underlying the region are recharged in winter. In summer, the water table may only be a few metres below the surface. Water is of generally good quality and there are no restrictions on the amount that may be used.

Management practices

Climatic conditions favour the development of fungal diseases such as downy mildew, bunch rot and oidium. Consequently, protective sprays are applied regularly during the growing season, often by aeroplane. As roots of young vines have difficulty penetrating the limestone layer, deep ripping is usually carried out before planting. Maintenance of a bare, compacted, weed-free soil surface from budburst onwards is essential to reduce frost damage.

Weed control has been mainly by cultivation, but non-tillage combined with the used of herbicides is increasing rapidly. Limited irrigation by fixed overhead sprinklers or travelling irrigator is common on larger vineyards. Average spacings for the area are 3.5 m (row) and 2.0 m (vine). The modern trellis is high (for frost protection) and suitable for machine harvesting. The most common trellis type has a single wire at 1.2 to 1.5 m. Low output overhead sprinklers are used for frost control (see Volume 2, Chapter 8). Much of the pruning is by machine, either severe hedging or light hedging (minimal pruning). Vine vigour varies from moderate to high depending largely on soil type and hence water-holding capacity. The main varieties are Cabernet Sauvignon, Riesling, Shiraz and Chardonnay (Table 2.3). Reasonably high yields may be produced in the region. Harvesting is mainly by machine.

Summary

Recognition of the high quality of wines from this region has led to extensive development by large wine companies. A combination of modern techniques and reasonably high yields has led to lower production costs than for most other areas. Potential for further vineyard development is limited by lack of suitable well-drained land. Other nearby parts of the south-east of South Australia and Victoria do, however, have good potential.

2.5.4 Great Western (Vic.)

The vineyards of Great Western (37°09′S, 142°51′E) are some 220 km north-west of Melbourne and at an elevation of 280 to 360 m. In its heyday early this century the area had 800 ha of vineyards but this declined for economic reasons. Today (mid 1980s) there are 160 ha principally owned by one large wine company. Production is limited by problems of frost, drought and mediocre soils.

Regional resources

The topography of the area is mildly undulating. The early vineyards were planted on flat land but to reduce frost risk newer vineyards are planted on slopes. The climate is warm and dry with moderate evaporation, radiation and relative humidity. Rainfall is slightly winter-dominant. Minimum temperatures are relatively low, leading to the likelihood of late

Plate 1. *A mechanical harvester of the vertical impactor type harvesting winegrapes at Waikerie (SA).*

Plate 2. *Vigorous vine growth in a cool grapegrowing region, Yarra Valley (Vic.).*

Riesling

Sultana

Muscat Gordo Blanco

Cabernet Sauvignon

Plate 3. Some common Australian grape varieties.

Grenache

Shiraz

Semillon

Doradillo

Photographs kindly supplied by CSIRO Division of Horticulture.

Ramsey 105mm	*K51-40* 145mm	*Freedom* 135mm
Dog Ridge 130mm	*K51-32* 155mm	*Harmony* 125mm
1616 150mm	*ARG1* 115mm	*du Lot* 100mm
1613 160mm	*1202* 120mm	*Riparia Gloire* 135mm

Plate 4. Rootstock varieties used in Australian viticulture (see Table 8.3). The approximate leaf width in millimetres is given for each variety.

Schwarzmann *145mm*	*3309* *90mm*	*99 R* *85mm*
101-14 *125mm*	*3306* *105mm*	*110 R* *110mm*
106-8 *135mm*	*5 C* *150mm*	*140 Ru* *115mm*
34 EM *150mm*	*5 BB* *150mm*	*1103 P* *105mm*

420 A   140mm

5 A   160mm

Plate 5. The three proles of Vitis vinifera. Left to right: Clairette, proles pontica; Riesling, proles occidentalis; Sultana, proles orientalis. (See 5.4.2)

(Photograph by courtesy of CSIRO Division of Horticulture)

Plate 6 (Figure 8.2) Chlorosis symptoms in the leaves of young vines of Muscat Gordo Blanco grafted to Harmony rootstock. Soil type: Irymple clay loam. Left: Whole vine. Above: Individual shoots.

Plate 7 (Figure 2.12) A vineyard at Coonawarra (SA) showing a high trellis for frost protection, mechanized hedge pruning (light on the left, severe on the right), and no cultivation (total herbicide).

Plate 8. (Figure 10.2) A contour-planted vineyard on sloping ground at Great Western (Vic.). Vineyards in the flats in this region are prone to frost damage.

Plate 9. (Figure 2.11) Frequent application of foliar fungicides for control of fungal diseases is essential in the Hunter Valley, NSW.

spring frosts, a major problem in the area. The common soil types are Yellow Duplex Soils on the flats and Red Duplex Soils on the hills. Soil reaction in the surface horizons is usually slightly acid to neutral (Badawy 1982, see also Chapter 3). The water resources in the region are limited to surface catchments as both creek-flow and underground supplies are limited and often saline.

Management practices
Downy mildew and oidium occur in the area but are routinely controlled with two to three fungicide sprays. Lightbrown apple moth is an occasional problem. There are no other major pests or diseases. Weed control is achieved with inter-row cultivation and undervine herbicides or cultivation. Cover crops are generally sown prior to vintage. In spring, vineyards are kept clean by cultivation and rolled to reduce frost damage. The traditional trellis of a single wire at 45 to 60 cm has been raised to 90 to 110 cm, thus assisting in frost control.

The principal varieties grown at Great Western are Shiraz, Chardonnay, Riesling and Cabernet Sauvignon. Cane pruning with two to four canes of 10 nodes is commonly used. Vine vigour and yields are low, primarily due to water stress.

Summary
The region has a reputation in Australia for sparkling wine. Red table wines are highly regarded. Expansion is limited by lack of available water resources.

2.5.5 Pyrenees (Vic.)
This relatively new vineyard area lies on the slopes of the Pyrenees Range, some 55 km north-east of Great Western at an elevation of 250 to 300 m and near to Avoca (37°5'S, 143°29'E) and Moonambel. Although vineyards were first planted in this area during the mid 1800s they had disappeared by the turn of the century. The present vineyard development commenced in 1963, initially for the production of grapes for brandy but the current emphasis is on table wine grapes, produced from approximately 300 ha.

The climate is similar to Great Western, with slightly higher temperatures (MJT = 20.9 °C) and lower rainfall during the growing season. Most vineyards have limited irrigation, mainly drip, supplied from dams or underground sources. The principal varieties are Cabernet Sauvignon, Chardonnay, Shiraz, Riesling and Trebbiano. Management practices are similar to Great Western.

2.5.6 The Southern Districts of Western Australia
The first plantings in this region took place in 1967, after the potential for table wine production was recognized by Olmo (1956) and Gladstones (1965). By the late 1970s, 500 ha had been planted, mainly in the areas of Busselton-Margaret River near the west coast (33°38' to 33°56'S, 115°04' to 115°20'E) and Mt Barker-Frankland near the south coast (34°20' to 34°43'S, 116°43' to 117°40'E). The present 600 or so hectares also includes small plantings near Bunbury (MJT = 22.0 °C) on the west coast and Albany (MJT = 19.6 °C) and Denmark on the south coast.

Regional resources
The topography of both areas is undulating (soils are listed in Table 3.4 and discussed in Chapter 3). The climate is characterized by warm summer temperatures with high, winter-dominant rainfall and high relative humidity. Although Margaret River is virtually free of spring frosts, they may cause problems in the Mt Barker-Frankland area (Figure 2.8 shows climatic data for Margaret River). Stored surface water may become saline in the Mt Barker area while underground water is limited in both regions. Chardonnay and Pinot Noir can burst as early as the beginning of July at Margaret River; this is a consequence of the relatively warm winter (mean temperature in July is 12.8 °C). Strong winds later in spring can cause severe shoot damage.

Management practices
The region is relatively free from diseases, probably a reflection of its newness and isolation. As elsewhere in WA, downy mildew has not been recorded, but oidium occurs spasmodically with damaging effects, particularly on Cabernet Sauvignon and Verdelho. Bunch rot may occur due to rainfall near vintage. Fruitset problems have been recorded for young Riesling, Traminer and Chardonnay vineyards, which may be due to wet and windy weather at fruitset, particularly in the Margaret River area. Row spacing has been decreased in new plantings from the standard 3.6 m to between 1.8 and 3.0 m. At Margaret River, tall cereals such as oats and rye are sown in alternate rows to act as windbreaks during early spring. Canopy management, by means of divided canopy training systems, shoot positioning and summer pruning is widely practised. Vigour and yields are low to moderate, varying mainly with soil depth. The main varieties are Cabernet Sauvignon, Shiraz, Chardonnay, Pinot Noir and Riesling. Yields are generally low.

2.5.7 Geelong (Vic.)

Geelong (38°07′S, 144°22′E) is 70 km south-west of Melbourne. Vineyards were established in this area in the early 1840s but were destroyed by phylloxera or Government uprooting programs in the period after 1875. The present 70 ha or so of vineyards were started in the mid 1960s.

The topography is moderately undulating. The climate is cool and dry with moderate evaporation and low radiation. Spring frosts can be a problem in low-lying areas. The common soil type is a red duplex with smaller areas of black cracking clays (see Chapter 3). Most vineyards have limited irrigation from surface storage. The main varieties are Cabernet Sauvignon, Shiraz, Chardonnay, Pinot Noir and Riesling. Yields are generally low.

2.5.8 Yarra Valley (Vic.)

The Yarra Valley vineyards are located near the town of Lilydale, 35 km north-east of Melbourne (37°45′S, 145°20′E). Vines were first planted in 1838 and by the 1870s there were 1200 ha. Vineyards had largely disappeared by the 1920s for economic reasons. There has been renewed interest in the region for table wine production since the late 1960s but the greatest expansion has taken place in the last decade to reach about 120 ha in the mid 1980s. Most vineyards are planted on gentle to moderately steep slopes.

Regional resources

The climate is cool with low radiation, high growing-season rainfall and relative humidity, leading to problems with fungal diseases. Low-lying vineyards are susceptible to spring frost damage. The main soil type is a red duplex soil with smaller areas of yellow duplex soil and deep red loam (see Chapter 3).

Management practices

Regular spraying is required for disease control. Bird pests, particularly starlings, are problems in most seasons. Many vineyards use limited irrigation, from surface catchment, to counter the effects of mid-summer water-stress. Excess vine vigour is a problem on the deeper soils and there has been greater interest in canopy management in recent times. Only table wines are produced: the main varieties are Cabernet Sauvignon, Shiraz and Pinot Noir for reds and Chardonnay and Riesling for whites. Yields vary from low to moderate.

Summary

This region has good potential for further development because of its close proximity to Melbourne.

2.5.9 The Granite Belt (Qld)

Most vineyards are found south of Stanthorpe, located to the south-west of Brisbane near the NSW border (28°39′S, 151°56′E); it is the main wine-producing region in Queensland. The high elevation (790 m at Stanthorpe) of this portion of the Great Dividing Range results in a very different climate to that at low elevations for the same latitude. The growing season is characterized by moderate temperatures, high growing-season rainfall and high humidities. The main soil types are Bleached Sands (Uc2.21) and Sandy-Mottled-Yellow Duplex (Dy5.41, 5.81).

Tablegrapes comprise more than 90% of the total vineyard area and have been grown here since the 1880s. The tablegrape industry (three-quarters of Queensland's production) is static at present; however, there is expansion in tablegrape production in other parts of Queensland. The main varieties are Muscat Hamburg (50 per cent of production), Waltham Cross and Cornichon. Muscat Hamburg ripens in late January.

Winegrapes are relative newcomers (main varieties are Shiraz, Cabernet Sauvignon, Semillon) and there are 10 small wineries at present. The main problems include fungal diseases, nematodes and birds (particularly silver-eyes).

2.5.10 Other Regions

These include vineyards in NSW and the ACT near Canberra (MJT = 20.2), on the more elevated sites of the King River Valley in north-east Victoria (more than 100 ha in the mid 1980s), the Mornington Peninsula south of Melbourne and the Adelaide Hills from Piccadilly to Lenswood (MJT = 19.5°C). The Adelaide Hills vineyards have expanded rapidly in recent years: in 1986, there were more than 70 ha, mainly Pinot Noir and Chardonnay.

2.6 Regions with MJT from 17.0 to 18.9°C

2.6.1 Macedon

This region lies to the immediate north-west of Melbourne, stretching from Sunbury in the south to Kyneton (37°15′S, 144°27′E) in the north, a distance of 50 km. It includes five sub-regions: Sunbury, Mount Macedon (MJT = 17.2°C), Romsey, Lancefield and Kyneton. The coolest sites are found near Kyneton and Romsey where most vineyards have been planted at elevations from 550 to 750 m. The first vines were planted at Sunbury in the 1860s. The present-day vineyards, of which there are about 100 ha, commenced in the early 1970s.

Regional resources

The climate at Kyneton (509 m) is cool with only moderate growing-season rainfall. Vineyards on more elevated sites than Kyneton would have lower temperatures. The strong, cold prevailing winds from the south inhibit shoot growth, reduce yields and probably delay maturity: the use of windbreaks is strongly recommended on most sites. Frost can also be a problem. Vineyards are planted on a range of soil types from deep loams to granitic sandy-loams.

Management practices

Some vineyards have limited irrigation from dams. Low autumn temperatures result in a very late harvest (see Table 7.4). Yields are low due to the combined effects of wind and water-stress. The main varieties are Cabernet Sauvignon, Shiraz, Pinot Noir, Riesling and Chardonnay.

Summary

There has been recent interest in the planting of Pinot Noir and Chardonnay for sparkling wine. However, commercial success in this region has yet to be adequately demonstrated.

2.6.2 Tasmania

Grapegrowing commenced in this state in the 1820s but remained insignificant until the 1970s when the first of the present-day vineyards was planted. The industry developed rapidly in the 1980s: in 1987, half of the 120 ha planted was non-bearing. Vineyards are found in five sub-regions within Tasmania: the north-east centred around Pipers Brook; the Tamar Valley, north of Launceston (41°26′S, 147°10′E); the south centred around Hobart; and the east and north-west coasts.

Regional resources

All sub-regions are very cool with rainfall varying from moderate to high. Most vineyards are located close to the coast and exposed to cold winds, however, frost risk is generally low. The preferred sites are 5 to 20 km inland or along river valleys, on ENE- to NNW-facing slopes with good wind protection and with well-drained soils. The main soil types are red gradational soils on Tertiary basalt (Pipers Brook), grey duplex soil on mudstones and siltstones (Tamar), brown duplex soils (Tamar) and black clays of uniform texture.

Management practices

Most vineyards have close row spacings, ranging from 1.2 to 2.4 m and vine spacings of 1 to 1.2 m; some newer vineyards have wide rows (3.6 m) with divided canopies, e.g. the 'lyre' system. Excessive vegetative growth is a problem in many vineyards: canopy management by summer pruning, shoot positioning and training system is essential. Regular spraying for fungal disease control is required. Cane pruning is most common. Most vineyards have drip irrigation to counter the effects of short-term droughts. Yields are generally low: the average yield in 1987 was 3.5 tonne/ha but plantings include a high proportion of young vines.

The degree of exposure to cold winds during flowering and fruitset (mid December to early January) has a large effect on yield; Cabernet Sauvignon and Merlot are particularly susceptible to poor set. Well-sheltered vineyards have recorded yields up to 15 tonne/ha. Harvest is very late (see Figure 7.6). The main varieties are Cabernet Sauvignon, Pinot Noir, Chardonnay, Riesling and Traminer—the non-bearing area is mainly Chardonnay and Pinot Noir.

Summary

There has been considerable recent interest in grapegrowing in this state, particularly for the production of fruit for sparkling wine.

2.6.3 Other regions

Heywood (38°105′S, 141°36′E) is representative of vineyards on coastal sites in Victoria, eg. Bairnsdale, Lakes Entrance, the southern portion of the Mornington Peninsula. There are many similarities to the vineyards of Tasmania. The climate is cool and maritime, with low radiation and evaporation and high relative humidity and raindays (Figure 2.9). The combination of excessive vegetative growth and climate leads to fungal disease problems, particularly bunch rot. There were about 55 ha in 1985, including 45 ha in Seppelt's Drumborg vineyard (this vineyard had 130 ha in the early 1980s).

Vineyards on inland elevated sites in Victoria above 450 m generally have an MJT less than 19.0°C. Small plantings are found near Ballarat (MJT = 18.5°C), Mansfield and Whitfield.

2.7 Concluding remarks

The following generalizations can be made about the viticultural regions of Australia:

(i) Water supply is a major factor limiting yield. Most areas have winter-dominant rainfall, and soil depth is rarely adequate to store a full year's requirements. The highest yields are obtained under irrigation.

(ii) The varietal spectrum has been limited and there is little regional specialization of specific varieties. Older regions have high proportions of varieties more useful for fortified than table wine production.

(iii) Most viticultural districts have a low incidence of fungal diseases due to low rainfall and humidity during the growing season. The Hunter Valley is a notable exception.

(iv) The majority of Australian vineyards are found in hot to very hot regions. Scope exists for vineyard expansion in warm to cool regions.

Further reading

Hall, N. (1972) Summary of Meteorological Data in Australia. Forestry and Timber Bureau, Canberra. Leaflet no. 114. Aust. Government Publ. Service, Canberra.

Halliday, J. (1985) The Australian Wine Compendium. Angus and Robertson.

Other references

Amerine, M.A., and Winkler, A.J. (1944) Composition and quality of musts and wines of Californian grapes. Hilgardia 15, 493-675.

Anon. (1955) The Committee of Enquiry into the Mid-Murray dried fruit area. Rep. 1955 (Mimeo).

Australian Bureau of Statistics (1981-1987) Viticulture Australia. Catalogue No.7310.0. Canberra.

Australian Bureau of Meteorology (1975a) Climatic Averages of Australia. Aust. Government Printing Service, Canberra.

Australian Bureau of Meteorology (1975b) Climatic Atlas of Australia. Map Set 2 (Global Radiation), Map Set 3 (Evaporation), Map Set 4 (Sunshine). Bureau of Meteorology, Melbourne.

Australian Bureau of Meteorology (1977) Rainfall Statistics. Bureau of Meterology, Melbourne.

Australian Bureau of Meteorology (1981) Climatic Averages (microfiche). Bureau of Meteorology, Melbourne.

Australian Bureau of Meteorology (1985) Evaporation (microfiche). Bureau of Meteorology, Melbourne.

Australian Bureau of Meteorology (1987) Climatic Averages (microfiche). Bureau of Meteorology, Melbourne.

Badawy, N.S. (1982) Soils of the vineyards of the Great Western district. Res. Project Series No. 133 Dept. of Agric., Victoria.

Black, J.N. (1956) The distribution of solar radiation over the earth's surface. *Arch. Met. Geo. Biokl. B.* 7, (2), 165-89.

Boehm, E.W. (1970) Vine development and temperature in the Barossa, South Australia, *Exp Record*, South Aust. Dept. Agric. 5, 16-24.

Branas, J., Bernon G., and Levadoux, L. (1946) Elements de Viticulture Generale. Ec. Nat. Agr., Montpellier.

Foley, J.C. (1945) Frost in the Australian Region. Bureau of Meteorology, Melb. Bull No 32.

French, R.J., Armstrong, F.W., Hodge, D., Rudd, C.L., Till, M.R., Moore, S.D., and Cirami, R.A. (1978) Vineyards of the Barossa. Dep. Agric. Sth Aust., Soil Cons. Rep. 17/78.

Gladstones, J.S. (1965) The climate and soils of south western Western Australia in relation to vinegrowing. J. Aust. Inst. Agric. Sci. 31, 275-88.

Hubble, G.D., and Crocker, R.L. (1941) A Soil Survey of the Red Cliffs Irrigation District, Victoria. CSIR Bull 137.

Northcote, K.H. (1959) Soils and Land Use in the Barossa District, South Australia. The Tanunda-Williamstown Area. CSIRO Div. Soils, Soils and Land Use Ser. No. 32.

Northcote, K.H. and de Mooy, C.J. (1957) Soils and Land Use in the Barossa District, South Australia. Part A. The Angaston-Springton Area. Part B. The Tanunda Creek-Trial Hill Area. CSIRO Div. Soils, Soils and Land Use Ser. No. 22.

Northcote, K.H., Russell, J.S., and Wells, C.B. (1954) Soils and Land Use in the Barossa District, South Australia. Zone 1. The Nuriootpa Area. CSIRO Div. Soils, Soils and Land Use Ser. No. 13.

Olmo, H.P. (1956) A survey of the Grape Industry of Western Australia. Vine Fruits Research Trust, Perth.

Penman F., Taylor, J.K., Hooper, P.D. and Marshall T.J. (1939) A Soil Survey of the Merbein Irrigation District Victoria. CSIR Bull. 123.

Penman, F., Hubble G.D., Taylor, J.K., and Hooper, P.D. (1940) A Soil Survey of the Mildura Irrigation Settlement, Victoria. CSIR Bull. 133.

Pym, L.W. (1955) Soils of the Swan Valley Vineyard Area, Western Australia. CSIRO Div. Soils, Soils and Land Use Ser No 20.

Smart, R.E. and Coombe, B.G. (1983) Water relations of grapevines, in: Water Deficits and Plant Growth. T.T. Kozlowski ed. Vol. VII, pp.138-96 Academic Press, New York.

Smart, R.E. and Dry, P.R. (1979) Vineyard Site Selection. Roseworthy Agric. Coll., South Australia, 163 pp.

Smart, R.E. and Dry, P.R. (1980) A climatic classification of Australian viticultural regions. Aust. Grapegrower and Winemaker, 196, 8-16

Smith, D. (1970) Viticulture in the Barossa Region-Prospects and Costs. Aust. Geog. Studies. 8, 101-20

Taylor, J.K., and Hooper P.D. (1938) A soil survey of the horticultural soils in the Murrumbidgee Irrigation Areas, N.S.W. CSIR Bull. 118.

CHAPTER THREE

Soils and Australian Viticulture

K. H. NORTHCOTE

Grapevines will grow in a wide range of soils, but, like all plants, they grow best when their requirements for nutrients and moisture are fully met (Northcote 1984). In Australia, the most important characteristic of a soil for growing grapevines is its capacity to supply moisture over the longest possible period, whilst at the same time remaining sufficiently well drained to avoid periodic oxygen deficiency arising from waterlogging of the root zone. Because of this, those properties that affect the water-holding status and the aeration of soil will be discussed in some detail. Similar considerations have been discussed for French soil environments ('*terroirs*') by Seguin (1986).

In the vineyard, grapevines planted at a given spacing have a fixed area of soil available to each vine. The depth of the soil then determines the volume of soil available to each grapevine for root growth. All but the border vines in a vineyard have a finite volume of soil in which to grow; for those illustrated in Figure 3.1 the volume of soil is at least 12 m^3 per vine. A deep soil is one in which vine roots grow abundantly to a depth of 70 cm or more, whereas one in which roots are sparse below 30 cm is described as shallow.

The importance of soil depth, particularly in providing an adequate reservoir of water, but at the same time in supplying adequate oxygen for the growth of roots, is the best reason for studying soils and their effects on the growth of grapevines. Unfortunately such studies are difficult. In Figure 3.1 the soil has been divided up into three more or less horizontal layers, the surface soil, subsurface soil, and subsoil, and a bottom layer termed the subsolum. The subsolum consists of the materials directly below the soil and must be considered here because vines are deep rooting. Of the three soil layers, the surface soil and the subsoil are always present whereas the subsurface soil may be absent.

In this chapter the physical and chemical properties of soils will be considered in relation to the requirements of the grapevine followed by descriptions of the most important soils for grape growing.

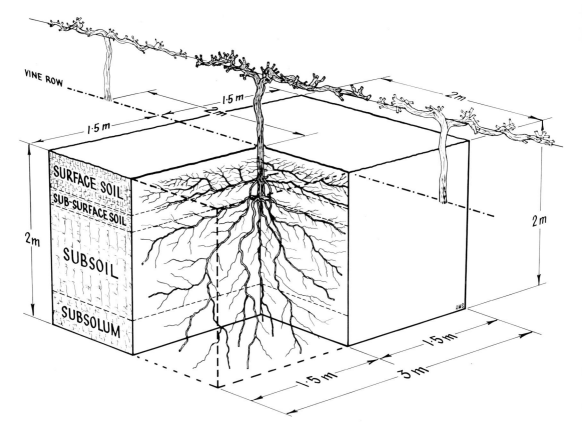

Figure 3.1. Diagrammatic representation of one quarter of the roots of a grapevine in a non-irrigated vineyard soil, showing also the volume of soil available to the roots to a depth of 2 m, together with the named layers of the soil encountered by the roots. (Drawn by R.M. Schuster, CSIRO, Division of Soils)

3.1 Physical properties of grapegrowing soils

The physical properties of a soil affect tillage operations, entry and passage of water through the soil, aeration, the growth of plant roots and the liability of the soil to erosion. Penkov (1974) has shown that grapevines respond to good physical soil conditions by developing vigorous root systems that permeate the soil evenly and deeply. The physical and chemical properties of soil interact closely, and both are reflected in the morphological, or descriptive, features of the soil. Before a site for a new vineyard is selected (see Chapter 10), the physical properties of the soil should be given particularly careful consideration because most soil physical characteristics cannot be readily changed.

3.1.1 Soil colour

Colour is the most noticeable feature of soil.

However, it is not always appreciated that it is often related to other factors affecting plant growth.

a. Surface soils

Generally, light coloured soils (such as Uc2, Bleached Sands — classifications are described in 3.3) reflect light and heat whereas dark coloured soils (such as Ug5.1, Black Cracking Clays) absorb and radiate heat, and thus warm up and cool down readily. The reflectivity of soils depends mainly on the content of organic matter and water, the texture, and the angle of the incident light. Over the whole solar spectrum, reflection coefficients range from about 10 per cent for dark soils rich in organic matter to about 30 per cent for light desert sand. There is a broad relationship between the colour of surface soils and their organic matter content. For a given soil, the darker the surface soil, the higher is its organic matter content; this in turn often indicates the quality of soil management. The darker coloured, well-managed surface soils more readily permit the entry of water and are less subject to erosion.

b. Subsurface soils

Light coloured (near white) subsurface soil indicates that leaching of nutrients has occurred and that the soil is periodically waterlogged. The amount of orange and rusty root-tracings and mottlings in the lower part of the subsurface layer increases with the frequency and duration of waterlogging.

c. Subsoils

Subsoil colour is a good indicator of the permeability of the entire soil to both water and air. Permeability decreases as soil colour changes from red to brown to yellow to dark (black to very dark brown) to gley (light greys to bluish and greenish greys). 'Gley' is a soil colour and is referred to as such on all soil colour charts. Mottled soils are less permeable than their unmottled counterparts. Undoubtedly, the very good permeability of red soils e.g. Dr. soils, is one reason why they are preferred for viticulture. Other properties, such as salinity and sodicity (sodium ion content), affect permeability; for example, a non-sodic brown or yellow soil may be more permeable than a sodic red soil (see 3.2.4).

3.1.2 Soil texture

Texture is probably the most important of all soil properties as it affects erodibility and available water capacity (3.1.6), factors which are highly significant under Australian conditions. Because such a wide range of soils have been used for grapegrowing, almost all textures are to be found in Australian vineyards.

Texture is a measure of the relative proportions of sand, silt and clay which are defined by their particle sizes. Sands range from 2 to 0.02 mm in diameter, silts from 0.02 to 0.002 mm, and clay particles are smaller than 0.002 mm. Texture grades range from sands, which contain 5 per cent or less of clay-sized particles through loams, with 25 percent of clay-sized particles, to heavy clays with 50 per cent or more of clay-sized particles. The amounts of organic matter, oxides of Fe and Al, Ca-Mg carbonates, the relative proportions of Ca to Mg and Na present on the clay-sized particles, and the type of clay minerals, all influence the behaviour of the different texture grades. So also do grits, gravels and stones which, because of their large sizes, decrease the available water capacity of the soil when present in it. However, gravel or stone beds on the soil surface help to conserve moisture in the surface soil besides reducing susceptibility to erosion. They also reflect light and heat onto the under parts of grapevines; lighter coloured stones or gravel reflect more than darker ones.

3.1.3 Soil friability

Soil friability expresses the ease with which soil material crumbles and retains the aggregated (crumbly) condition. It is a complex attribute dependent on texture, structure and consistence. Organic matter improves friability while sodicity (3.2.4) adversely affects it for both surface soils and subsoils. The rate of movement of water and air through the soil is directly proportional to soil friability. Thus the more friable the soil, the better is the growth of the grapevine; see also Wall (1987). Soil friability also affects the ease with which machinery can be moved in the vineyard.

a. Surface and subsurface soils

Most surface and subsurface soils, except for sand textures (Dy5 and some Uc soils), soils naturally well supplied with organic matter (Gn4, Dr4 soils) and self-mulching soils (Ug5.1, Ug5.2, Ug5.3 soils) set hard when dry. This hardsetting property, common to most Australian soils, increases with increasing clay content. Hardsetting soils should be cultivated while they contain optimum moisture. For most, this period is short, often the day following thorough wetting of the surface. Continued clean cultivation increases the strength of hardsetting because organic matter is destroyed; conversely, a green-manure crop, sod-culture, or the introduction of a pasture phase provides extra organic matter and so ameliorates the hardsetting condition. Where sodicity has influenced soil formation e.g. Dr2.33, Dy3.43 soils, or where the content of exchangeable calcium is less than about 50-60 per cent, the application of gypsum makes the soil more friable, as does increasing the soil organic matter content. Self-mulching surface soils with high clay contents remain friable over only a limited moisture range and rapidly become sticky as moisture exceeds this range. This stickiness restricts the time available for cultivation and may impede the movement of machines in the vineyard.

b. Subsoils

Friability in subsoils largely depends upon the size and strength of the aggregates or fragments resulting when the soil is disturbed. Friable to semi-friable subsoils break readily into small units, 2 cm or less in size, that in turn crumble easily between the fingers. Non-friable subsoils have larger units and even when moist, do not break up readily; they are usually sticky when moist. Poor friability may be found in sandy loam to loam subsoils, but is especially important in clay-textured ones. Friable subsoils (as in Uf5.31, Dr2.2 and Dy3.2) allow water and air to move readily through the soil thus providing a good medium for root growth. Non-friable subsoils (as Dr2.3, Dy3.4, Dy5.4 and Dy5.8) impede water and air movement and in extreme cases perched water-tables may develop, thus creating conditions unfavourable for root growth. Both sodicity and the content of soft fine carbonates (3.2.5) affect the friability of subsoils. Friability may be improved by applying gypsum directly into the subsoil.

3.1.4 Soil depth

The depth of surface soil is important because it influences the supply of nutrient elements; it is the layer which contains most nutrients to which fertilizers are often applied. Where it is thin or where cultivation destroys surface feeding roots in the top 8-15 cm of soil the supply of nutrients may be limited. Deep surface soils, of 15-30 cm or more with fertilizer placed within the layer, will usually support vigorous grapevines. Another important soil depth is that to an impeding layer.

3.1.5 Impeding layers

Impeding layers obstruct both root growth and water movement, and (in the latter case) they can cause waterlogging. Unless an impeding layer occurs at great depth, both the layer itself and its effect on the supply of water and oxygen will affect root growth. Under natural rainfall, grapevines should not be grown in soils with impeding layers at depths of less than 1-2 m unless other favourable conditions prevail such as a gently-sloping and naturally-draining topography. Where vines are grown under irrigation both soils and subsola should be free of impeding layers to a depth of 3 m unless drains have been installed.

There are four kinds of layers that obstruct root growth and water penetration in grapegrowing soils; country rock, calcrete, subsoil clays, and cemented pans.

a. Country rock

Rock occurs at less than 1 m depth below a number of soils used for grapegrowing (e.g. Uc1.4, Uc6.11, Um6, Dr2, Db1, Dy2, Dy3). The denser rocks (some sandstones, quartzites and granites) almost totally restrict root and water penetration. Rocks in which fissures, cracks and cleavages occur (schists, phyllites) allow some root and water penetration and may prove satisfactory for grapegrowing especially if they occur in close association with soils 1 m or more deep, as on some Barossa hillslopes. Where rocks outcrop and physically occupy land area, the establishment and maintenance of a vineyard may be hindered.

b. Calcrete

The term calcrete is used for all hardened to semi-hardened accumulations of Ca-Mg carbonates (usually Ca-predominant) that occur either in subsoils or subsola of soils used for grapegrowing. Calcrete also occurs as a secondary capping on aeolianite and calcarenite, terms used for wind-drifted sandy forms of limestones. There seem to be several kinds of calcrete, but it is convenient to consider them in two groups:

(i) The first group of calcrete (found in Gc and Uc5.1 soils) have several kinds of carbonate layers each with different permeabilities (Wetherby and Oades 1975). These layers consist of hard calcretes and/or finely divided, soft carbonates within the fine earth matrix (all soil particles less than 2 mm in size). Generally, the hard calcretes form a physical barrier to root and water penetration which does not alter with irrigation time (in years). Therefore shallow soils with hard calcretes are not suited to irrigated viticulture. The finely divided soft carbonates conversely present a chemical barrier which shows decreasing permeability with irrigation time, except where the fine earth matrix is sandy (3.2.5).

(ii) The second group of calcretes have varying porosity, but in general do not impede water movement (e.g. in the subsola of Uc1.2, Uc2.2, Uc4.2, Uc6.13, Um6.2, Uf5.31 and shallow Dr2.23 soils). Indeed, vines grow well where a water-table sits below the calcrete as at Coonawarra. The volume of soil for root exploration may be limited by calcrete, but in some cases roots can penetrate these layers, especially if the layers have been 'ripped' (see 3.3.1, Uf5.31).

c. Subsoil clays

Impeding subsoil clays (claypans) may occur in duplex soils (3.3.3) and some other soils e.g. Gn2.34 and Gn2.74. Claypans obstruct root and water penetration and are the main reason for waterlogging in duplex soils. Impermeability problems caused by subsoil clays are accentuated under irrigation because these clays, once sealed by water, cannot cope with any extra water.

d. Cemented pans
These pans are mainly sands and gravels cemented by the infilling of coatings of clays and sesquioxides, but there is considerable variation in their thickness and composition. Many are related to subsola formed from layered deposits as in parts of the riverine plains of south-eastern Australia. Others occur below some of the Dy5.81 soils in the Swan Valley where ironstone-gravels may be strongly cemented. Such pans prevent root and water penetration, and are a problem under irrigation. Amelioration of the pans is often difficult or impossible due to their depth.

3.1.6 Available water capacity
The available water capacity is an estimate of the soil's store of water. It is the difference between field capacity and wilting point, where the former is the upper limit of available water when the addition of more water is lost by drainage, and the latter is the lower limit of available water when water is so tightly held by soil that plant roots cannot extract it. The available water capacity represents the extreme of water availability and is a useful indication of the maximal amount of water that may be stored for plant use by a soil. Coarse sands have a low available water capacity of 0.08 cm³/cm³ while the other textures from sands to clays have values of around 0.15 cm³/cm³ (Salter and Williams 1967).

The available water for a Dr2.23 soil, Dorrien loamy fine sand, from the Barossa Valley is estimated to be 2000 L for a 12 m³ volume of that soil (Figure 3.1). A similar volume of coarse sand is estimated to have only 1000 L whereas the deeper cracking clays (Ug5 soils) may have values from 1300 L to 1800 L. These are theoretical values. Experimental results for a Dr2.23 soil, and a Ug5.15 soil both at Glen Osmond, South Australia were, respectively, 1560 and 1320 L available water held per 12 m³ of soil between the limits of wetting and drying. More measurement of water storage and availability are required for grapegrowing soils. In non-irrigated areas, where water is often the major limiting factor, rootstocks of varieties selected for their performance under dry conditions would be valuable.

3.1.7 Soil permeability
Permeability is a measure of the ability of soil to transmit water vertically. Generally, soil permeability depends on the size and number of natural voids, and the amount of clay and its swelling properties. Sandy soils have many voids and little clay, so permeability remains high even when the soil is saturated. Conversely many clay soils, which have smaller and fewer voids, have low permeability when saturated. In the Cracking Clays, the initial rate of entry of water into the cracks is rapid but, as swelling closes the cracks, water either ponds on the surface or runs off depending on the topography. Permeability is related to the physical properties of texture, friability and impeding layers and to the chemical properties of salinity, sodicity and the contents of organic matter and carbonate.

3.1.8 Waterlogging
Waterlogging is a serious problem as grapevines prefer soils that are well-drained. Where stagnant soil water occurs, the roots of grapevines are weakened and may be attacked by root-rotting organisms causing loss of vigour and eventual loss of the vine. There are two main kinds of waterlogging, surface and subsurface.

a. Surface waterlogging
Surface waterlogging has two main causes. One is the slow permeability of surface soils in which water entry has become very slow as a result of the loss of friability (3.1.3). This is often due to poor soil management. Applications of gypsum and organic matter usually correct this condition. The second is due to thin surface soils overlying claypan subsoils (3.1.5). This condition can be corrected by incorporating gypsum into the claypan subsoil.

b. Subsurface waterlogging
This occurs mostly in soils on low-lying or flat terrain where the surface soil is more than 20 cm thick and overlies claypan subsoil. The grapegrowing duplex soils (see 3.3.3) particularly subject to subsurface waterlogging are Dr2.4, Dr3.4, Db1.4, Db2.4, Dy2.4, Dy2.6, Dy3.4, Dy3.6, Dy3.8, Dy5. Of these, the Sandy, Mottled-yellow Duplex Soils (Dy5) are often the most severely affected, because their sand surface soils are highly permeable whereas their claypan subsoils are only very slowly permeable.

One consequence of subsurface waterlogging is that water moves relatively rapidly over the impeding subsoil clay and is lost to creeks and often similar but smaller natural drainageways. Another result is the formation of plough soles or traffic pans, which result from cultivating soil that is too wet or from the indiscriminate and frequent use of heavy equipment in the vineyard. Such pans have been recorded at depths of 12-23 cm in sandy, Mottled-yellow Duplex Soils (Dy5.81) in the Swan Valley, W.A. In these circumstances, traffic and cultivation should be kept to a minimum and timed carefully. Longer term remedial measures include deep ripping of the clay subsoil together with deep placement of gypsum, followed by cover cropping with deep-rooted species. These measures should help water to penetrate the subsoil and improve the moisture regime of the soil.

3.1.9 Topography

The surface configuration of land influences, and is influenced by, the physical and chemical properties of the soil. Most of these relationships are fairly obvious. To the grapegrower, the topography is especially important as it affects water infiltration and drainage on the one hand and soil erosion on the other.

The dune-swale topography that predominates throughout the Riverland, Mildura-Robinvale and Swan Hill grapegrowing areas is conducive to the development of seepage, waterlogging and attendant salinity problems. This, together with the nature of the soils and the subsola, makes drainage with agricultural drains essential. The need for drains was recognized in the early years of these districts (Thomas 1939, Northcote and Boehm 1949) but disposal of the drainage water presents problems which are still receiving attention. The first or front slopes — gentle slopes between the highland dune-swale areas and the river terraces and flats — are the only areas where artificial drainage may not be necessary.

Elsewhere the general principle to follow is that seepage, water-logging and salinity develop where slopes grade into or abut flats. The problems are accentuated by differences in the relative per-meabilities of soil and/or subsola layers (Cockroft 1965). On flat or nearly flat land, the permeability of the surface soil is all important.

Water erosion in grapegrowing soils is of two types: the sheet removal of soil particles suspended in water as it flows over the soil surface, and the formation of gullies where water concentrates and 'knifes' through the soil. The degree of either form of erosion on any given soil type increases directly with increasing slope (Northcote et al. 1954). Often the most obvious effects of water erosion are found on the duplex soils, even on slopes of only 1-1.5 per cent. Certainly on slopes of more than this

vineyards should be planted in such a way as to minimize erosion. Both friable (3.1.3) and dispersible subsoils (3.2.4) are particularly liable to gully erosion.

Water erosion is prevented by maintaining a rough, cloddy soil surface that will not slake down on wetting, and which reduces the velocity of water moving down the slope (see Volume 2, Chapter 8).

3.2 Chemical properties of grapegrowing soils

The chemical properties of soil affect not only the nutrition of plants, but also the physical soil conditions and thus the moisture regimes. Since the grapevine can grow in a wide range of soils, it is able to obtain adequate moisture and nutrition under a variety of chemical soil conditions. However, some soils suit the grapevine better than others, and it is easier and cheaper to manage vineyards on the more suitable soils. The subjects discussed in this section include nutrition, salinity, sodicity and carbonate content. Some chemical properties of grapegrowing soils are set out in Tables 3.1, 3.2 and 3.3. These data are representative only and should be used as an indication of the range of chemical properties that exist in grapegrowing soils.

3.2.1 Soil reaction; pH

Measurement of pH is probably the most commonly made soil test. The colorimetric pH kits make it one of the few chemical tests that can be made in the field. It is not enough, however, to test the surface soil alone as this may give pH values varying by up to 1.5 pH units due to fertilizer high spots, urine patches and natural soil variability. However, by making 2 or 3 pH tests on a soil profile, including the surface soil and subsoil, it is possible to gauge the reaction trend of the soil profile. Three broad classes of reaction trend are recognizable: acid, with subsoils of pH less than 6.5; neutral, with subsoils of pH 6.5 to 8.0, and alkaline, with subsoils of pH higher than 8.0. Examples of each class are listed in Tables 3.1-3.3. Grapevines grow in soils within each of these classes.

Soil pH is controlled by the cation exchange capacity. The amount of exchangeable cations per unit mass of soil is often measured as milliequivalents per 100 g of soil. It also largely determines the availability of nutrient cations (e.g. Ca, Mg, K) to plants. Thus the simple pH test gives good clues about the level of nutrients in the soil; a pH value greater than 8 indicates the presence of calcium carbonate, and a pH value greater than 9 indicates

Table 3.1 Analytical data for soils with acid reaction trends

PPF	Soil Layer	Depth cm	pH	Clay %	CaCO₃ %	TSS %	NaCl %	N %	Total* P %	Total* K %	CAP. meq	Ca meq	%	Mg meq	%	K meq	%	Na meq	%†	H meq	%
Uc2.21 surface		0-5	6.2	—	0	0.01	<0.01	0.07	<0.01	0.04	6.2	1.8	29	0.5	8	0.1	2	<0.1	1	3.8	60
	subsoil	69-107	6.0	—	0	<0.01	<0.01	0.03	<0.01	0.03	1.5	0.4	28	0.3	21	0.1	6	0.2	10	0.5	35
Uc2.33 surface		0-15	6.5	2	0	<0.01	<0.01	0.23	<0.01	—	14.0	10.0	71	2.2	16	0.2	1	0.2	1	1.4	10
	subsurface	30-46	5.5	1	0	<0.01	<0.01	0.07	—	—	7.0	4.7	67	1.1	16	—	0	0.01	2	1.1	16
	subsoil pan	142-147	6.1	—	0	<0.01	<0.01	0.03	0.01	—	8.0	—		—		—		—		—	
Uc4.21 surface		0-10	4.9	—	0	0.05	0.03	0.07	0.01	0.02	8.0	2.2	27	3.7	46	0.2	3	0.2	3	2.7	33
	subsoil	81-119	5.6	17	0	0.01	0.01	0.01	—	—	4.0	1.0	25	1.2	29	0.1	3	0.1	3	1.6	40
Uc5.22 surface		0-10	5.5	14	0	0.03	<0.01	0.01	0.01	0.16	4.0	0.5	13	0.8	20	0.1	3	0.1	3	2.5	63
	subsoil	60-90	4.8	13	0	0.12	0.11	0.01	<0.01	0.18	3.0	0.8	26	0.4	13	0.1	3	0.8	26	0.9	29
Uc6.11 surface		0-3	6.3	11	0	0.04	0.01	0.30	0.04	—	—	6.2		1.6		1.0		0.3	3††		—
	subsoil	10-28	5.8	12	0	0.01	<0.01	0.09	0.03	—	—	2.3		1.1		0.2		0.1	3††		—
Gn2.74 surface		0-10	5.4	3	0	0.02	0.01	0.09	0.02	0.07	3.0	1.6	52	0.2	7	0.3	10	0.1	3	0.8	26
	subsoil	50-75	4.8	23	0	0.01	<0.01	0.01	<0.01	0.09	3.0	0.1	3	0.4	13	0.0	0	0.1	3	2.4	78
Dr2.21 surface		0-4	5.6	14	0	0.01	<0.01	0.11	0.01	—	—	2.7		1.4		0.7		0.2	3††		—
	subsoil(u)	15-48	5.2	60	0	0.02	0.01	—	0.01	—	—	0.1		3.0		0.6		0.3	6††		—
Dr4.11 surface		0-10	6.8	39	0	0.03	0.01	0.17	0.06	0.37	22.0	2.0	55	5.9	27	1.5	7	0.1	1	2.5	11
	subsoil	46-61	5.7	52	0	0.07	0.05	0.02	0.02	0.34	13.0	4.0	31	6.5	50	0.2	2	0.5	4	1.8	14
Dy3.41 surface		0-2.5	5.4	14	0	0.02	0.01	0.17	—	—	11.0	1.4	13	2.6	24	0.3	3	0.5	5	6.2	56
	subsoil(u)	30-53	5.5	42	0	0.01	0.01	—	—	—	10.0	0.1	1	3.6	36	0.1	1	0.5	5	5.7	57
	(l)	76-117	5.2	48	0	0.02	0.01	—	—	—	11.0	0.2	2	3.0	27	0.1	1	0.4	4	7.3	66
Dy3.61 surface		0-9	6.0	10	0	—	—	—	0.01	0.09	7.2	1.8	25	0.6	8	0.2	3	0	0	4.6	64
	subsoil	25-41	6.3	74	0	—	—	—	0.02	0.29	22.7	5.1	23	6.2	27	0.4	2	0.3	1	10.7	47
Dy3.81 surface		0-14	6.1	4	0	0.01	<0.01	0.04	—	—	4.6	2.0	43	0.4	9	0.1	2	0.1	2	2.0	43
	subsoil (u)	46-51	6.1	41	0	0.02	<0.01	0.03	<0.01	—	9.3	1.6	17	3.4	36	0.3	3	0.4	5	3.6	39
	(l)	104-130	5.9	60	0	0.04	0.02	—	—	—	13.0	1.1	4	5.3	40	0.1	1	0.9	3	5.6	43
Dy5.41 surface		0-10	6.3	9	0	0.01	<0.01	0.05	0.01	0.11	5	2.2	44	1.0	20	0.2	4	0.1	2	1.5	30
	subsoil (u)	40-60	6.3	63	0	0.04	0.01	0.02	0.01	0.57	18	4.3	24	11.0	61	0.5	3	1.3	7	0.9	5
	(l)	90-100	5.5	49	0	0.06	0.02	0.01	0.01	0.45	15	2.6	17	6.9	46	0.2	1	1.5	10	3.8	25

Notes. CaCO₃ = calcium carbonate, TSS = total soluble salts, NaCl = sodium chloride, N = nitrogen, P = phosphorus, CAP = cation exchange capacity, K = potassium, Ca = calcium, Mg = magnesium, Na = sodium, H = hydrogen.
* Soluble in boiling hydrochloric acid, meq = milliquivalents per 100g of soil, % = percentage composition, † Percentage of exchange sodium, †† Metal cations only — = not available, u = upper, l = lower.

sodium bi-carbonate. Values greater than 9 indicate that the soil may be saline and sodic, though not all sodic soils have high pH. However, pH should be considered in relation to soil texture and the Principal Profile Form. For example, sands (5 per cent clay) contain smaller amounts of plant nutrients than say loams (25 per cent clay) of similar pH.

Soil pH can be altered by the addition of some fertilizers. For example, application of ammonium sulphate to the soil surface over 10 years can lower pH by about one pH unit to a depth of about 30 cm. Below that depth the effect decreases to 0.2-0.3 of a pH unit by 60 cm. Such a reduction in pH may well reduce the availability of some nutrient elements, including phosphorus, which is often low in Australian grapegrowing soils. Furthermore, low pH may induce metal toxicities, for example aluminium and manganese toxicity (Dry and Smart 1985).

3.2.2 Nutrient elements

A guide to the reserves of mineral nutrients in soils may be obtained from the soil chemical properties, particularly the Cation Exchange Capacity and the exchangeable cations considered in relation to the Profile Forms (Section 3.3). The acid soils (Table 3.1) have low Cation Exchange Capacity with a predominance of hydrogen, while the alkaline soils (Table 3.3) have relatively high Cation Exchange Capacity with a predominance of the metal ions (Ca, Mg, K and Na). The values for neutral soils (Table 3.2) lie between. Thus, in general, the acid soils have low nutrient element reserves, the neutral soils moderate reserves, and most alkaline soils have high reserves. Such comparisons should only be made between similar soils, that is a sand soil with other sand soils and not with a cracking clay or a duplex soil.

There is a delicate balance between nutrients in acid soils which is easily upset by over-cropping or continued applications of one fertilizer; such an imbalance can induce deficiencies of other nutrient elements. Alkaline soils containing a lot of free calcium carbonate, especially the Calcareous Earths (Gc), also have a delicate nutrient balance that may be easily upset by heavy applications of fertilizer. For example, Zn deficiency may be induced by heavy applications of phosphatic fertilizers.

The nutrient elements required for plant growth are carbon, hydrogen, oxygen, nitrogen, phosphorus, potassium, sulfur, iron, calcium, magnesium, boron, manganese, copper, cobalt, zinc, molybdenum, and chlorine. Carbon is obtained by green plants from the carbon dioxide in the air, hydrogen and oxygen are obtained mainly from water and the remaining elements are obtained from the soil.

Nitrogen (N) and organic matter

The decomposition of plant remains and soil organisms provides most of the organic matter and N in the soil. N is also fixed by organisms that form nodules on the roots of leguminous plants. Generally all nitrogenous compounds in soil are oxidized by soil organisms to nitrates, a form which is readily available to plants. With a few exceptions, nitrogen is moderate to low (0.25 to 0.1 per cent N) in Australian grapegrowing soils. It reflects their organic matter status which is related more to soil management than to the kind of soil. In the Barossa Valley, for example, an area under an improved pasture including subterranean clover contained more than twice as much N as an adjoining vineyard on the same soil under continuous clean-cultivation. In Western Australia, it was shown that the vigour of grapevines increased markedly as the level of soil N rose from 0.02-0.04 per cent N to 0.12-0.26 per cent N. Nitrogen is one of the most mobile elements in soil and can be readily leached from the soil system. Thus very low N levels are particularly likely on shallow soils, leached acid soils and sand soils. Low levels of soil N reflect low soil fertility. The implications of this for water relations, soil management, and fertilizer program in Australian vineyards are discussed in Volume 2, Chapters 6, 8 and 9 respectively.

Phosphorus (P)

With few exceptions, Australian grapegrowing soils are notoriously low in P, often containing 0.01 per cent or less total P (see Tables 3.1-3.3). Even where somewhat higher values (0.05 per cent) are recorded, P deficiency is likely. The dual deficiencies of N and P, common in most Australian soils, led to the now well established and successful remedy of growing legume-rich green manure crops or pasture leys with superphosphate fertilizer. Grapevines in the Barossa Valley, growing on Red Duplex Soil (Dr2.23) gave significantly improved fruitset and yield after fertilization with superphosphate (Tulloch and Harris 1970). This is one of the few such findings in world horticulture. P, unlike N, is relatively immobile in the soil, and therefore must be placed close to the root system. Since surface cultivation and lack of moisture in the cultivation zone nearly eliminate feeder roots in the top 15 cm of many vineyard soils, it is important to place phosphatic fertilizers below

Table 3.2 Analytical data for soils with neutral reaction trends

Exchangeable Cations span the Ca, Mg, K, Na and H columns.

PPF	Soil Layer	Depth cm	pH	Clay %	$CaCO_3$ %	TSS %	NaCl %	N %	Total* P %	Total* K %	CAP. meq	Ca meq	Ca %	Mg meq	Mg %	K meq	K %	Na meq	Na %†	H meq	H %
Uc1.22	surface	0-15	6.3	7	0	0.01	—	0.05	—	—	—	1.4		0.6		0.9		0.03	1††	—	
	subsoil	66-94	7.3	7	0	0.01	0.01	—	—	—	—	2.5		1.7		0.5		0.04	1††	—	
Uc1.43	surface	0-14	7.9	18	0	—	—	—	—	—	6.2	3.8	61	1.1	18	1.2	19	0.2	2	0	
	subsoil	76-89	7.8	18	0	—	—	—	—	—	16.0	11.7	72	2.9	18	1.1	7	0.5	3	0	
Uc6.13	surface	0-10	7.1	15	0.39	0.05	0.01	0.12	0.03	0.67	7.0	4.6	66	0.9	13	0.5	7	0.1	1	0.9	13
	subsoil	50-60	7.1	17	0	0.10	<0.01	0.04	0.02	0.64	7.0	4.4	63	1.1	16	0.2	3	0.1	1	1.2	17
Um4.31	surface	0-15	6.4	17	0	—	0.01	0.11	—	—	—	10.0	—	3.8	—	1.3	—	0.8	5††	—	
	subsoil	109-152	7.1	25	0	—	—	—	—	—	—	—		—		—		—		—	
Uf5.31	surface	0-10	7.4	43	0.13	0.04	<0.01	0.24	0.03	—	—	18	—	1.8	—	1.8	—	0.2	<1††	—	
	subsoil	28-46	6.9	56	0	0.08	<0.01	0.09	0.03	—	—	12.6		2.0		1.4		0.4	2††	—	
Gn2.12	surface	0-10	6.0	22	0	0.02	0.01	0.12	0.04	1.9	14.0	4.7	34	2.0	14	1.4	10	0	0	5.9	42
	subsoil	80-90	6.6	57	0	0.01	<0.01	0.03	0.04	1.7	16.0	4.8	30	4.9	30	0.9	5	0.1	<1	5.3	34
Dr2.22	surface	0-3	5.6	12	0	0.03	<0.01	0.24	0.03	1.1	25.0	10	40	1.7	6	1.1	4	0.2	<1	12.6	50
	subsoil	20-30	7.0	41	0	0.01	<0.01	0.04	0.01	0.8	18.0	10	56	4.9	27	1.0	6	0.5	3	1.6	9
Dr2.42	surface	0-4	5.5	17	0	0.12	0.04	0.60	0.08	0.35	26.0	8.7	31	2.1	8	1.8	7	0.3	1	13.1	53
	subsoil (u)	40-50	6.1	65	0	0.06	0.02	0.07	0.02	0.33	20.0	6.6	33	6.7	34	0.1	<1	0.5	2	6.1	31
	(l)	90-120	6.5	53	0	0.08	0.03	0.02	0.02	0.13	15.0	3.0	20	8.1	54	0.4	3	2.4	16	1.1	7
Dy2.62	surface	0-6	6.1	17	0	0.01	<0.01	0.10	0.01	0.05	—	—		—		—		—		—	
	subsoil	84-114	6.5	56	0	0.03	0.02	—	—	0.12	—	3.7		10		0.3		0.8	5††	—	
Dy3.22	surface	0-5	6.0	6	0	0.03	0.01	0.26	0.03	0.33	14.2	3.8	27	1.6	11	0.5	3	0.4	3	7.9	56
	subsoil	48-61	6.3	43	0	0.02	0.01	0.06	0.05	0.78	25.1	6.5	26	9.1	36	0.3	1	1.0	4	8.3	33
Dy3.42	surface	0-10	5.3	19	0	—	<0.01	0.11	0.02	—	9.0	3.7	41	1.5	17	0.2	2	0.3	3	3.3	37
	subsoil (u)	36-46	6.5	31	0	—	0.01	—	0.01	—	13.0	2.6	20	6.8	52	0.1	<1	2.1	16	1.4	11
	(l)	56-86	6.9	54	0	—	0.02	—	0.01	—	21.0	3.9	19	12.0	57	0.3	1	5.1	24	0	0
Dy5.42	surface	0-18	5.9	5	0	0.03	0.01	0.09	0.01	0.05	—	—		—		—		—		—	
	subsoil (u)	69-114	6.8	27	0	0.01	0.01	—	—	—	13.0	6.6	51	3.2	25	0.1	1	0.8	6	2.3	18
	(l)	127-178	7.6	56	0	0.06	0.02	—	—	—	34.0	21.0	62	8.0	24	0.3	<1	0.3	<1	4.4	13
Dy5.82	surface	0-4	6.5	—	0	0.03	0.01	0.10	—	—	5.5	3.4	60	0.8	15	0.3	5	0.2	3	0.8	15
	subsoil (u)	94-107	7.6	22	0	0.03	0.01	0.02	<0.01	—	6.3	2.0	32	3.0	49	0.3	3	1.0	16	0	0
	(l)	145-183	7.1	24	0	0.18	0.10	—	—	—	9.6	1.6	17	3.6	38	0.3	4	2.4	25	1.7	18

Notes. $CaCO_3$ = calcium carbonate, TSS = total soluble salts, NaCl = sodium chloride, N = nitrogen, P = phosphorus, CAP = cation exchange capacity, K = potassium, Ca = calcium, Mg = magnesium, Na = sodium, H = hydrogen.
* Soluble in boiling hydrochloric acid, meq = milliquivalents per 100g of soil, % = percentage composition, † Percentage of exchange sodium, †† Metal cations only
— = not available, u = upper, l = lower.

this depth so that the phosphorus is more readily accessible to vine roots. This is true for potassic fertilizers too, as K is also relatively immobile in soil.

Potassium (K)

The K content of grapegrowing soils varies widely, both in regard to total and exchangeable forms. Total K includes all the K present in the soil, while exchangeable K refers only to that part of the total associated with the clay minerals. It is this latter form that is most readily available to plants, and equates well with the nutrient status of the soil. Low exchangeable potassium values of 0.4 meq per 100g or less are usual in acid soils (Table 3.1), whereas alkaline soils have higher values of 1 meg per 100g or more (Table 3.3). Such wide variation suggests that some soils may be deficient, while others may be very well supplied. K deficiency in grapevines has been reported on Yellow Duplex Soils (Dy3.81) in Western Australia; their subsoils contain 0.1 meq K per 100g but become depleted in long established vineyards to as little as 0.05 meq per 100g. In the Southern Districts of South Australia, subterranean clover as a cover crop in vineyards on a Bleached Sand (Uc2.21) responds to K. Since both these soils occur at Stanthorpe in Queensland (Table 3.4), vineyards there may also be deficient in K. The few figures available for acid Red, Brown and Yellow Duplex soils from some Hunter Valley vineyards (exchangeable K of 0.2-0.5 meq per 100g) suggest that potassium deficiency is likely there too.

While some acid and neutral soils may be deficient in K, the reverse seems to apply in some alkaline soils. An 'oenological excess' of total cations, particularly K, in the skin of some red grape varieties has been associated with lower quality in dry red wines (Somers 1975). Alkaline soils with high exchangeable K contents are possibly implicated as the source of such K. In this connection it is interesting to note that French grapegrowing soils have cation (and K) contents comparable with those found in Australian acid soils.

Sulfur (S)

Although S deficiencies have been widely reported in New South Wales in pastures, mainly on acid soils, but also some Ug5.1 and Dr2.33 soils, no S deficiency has been reported in grapevines. The wide use in Australian vineyards of superphosphate fertilizer which contains 11 per cent S may have prevented S deficiency in grapevines. The use of fungicides containing S may also have contributed.

Calcium (Ca)

Deficiencies of Ca have been recorded for a range of crops largely on acid soils and peats, but not in grapevines. However, vines growing in acid soils with very low contents of exchangeable Ca ($<$ 1 meq per 100g) in their subsoils (Table 3.1) must be suspect. Subsurface waterlogging (3.1.8) may result in an induced Ca deficiency in some shallow-rooted plants, such as the green manure crops grown in vineyards. Ca hydroxide or carbonate, often applied as agricultural lime, raises the soil pH, improves the availability of Mo, and secures the establishment of legumes on acid soils. Indeed, on some acid soils a light dressing of lime plus molybdenum-superphosphate is necessary to ensure adequate nodulation in legumes.

Magnesium (Mg)

Magnesium deficiency is comparatively rare in Australia because of the large content of exchangeable Mg in most soils. The soils most likely to show a deficiency are those with less than 1 meq per 100g of Mg in both surface soil and subsoil. Indeed, citrus grown on such a soil (Gn2.74) near Sydney has shown magnesium deficiency. No Mg deficiency has been reported in grapevines in Australia, apart possibly from Queensland (see Volume 2, Chapter 9), but it is common in the older European grapegrowing areas where it is often associated with an excessive use of K fertilizer.

Iron (Fe)

Iron deficiency occurs widely in horticultural crops, including grapevines, and in most cases takes the form of chlorosis associated with high pH. The high pH may be associated with high lime (carbonate) content or with poor soil drainage. In both cases, Fe is rendered unavailable to the grapevine. When due to poor soil drainage, the chlorosis may disappear with warmer weather as the soil dries and the Fe again becomes more readily available. Lime-induced chlorosis is common on high lime soils such as the Calcareous Earths (Gc, Table 3.3) and some other alkaline soils. It is particularly evident in spring when the soil is cold and wet (see also Leamon 1981). Generally, *Vitis vinifera* varieties on their own roots are much less sensitive to lime-induced chlorosis than are some American *Vitis* species (see Chapter 8).

Boron (B)

The only B deficiency recorded in grapevines in

Table 3.3 Analytical data for soils with alkaline reaction trends

PPF	Soil Layer	Depth cm	pH	Clay %	CaCO₃ %	TSS %	NaCl %	N %	Total* P %	Total* K %	CAP. meq	Ca meq	Ca %	Mg meq	Mg %	K meq	K %	Na meq %††	Na	H meq	H %
Uc5.11	surface	0-56	9.0	5	1	0.02	<0.01	0.02	0.02	–	–	–		–		–		–		–	
	subsoil	167-213	9.1	9	4	0.03	<0.01	–	–	–	–	–		–		–		–		–	
Um6.11	surface	0-10	7.7	21	0.04	0.03	0.01	0.17	0.11	1.4	30.1	21.0	70	7.9	26	0.8	3	0.4	1	0	
	subsoil	61-76	8.0	23	0.02	0.03	0.01	0.09	0.12	1.4	33.8	23.0	68	9.8	29	0.4	1	0.6	2	0	
Uc5.15	surface	0-13	6.6	35	0	0.02	0.01	0.21	0.03	–	37.3	25.2	68	10.2	27	1.48	4	0.4	1	0	
	subsoil	86-102	8.6	61	3.2	0.42	0.23	–	–	–	37.6	16.4	44	14.3	38	0.55	1	6.3	17	0	
Um5.24	surface	0-4	6.6	43	0	0.02	0.01	0.11	–	–	15.7	6.9	45	6.8	44	1.2	8	0.4	3	0	
	subsoil	23-33	8.7	58	1.0	0.21	0.10	–	–	–	23.1	7.5	33	12.1	52	0.7	3	1.8	12	0	
Gc1.12	surface	0-18	8.9	14	9	0.04	0.01	0.04	0.01	1.7	–	–		–		–		–	–		
	subsoil	106-130	9.6	15	34.0	0.40	0.16	–	–	–	12.4	2.5		4.8		1.0		4.1	33††	0	
Gc1.22	surface	0-20	9.0	9	0.5	0.04	0.01	0.03	0.01		–			–		–		–		–	
	subsoil	75-108	9.1	12	17.8	0.31	0.14	–	–	–	16.9	11.0		4.1		0.8		1.0	6††	–	
Gn1.13	surface	0-15	7.9	7	–	0.03	0.01	0.04	0.01	1.0	–	–		–		–		–		–	
	subsoil (u)	53-96	9.1	10	1.0	0.09	0.04	–	–	–	–	–		–		–		–		–	
	(l)	96-120	9.3	15	13.0	0.24	0.12	–	–	–	15.0	8.9	59	4.2	28	0.6	4	1.3	9	0	
Dr1.43	surface	0-6	8.4	13	–	0.03	0.01	0.06	0.02	–	–	–		–		–		–		–	
	subsoil (u)	27-47	9.2	44	4.0	0.41	0.20	–	–	–	–	–		–		–		–		–	
	(l)	48-81	9.2	34	17.0	0.55	0.25	–	–	–	32.6	13.4	41	11.7	36	1.3	4	6.2	19	0	
Dr2.23	surface	0-11	6.5	8	0	0.03	0.01	0.06	0.02	–	4.6	3.5	77	0.5	10	0.5	10	0.2	3	–	
	subsoil (u)	30-69	6.8	60	0	0.04	0.02	0.06	0.02	–	23.8	15.3	64	6.1	26	1.3	6	1.1	4	0	
	(l)	79-122	8.8	35	6.3	0.08	0.02	0.02	0.01	–	18.9	12.4	66	4.8	25	0.8	4	0.9	5	0	
Dr2.33	surface	0-10	6.4	23	0	0.02	0.01	0.16	0.04	1.6	10.4	6.0	57	3.1	30	1.1	11	0.2	2	0	
	subsoil (l)	79-102	8.5	43	0.9	0.30	0.20	–	0.01	1.9	19.8	5.2	26	9.4	47	1.1	6	4.1	21	0	
Dy2.43	surface	0-16	6.0	14	0	0.01	0.01	0.13	0.03	–	6.3	4.1	65	1.2	19	0.9	15	0.04	1	–	
	subsoil (u)	25-41	7.2	60	0	0.06	0.02	–	–	–	15.2	4.5	29	8.7	58	0.8	5	1.2	8	0	
	(l)	91-114	8.7	43	17.2	0.33	0.20	–	–	–	14.4	5.1	35	6.3	44	0.6	4	2.4	17	0	
Dy3.43	surface	2.5-9	6.9	8	0	0.02	<0.01	0.14	–	–	11.8	10.3	87	1.1	9	0.2	2	0.2	2	0	
	subsoil	23-58	8.4	52	<0.01	0.37	0.23	0.04	0.01	–	25.8	8.4	33	9.8	38	1.2	4	6.4	25	0	
Dy5.43	surface	0-10	6.2	50	0	0.01	<0.01	0.07	–	–	2.8	1.8	64	0.7	25	0.2	8	0.1	3	–	
	subsoil (u)	48-61	6.5	46	0	0.04	0.01	0.04	0.01	–	13.6	3.2	25	6.0	44	0.7	5	2.7	20	1.0	7
	(l)	107-127	8.9	29	0.1	0.25	0.13	–	–	–	14.1	3.6	27	6.2	46	0.4	3	3.3	24	0	
Dd1.43	surface	0-3	6.9	29	0.03	0.08	0.04	0.60	0.13	–	32.7	17.0	50	9.8	29	5.2	16	0.7	2	0	
	subsoil	64-76	9.1	53	0.38	0.41	0.26	–	–	–	41.7	10.0	24	20.0	48	0.7	2	11.0	26	0	

Notes. CaCO₃ = calcium carbonate, TSS = total soluble salts, NaCl = sodium chloride, N = nitrogen, P = phosphorus, CAP = cation exchange capacity, K = potassium, Ca = calcium, Mg = magnesium, Na = sodium, H = hydrogen.
* Soluble in boiling hydrochloric acid, meq = milliquivalents per 100g of soil, % = percentage composition, † Percentage of exchange sodium, †† Metal cations only
– = not available, u = upper, l = lower.

Australia is at Stanthorpe (Jardine 1946) on acid sandy soils. B toxicity is a greater problem. In the Murray River districts, excess B arises from the soil. B levels are higher (about 1 ppm in some surface soils to more than 10 ppm in some subsoils) in soils whose parent materials have been derived from sediments laid down below the sea. The B content in these soils is lowest in those with sand surface soils, probably slightly higher in the sandy loams and highest in those with loam surface soils. As the irrigation water is low in B it can be used to leach the B from the soils, provided they are adequately drained. Such drainage waters may contain 5-10 ppm of B as compared with 0.1 ppm or less in the original irrigation water.

Manganese (Mn)
Manganese deficiency has been reported in a variety of plants including peas, cereals, legumes and many fruits. These deficiencies occur largely on alkaline soils, and on soils with thick limestone subsola, such as the Calcareous Earths (Gc); the intake of Mn by the plant becomes restricted where the soil pH rises above 6.5. Usually the supply of Mn is ample in acid soils except for some highly leached sands (Uc2.2, Uc2.3) and some leached ironstone soils (Dy2.61, Dy3.81); indeed, an example of Mn deficiency in grapevines has been reported on the leached ironstone soils in Western Australia. The application of lime to acid soils may induce Mn deficiency where the soil pH is raised above 6.5. This has occurred in vegetables on acid soils near Melbourne.

Zinc (Zn)
Of the trace elements — copper, cobalt, zinc, molybdenum, manganese, boron, iron, chlorine — probably the most important for grapevines and many other fruits is Zn. A mild deficiency of Zn, in which leaf symptoms are not obvious but yield is suppressed, occurs in the Riverland, Sunraysia and the MIA. Zn deficiency is usually found in alkaline soils, but has been recorded on acid and neutral soils in Western Australia, especially those subject to subsurface waterlogging. The most common associated deficiencies are P, Cu and Mn.

Copper (Cu)
The use of Cu sprays for the control of diseases in many vineyards has probably prevented Cu deficiency in grapevines. The poor growth of grapevines on Uc5.2 soils near Gingin, Western Australia (Teakle

et al. 1943) was corrected by both foliar sprays of Bordeaux mixture and applications of copper sulphate to the soil. This seems to be the only recorded deficiency of Cu in Australian vineyards. Cu deficiency is always associated with P deficiency and commonly with deficiencies of Zn, Mo and K. The soils most likely to develop Cu deficiency are acid soils with low Cation Exchange Capacities, highly calcareous soils and duplex soils subject to subsurface waterlogging.

Cobalt (Co)
Cobalt is needed in very small amounts by legumes but otherwise is not regarded as an essential element for higher plants. Supplies of Co are likely to be poor in soils which are low in Cu. As with Cu, Zn and Mn, Co becomes less available as pH rises.

Molybdenum (Mo)
Molybdenum deficiency is usually associated with a deficiency of P, often with S or K and sometimes with Cu. It has not been recorded as a simple deficiency. While no responses to Mo have been reported in grapevines, it is common to find marked responses in legumes grown as green manure crops and pasture leys in vineyards. Mo is required by the plant itself and for N fixation in the nodules. Deficiencies of Mo may be associated with its low availability, especially in acid soils. Liming acid soils to increase the soil pH may improve availability, however there are some acid soils which lack Mo as such. On highly calcareous and often alkaline soils, Mo deficiency has been observed in cauliflowers.

3.2.3 Salinity
A high concentration of soluble salts in the soil can limit plant growth, or even kill a crop, by creating an osmotic potential so high that plants have difficulty in obtaining water and nutrients from the soil solution. Alkaline soils (Table 3.3) generally have higher surface and subsoil salinities than acid and neutral soils as shown by their total soluble salt and sodium chloride (NaCl) contents. Generally, NaCl makes up two-thirds or more of the soluble salts, and bicarbonate, sulphate and other salts make up the rest. Non-saline soils have less than 0.05 per cent total soluble salts in their surface soils and less than 0.10 per cent in their subsoils.

Salinity becomes a problem when surface soils have 0.15 per cent or more total soluble salts or when subsoils contain 0.30 per cent or more. Soils with contents of total soluble salts between these levels must be irrigated with care. Subsoils containing 0.3 per cent total soluble salts have 40 tonnes of salts per hectare in each metre depth. Poor irrigation practice may cause a water-table to develop in the soil which can concentrate much of this salt in the top of the water-table zone causing severe salinity.

In soils rich in soft carbonates (3.2.5) a significant proportion of the salts in the soil solution are sodium carbonate and bicarbonate. These salts intensify the osmotic potential, render the soil less permeable due to increased sodicity (3.2.4), raise the soil pH to 9 or higher, and decrease the availability of some nutrient elements.

Soils particularly prone to salinity problems are, in order of decreasing severity, Gc1.12, Dr1.43, Gc1.22, Ug5, Dd1.43, Dy5.43, Dy3.43, Dr2.43 and Dr2.33. Their salt contents in some areas are often higher than those reported in Table 3.3. Small areas of some neutral and acid soils may also contain more salt than usual. The relationship between salinity and irrigation, the effect of salinity on grapevines and the treatment of salinity problems in vineyards is discussed in Volume 2, Chapter 7.

3.2.4 Sodicity

The friability and permeability of soils are strongly influenced by their sodium ion content, which if high enough will cause soil clay to disperse and block the passage of water through the soil pores. The exchangeable sodium percentage (shown as Na % in Tables 3.1-3.3) is a measure of the sodium content, or sodicity, of a soil. Exchangeable sodium percentages of 6 or more indicate that the soil is sodic (Dy5.41, Table 3.1) and 15 or greater (Dy3.42, Table 3.2) that the soil is strongly sodic. Sodicity increases with pH. Sodicity in many surface soils is commonly less than 6, but if the exchangeable sodium percentage of the subsoil is 6 or more it is probable that the surface soil has been more sodic during its formation. Soils with sodic to strongly sodic surface soils are not usually used for grapegrowing.

Magnesium ions are also thought to increase the dispersion of soil clay. This may be due either to the actual presence of high concentrations of Mg ions or to the low concentrations of Ca ions found in such soils, e.g. 47 per cent Mg and 26 per cent Ca in Dr2.33 subsoil (Table 3.3). The importance of Ca ions in maintaining or improving soil friability and permeability by keeping soil clays flocculated and stable is well-known. It is also clear that the content of Ca ions needs to be high in relation to the combined total of Na and Mg ions.

Soil permeability (3.1.7) generally decreases as the exchangeable Na and Mg contents increase. This is particulary so in subsoils, where Na ions cause the clay to disperse as it wets. Thus sodic soils lose friability (3.1.3) rapidly when wetted. Extreme examples are found in Sodic Yellow Duplex Soils (Dy3.4 and Dy5.4). Water ponded directly on such sodic subsoils does not even enter those subsoils during a 24 hour period; consequently, severe subsurface waterlogging can develop. The surface soils of sodic soils (Dy3.4, Dr2.3), except where they are sands (Dy5), also show low permeabilities and pronounced hardsetting properties, even where their exchangeable sodium percentage is less than 6. Thus water entry is low and run-off high. The remedy for both surface soils and subsoils is to improve soil friability, as in the Tatura method (Adem and Tisdall 1983).

Under Australian conditions, gypsum ($CaSO_4$) is the most useful improver of friability for both surface soils and subsoils. Because gypsum is only slowly soluble it should be placed in the soil layer requiring treatment. About 16 tonne/ha of gypsum are needed to remove 5 meq per 100 g of Na ions from 30 cm of soil. Ca ions released by the gypsum displace the Na ions which together with the sulphate are leached from the soil.

Powdered S can also be used to remove Na from the soil. The S is rapidly oxidized to sulphuric acid which in turn forms sodium sulphate. S has not been used extensively in Australia, but may be useful where the soil contains moderate amounts of calcium carbonate or the exchange complex of the soil is well supplied with Ca.

Sodicity also affects plant nutrition. Evidence is being accumulated that for some plants (e.g. almonds) the availability of nutrient elements, and/or the ability of plants to take up nutrient elements from sodic soils, is restricted and causes some nutritional imbalance. Whether this is due to a chemical antagonism or to the poor physical state of sodic soils is not known. No data are available for grapevines.

3.2.5 Soft carbonates

The soft carbonates, as distinct from hard limestone and calcretes (3.1.5), occur within the fine earth fraction (particles less than 2 mm diameter) of the soil. They consist of Ca-Mg carbonates with Ca predominating. They affect the availability of some nutrient elements, cause lime-induced chlorosis and decrease the permeability of the soil. In soils in which the soft carbonates are important (e.g. Uc5.1, Gc and Gn1.13) significant amounts are found in the

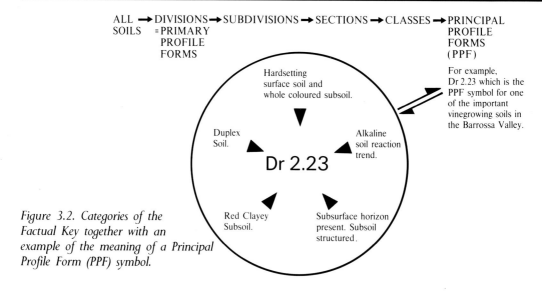

ALL → DIVISIONS → SUBDIVISIONS → SECTIONS → CLASSES → PRINCIPAL
SOILS = PRIMARY PROFILE
PROFILE FORMS
FORMS (PPF)

For example,
Dr 2.23 which is the
PPF symbol for one
of the important
vinegrowing soils in
the Barrossa Valley.

Hardsetting
surface soil and
whole coloured subsoil.

Duplex
Soil.

Alkaline
soil reaction
trend.

Dr 2.23

Red Clayey
Subsoil.

Subsurface horizon
present. Subsoil
structured.

Figure 3.2. Categories of the Factual Key together with an example of the meaning of a Principal Profile Form (PPF) symbol.

three fractions — sand, silt and clay. These soils have horizons of maximum carbonate accumulation at depths ranging from less than 0.3 m to more than 1 m, and contain about 5 to more than 35 per cent of carbonate, calculated as calcium carbonate, up to one-third of which exists in the silt and clay fraction. That is, the silt plus clay fraction forms the active carbonate which enters into chemical reactions. Any sodium present intensifies this reactivity. Where carbonate-rich soil layers are free from Na the soil pH does not exceed 8.5 but where Na is present the soil pH will rise to 9 and even 10 (e.g. carbonate horizons of Uc5.1, Gc and Gn1.13 soils). At this pH, nutrients such as P, Fe, Zn and Mn become unavailable to plants and lime-induced chlorosis develops in susceptible varieties. Moreover, soil friability, permeability and aeration are poor because the clay particles are dispersed. Viticulture on soils containing soft carbonates is more satisfactory when at least 45 cm of soil with relatively low carbonate (preferably less than 5 per cent) occurs above the horizon of maximum carbonate.

3.3 Classification and description of Australian grapegrowing soils

In Australia, until recently, soils were classed into various poorly co-ordinated, loosely described groups termed the Great Soil Groups, some of which have unusual names, e.g. solodized-solonetz. Many people, including grapegrowers and winemakers, have attempted to classify their local soils, and this has resulted in much confusion. Often a soil has different names in different districts; or different soils may be given the same name; or a soil may be termed 'basaltic' in one area just because it is red, and in another area be so named because it is black! Clearly, this is not satisfactory. It means that one grower's experience cannot be confidently applied elsewhere, nor can the results of new research be easily communicated. Good classification understood by everyone means good communication.

The modern co-ordinated soil classification first published in 1960 achieves this objective. Known as *A Factual Key for the Recognition of Australian Soils* (Northcote 1979), it was used to classify and map the soils of Australia between 1958 and 1968. These maps have been published as an *Atlas of Australian Soils* and described in *A Description of Australian Soils* (Northcote *et al.* 1975). These three publications furnish comprehensive data on the recognition of Australian soils, their geography, their general features, description, occurrence and land use, and the sources of analytical data.

The Factual Key is here adapted to cover the soils used for Australian viticulture. It uses a small number of properties of each of the two or three soil layers shown in Figure 3.1 to class a soil. There are four primary groups of soils in Australia denoted by the letters O, U, G and D. The O soils are those composed mainly of organic materials, such as peat, and because grapevines are not grown on these soils, they will not be considered further. Grapevines are, however, grown on soils in each of the three primary groups of mineral soils, U, G and D.

In all the soils of the U group there is little change in texture between surface soils and subsoils; their texture profiles are Uniform. Thus the U group includes soils that range from sandy throughout, Uc, through those that are loamy throughout, Um, to those that are clayey throughout, Uf and Ug.

In the G group soils there is a gradual increase in fine particles so that texture becomes more clayey from the surface soil down and into the subsoil; their textures profiles are Gradational.

In the D group there is a sudden change from sandy or loamy surface soils to decidedly more clayey subsoils; the profiles have a texture contrast and are Duplex. Each primary soil grouping is further subdivided to obtain the Principal Profile Forms that form the main operational units of the classification.

The principal profile form symbol, e.g. Dr2.23, is a shorthand description of a soil (see Figure 3.2). In the discussion that follows, however, the description of the principal profile forms includes, in addition to the identifying properties, others of particular interest to the grapegrower which may be termed land use properties.

Soils that are known to occur in the grapegrowing districts are listed in Table 3.4; the commoner soils used for grapegrowing are described.

Table 3.4 Soils of the grapegrowing areas

Grapegrowing areas	Most common soils	Some other soils
New South Wales		
Forbes-Cowra	Dr2.22, Dr2.23, Dr2.33, Dr2.42	Gn2.12, Db1.22, By3.43
Hunter Valley, Lower	Dy3.41, Dy3.42, Ug5.13, Ug5.14, Ug5.15, Ug5.32, Dr2.21, Dr2.22, Dr2.41, Dr2.42	Dr4.11, Dr4.12, Dr2.23, Dr3.41, Db1.41, Db1.42, Dy3.21, Dy3.22, Gn2.25, Um6.11
Hunter Valley, Upper	Um6.11, Dr2.23, Dr2.33, Dr2.43	Dr2.22, Dr2.42, Db1.22, Db1.23, Db1.33, Db1.42, Dy3.42, Dy3.43, Dy5.41, Dy5.42, Dd1.43, Ug5.13, Ug5.14, Ug5.15, Ug5.32, Uc1.2
Mudgee	Dr2.22, Dr2.32, Dr2.42, Dy3.41, Dy3.42	Db1.22, Dy2.22, Gn2.12, Gn2.15, Um6.11, Ug5.1
Riverina	Dr2.33, Dr2.23, Gn2.46, Gn2.13, Gn1.13	Dr2.43, Db1.33, Db1.43, Dy2.33, Dy2.43, Dy3.43, Dy5.43, Dd1.43, Ug5.24, Gc1.12, Gc1.22
Rooty Hill	Dr2.21	Ug5.1, Dy3.41, Dy3.42
Victoria		
Avoca	Dy3.41, Dy3.42, Dr2.21, Dr2.22	Dr2.32, Dr3.41, Dr3.42, Dy3.43
Drumborg	Gn4.11, Dy3.61	Db1.22, Db2.22, Db2.42
Geelong	Dr2.23	Ug5.15, Ug5.16
Glenrowan-Milawa	Dr2.22, Uc1.21, Uc1.22, Dy5.41, Dy5.42	Dr2.21, Dy3.42, Dy3.43
Goulburn Valley	Dr2.22, Dr2.62, Dr2.33, Dr2.23	Uc1.22, Uc1.23, Db1.42, Dy3.33, Dy3.41, Dy3.42, Dy3.43
Great Western - Ararat	Dy3.41, Dy3.42, Dr2.21, Dr2.22	Dr2.41, Dr2.42, Dr3.41, Dr3.42, Dy3.43
Lilydale	Dr2.21, Dr2.22	Dy3.42, Dy3.41
Mildura-Robinvale*	Gc1.22	Gc1.12, Gn1.13, Dr1.33, Dr1.43, Uc5.11, Uc5.12, Ug5.25, Uc1.4
Rutherglen-Corowa* (includes Barooga)	Dr2.22, Dr2.33, Dr2.23	Uc1.22, Uc1.23, Uc1.4, Ug5.2, Dr3.42, Dr3.43, Dy3.41, Dy3.42, Dy3.43
Swan Hill*	Gc1.22	Gc1.12, Gn1.13, Dr2.33, Uc5.1, Ug5.2

Table 3.4 (continued)

Grapegrowing areas	Most common soils	Some other soils
Queensland		
Roma	Dy3.43	Db1.33, Uc1.21
Stanthorpe	Uc2.21, Dy5.41, Dy5.81	Uc2.12, Dy3.41, some Gn2 soils
Other areas e.g. Coominya, Inala, Inglewood, Warwick		Dy3.42, Um4.31, some Gn2 soils
South Australia		
Adelaide Metropolitan and Angle Vale	Dr2.23	Ug5.1, Um6.2, Um6.4, Uc1.2, Gc1.12
Barossa Hills	Dy3.22, Dy3.61, Dr2.23, Uc6.11	Dy2.41, Dy3.42, Dy3.43, Dy5.42, Dy5.43, Dy5.82, Uc1.4, Uc2.22, Dy2.22
Barossa Valley (includes Lyndoch)	Dr2.23, Dr3.23, Dy5.43, Dy5.82, Dy5.83	Dr2.33, Dr2.43, Db1.33, Db2.43, Dy3.43, Dy3.61, Dy3.81, Uc1.4, Uc2.21, Um6.21, Um6.24, Ug5.16
Clare-Watervale	Dr2.23	Ug5.15, Ug5.16, Uc1.4, Dy3.22, Dy3.42, Dy3.43, Dr3.43, Um6.23, Um6.24
Coonawarra	Uf5.31, Um6.41, Ug6.42, Um6.43	Dr2.23
Langhorne Creek	Uc1.43, Uc1.44, Ug5.15	Dr2.23, Dd1.13, Uc4.22
Padthaway-Keppoch	Dr2.23	Uc2.21, Uc6.13, Um6.41, Um6.42, Um6.43, Uf5.31, Db1.23, Db2.23, Dy3.43, Dy5.83
Riverland (Murray River districts in S.A.)	Gc1.22	Gc1.12, Gn1.13, Dr1.33, Uc5.11, Uc5.12 Ug5.25
Southern Vales District (Blewitt Springs, McLaren Vale etc.)	Dr2.23, Dy3.43, Uc2.21, Dy5.42	Ug5.14, Ug5.16, Dy3.61, Dr2.22, Um6.2, Um6.4
Northern Territory		
Alice Springs	Uc5.21, Uc1.43	
Western Australia		
Margaret River	Uc4.22 and Uc4.21, Uc1.22, Dy5.81	Gn2.22, Gn2.15, Dr2.61, Dr2.21, Dy3.21, Dy3.61, Uc2.21
Mt. Barker, Frankland River	Dy3.61, Dy3.62, Dy3.81, Dy3.82	Dy3.21, Dy3.41, Dy5.42, Dy5.81, Dr2.21 Dr2.22, Uc2.33
Swan Valley, Wanneroo, Gingin, and Toodyay	Dy5.81, Gn2.15, Gn2.25, Dy2.61	Dy3.61, Dy3.81, Dy3.82, Um6.11, Gn2.24, Gn2.14, Dr2.21, Dy3.21, Uc4.21, Uc4.22, Uc5.21, Uc5.22

* Includes adjacent areas in New South Wales.

3.3.1 Uniform texture profiles, the U soils

Sands, the Uc soils

At least 16 different kinds of sand soils are used for viticulture. Some are illustrated diagrammatically in Figure 3.3. Collectively, they are permeable soils suitable for vineyards where moisture and nutrient requirements can be met and maintained. As available water capacities are very low where sands are coarse or shallow, frequent irrigation may be necessary.

(i) Siliceous Sands - Uc1.21, Uc1.22

These dominantly quartzose sands range from fine to coarse; some may be gritty or gravelly. Surface soils are brownish grey to grey-brown in Uc1.21 and Uc1.22; subsoils are light yellow to light grey in Uc1.21 and yellowish brown through brown to yellowish red in Uc1.22. Soil depth varies from 0.3 to more than 6m.

These highly permeable and excessively drained soils are mildly acidic to neutral sands and are susceptible to wind erosion where there is little plant cover. Deficiencies of P, N and Zn are known to occur, and other deficiencies, including S, K, Ca and Mg, are likely with intensive use.

These soils are found on dunes and sand-sheets adjacent to channels of both active and non-active drainageways (as in the Goulburn Valley, and elsewhere in the riverine plains of south-eastern Australia), on subcoastal dunes (as near Margaret River) and in hilly areas of siliceous rocks on ridge crests and slopes (as near Glenrowan). Subsolum materials, which include aeolianite (near Margaret River) and siliceous rocks (Glenrowan), affect the moisture regime of these soils.

(ii) Firm Siliceous Sands - Uc1.43, Uc1.44

These loamy sand to sandy loam soils have a sand fraction that ranges from coarse through medium to fine. Uc1.43 soils are red-brown in colour; Uc1.44 soils, are dark grey. Their firm consistence means that wind erosion is not such a hazard as with Uc1.2. They are highly permeable, well-drained soils and their available water capacity is strongly influenced by the grain size of the sand; fine sandy forms contain more available water than do the coarse ones. The inherent fertility of these mildly acidic to neutral sands varies greatly, but phosphorus and nitrogen contents are often low.

The Uc1.4 soils occur mainly in two topographic positions: on hill slopes where they are usually less than 0.6 m deep and overlie rock: and on alluvial plains and terraces where they are usually more than 0.6 m deep and overlie layered alluvial sediments which often exceed 2 m. This latter situation is often very suitable for vineyards, as at Langhorne Creek (Table 3.4). However, soil conditions vary greatly over short distances and in some cases recent deposits of silty loam may cover the sandy soil. Such local variability makes recommendations difficult. Grapevines are also grown on alluvial plains of Uc1.43 at Alice Springs. The shallower forms of Uc1.4

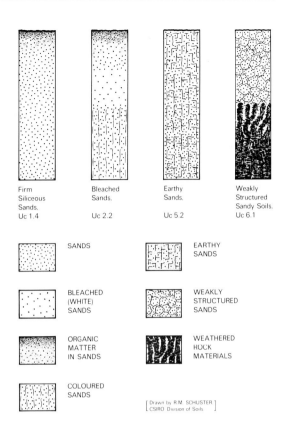

Figure 3.3. Profile diagrams of some sand soils — Uc — used for viticulture.

are used for vineyards only where they are closely associated with deeper soils.

(iii) Bleached Sands - Uc2.21, Uc2.22, and Uc2.33

Bleached sands are distinguished by the white subsurface sand visible in the dry soil. It is overlain by a grey to black surface soil that appears strongly speckled because of a mixture of discrete organic particles and sand grains. The Uc2.2 soils vary in depth from 1 to 6 m. They are all highly permeable when moist, but the surfaces of some are difficult to wet when dry. Severe wind and water erosion are fairly common where there is little plant cover.

As a general rule, these acid Uc2 sands are very deficient in phosphorus, very low in K and Ca, low in N and deficient in a range of other nutrients including Zn, S, Mo and Cu. The Uc2 soils are widespread in Australia on dunes and sand-sheets, and overlie a variety of subsola. Where subsola are clayey and occur at shallow depths, the soil moisture may be adequate for vineyards. This is the case in the Southern Districts (Blewitt Springs), where extensive vineyards are planted on Uc2.21 soils, and may be so at Stanthorpe. In Padthaway-Keppoch, dunes of Uc2.21 are underlain by limestones. In the Barossa Hills, Uc2.22 soils (mottled sand subsoils) on creek flats are sometimes used for viticulture, but they suffer from seasonal waterlogging as do Uc2.33 soils (dark brown to black subsoil hardpan) near Mt Barker in Western Australia.

(iv) Pale Sands with Yellowish or Brownish Subsoils - Uc4.21, Uc4.22

Surface soils are usually grey-brown loamy sands, but range from dark grey to dark red-brown and from gritty sand to sandy loam. They pass into pale yellow or brown subsurface soils which grade into stronger yellow and brown subsoils in Uc4.21 and Uc4.22, respectively. Subsoils are commonly clayey sand, but vary from sand to light sandy clay loam.

These soils are commonly 1-2 m thick, and are highly permeable when moist. When dry, some are difficult to wet and they shed water from sloping sites. Those on dune formations are susceptible to wind erosion where there is little plant cover. In general, these acid to neutral sands are low in P, low to moderate in K and Ca, and probably have some trace-element deficiencies.

In Western Australia these soils are used for viticulture in the Swan Valley and near Margaret River. Available water capacities are low, especially for Uc4.22 soils on older dune formations underlain by aeolianite. However, where Uc4.22 occur on levees and fans, and where Uc4.21 occur on terraces, available water capacities are higher. At Langhorne Creek, Uc4.22 soil occurs on dunes bordering the alluvial plains of the Bremer River. Here, too, available water may be fair because of alluvial sediments at depth. However, wind erosion remains a serious problem.

(v) Brownish Sands - Uc5.11, Uc5.12

These Uc5.1 soils are loose sands, predominantly brownish or reddish in the surface and gradually becoming paler and yellower in the subsoil owing to accumulations of carbonates (lime). Where these soils have developed on dunes and sand-sheets they are usually about 2 m thick. They are generally alkaline sands of low fertility, and are liable to wind erosion. Uc5.1 soils have developed mainly in drier inland areas.

Where irrigation water is available, as along the Murray River, some Uc5.1 soils have been used for viticulture, although larger areas are planted to citrus. Careful management with particular attention to subsoil drainage is necessary, especially in Uc5.12.

(vi) Earthy Sands - Uc5.2

Uc5.2 soils have dull, pale yellowish or reddish brown to dark brown sand to sandy loam surface soils. The subsoils are massive and porous sand to sandy loam, and are coloured red or yellow by clayey and oxidic coatings on the sand grains. Commonly, these soils are about 1 m deep but range from 0.25 to 2 m. Some overlie hardpans or truncated laterites.

While the soils are highly permeable, internal drainage may be restricted by the relatively impervious subsola. This limitation is important where irrigation is proposed. Uc5.2

soils have formed from strongly weathered siliceous materials. Very low P, N and K contents are general, and trace-element deficiencies, in particular Mo and Cu, are likely in these acidic sands. Uc5.21 soils are used for viticulture in Western Australia and the Northern Territory in areas where the deeper forms occur on gentle slopes and plains.

(vii) Weakly Structured Sandy Soils - Uc6.11, Uc6.13

These soils have weak crumb, granular or subangular blocky structure, especially evident when the soil is moist. They are grey-brown (Uc6.11) to red-brown (Uc6.13). Texture is commonly sandy loam but may be loamy sand or sandy clay loam. They are shallow soils, 0.6 m thick or less, and thus can store only a limited volume of moisture. They are permeable soils, low to moderate in P content and moderate in N and K. Responses to trace elements, including Zn, Cu and Mn, have been obtained in some areas of these mildly acidic (Uc6.11) to mildly alkaline (Uc6.13) soils.

The Uc6.11 occur on hillslopes in the Barossa Hills where they are underlain at shallow depth by weathered mica-schists which often outcrop. It is doubtful if they would be favoured for vineyards on their own, but their intimate association with Dy3.22 soils, which have a greater capacity to store moisture, means that they are often included in vineyards by expedience.

The Uc6.13 occur on old stranded beach ridges and dunes in the Padthaway-Keppoch area where they are underlain by dune limestone (calcarenite) at depths of 0.1-0.6 m, which may outcrop. The limestone often has a hard capping, but it becomes softer and more porous with depth. The limestone may exceed 3 m in thickness. Water-tables are from 2 to 10 m in depth. The capacity of these shallow sandy Uc6.13 soils to store moisture is limited, but is probably greater in the limestone subsolum. On account of their colour, the Uc6.13 soils have sometimes been called Terra Rossa; however, their sandy textures clearly separate them from the red but clayey Coonawarra soils, Uf5.31.

Loams, the Um soils

The loam soils used for viticulture are either moderately deep to deep soils or shallow soils overlying limestone. Some are illustrated in Figure 3.4

(i) Pale Loams with Rough-ped* Subsoils - Um4.31.

These moderately deep soils have developed on the thick alluvia of river terraces and levees, notably in southern Queensland where small areas are used for viticulture. They seem well suited to the needs of grapevines, although

---

* Definition of ped: a ped is an individual natural soil aggregate, whereas clods, or fragments, result from soil ruptured by an applied force, e.g. a plough. Rough-ped means that ped faces are porous, and contrasts with smooth-ped where ped faces are smooth (matt to shiny).

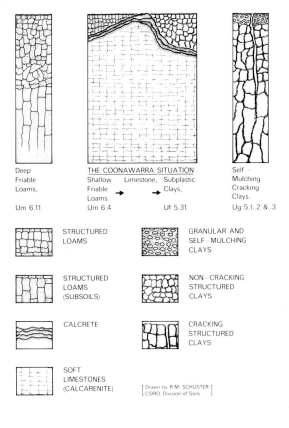

Deep Friable Loams. Um 6.11	THE COONAWARRA SITUATION		Self — Mulching Cracking Clays. Ug 5.1,.2 & .3
	Shallow Friable Loams. Um 6.4 →	Limestone, Subplastic Clays. → Uf 5.31	

	STRUCTURED LOAMS		GRANULAR AND SELF—MULCHING CLAYS
	STRUCTURED LOAMS (SUBSOILS)		NON—CRACKING STRUCTURED CLAYS
	CALCRETE		CRACKING STRUCTURED CLAYS
	SOFT LIMESTONES (CALCARENITE)		[Drawn by R M. SCHUSTER] [CSIRO Division of Soils]

Figure 3.4. Profile diagrams of some loam and clay soils — Um. Uf. Ug — used for viticulture

the surface seals with continued cultivation and reduces water entry. Dark brown loams, friable when moist, overlie red-brown blocky subsoils. Soil permeability and available water capacity are good. Inherent fertility is moderate, the main deficiencies being P and N.

(ii) Friable Loams with Rough-ped Subsoils - Um6.11
The Um6.11 are deep friable loamy soils. Surface soils are black to very dark brown; they are silty or fine sandy loams to clay loams that are strongly structured. The subsoils are also black to very dark brown loams to clay loams with prismatic to coarse blocky structure which may break down to finer units. There may be some soft and hard carbonate (lime) patches or nodules in the deeper subsoil.

Um6.11 are usually 0.6 to 1.5 m thick and grade into subsola or alluvial sediments that range from sandy to clayey. They are permeable and moderately fertile soils, mildly acid to neutral in the surface and becoming neutral to alkaline at depth. Some areas of Um6.11 may not require phosphatic fertilizers. The available water capacity should be moderate to high. Um6.11 soils occur mainly on young river terraces and alluvial fans, notably in the Hunter River, Mudgee and Swan Valley districts.

(iii) Shallow Friable Loams with Rough-ped Fabric - Um6.21, Um6.23, Um6.24
These black (Um6.21), brown (Um6.23) or red (Um6.24) loams, sandy clay loams or clay loams are well-structured and friable with rough-faced porous peds. In some there is a distinct organic darkening in the surface few centimetres. They are shallow (0.2 - 0.6 m thick) and in the viticultural areas commonly have a soft to moderately hard calcrete (limestone) layer immediately below the soil with hard rock (e.g. shale) or clay sediments below the calcrete.

Although the soils are permeable, their available water is restricted by their shallow depth and thus the moisture regime depends a great deal on the nature of the underlying sediments or rock. Although the natural fertility of Um6.2 soils is probably moderate, deficiencies of P, N, Zn, Cu and Mn have been recorded in these mildly acid to aklaline loam soils. Um6.2 occur on moderate to steep slopes in the Barossa Valley and Clare-Watervale.

(iv) Shallow Friable Loams with Smooth-ped Fabric - Um6.41, Um6.42, Um6.43
These shallow soils are similar to the previous group but have dense smooth-faced peds. They mostly range from a few to 50 cm thick and have a soft to hard calcrete layer immediately below the soil, and softer limestones below that. Although they are permeable soils, their available water is restricted by the shallow depth of soil and the moisture available to the grapevine depends greatly on the underlying limestones. Natural fertility is probably moderate, and similar to that of Um6.2. At Coonawarra, Padthaway and Keppoch, Um6.4 soils occur on gentle slopes and plains underlain by limestones (calcarenite), and with water-tables at depths of 2 to 10 m.

Non-cracking clays, the Uf soils
Relatively small areas of non-cracking clays are used for viticulture, but the red clays of the Coonawarra District (Figure 3.4) are reputed to be outstanding for winegrape production.

(i) Non-cracking Subplastic Clays - Uf5.31.
The Uf5.31 soils include the celebrated Coonawarra loam, so-called because of its excellent friable nature. In fact the surface soil is a subplastic medium clay. The term subplastic indicates that such clays do not show their full plastic potential as clays unless a great deal of mechanical work is done on them either by kneading a specimen in the hand or by machinery in the paddock.

The surface soils, 0.1-0.15 m thick, are dark brown to dark reddish brown subplastic medium clays that initially feel like loams, clay loams or light clays. Their structure is strong granular or subangular blocky. They merge into the brighter subsoil of red-brown to dark red medium to heavy clays that initially feel like light clays or fine sandy clays. Structure is moderately to strongly

not used extensively for viticulture, but occur in several grapegrowing areas and are generally suitable for grapes. Red Massive Earths, Gn2.1 are among the most widespread of Australian soils, but development has been limited by their low-activity kaolinitic clays and low moisture-holding capacity.

(i) Red Massive Earths - Gn2.1
Surface soils range from sandy to loamy and from brown or red-brown to dark red. Subsurface soils found in Gn2.13 and Gn2.15 are light reddish brown and are slightly more clayey than the surface soils. These surface and subsurface soils grade into subsoils which are typically red, massive and porous, sandy clay loams to clays. Surface soils are mildly acid to neutral; subsoils vary from mildly acid to mildly alkaline. Small patches of carbonate occur in the deeper subsoil of Gn2.13. Inherent fertility is generally low; deficiencies of N, P and K are common, and deficiencies of S, Cu, Zn, Mo and B have been reported.

The Gn2.1 are highly permeable soils and are commonly 1-2 m deep. Subsola vary from sandy or clayey sediments to weathered rocks, which reflect the wide range of land forms (from stream terraces and levees to plains, hill clopes and tableland crests) on which Gn2.1 soils occur. At present small areas on slopes are used for vineyards in the Forbes-Cowra area, on plains and undulating land in the Riverina (where Gn2.13 soils are associated with Dr2.33 soils in some localities), and on terraces and slopes at Mudgee, the Swan Valley and Margaret River. The Gn2.1 occur widely in south-eastern Australia and are suitable for grapes if nutrient requirements can be met.

(ii) Yellow Massive Earths - Gn2.2
These soils are the yellow counterparts of the Gn2.1 soils. They have greyish, brownish or yellowish sandy to loamy surface soils that grade through lighter coloured subsurfaces into yellowish massive and porous sandy clay loam to clay subsoils. Surface soils range from slightly to moderately acid. Nutrient status is generally low and deficiencies similar to those for Gn2.1 soils are likely. The Gn2.2 are moderately permeable soils from 1 to 2 m thick and over lie as wide a range of subsola as those under Gn2.1 soils. Only small areas are used for viticulture.

(iii) Brown or Mottled-red Massive Earths - Gn2.46
These soils are the brown and mottled-red counterparts of the Gn2.1 soils. Surface soils are brownish to yellowish with a paler subsurface, and are sands to sandy loams. Subsoils are brown to mottled-red sandy clay loams to clay loams with segregation of carbonates at a depth of about 0.6 m; sobsola which occur at depths of 1-2 m are clayey sediments. Surface soils are mildly acid to neutral, but subsoils are strongly alkaline.

Inherent fertility is generally low. The sandy surface soils, which are liable to wind erosion when not vegetated,

are highly permeable. However, permeability decreases rapidly with depth, and waterlogging is often experienced. Gn2.46 soils occur on sandy sheets and low sandy ridges in the Riverina, which seems to be the only place where they are used for grapegrowing.

Rough-ped earths, the Gn4 soils
These soils have gradational texture profiles like the Gn2 soils, but are distinguished by their well-structured profiles in which the peds are soft and porous (Figure 3.5).

(i) Red Rough-ped Earths - Gn4.11
Surface soils are black to dark reddish brown loam to light clay, with large amounts of organic matter. They are well-structured (crumb to granular) and very friable especially when moist. Clay contents increase steadily from 20-40 cm depth down to the light to medium clay subsoil, which is also well-structured and friable. The dark reddish brown to dark red clay subsoils are often 2 m or more thick and pass into weathered basic rocks or colluvium derived therefrom. Gn4.11 are highly permeable, acid soils that retain their very good physical condition under continued cultivation. They are fertile in their natural state, but levels of organic matter, N and P rapidly decline with intensive use. Responses to these nutrients and to S, Mo and K have been obtained after prolonged use. Though not extensively used for viticulture, these soils feature in the Drumborg area (Table 3.4)

3.3.3 Duplex texture profiles, the D Soils
The range of duplex soils found in Australia is probably greater than that in any other country. Some of our most important agricultural soils are duplex, and so, as may be expected, are many of the viticultural soils (Table 3.4). The most notable exceptions are the Murray River irrigation districts where the Calcareous Earths and Brownish Sands predominate. Variations within the duplex soils (Figure 3.6) are determined largely by the nature of the surface soils and the differences in drainage of the subsoils. In general, the sequence of subsoil colour from red (Dr) → brown (Db) → yellow (Dy) → black (Dd) → gley (Dg) also represents decreasing subsoil permeability and aeration. No grapevines are grown on the Dg soils.

Red duplex soils, the Dr soils
All Dr soils have red-brown to red clayey subsoils. They include some of the most important grapegrowing soils in south-eastern Australia, especially Dr2 soils.

(i) Crusty Red Duplex Soils - Dr1.33, Dr1.43
The loamy surface soil which is brown or reddish brown forms a soft surface crust and is only 5-10 cm thick. Below this the very thin subsurface may form a continuous bleached layer in Dr1.43, or a sporadic one in Dr1.33, no more than 1-2 cm thick. It passes sharply to a red to red-brown clay subsoil which tends to have prismatic

or columnar structure. In the lower subsoil, carbonate and often gypsum segregations are present. The underlying subsola which occur at depths of 1-2 m vary from sandy clay loam sediments to hard, white sandstone.

These alkaline soils contain appreciable amounts of soluble salts: NaCl content may exceed 0.3 per cent in the subsoil. However, the salts are readily leached during irrigation. Inherent fertility is low to moderate, and P and N deficiencies are likely. Such soils, for example Boeil loam, mainly occur in the Riverland and at Mildura on the Murray River, where they occupy the lower-lying plains and interdune flats. As their permeability is generally moderate, they are not liable to waterlogging unless seepage from dunes occurs. Artificial drainage would then be necessary.

(ii) Hard Red Duplex Soils - Dr2.21, Dr2.22, Dr2.23, Dr2.32, Dr2.33, Dr2.41, Dr2.42, Dr2.43, Dr2.61, Dr2.62

Dr2 soils occur to a greater or lesser extent in almost all the grapegrowing districts of south-eastern and Western Australia. They are particularly important in the dryland grapegrowing areas where winegrapes predominate. The Dr2 (Figure 3.6) have brownish surface soils ranging from loamy sand to clay loam. Subsurface

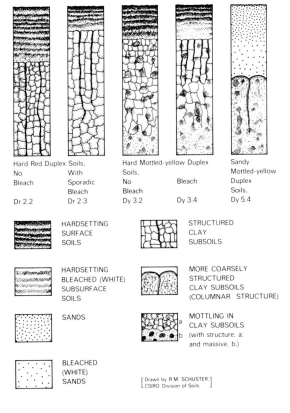

Hard Red Duplex Soils.
No Bleach
Dr 2.2

With Sporadic Bleach
Dr 2.3

Hard Mottled-yellow Duplex Soils.
No Bleach
Dy 3.2

Bleach
Dy 3.4

Sandy Mottled-yellow Duplex Soils.
Dy 5.4

	HARDSETTING SURFACE SOILS		STRUCTURED CLAY SUBSOILS
	HARDSETTING BLEACHED (WHITE) SUBSURFACE SOILS		MORE COARSELY STRUCTURED CLAY SUBSOILS (COLUMNAR STRUCTURE)
	SANDS		MOTTLING IN CLAY SUBSOILS (with structure, a; and massive, b.)
	BLEACHED (WHITE) SANDS		

[Drawn by R.M. SCHUSTER]
[CSIRO Division of Soils.]

Figure 3.6. Profile diagrams of some duplex soils — D — used for viticulture

soils vary from no development to a fully bleached subsurface. They all set hard when dry, vary in thickness from less than 10 to 50 cm and pass directly, and often very sharply, into the red-brown clay subsoils.

The soil profile varies in total thickness from 0.3-2 m. Dr2 soils are moderately permeable, well-drained, and have good available water capacities. These properties, however, are modified considerably by the various subsola that range from rock to clayey or sandy sediments. The soil environment is relatively drier when rock rather than sediment occurs. Furthermore, where soil overlies rock subsolum, the shallower the soil is, the drier the soil-subsolum environment. The topography gives a broad guide. Where Dr2 soils with rock subsolar extend from upper hill slopes to valleys, as at Clare-Watervale, the moisture environment improves downslope. In the Barossa Valley, deep clay sediments below Dr2 soils provide a moister situation. Dr2 soils on plains, terraces and levees, and even those on rolling terrain, are underlain by moisture-retaining sediments (as in the Southern Districts) and have better available water capacities than those on hillslopes underlain by hard rock.

Dr2 soils are moderately fertile, but most are low in P and N. K levels are moderate. Mo deficiency is associated with some Dr2.21 soils and is likely in Dr2.61 soils; low Zn availability is common on the more calcareous Dr2.23 and Dr2.33 soils. Dr2.2 soils have light coloured, but not bleached, subsurface soils, and very friable subsoils that are not sodic (see 3.2.4). They are the best of the Dr2 soil range for all agricultural purposes, including viticulture.

Dr2.3 soils have sporadic bleaching, whitish spots and patches in the subsurface of the dry soil just above the clay subsoil. The subsoils are less friable than Dr2.2 subsoils and are sodic. Thus Dr2.3 subsoils are less permeable than Dr2.2 subsoils. As the surface soils are very hardsetting, applications of gypsum to both surface and subsoils is desirable to help overcome this. Dr2.4 soils have fully bleached, whitish when dry, subsurface soils just above the clay subsoil. Again, this subsoil is less friable than that in Dr2.2 soils and is sodic. Slight, temporary waterlogging of the subsurface may occur after prolonged or heavy rain. Dr2.6 soils have unstructured, though friable clay subsoils, whereas all the previous Dr2 have structured subsoils. They may perform as well as Dr2.2, but experience is limited.

The surface soils of Dr2.21, Dr2.41, Dr2.61, Dr2.22, Dr2.32, Dr2.42 and Dr2.62 are slightly acid. In the first three, acidity either remains fairly constant or increases with depth, while in the others the pH increases in the subsoil to within the range 6.5-8.0. In Dr2.23, Dr2.33 and Dr2.43, surface soils range from slightly acid to slightly alkaline and subsoils are alkaline with free carbonate (lime) segregations in the deeper parts. Carbonate occurs either as low amounts, 1-35 per cent $CaCO_3$ at depths of 0.5-1 m, or as a more conspicuous layer at about 0.6 m in depth containing 20 to 50 per cent $CaCO_3$. The available water capacity of soils with the high carbonate layer is lower than that of soils low in carbonate. The soil thickness above the carbonate layer thus becomes particularly significant.

The Dr2.23 soils and the closely related Dr2.22 are among the most widely used soils for grapegrowing in south-eastern Australia (Table 3.4). The Dr2.23 soils were formerly named Red-brown Earths. Unfortunately, many people also regard Dr2.33 and Dr2.43 soils as Red-brown Earths; they fail to appreciate their sodic and, in some cases, saline properties that make them less desirable viticultural soils.

(iii) Hard Mottled-Red Duplex Soils - Dr3.23, Dr3.41, Dr3.42, Dr3.43

These soils are not widely used for viticulture. They are similar to the corresponding Dr2 soils, but are distinguished by the presence of brown, yellow-brown and/or grey mottling in their clay subsoils which indicates that they are less permeable than the Dr2 soils. This is most pronounced in Dr3.4 soils, in which the subsurface soil becomes saturated during prolonged or heavy rainfall more readily than it does in Dr2.4. Infiltration of the dry surface soils is initially slower in Dr3 soils than in Dr2 soils, causing more run-off of heavy rains in Dr3.

(iv) Friable Red Duplex Soils - Dr4.11, Dr4.12

The Dr4.1 soils are identified by their dark (black to very dark reddish brown), highly structured, loamy surface soils that are always friable, that is, they do not set hard (Figure 3.6). They are about 20cm thick and pass clearly, and often sharply, to red-brown, well-structured clay subsoils. These permeable, well-drained soils have moderate to high inherent fertility, but phosphatic and nitrogenous fertilizers are required to maintain yields. Surface soils are acid and the soils either remain acid into the subsoils, Dr4.11, or pH values rise to 6.5-8.0 in Dr4.12.

These soils occur mainly on hillslopes and ridges in rolling to hilly lands, and at depths of 0.4-1.8 m pass into subsola of weathered basic rocks or clayey sediments derived from them. Areas of Dr4.1 soils are not large and the only plantings of grapevines on them occur in the lower Hunter Valley.

Brown Duplex Soils, the Db Soils

All Db soils have brown clayey subsoils. Although not as extensive in area as the Dr soils, they are often associated with them, perhaps even more extensively than has been realized.

(i) Hard Brown Duplex Soils - Db1.22, Db1.23, Db1.33, Db1.43

Db1 soils have brownish grey to brown loamy sand to clay loam surface soils with lighter coloured subsurface soils in Db1.2, sporadic bleaching in the subsurface in Db1.3, and a fully bleached subsurface in Db1.4. These all set hard when dry, are 5-30 cm thick, and pass sharply into brown, well-structured clay subsoils. Surface soils are

slightly acid to slightly alkaline, while subsoils have a pH greater than 8.0, except for Db1.22 which is somewhat lower.

The Db1.33 and Db1.43 soils are sodic. The Db1.2 are moderately permeable and moderately well-drained soils, but the other Db1 soils have slowly permeable subsoils and some seasonal waterlogging of the surface soil results. These soils are found mainly on plains, terraces and hillslopes, and are often more low-lying than the Dr soils. Subsola of weathered rocks or clayey sediments are found at depths of 0.5-2 m and modify the available water capacities.

(ii) Hard Mottled Brown Duplex Soils - Db2.23, Db2.43

The Db2 soils are generally similar to Db1 soils, except for the reddish, yellowish and greyish mottles found in their brown clay subsoils. The mottling indicates that their subsoils are only slowly permeable and that periodic waterlogging occurs. Otherwise, Db2 soils are generally similar to the corresponding Db1 soils, for example, Db2.23 with Db1.23. The most satisfactory Db soils for viticulture are Db1.22, Db1.23 and Db2.23 which compare moderately well with Dr2.22 and Dr2.23 soils.

Yellow and yellow-grey duplex soils, the Dy soils

All Dy soils have yellow to yellow-grey clayey subsoils. With the exception of the Murray River irrigation districts, they occur in almost all the grapegrowing areas of Australia (Table 3.4).

(i) Hard Yellow Duplex Soils - Dy2.22, Dy2.33, Dy2.41, Dy2.43, Dy2.61

Probably only small areas are used for viticulture. Dy2 clay subsoils are more permeable than the mottled Dy3 subsoils, and thus slightly less subject to waterlogging. Otherwise the general properties of Dy2 are comparable with those of the corresponding Dy3 soils.

(ii) Hard Mottled Yellow Duplex Soils - Dy3.21, Dy3.22, Dy3.41, Dy3.42, Dy3.43, Dy3.61, Dy3.62, Dy3.81, Dy3.82

These soils are the most widespread Dy soils in south-eastern and south-western Australia; they are prominent in most dryland grapegrowing areas, e.g. Southern Districts and the Hunter Valley (Table 3.4). Dy3 soils have grey through grey-brown to brown surface soils ranging from loamy sands to clay loams. In Dy3.2 and Dy3.6, the subsurface soils, although lighter in colour, are not bleached as they are in Dy3.4 and Dy3.8.

All these surface and subsurface soils vary in total thickness from 5-60 cm and set hard when dry. They pass directly, and often sharply, into yellow-brown through grey-brown to brownish grey clay subsoils with distinct mottles in shades of red, yellow and light grey. The soil profile varies from 0.5-3 m. Subsola vary from weathered rock to clayey sediments, and modify the moisture regime. Ironstone nodules (gravels), quartz gravels and rock fragments are present in the surface and subsurface of many Dy3 soils. Dy3.6 and Dy3.8 soils may contain up to 70 per cent ironstone nodules.

Surface soils are fairly permeable, although the loamy types tend to seal and readily shed water from sloping sites. The subsoils have much lower permeability, and this results in intermittent perched water in the subsurface horizon and partial saturation of the upper subsoil during wet seasons, especially on flatter sites. Generally, the Dy3.8, Dy3.4 and Dy3.6 soils suffer more severe waterlogging in winter and spring than do the Dy3.2 soils. One consequence is that water is slowly lost laterally to creeks and other natural drainageways, instead of being stored in the deeper subsoil. Inherent fertility levels are low to moderate for Dy3.2 and low to very low for Dy3.4, Dy3.6 and Dy3.8. Severe deficiencies of P and N are usual. K contents are moderate in Dy3.2, but low in the others. Some Dy3.41, Dy3.61 and Dy3.81 soils have low Ca status. Responses to Mo, S, Cu and Zn have been observed. The profitability of adequate fertilizer use on such low nutrient soils has been demonstrated recently in Western Australia (Cripps, Goldspink and Elliott 1987).

Dy3.2 soils have light coloured, but not bleached, subsurface soils and moderately friable structured subsoils that are not sodic (see 3.2.4). They are the best of the Dy3 soils for grapevines and occur on crests and upper to mid-slopes in undulating lands. Dy3.4 soils have bleached subsurface soils above structured clay subsoils which are hard when dry and sticky when wet. Dy3.4 are friable only over a very limited moisture range and their subsoils are sodic. They occur mainly on plains and lower hillslopes. The Dy3.6 soils have light coloured, but not bleached, subsurface soils, and unstructured subsoils that, with repeated wetting and drying, fret to irregular fragments on exposed faces. They are not usually sodic and occur mainly in gently undulating to hilly lands. The Dy3.8 soils have fully bleached subsurface soils above sodic massive clay subsoils. They occur mainly on crests and slopes of hilly lands.

The surface soils of Dy3.21, Dy3.41, Dy3.61, Dy3.81, Dy3.22, Dy3.42, Dy3.62 and Dy3.82 are acid. In the first four, acidity is either fairly constant or increases with depth, while in the others acidity decreases in the subsoils to pH 6.5-8.0. Surface soils range from acid to slightly alkaline in Dy3.43 and pH values increase, often to strongly alkaline, in their subsoils. Free carbonate (lime) segretations occur in the deeper subsoils of Dy3.43 and soluble salt contents are often moderate to high.

(iii) Sandy Mottled Yellow Duplex Soils - Dy5.41, Dy5.42, Dy5.43, Dy5.81, Dy5.82, Dy5.83
Though less widespread than Dy3, Dy5 soils (Figure 3.6) are important viticultural soils in the Barossa Valley, Swan Valley and probably at Stanthorpe (Table 3.4). Dy5 soils have light brownish grey to dark grey-brown sand surface soils that become paler with depth and gradually change to the comparatively thick, strongly bleached (white, very pale brown or yellowish white) subsurface sands. These

surface and subsurface sands do not set hard and may be up to 1 m or more thick. They pass sharply, but often unevenly with projections of bleached sand between subsoil cracks, into the clayey subsoils. These subsoils are mottled light brownish grey and yellow-brown with subsidiary mottling in red, yellow and brown, and their structure ranges from blocky to columnar in Dy5.4 to massive in Dy5.8. Profiles are 1-2 m thick and usually grade into sandy clay sediments where Dy5 soils occupy plains and fans, or into weathered siliceous rocks where they cover hillslopes.

The surfaces of many of these soils accept water slowly when dry, but when moist are highly permeable with an infiltration rate far exceeding that of the clay subsoil. This results in short-term saturation of the subsurface sand as well as perched, seasonal water-tables after prolonged rains. Thus, these are often 'spewy' soils. Lateral losses of water to drainageways along the top of the subsoil are considerable, thus lessening water penetration and storage of water in the deeper subsoil.

In these soils deficiencies of P and N are severe. K contents are low to very low, especially in surface soils, but may be a little higher in some subsoils. The more acid soils Dy5.41 and Dy5.81 contain only small amounts of Mg and Ca, and are likely to respond to Zn, Cu and Mo. The sandy surface and subsurface soils accept water slowly when dry and have low fertility. They are susceptible to wind erosion, particularly when planted to row crops. The erosion hazard becomes marked where the sand is deeper than 0.5 m.

The surface soils are mildly acid, the top of the clay subsoil may be moderately acid to neutral and the deeper subsoil ranges from acid in Dy5.41 and Dy5.81, near neutral (pH 6.5-8.0) in Dy5.42 and Dy5.82, to alkaline in Dy5.43 and Dy5.83. The last two contain segregations of free carbonates (lime) in their deeper subsoils; they are also very sodic with exchangeable sodium percentages usually over 20 per cent and up to 50 per cent in their deeper subsoils. Dy5.42 and Dy5.82 also contain low to moderate amounts of exchangeable Na, but Dy5.41 and Dy5.81 contain few exchangeable metal cations, Na, Mg and Ca, in their subsoil clays.

Black duplex soils, the Dd soils
All Dd soils have very dark coloured clayey subsoils. Not many of these soils are recorded in the viticultural areas, though early soil workers may have failed to distinguish them.

(i) Hard Black Duplex Soils - Dd1.13, Dd1.33, Dd1.43
The surface soils range from grey to brown sandy loams to clay loams, 5-20 cm thick. No subsurface soil layer occurs in Dd1.1. The subsurface in Dd1.3 is paler than the surface with white bleached patches, and in Dd1.4 it is fully bleached. The surface and subsurface soils set hard when dry and pass sharply to the clay subsoils which vary from very dark grey or black to very dark brown.

Accumulations of free carbonates (lime) are present in the deeper subsoils. The soils range from 0.5 to 1 m deep and are underlain by clayey sediments when they occur on plans.

Dd1 soils are only slowly permeable and most are seasonally saturated above the clay. While surface soils are slightly acid to neutral, subsoils are alkaline to strongly alkaline and sodic (see 3.2.4). Natural fertility ranges from low to moderate, N and P being the main deficiencies, but experience is limited and deficiencies of trace-elements, such as Zn, seem likely.

3.4 Soils used for grapevines in other countries

The world's oldest grape-growing region extends from around the Mediterranean, north into Germany and Czechoslovakia and east into the U.S.S.R. around the Black and Caspian Seas. These vineyards cover more than 8.5 million hectares. In contrast, the rest of the world's vineyards cover less than 1 million hectares. They are widely distributed from the Americas, to South Africa, Japan, New Zealand, Australia and parts of Asia.

3.4.1 The general nature of the soils

The considerable natural variation in the soil of European vineyards has been amplified by man's activities over the centuries: for example, terracing on 60^0 slopes of slate and granite along the hillsides above the Upper Douro River in Portugal has allowed soil to develop on the terraces between the walls. Even so it is possible to recognize five broad soil groupings, though it must be emphasized that these groupings do not cover all soil formations.

(i) In Western Europe there is a range of brown gradational loamy to clayey soils with long agricultural histories. They are thus highly artificial, are usually less than 2 m deep, have good drainage, range in pH from acid to neutral and are underlain by acidic rocks, sediments, loess or calcareous rocks. These soils respond well to fertilizers and some acid ones are liable to trace element deficiencies. No Australian soils fit satisfactorily in this grouping.

(ii) Leached, acid, sandy soils derived from a great variety of siliceous rocks, sediments and aeolian deposits occur throughout Europe. A feature of the Bordeaux area are the thick gravel beds, some of which are regarded highly for grapevines. On the great plain in Hungary, grapevines were used to reclaim shifting dune sands, and in Rumania grapevines are planted in pockets 3 m down in the sand so that their roots can more rapidly enter the underlying materials; the vines then have to grow up to ground level! These vines produce light wines where nothing grew before. The soils in this grouping often require drainage and fertilizers. The Australian Uc2 soils belong to this grouping.

(iii) Of very wide distribution are the various red, brown and black, mostly loamy, sometimes clayey soils formed from limestones, and from some shales and volcanic rocks. They are generally of such variable depth that deep and shallow soils alternate within short distances. The content of metal cations in the subsoils varies from medium to high, and fertility is moderate.

This grouping includes not only the better soils of Champagne but also the 'Albarizas', the sherry soils, of Spain. The underlying limestone (chalk) is judged to be a most important feature for grapevines. Cracking clay soils are often associated with bottom lands whereas the red, brown and black 'limestone' soils dominate the slopes. The Coonawarra soil-subsolum complex may be regarded as belonging to this grouping.

(iv) In parts of Eastern Europe from Lower Australia to the U.S.S.R. occur a range of soils with black, loamy to clayey, granular surfaces, that contain soft carbonates in their subsoils; they are easily worked productive soils, alkaline throughout their profiles and are largely derived from loess. Both shallow and deep forms are used for grapevines. The Um6.11 soils of the Hunter River terraces could be placed in this grouping.

(v) A range of greyish-brown to yellowish-brown soils with dark loamy to clayey, granular surfaces, soft carbonates in the subsoil, generally alkaline and often developed on alluvial sediments occur in some vineyards of Eastern Europe, for example, in the Digomi and Mukharani plains of Georgia. No Australian soils fit satisfactorily into this grouping, although some of the Db and Dy soils would if they did not have such pronounced duplex profiles.

The range of soils and soil properties found in Australian viticultural areas, as described in Section 3.3, illustrates the variability that may be encountered within one country. If the soils of all the grapegrowing countries are considered in detail, the variation would be even greater. For example, in California, there are soils with colour, and (often) structure, profiles similar to some of the Australian Dr and Db soils. However, such Californian soils have only clay loam to light clay subsoils instead of medium to heavy clay subsoils and are gradational rather than duplex in texture profile.

3.4.2 Physical and chemical properties of the soils

Throughout the grapegrowing areas of the world, physical soil properties are universally recognized to be of major importance. The most important physical consideration is to have soils that are well-drained, but which provide moisture throughout the growth cycle of the grapevine. Poor soil drainage and aeration affects not only the health of the vine, but also management of the vineyard, and the ease with which machinery can be moved.

Soil depth is next in order of importance. As in Australia, soil depth must include not only the soil but also the subsola (often soil parent materials in Europe and America) for the grapevine roots deeply under favourable conditions and growth will be restricted unless both soil and subsola can be easily penetrated by both roots and water.

The excellent performance of grapevines in some Bordeaux areas, group (ii), is attributed to the subsola below the leached sand soils. The fame of vineyards on soils of group (iii) is due to the grapevine being able to penetrate the calcareous parent materials (subsola) below the often thin soil. The success of grapevines on soils of groups (iv) and (v) can be attributed to the deep and friable nature of these soils, paralleled in Australia by Um6.11 and Dr2.23 soils. Finally, in the vineyards of Western Europe, stones and gravels on the soil surface are especially esteemed for trapping sunlight and its warmth and directing these onto the underside of the vine and its bunches of grapes, a factor of importance when growing grapes towards the cooler limits of their climatic range.

There are significant differences in the chemical properties of Australian grape soils and those used elsewhere. In general, more fertilizer is used in European vineyards, perhaps because of their long use for viticulture. In Australia, P is widely deficient and frequently applied. Elsewhere, fertilizing with K is widely practised, but in Australia K levels are generally adequate. But perhaps the most significant feature of Australian viticulture is the greater use of saline and sodic soils. The Gc and Dr2.33 soils, for example, are more alkaline and have higher soluble salt contents than do soils used elsewhere, except in some Eastern European areas.

3.5 The potential of soils for grapegrowing

3.5.1 Finding new viticultural areas

The art of gauging the viticultural potential of new areas depends on many factors besides land; climate, the kind of grape product wanted, and various economic considerations are all important. But assessment of the suitability of the soil is a fundamental starting-point. Probably in the early stages of enquiry, soil-landscape maps such as the *Atlas of Australian Soils* (Northcote *et al.* 1960-68) provide a useful guide to soils and topography. After several areas have been chosen a pedologist who specializes in soil-plant relationships should be consulted. His task is to evaluate and rank the likely areas in order of their ease of management from the standpoint of soils and topography. Aerial photographs and the information provided in this chapter would assist in this evaluation. When a final choice is made, the soil-topographic units of the proposed new vineyard should be defined, mapped and used as a basis for its management. This work can be carried out by vineyard personnel under the guidance of the pedologist. Where this is done, the properties of the vineyard soils become better appreciated by those using them.

3.5.2 Plants as indicators of soil conditions

Though not a substitute for examining the soil itself the study of native and exotic vegetation growing on an area can provide useful pointers to soil conditions (Table 3.5) and as a guide to vineyard site selection (Due 1979). The extent and mixing of plant species, especially of shrubs and trees, and variations in the growth of individual species may indicate strengths and weaknesses of a particular soil for the growing of grapes. Care is necessary however. A species may give a good indication of viticultural potential in one locality but not in another, i.e. its adaptability to a range of soil conditions may be wider than that of the grapevine. Solitary individuals should also be regarded cautiously.

As an example, the relationship between soils and the type of native vegetation found in the warm temperate semi-arid zone of the Murray Mallee highland areas of south-eastern Australia are listed below. The soils are described in Section 3.3

(a) Dry Savannah (grassy) Forests to Dry Savannah Woodlands both characterized by *Callitris* spp. (native pine) occur on Gn1.13 sands.

Table 3.5 Some Australian soil-plant relationships

Soil	Plants
Calcareous soils	
Carbonates in surface soil	*Marrubium vulgare* (horehound)
Sandy soil, often duplex, with calcareous suboils or calcrete	*Hakea vittata* (striped hakea)
Shallow loamy, often alkaline soils, on calcrete	*Melaleuca lanceolata* (moonah, dryland tea-tree, black tea-tree
Clay soils	
Clay soils (Ug5) or duplex soils (D) with thin, often loam surfaces e.g. Dr2.33, Db1.43	*Eucalyptus microcarpa* (grey box) *Allocasuarina luehmannii* (buloke)
Clay soils, poorly drained	*Eucalyptus largiflorens* (black box)
Clay or clayey soils waterlogged in winter	*Marsilia drummondii* (nardoo)
Clay or clayey soils often wet but not saline	*Craspedia uniflora* (billybutton)
Clay or clayey soils often saline	*Nitraria schoberi* (dillon bush)
Clay or clayey soils usually swampy	*Muehlenbeckia cunninghamii* (lignum)
Duplex soils	
Sandy loam surfaces, Dr2.33, probably Dr2.23	*Eucalyptus melliodora* (yellow box)
Ironstone gravelly soils	*Eucalyptus marginata* (jarrah) *Eucalyptus calophylla* (marri) *Eucalyptus baxteri* (brown stringybark)
Moisture status of site over 12 months	
Dry (periodic waterlogging likely)	*Eucalyptus marginata* (jarrah) *Eucalyptus calophylla* (marri) *Eucalyptus baxteri* (brown stringybark)
Moist	*Eucalyptus camaldulensis* (red gum) *Eucalyptus diversicolor* (karri)
Wet — including seepage patches	*Juncus pauciflorus* (loose-flower rush)
Natural soil fertility	
Moderate to high	*Eucalyptus camaldulensis* (red gum) *Eucalyptus diversicolor* (karri)
Low	*Eucalyptus marginata* (jarrah) *Eucalyptus calophylla* (marri) *Eucalyptus baxteri* (brown stringybark)
Saline soils	
Highly saline	*Halosarcia* spp. (samphire) *Atriplex* spp. (saltbush) *Crithmum maritimum* (samphire) *Melaleuca halmaturorum* (swamp paper-bark) *Mesembryanthemum* spp. (iceplant) *Sclerostegia* spp. (glasswort) *Suaeda maritima* (seablite)
Moderate salinity	*Hordeum* spp. (barley grass) *Nitraria schoberi* (dillon bush) *Parapholis incurva* (curly rye grass) *Polypogon monspeliensis* (annual beard grass)
Sandy saline soils	*Distichlis distichophylla* (saltgrass) *Sporobolus virginicus* (salt couch)

Table 3.5 (continued)

Soil	Plants
Sand soils	
Sandy soils e.g. Uc1.22, Uc2.21, Gn2.46 and sandy surfaced duplex soils e.g. Dy5.42	*Callitris* spp (native pine)
	Banksia spp.
Sandy soils with bleached subsurfaces e.g. UC2.21, Uc2.3, Dy5.4 (occasionally on other well-drained sites)	*Pteridium esculentum* (bracken)
Sandy loams, well drained	*Lepidium hyssopifolium*
Sodic soils	*Eucalyptus albens* (white box)
	Eucalyptus melliodora (yellow box)
	Eucalyptus odorata (peppermint box)
	Eucalyptus tereticornis (forest red gum)
	Melaleuca uncinata (broombush)

(b) Dry Savannah Woodlands characterized by *Eucalyptus spp.* (large mallee) with native pine occur on Gc1.2 sands.

(c) Dry Savannah Woodland to Dry Savannah Scrub both characterized by *Casuarina* sp. (belar or belah) occur on Gn1.13 sandy loams, Gc1.22 sands and sandy loams, Gc1.12 sandy loams and loams, and Dr1.43 loams.

(d) Dry Savannah Mallee Scrub characterized by *Eucalyptus* spp. (mallee), sometimes with belar, occurs on Gc1.12 sands and sandy loams (see 3.3).

(e) Grasslands characterized by *Stipa* spp. occur on Dr1.43 loams.

Comparable data on vegetation and soils is not available for the other grapegrowing areas. Nevertheless, it can be said that sclerophyllous plant communities (plants with hard leaves that minimize water loss), including heaths, are mostly confined to the more arid soils of lower fertility than those on which the savannah woodland communities occur. Savannah woodlands characterized by *Eucalyptus camaldulensis* (red gum) and/or *E. leucoxylon* (blue gum) probably occur on non-sodic soils, whereas *E. odorata* (peppermint gum) savannah woodlands are often found on sodic soils. Sclerophyll mallee or mallee-broombush (*Eucalyptus* spp., often *E. incrassata*, *Melaleuca uncinata*) commonly occurs on Dy5.43 soils. Finally, open grassland communities may occur on the cracking clays (Ug5), but savannah woodlands may develop on these soils also.

3.5.3 The criteria for good grape soils

Of the physical aspects, the principal requirements for good grapegrowing soils are an adequate supply of soil moisture, good soil drainage and aeration, and a stable non-eroding soil. The physical properties that influence these three requirements have been discussed in Section 3.1. A good physical soil system would be surface and subsurface soil of loamy fine sand, sandy loam, loam, silt loam, clay loam, or subplastic clay texture at least 15 cm thick and friable passing to a free-draining subsoil (which, if clay, must be friable) passing to free-draining subsola with no impeding layer to a depth of preferably 3 m, especially if the vineyard is to be irrigated. Perhaps the best soils — soils where these requirements are most commonly met — are Dr2.2, Dy3.2, Gn1.13, Um6.11, Uc1.4 and Uc4.2 (but only on flat areas with no impeding layers to 3 m) with the Coonawarra Uf5.31 - Um6.14 limestone complex being a special case. Other soils not used at present could be suitable: for example, the red smooth-ped earths (Gn3.1) of the Wellington district in N.S.W. In all cases good soil management is necessary to maintain grapevine health, vigour and productivity.

From the chemical viewpoint, soils should be sufficient in nutrient elements and neither saline, sodic nor too high in soft carbonates. The soils listed above meet these requirements except for nutrients — phosphorus is deficient in most, and zinc deficiency occurs even in Dr2.23 soils. However, once properly diagnosed, nutrient deficiencies can be corrected and rarely do they seriously limit the use of a soil — on the other hand toxicities such as those due to aluminium and manganese in acid soils can be serious limitations (see 3.2.1). It is important to have a satisfactory supply of water and oxygen at depth, and an absence of toxic substances, so that roots can grow vigorously and penetrate deeply.

Further reading

Delmas, J. (1971) Vineyard soils (in French) in: Sciences et Techniques de La Vigne, eds. Riberau-Gayon, J., and Peynaud, E., Tome 1 - Biologie de la vigne: Sols de vignobles. pp. 725. Dunod, Paris.

Northcote, K.H., Hubble, G.D., Isbell, R.F., Thompson, C.H. and Bettenay, E. (1975) A Description of Australian Soils. CSIRO, Australia. 170 pp.

Northcote, K.H. (1984) Significance of soil properties in the agricultural context. In: Soils, Soil Morphology and Soil Classification: Training Course Lectures. Div. Soils CSIRO Aust. p. 62. Rellim Techn. Pub. Pty Ltd Adelaide, S.A.

Seguin, G. (1971) Natural factors influencing wine character (in French) in: Sciences et Techniques de La Vigne, eds. Ribereau-Gayon, J. and Peynaud, E. Tome 1 - Biologie de la vigne : Sols de vignobles. pp. 725 Dunod - Paris.

Seguin, G. (1986) 'Terroirs' and pedology of wine growing, Experientia 42 (1986), Birkhäuser Verlag, CH-4010 Basel, Switzerland.

Tulloch, H.W. and Harris, W.B. (1970) Fertilizer responses with non-irrigated Shiraz grapevines 1944-66. Aust. J. Agric. Res., 21, 243-52.

Other references

Adem, H.A. and Tisdall, J.M. (1983) Reconditioned soil : the key to better crops. The Australian Grapegrower and Winemaker. 238 Oct. 1983, p. 18.

Cockroft, B. (1965) Pedology of the Goulburn Valley area, Victoria. Dep. Agric. Vic. Tech. Bull. No. 19.

Cripps, J.E.L., Goldspink, B.J. and Elliott, J.E. (1987) Fertilizer trial results and fertilizer costs for wine grapes in Western Australia. The Australian Grapegrower and Winemaker 278. Feb. 1987 p. 19.

Dry, P. and Smart, R. (1985) Watch out for acid soils. The Australian Grapegrower and Winemaker. 253. Jan. 1985 p. 26.

Due, G. (1979) The use of vegetation as a guide to site selection. In: 'Vineyard Site Selection', eds. R.E. Smart and P.R. Dry. Roseworthy Agricultural College, pp. 79-89.

Jardine, F.A.L. (1946) The use of borax on Waltham Cross grapes in the Stanthorpe district. Qld Agric. J. 62(2), 74-8.

Leamon, K. (1981) Iron deficiency showing up. The Australian Grapegrower and Winemaker. 215, Nov. 1981 p. 7.

Northcote, K.H. (1979) A Factual Key for the Recognition of Australian Soils, 4th Ed. 124 pp. Rellim Technical Publications, Adelaide.

Northcote, K.H., and Boehm, E.W., (1949) The Soils and Horticultural Potential of the Coomealla Irrigation area. C.S.I.R.O. Div. of Soils, Soils & Land Use Series No. 1.

Northcote, K.H., Russell, J.S. and Wells, C.B. (1954) Soils and Land Use in the Barossa district, South Australia. Zone 1. The Nuriootpa area. C.S.I.R.O. Div. Soils, Soils & Land Use. Ser. No. 13.

Northcote, K.H. with Beckmann, G.G., Bettenay, E., Churchward, H.M., van Dijk, D.C., Dimmock, G.M., Hubble, G.D., Isbell, R.F., McArthur, W.M., Murtha, G.G., Nicholls, K.D., Paton, T.R., Thompson, C.H., Webb, A.A. and Wright, M.J. (1960-68) Atlas of Australian Soils, Sheets 1-10, with explanatory booklets. C.S.I.R.O. and Melbourne University Press, Melbourne.

Penkov, M. (1974) Influence of the soil profile on the disposition of the root system of grapevine. Trans. 10th Int. Cong. Soil Sci. Vol. 1., 246 English Summary.

Salter, P.J. and Williams, J.B. (1967) The Influence of Texture on the Moisture Characteristics of Soils. J. Soil Sci. 18(1), 174.

Somers, T.C. (1975) In search of quality for red wines. Food. Technol. in Aust. 27(2) 49-56.

Thomas, J.E., (1939) An investigation of the problems of salt accumulation on a mallee soil in the Murray Valley irrigation area. CSIRO Bull. 128.

Teakle, L.J.H., Johns, H.K., and Turton, A.G. (1943) Experiment with micro elements for the growth of crops in Western Australia. J. Dep. Agric. West. Aust. 20, 171-84.

Wall, P. (1987) - Don't be misled by the vine's capacity for adaption. The Australian Grapegrower and Winemaker. 277, Jan. 1987 p. 23.

Weatherby, K.G. and Oades, J.M. (1975) Classification of carbonate layers in highland soils of the Northern Murray Mallee, S.A., and their use in stratigraphic and land-use studies. Aust. J. Soil Res. 13(2), 119-132.

CHAPTER FOUR

Climate and Viticulture in Australia

D. I. JACKSON and M. B. SPURLING

Climate has a major influence on both the quantity and quality of grape production, but how climate brings about its effects is only partially understood. Many theories have been proposed yet many do not stand up to close scrutiny.

The quality of wine is an ephemeral thing but it is the factor whose determination adds to the charm and mystique of grapegrowing, winemaking and wine evaluation; however, it also creates frustration and sometimes despair for those engaged in its production. For scientists studying grapes its evaluation poses difficult problems in measurement and determination. The most highly sophisticated

chemical analysis will not yet indicate quality reliably; this must still be judged, ultimately, by the consumer. Yet although the wine consumer is the final arbiter, even he or she may not be able to agree, since standards for quality are not irrevocably determined. The quality of raisins and table grapes is not so difficult to quantify.

This chapter will consider the effect of climate on vine growth and grape production and, in addition, its role as a contributor to quality. Firstly, however, those aspects of climate whose effects may influence growth and development need to be distinguished.

4.1 Climatic variables

Vine growth and development can be influenced by the following factors: temperature, rainfall, hail, wind and sunshine. This influence can be profound and will be a critical factor in determining the use and value of the grapes that are produced.

4.1.1 Temperature

Temperatures during the growing season
Generally, if growing-season temperatures are high, development will be more rapid and grapes will be harvested earlier. This important aspect will be discussed later in this chapter.

Specific responses to temperature are important; for example, if temperatures are high and the sky clear, sunburn may occur on the berries. This in itself seems to be of several types. High temperature burn occurs when temperatures reach 35-40°C or above; unshaded berries scorch and the exposed side turns brown to black and part or the whole of the berry may shrivel and die. Lower temperatures will sometimes cause burning, especially if previously-shaded berries become exposed to sunlight. Sometimes berries exposed to continuous sun will display milder symptoms where the skin turns brown but death and shrivel are not consequent.

Frost during spring or autumn is very significant. Unlike many other plants where frost kills only the flowers or fruit, frost on grapes kills the whole shoot, i.e. stem, leaves, flowers and fruit. The compound bud (winter bud) of grapes has three growing points (Pratt 1979). The central or primary bud may be the only one which normally grows, however if the shoot is killed, the secondary and even the tertiary bud will usually develop. Unfortunately the secondary and tertiary buds have low fruitfulness. In one New Zealand study with 13 varieties, shoots from secondary buds produced an average of one third of the number of berries compared with those arising from the primary bud; those from the tertiary buds were barren (Jackson 1984). Even one third can be regarded as a bonus when compared with, say apples and peaches, which do not get a second chance to fruit after death by spring frosts.

Frost occurs occasionally in certain Australian vineyards, especially those in low-lying, 'frost pockets'; there special measures are needed to reduce its incidence. The buds of many varieties of grapevine burst relatively later than some deciduous temperate fruits, e.g. stone fruit, thereby avoiding some of the danger period. There is considerable variability in the time of budburst of grape varieties—an early variety like Chardonnay may burst almost two weeks ahead of a later one such as Cabernet Sauvignon; it will therefore have more chance of succumbing to spring frost. Frost control will be discussed in more detail in Volume 2, Chapter 8.

Autumn frost may kill the leaves before the crop is mature and interfere with the ripening process; severe autumn frosts may also damage the berries, which will then rot if not picked soon after. Such frosts are not common in Australia.

Winter temperatures

Being a temperate plant the grapevine needs a distinct winter period. This is the period of dormancy which precedes budburst in the spring. Grapes are occasionally grown in tropical areas but growth of the vine and production of fruit involves special methods; the dormant period is circumvented by pruning after fruiting, and with careful management, two crops a year may be achieved. Despite these problems the advantages of earliness bestowed by

such areas can make such an activity economic. Vineyards in north Queensland are able to supply tablegrapes for southern markets in September and October.

Grapes can be damaged by very cold winter temperatures but this is rare in Australia. For *Vitis vinifera*, temperatures below $-15^{\circ}C$ can cause freeze injury to the dormant buds and wood. Where there is a possibility that the temperature may fall below $-20^{\circ}C$ once during a 20-year period, the profitability of viticulture in that location is considered doubtful (Becker 1985). It is also believed that if the mean temperature of the coldest month is below $-1^{\circ}C$ the likelihood of winter injury is too high (Prescott 1965, Becker 1985). The physical damage induced by cold temperatures is often followed by the disease organism crown gall (*Agrobacterium tumefaciens*), which accentuates the destruction of part of the whole vine. American *Vitis* species such as *V. labrusca* are more resistant to winter cold.

Soil temperatures

The growth of the vine's roots is temperature-dependent, and warm temperatures in the root zone can induce more rapid vegetative growth in above-ground parts and can improve fruitset (Woodham and Alexander 1966, Zellecke and Kliewer 1980). Root growth will begin earlier in the year if the soil warms up more rapidly. Since sandy soils warm up more rapidly than clay soils, root development is likely to be more advanced in sands. It may be postulated, although it has not been proven, that this will generally benefit early growth of the vine. Sandy soils also induce higher temperatures in the above-soil microclimate.

4.1.2 Rainfall

The importance of water will be discussed later in this chapter and again in Volume 2, Chapter 6. In general, rainfall has the following consequences.

Low rainfall

Inadequate rain which is not supplemented by irrigation will reduce the length of the vegetative growing season, induce early leaf senescence and reduce yield. Some water stress may improve quality of winegrapes (McCarthy and Coombe 1985, Bravdo and Hepner 1987) but severe stress is almost certain to lower it (Hofäcker *et al.* 1976).

High rainfall

The most serious consequence of high rainfall is an increased likelihood of disease, both above and below the ground (see Volume 2, Chapters 10 and 11). Heavy rain will often cause splitting and consequent deterioration of the berries, especially if it falls between veraison and harvest. Heavy rain prior to harvest induces excessive uptake of water which, in addition to causing splitting, has been said to cause undesirable dilution of the juice. Such problems—rot, splitting and dilution—reduce grape quality directly; quality may also be reduced indirectly by picking at an earlier stage than optimal in the hope of avoiding rain damage.

Most Australian grapegrowing regions have low rainfall and low humidity compared with European regions, particularly during the ripening period (Table 4.1). Thus fungal diseases are usually of less significance compared with Europe. Rain at flowering will reduce the ability of inflorescences to retain fertilized berries. The combination of rain and low temperature seem to be most damaging at this time (Champagnol 1984).

Table 4.1. Rainfall and humidity characteristics of wine-producing areas in Australia and France during mid-summer.[1]

Region	Relative Humidity (at 3 pm)[1]	Rainy days[2][3]	Precipitation (mm) [3]
Australia			
Swan Valley, WA	38	6	27
Griffith, NSW	28	9	65
Pokolbin, NSW	46	23	178
Loxton-Berri, SA	28	8	48
Magill, SA	38	11	49
Mudgee, NSW	43	11	112
Rutherglen, Vic.	33	10	79
Clare, SA	30	9	50
Great Western, Vic.	34	9	60
Barossa Valley, SA	32	8	44
Coonawarra, SA	40	13	54
Drumborg, Vic.	48	20	73
Pipers Brook, Tas.	62	15	85
France			
Bordeaux	55	23	150
Champagne	58	22	96

1. January-February (inclusive) in the southern hemisphere and July-August (inclusive) in the northern hemisphere.
2. Days with rainfall exceeding 1 mm (France) or 0.2 mm (Australia).
3. February-March (inclusive) in the southern hemisphere and August-September (inclusive) in the northern hemisphere. Adapted from Pirie (1978).

There is evidence that the amount of rainfall can alter the rate of vine and berry development. Hofäcker et al. (1976) found that the growth rate of berries was more dependent upon the precipitation received in stages I and II of growth than on the temperature at the time; only in stage III was temperature more significant. Higher rainfall delayed berry development. In a seven-year study of 58 varieties, Alleweldt et al. (1984) showed that precipitation was a significant factor affecting rate of growth of berries in stages I, II and III. Even pre-flowering rainfall was found to shorten stage I. High rainfall delayed growth, an effect which was not simply a response to associated low temperatures.

Areas with high rainfall often have problems with excessive vigour. The vigorous vine may need considerable summer pruning and canopy management, and the self-shading of shoots may reduce inflorescence initiation (May and Antcliff 1963, Morgan et al. 1985). Vigour may affect factors such as sugar, acid and pH levels (and thus influence quality) either directly (Jackson 1986), or indirectly through increased shade (Smart et al. 1985a, b) associated with undesirably dense canopies.

4.1.3 Hail

Hail can reduce leaf area, damage berries and, as a consequence, increase disease, which in turn reduces yield and quality. By its very nature hail is unpredictable, but it is known to be more common in certain areas of Australia, for example the Granite Belt of Queensland and the Hunter Valley in NSW. While some control is claimed by the use of rockets and cannons, by the seeding of storm clouds with dry ice or by covering vineyards with nets, these measures are rarely employed on grapes in Australia.

4.1.4 Wind

Wind can have a deleterious effect on grapevines. If severe it can cause physical damage (Hamilton 1988); for example, young shoots can be broken before the shoot base becomes lignified, usually when shoots are less than 30 cm long. However, there is increasing evidence that constant exposure to low and moderate velocity winds also has large and general effects on vine-growth and productivity: exposed vines have reduced shoot lengths, shorter internodes, smaller leaves, fewer bunches per vine and berries per bunch, and lower fruit weight per vine (Ewart et al. 1987, Hamilton 1988; Dry et al. 1988). Wind speeds greater than three m/sec significantly reduce stomatal conductance and photosynthetic activity (Kliewer and Gates 1987).

Windy sites are generally cooler than sheltered areas; this may have undesirable consequences in cool climatic zones. Growth of vines in exposed locations is slower and hence such vineyards take longer to reach full production.

By and large Australian viticulturists have paid little attention to the effect of wind on grapevines, yet many vineyard areas are relatively windy. Table 4.2 shows the wind speed in various Australian and overseas locations. Clearly the Australian sites are no less windy than those in other grapegrowing areas. The careful selection of sites less exposed to wind and the use of living and artificial shelterbelts in areas where wind is persistent and strong would seem to be wise precautions.

4.1.5 Sunshine
Generally Australia has high sunshine hours (Table 4.2) and low pollution, giving adequate high-intensity light. The sunshine contributes to the heat of a site and influences photosynthesis.

Under normal conditions sunshine received by the outside leaves is more than adequate for photosynthesis; internal leaves are more dependent on transmitted and reflected light. Since, in a given site, sunlight cannot be changed directly, the optimum use of given sunlight is the management tool available to growers. This will be discussed in Volume 2, Chapters 3 to 5.

4.2 Climatic effects on grapevine growth and development

4.2.1 Vegetative growth
In temperate zones the endodormancy of grape buds develops during summer and is removed during cold weather in autumn and early winter. Thereafter the buds burst if the temperatures exceed certain threshold levels, generally 7 to 11°C (Pouget 1968). After budburst, the growth of the shoots—formation of new nodes and elongation of internodes—is very sensitive to temperature, both day and night. Warm temperatures, up to about 25°C, will promote growth but temperatures of 30°C and above are less conducive (Buttrose 1968). Other climatic variables that may vary the overriding influence of temperature on shoot growth are light intensity (high light increases dry matter production), wind (moderate to strong winds inhibit shoot and leaf growth), and humidity (humid air promotes growth).

The shoots of each vine collectively form its canopy. If their growth rate is rapid (i.e. if the vine is vigorous), leaves and lateral shoots are large and the canopy may be dense; dense canopies favour increased air humidity and are more susceptible to disease.

The slowing of shoot growth during mid-summer is due to high temperatures and water-stress created by dry air and dry soils; prolonged shoot growth is

Table 4.2. Wind speed and sunshine hours in various Australian and overseas places.

Place	Annual	Mean wind speed (m/sec) Dec-Feb[1] (Jun-Aug)	Mar-May[2] (Sept-Nov)	Annual average bright sunshine (hours per day)
Adelaide (SA)	4.3	4.5	3.9	6.9
Sydney (NSW)	4.0	4.5	3.5	6.7
Melbourne (Vic.)	4.4	4.3	4.1	5.6
Perth (WA)	4.7	5.1	4.4	8.0
Launceston (Tas.)	4.6	5.1	4.1	5.9
Napier (N.Z.)	4.7	5.0	4.4	6.1
Strasbourg (France)	2.5	2.3	2.2	4.6
Bordeaux (France)	3.2	3.0	2.7	5.6
Trier (W.Germany)	3.9	3.3	3.8	4.3
Sacramento (USA)	3.4	3.9	2.9	—
Portland (USA)	3.6	3.3	3.2	—

1. Dec-Feb in the southern hemisphere
   June-Aug in the northern hemisphere

2. Mar-May in the southern hemisphere
   Sept-Nov in the northern hemisphere

a feature of regions and seasons with high air humidity and moist soils. Leaf fall varies with all of the preceding factors that affect shoot growth, but is hastened by low temperatures at the end of autumn.

4.2.2 Reproductive growth

As with vegetative growth, temperature is the overriding climatic factor influencing each of the many components that make up the reproductive development of the grapevine. However other climate variables contribute in varying degrees.

The reproductive cycle begins with the initiation of inflorescences during the season before the fruiting year (Figure 7.1). Induction occurs in buds when the subtending leaves are immature (1.5 to 2 cm across) although primordial initials are not seen microscopically until several weeks later (starting at flowering time in basal buds). The whole process is very sensitive to temperature, especially at this early stage (Buttrose 1970, Palma and Jackson 1981) and also to water stress and light impingement on the bud and subtending leaf, these possibly having their effects later in the spring (May and Antcliff 1963). Temperature during spring also affects the number of flowers formed on inflorescences and the timing of flowering; the latter is linked to the rate of node formation in the shoot and hence is subject to the same climatic influences as outlined in 4.2.1.

Fruitset, as noted above, is especially sensitive to the weather: cold cloudy conditions, high winds, and weather that creates water stress in the vines all reduce berry set (Champagnol 1984). The growth and development of grape berries is altered by climatic factors more in rate than degree. The rapid growth which follows high temperatures enables production of early tablegrapes grown under glass. Controlled-temperature experiments have shown that an increase of temperature from 20 to 30°C has different effects on individual components of a berry as shown in Figure 4.1: the major effect is the large decrease in malate concentration; the increase in sugar is relatively small. Hale and Buttrose (1974) found that sugar was increased more when high temperatures were imposed early during berry growth rather than during ripening.

There is an important influence on grape composition caused by exposure of the berries to light (Morrison 1988): shading of bunches leads to decreased anthocyanin content and a reduction in total phenolics in the berries. This is an important effect of light on grape composition since phenolics affect the colour and flavour of wine and tablegrapes. It has also been claimed that a shaded microclimate, i.e. shading of leaves as well as berries, causes potassium accumulation in shoots before veraison, which is then associated with high potassium levels and high pH in the fruit (Smart et al. 1985 a, b). Shading may increase acid levels in juice, cause a lower soluble solids/acid ratio, increase nitrogen content and induce 'grassiness' in wines made from such grapes (Kliewer et al. 1967, Pszcolkowski et al. 1985). These factors are more commonly a consequence of micro- rather than macroclimate; further discussion may be found in the chapter on canopy management (Volume 2, Chapter 5).

Grapes grown for drying, where sugar production is the main objective, benefit from ripening during hot weather, which also assists the drying processes. Tablegrapes grown outdoors are also favoured by warm dry climates, with early and late cultivars being chosen to extend the harvest season. Climatic factors have an important influence on the composition and quality of tablegrapes (Volume 2 Chapter 12).

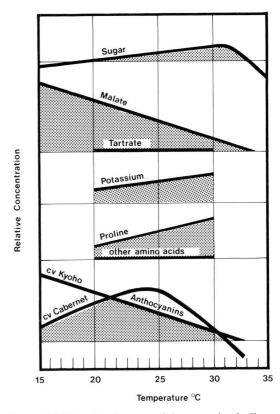

Figure 4.1 Tentative diagram of the generalized effects of temperature treatments on the concentration of some compounds in grape berries (from Coombe 1987).

The effect of climate on winegrapes is considered to be of paramount importance. The geographic distribution of grapes from so-called 'cool' to 'hot' climates is marked by a corresponding change in style. The conventional wisdom on this relationship is well expressed by Becker (1977) as follows:

Under cool conditions white wines tend to be fresher, more acidic and of finer bouquet and aroma. In warmer zones the aroma forfeits its freshness and the wines have more alcohol and often lack balance. High quality white wines generally come from cooler zones whereas the optimum for red wines is somewhat warmer. . . In very warm regions wines are high in alcohol and short on taste and aroma; such zones are suitable for dessert wines.

In commenting on this, Coombe (1987) has pointed out that generalizations about the relationship between climate and wine quality should be treated cautiously because of the complications that may be caused by errors in estimating harvest date and the more difficult vinification in hot climates. His argument is that ripening in a hot climate occurs rapidly and the time of optimum ripeness is commensurately brief; thus the chance of picking over- or under-ripe fruit is greater. With respect to vinification new methods of handling hot-climate grapes appear to be improving their general quality. Due (1988) also questions the validity of the conventional arguments, claiming that much of the reputation of hot versus cool region wines is derived from historical forces, not viticultural performance. Nevertheless, within Australia, cooler sites have developed a reputation for the production of fine table wines, for example: the Adelaide Hills, Coonawarra and Padthaway in South Australia, Tasmania, parts of southern Victoria, Geelong, Drumborg, Yarra Valley, and south-west Western Australia; the present reputation of table wines from hot inland areas relates to their quantity rather than their quality.

4.3 Determining climatic variables and indices

4.3.1 Important climatic variables and indices
The following factors influence grapevine growth and ripening capacity of a district: heat accumulation, length of the growing season, sunshine hours, rainfall, diurnal temperature range, evapotranspiration and humidity. From these factors an array of climatic indices have been devised since it is useful to be able to predict from climatic and other data the suitability of a new district for grape production.

Heat accumulation
The most common index used has been Degree Days or Heat Units (see Winkler *et al.* 1974). These are calculated by taking the mean temperature of the month, subtracting a base value such as 10, and multiplying by the number of days of the month. The mean temperature is the mean of the mean maximum and the mean minimum daily temperatures. Thus if January had a mean maximum of 25°C and a mean minimum of 15°C, then Degree Days would be (20−10) × 31 = 310. Seasonal Degree Days are the total for the seven months October to April (southern hemisphere) or April to October (northern hemisphere). Degree Days may be more accurately calculated on a daily basis; this method appears to give a better correlation between values for districts and the grapes that can be ripened (Jackson and Cherry 1988). Unfortunately it is seldom stated in the literature whether figures quoted have been calculated on a monthly or daily basis. The latter is higher and can be estimated from the former by a formula determined by Wendland (1983).

While the degree days index has been commonly used, it has significant limitations; reliance on this index may have been responsible for the late arrival of grapes in such cool areas as Tasmania. Comparison of Tasmanian figures with those of European wine-producing districts suggests that the climate is marginal for grapes, but subsequent development of the industry has clearly shown it is not.

Ten degrees Celsius has been chosen as a base temperature on the assumption that little or no growth occurs below 10°C (Winkler *et al.* 1974). Some authors have suggested that other base temperatures are more appropriate. Boehm (1970) found that 8°C was a better base temperature for predicting the interval from budburst to flowering and 3°C better for the interval flowering to veraison. Jackson and Cherry (1988) found degree days at base 10°C distinguished between areas growing cool-climate grapes (<1100°C days) but lower base temperatures were better for warmer districts. McIntyre *et al.* (1987) showed that a calculation of the average duration for various growth stages over a number of years provided an equal and possibly better prediction of future durations than did the degree days for each period. Boehm (1970) found poor correlation between degree days and the interval veraison to harvest. Coombe (1987) has summarized work which shows that degree days may, or may not, predict duration of berry growth periods; in short it was found to be a good predictor for some varieties and not others, and only for some growth stages.

Gladstones (1965), in trying to define areas suitable for grapegrowing in Western Australia, attempted to refine the calculation for degree-days to give a better correlation with observed grapevine performance. He used the base of 10°C but truncated the temperature summations at 19°C (i.e. all further increases in mean temperature above 19°C are disregarded). He found that this calculation of degree days, 'effective' 19/10 day-degrees, gave a better fit with the observed ripening dates in established grapegrowing districts.

Mean January temperature (MJT) or mean temperature of the warmest month (MTWM)
To calculate degree days, monthly, and preferably daily temperature means are required. A simpler index of temperature advocated by several Australian authors is the 'mean temperature of the warmest month' or 'mean January temperature' ('mean July temperature' in the northern hemisphere) (Smart and Dry 1980, Dry and Smart 1984). Within Australia or France for example there is a good correlation between these indices and degree days. Generally however, in Australia there are higher degree days for a given mean January (July) temperature than in France. This is due to lower winter temperatures in France, that is, there are more days below 10°C. This difference between summer and winter temperatures—termed 'continentality—is seen as a useful adjunct to MJT by Smart and Dry (1980). Thus where continentality is high, as in Europe, the figure for MJT overestimates ripening capacity.

Length of the growing season and latitude
This is sometimes referred to as the frost-free season and indicates the average number of days elapsing between the last damaging frost of winter and the first in autumn. It is normally considered that a minimum of 180 frost free days is required (Tukey and Clore 1972) although early varieties can sometimes be grown with less. Australia is unlikely to have any potential viticultural areas with less than 180 frost-free days but the use of a measure of growing season length can be useful and may explain some anomalies of degree days and MTWM.

Australia and New Zealand have many areas where the degree days, MTWM and MJT are low by European standards. Drumborg, Ballarat and Launceston, for example, have an MTWM below the 18.7°C which Prescott (1965) says is the cool

limit for viticulture in Europe, yet these areas can ripen Cabernet Sauvignon which in Europe is said to require 20°C.

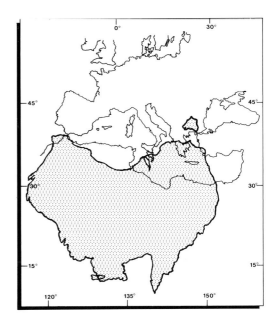

Figure 4.2 Comparative latitudes of Australia and Europe (from Smart 1977).

Even in the coolest Australian areas, latitudes are lower than most European areas (Figure 4.2). In Australia there is an antarctic influence on the weather and the coast does not have the benefit of a warm ocean stream. The result is that Australian summer temperatures of equivalent latitudes are lower, yet the season is just as long as areas of similar latitude in Europe. Figure 4.3 shows monthly temperature for Launceston, Geisenheim (Germany) and Bordeaux (France). The length of the growing season for Bordeaux and Launceston is similar and both can ripen Cabernet Sauvignon. Geisenheim has higher MTWM than Launceston but cannot ripen Cabernet Sauvignon (Johnson 1985, Jackson and Schuster 1987). Latitude can usefully indicate the length of the growing season above a certain temperature and has been shown to be as good as degree days or MTWM in separating cool-climate districts on the basis of ripening capacity (Jackson and Cherry 1987). The latitude-temperature index (LTI) combines a factor of latitude (which indicates length of season) and MTWM (a measure of summer

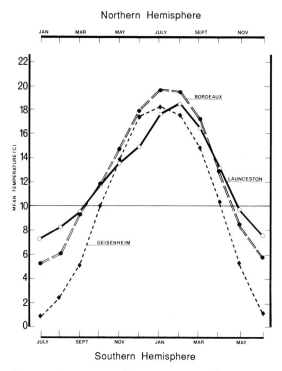

Northern Hemisphere

Figure 4.3 Mean monthly temperatures of Launceston (Tas.), Geisenheim (W. Germany) and Bordeaux (France).

maxima) into a formula, viz. LTI = MTWM (latitude - 60) (Jackson and Cherry 1988). LTI was found to be more effective than other indices in predicting the grape varieties that would ripen in a specific district and it appears to have special value in cool-climate districts.

Sunshine hours
Sunshine hours are generally higher in warmer climates and lower latitudes. To our knowledge no research shows any special merit in using sunshine hours or total radiation for determining the suitability of a site for viticulture, although Becker (1985) suggests that where less than 1250 hours are received between April and October (northern hemisphere), ripening, inflorescence initiation and yields will be unsatisfactory.

Evapotranspiration (ET)
ET refers to the amount of water lost to air from a specific area of land. It is a summation of the evaporation from the soil (and plant surfaces) plus transpiration through plants. Its value for determining irrigation will be discussed later (Volume 2, Chapter 6). Since ET is correlated with the summer accumulation of heat it has been suggested as an

alternative to degree days. Aney (1974) used Thornthwaite's potential evapotranspiration index as an arbiter of climatic suitability for grapegrowing in Oregon. However, a later comparison of this with other indices showed that it had little merit (Jackson & Cherry 1988).

Rainfall
Rainfall is not a factor used in the development of any of the common climate indices for grapes, yet high rainfall may delay maturity and have a number of undesirable effects on grape and wine quality (4.1.2). There is some evidence that areas with high rainfall tend to have lower ripening capacity than temperature indices predict (Jackson and Cherry 1988). Nevertheless, because of Australia's generally warm climate and low rainfall (Table 4.1), such problems are less common than in cooler viticultural climates.

4.3.2 The value of climatic indices
Sufficient evidence has been presented to indicate that many, if not all, climatic indices have limitations for the evaluation of the potential of a district for grapegrowing. They do not adequately explain responses in already proven areas. Some (e.g. LTI) may be suitable for evaluating cooler climates but the majority of Australian locations are—in world viticultural terms—warm to hot. In this volume the broader approach used in Chapter 2 has been adopted. The climatic indices used are:
1. mean January temperature (MJT)
2. contintentality — January mean minus July mean (MAR)
3. sunshine — mean daily hours between October and March
4. aridity — (0.5 × evaporation) minus rainfall
5. humidity — 9 am January relative humidity.

These give a composite picture of a region and allow viticulturists and processors a more realistic opportunity to assess the region's likely advantages and disadvantages.

4.4 The climate of Australian grapegrowing districts

In the discussion so far a number of aspects of the Australian climate have already become apparent. These are as follows:

1. Australia is a warm continent and only the southern portions may be regarded as temperate.
2. Since the cooler areas are generally relatively close

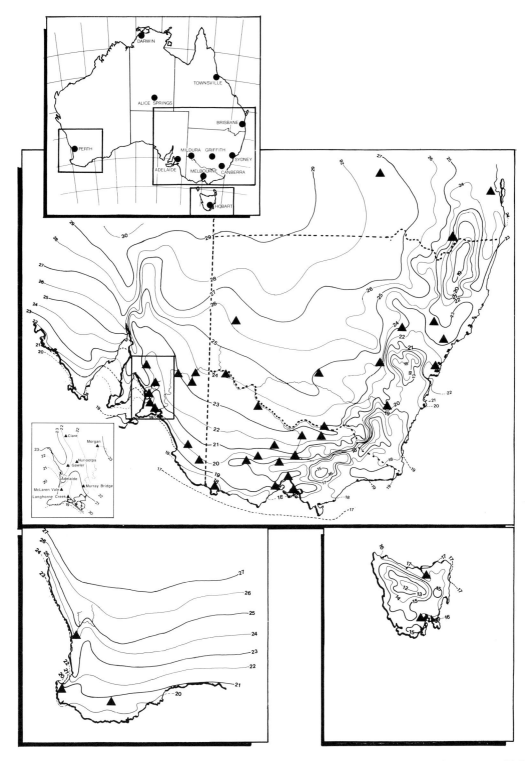

Figure 4.4 Isotherms of mean January temperature (MJT). Redrawn by G.P. Lavis and P.R. Dry from an unpublished figure supplied by the Australian Bureau of Meteorology. Triangles indicate the location of major grapegrowing regions in Australia (refer to Figure 2.1).

to the coast, the climate is less continental than many regions of Europe; winters are comparatively mild.

3. Overall heat accumulation (degree days) tends also to be lower than in areas of Europe with similar latitudes. Western Europe is relatively warm due to the influence of the Gulf Stream but southern Australia has no such moderating influence.

4. Australia has no problems with winter freeze injury although spring frost is troublesome in some areas.

5. Despite the fact that Australia is, on the whole, a dry continent, some grapegrowing areas are in moist climates and fungal diseases are a bigger problem in these areas.

6. The range of climates used for viticulture—from warm to hot temperate and sub-tropical—enables the production of grapes for three main purposes: drying, table and wine. The availability of tropical climates is enabling the production of out-of-season tablegrapes by the use of special management methods.

4.4.1 Temperature

Figure 4.4 shows the mean January temperature (MJT) over southern Australia.

Two of the warmest regions where grapes are grown commercially are at Roma (Qld) and Alice Springs (NT); the coolest are in Tasmania, e.g. Launceston and Hobart. The type of temperature distribution is illustrated in Figure 4.5. Several important points are demonstrated in this graph.

1. Although its use as a base temperature has been questioned (4.3.1) it is likely that grapevines make little growth below 10°C. Of the stations selected only two have any month below this temperature. Failure to ripen grapes before winter is rarely a factor in Australia because of the long growing season (Figure 4.5).

2. The graphs also show the differences between maritime and moderately continental climates. Nuriootpa in the Barossa Valley (SA) shows big differences between summer and winter temperatures compared with Mt Barker (WA), which has a strong maritime influence. Both have similar latitudes.

3. The skew of the graphs to the right in the cooler Australian districts is rather typical of Australian and New Zealand climates and contrasts with the more regular European and Northern American climatographs (compare Figures 4.3 and 4.5). This skew is due to the anticyclones which, in spring,

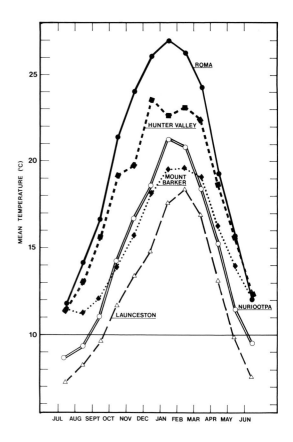

Figure 4.5 Mean monthly temperatures for Roma, Qld (latitude 26° 30′, mean annual temperature 19.9°C), Singleton, Hunter Valley, NSW (32° 37′, 17.5°C), Nuriootpa, SA (34° 29′, 14.6°C), Mt Barker, WA (34° 57′, 15.1°C), Launceston, Tas. (41° 27′, 12.3°C).

are centred further to the south than they are in the autumn; therefore they bring a greater frequency of cool spring air flows to the southern areas. The graphs also illustrate the effect of latitude on temperature — as expected, lower latitudes have warmer temperatures.

The close relationship between latitude and mean annual temperature is shown in Figure 4.6 and illustrates why latitude can give a good indication of a district's ripening capacity (4.3.1). It also shows another interesting feature — the effect of elevation: grouped below the line of best fit are a series of stations whose mean temperature is lower than that which latitude would predict. These are all stations where the elevation is above 240m. Clare (SA) for example is 400m above sea level; Mt Barker (SA) 330m. The cooling effect of elevation is well known and is of the order of 0.6°C per 100 m rise above sea level.

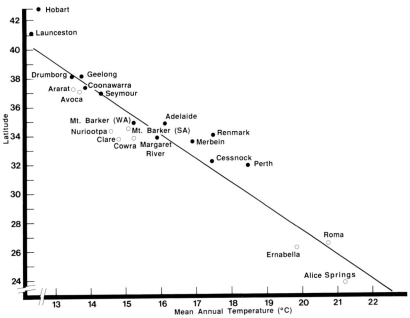

Figure 4.6 The relationship between mean annual temperature (°C) and latitude. Open circles represent those stations with elevation greater than 240m.

4.4.2 Sunshine

Sunshine hours indicate the amount of total radiation potentially available to vines. Australia is well endowed with high radiation (Figure 4.7). Sunshine hours in Australian grapegrowing regions are generally lower than in central and northern Australia but they are still high by comparison with elsewhere in the world (Table 4.2).

4.4.3 Rainfall, humidity and aridity

There is a marked variation in rainfall distribution in Australia, from the monsoonal areas in the north where 60 to 70% falls in the summer, to the southern and western districts where summer is the driest season and winter the wettest. A high proportion of Australian vineyards are in the latter areas. Median annual rainfalls are shown in Figure 4.8.

The significance of rainfall for fungal disease incidence and splitting has been discussed (4.1.2). The relationship between rainfall and evapotranspiration contributes to the aridity of a region and thus is a significant factor in Australian viticulture. Areas where the effective evaporation exceeds rainfall for much of the year (e.g. Mildura, Vic.) contrast markedly with districts where rainfall exceeds evaporation, except briefly in midsummer (e.g. Hunter Valley, NSW).

Water loss from a mature Australian vineyard is about one quarter to one half the evaporation from a water surface (see Volume 2, Chapter 6). An indication of the water balance of a region during a specific interval is given by the Waite Index which is calculated as

$$\frac{rainfall\ (R)}{evaporation\ (E)^{0.7}}$$

(Gentilli 1971)

A figure for the growing season below 0.25 would be considered *very arid*—irrigation would be required every season; 0.25-0.50 is *arid*—irrigation required most seasons; 0.50-1.00 *slightly arid*—irrigation required some seasons; >1.00 *not arid*—irrigation not required. Figure 4.9 shows the water balance for Australia during the months of November, January and March. The monthly water balance for November shows that large parts of the southern Australian, inland Victorian and western Australian viticultural regions are in water deficit; by January this extends to coastal Victoria and South Australia, but eastern coastal Australia is still in water balance.

Humidity (Figure 4.10) tends to correspond to rainfall data and aridity. Low humidity exacerbates the loss of water by evapotranspiration but reduces the incidence of diseases such as downy mildew, botrytis and other bunch rots.

4.4.4 Wind

The wind run in selected Australian and overseas locations is shown in Table 4.2. Wind in midsummer over southern Australia is shown by the wind roses in Figure 4.11. They emphasize the strong coastal influence in wind incidence, especially where strong winds are prevalent.

The direction and strength of strong winds during spring, particularly from the south and south-west, have the greatest influence on the vineyard canopy. The hot, dry northerlies that occur in summer have an all-pervading influence on the weather of southern Australia, even extending across Tasmania; they may create severe water stress in plants which, together with sudden elevation in temperature, can have important effects on vine physiology, including initiation of inflorescences, setting and early berry development.

4.5 Concluding remarks

There is no doubt that the varied climate of Australia provides enormous potential for viticulture. Few other countries in the world allow the possibility of combining subtropical viticulture, hot-climate viticulture for dried grapes, table grapes and bulk wine, and the cool to warm-climate production of quality table and fortified wines. That viticulture is spreading northward to new tropical areas in Queensland and southward to cool/warm climates of southern Victoria and Tasmania is an indication of the varied and interesting future in store.

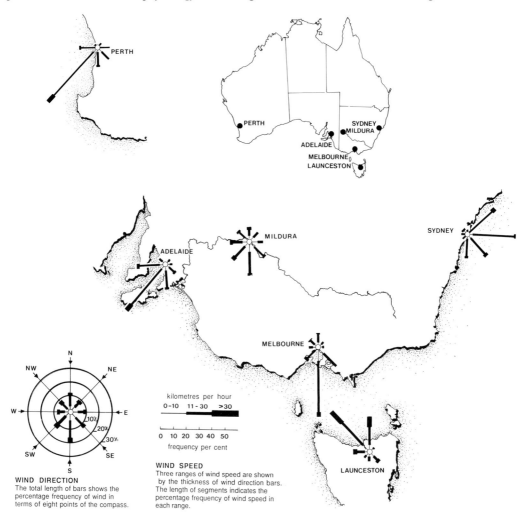

Figure 4.11 Wind roses, 3pm, January for Perth (WA), Adelaide (SA), Mildura (Vic.), Melbourne (Vic.), Launceston (Tas.) and Sydney (NSW). (Redrawn from Climatic Atlas, Map Set 8, Australian Bureau of Meteorology and Atlas of Australian Resources (1986) p.38).

Further readings

Atlas of Australian Resources (1986) 3rd series, Volume 4 — Climate. Division of National Mapping, Canberra, ACT.

Daubenmire, R.F. (1974) Plants and Environment. A Textbook of Autecology. Wiley, N.Y.

Gentilli, J. (1972) Australian Climate Patterns. Nelson, Melbourne.

Slatyer, R.O. (ed). (1973) Plant Response to Climatic Factors. Proc. Uppsala Symp. 1970, UNESCO.

Other references

Alleweldt, G., Düring, H. and Jung, K.H. (1984) Zum Einfluss des Klimas auf Beerenentwicklung, Ertrag und Qualitat bei Reben. Vitis 23, 127-42.

Aney, W.W. (1974) Oregon climates exhibiting adaptation potential for vinifera. Amer. J. Enol. Vitic. 25, 212-8.

Becker, N.J. (1977) The influence of geographical and topographical factors on the quality of the grapecrop. OIV Symp. on the Quality of the Vintage; OVRI, Stellenbosch, South Africa, 169-180.

Becker, N.J. (1985) Site selection for viticulture in cooler climates using local climatic information. Heatherbell, D.A. et al. (eds.) Proc. Int. Symp. Cool Climate Vitic. Enol., 25-28 June 1984; Eugene, Or.; Oregan State Univ. Tech. Public. 7628, Corvallis, Or.: 20-34.

Bochm, E.W. (1970) Vine development and temperature in Barossa, South Australia. Experimental Record, Dept. Agric. Sth Aust. 5, 16-24.

Bravdo, B.A. and Hepner, Y. (1987) Irrigation management and fertigation to optimise grape composition and vine performance. Acta Horticulturae 206, 49-67.

Bureau of Meteorology, Australia (1979) Climatic Atlas of Australia. Mapset 8, Wind Roses. Aust. Govt. Publ. Service, Canberra, ACT.

Buttrose, M.S. (1968) Some effects of light intensity and temperature on dry weight and shoot growth of grapevines. Ann Botany 32, 753-65.

Buttrose, M.S. (1970) Fruitfulness in grapevines: the response of different cultivars to light, temperature and day length. Vitis 9, 121-25.

Champagnol, F. (1984) Elements de physiologie de la vigne et de viticulture generale. Publ. by the author. B.P. 13 Prades-le-Lez, 34980 Saint-Gely-du-Fesc. France.

Coombe, B.G. (1987) Influence of temperature on the composition and quality of grapes. Acta Horticulturae 206, 25-35.

Dry, P.R., Reed, S. and Potter, G. (1988) The effect of wind on the performance of Cabernet Franc grapevines. Acta Horticulturae (in press).

Dry, P.R. and Smart, R.E. (1984) An evaluation of heat degree days as a climatic index in Australia. Aust. Grapegrower & Winemaker No.248, 12-14.

Due, G. (1988) History, geography and the 'cool climate' dogma. Aust. & N.Z. Wine Industry J. 2(6), 42-4.

Ewart, A.J.W., Iland, P.G. and Sitters. J.H. (1987) The use of shelter in vineyards. Aust. Grapegrower & Winemaker No. 280, 19-22.

Gladstones, J.S. (1965) The climate and soils of south-western Western Australia in relation to grapegrowing. J. Aust. Inst. Agric. Sci. 31, 275-88.

Gentilli, J. (ed) (1971) Climates of Australia and New Zealand. Vol. 13 of World Survey of Climatology (ed) H.E. Landsberg. Elsevier, Amsterdam.

Hale, C.R. and Buttrose, M.S. (1974) Effect of temperature on ontogeny of berries of Vitis vinifera L. cv. Cabernet Sauvignon. J. Amer. Soc. Hort. Sci. 99, 390-4.

Hamilton, R.P. (1988) Wind effects on grapevines. Proc. 2nd Int. Symp. for Cool Climate Vitic. and Oenol., N.Z. Soc. Vitic. Oenol., Auckland, N.Z., 65-8.

Hofäcker, W., Alleweldt, G. and Khader, S. (1976). Einfluss von Umweltfaktoren auf Beerenwachstum und Mostqualitat bei der Rebe. Vitis 15, 96-112.

Jackson, D.I. (1984) The grape experiments at Lincoln College. Department of Horticulture, Lincoln College, Bulletin 36, 131 pp.

Jackson, D.I. (1986) Factors affecting soluble solids, acid, pH, and colour in grapes. Amer. J. Enol. Vitic. 37, 179-83.

Jackson, D.I. and Cherry, N.J. (1988) Prediction of a district's grape-ripening capacity using a temperature-latitude index (LTI). Amer. J. Enol. Vitic. 39, 19-28.

Jackson, D.I. and Schuster, D. (1987) Production of grapes in cool climates. (Nelson, Melbourne).

Johnson, H. (1985) The World Atlas of Wine. (Mitchell Beazley, London).

Kliewer, W.M. and Gates, D. (1987) Wind effects on grapevine growth, yield and fruit composition. Aust. & N.Z. Wine Industry J. 2, 30-7.

Kliewer, W.M., Lider, L.A. and Schulz, H.B. (1967) Influence of artificial shading of vineyards on the concentration of sugar and organic acids in grapes. Amer. J. Enol. Vitic. 18, 78-86.

McCarthy, M.G. and Coombe, B.G. (1985) Water status and winegrape quality. Acta Horticulturae 171, 447-56.

McIntyre, G.N., Kliewer, W.M. and Lider, L.A. (1987) Some limitations of the degree day system as used in viticulture in California. Amer. J. Enol. Vitic. 38, 128-32.

May, P. and Antcliff, A.J. (1963) The effect of shading on fruitfulness and yield in the sultana. J. Hortic. Sci. 38, 85-94.

Morgan, D.C., Stanley, C.J. and Warrington, I.J. (1985) The effects of simulated daylight and shade-light on vegetative and reproductive growth in kiwifruit and grapevine. J. Hortic. Sci. 60, 473-84.

Morrison, J.C. (1988) The effects of shading on the composition of Cabernet Sauvignon grape berries. Proc. 2nd Int. Symp. for Cool Climate Vitic. Venol. N.Z. Soc. Vitic. Oenol. Auckland, NZZ, 144-6.

Palma, B.A. and Jackson, D.I. (1981) Effect of temperature on flower initiation in grapes. Bot. Gaz. 142, 490-3.

Pirie, A.J.C. (1978) Comparison of the climates of selected Australian, French and Californian wine producing areas. Aust. Grapegrower & Winemaker No.172, 74-8.

Pouget, R. (1968) Nouvelle conception du seuil de croissance chez la vigne. Vitis 7, 201-5.

Pratt, C. (1979) Shoot and bud development during the pre-bloom period of Vitis. Vitis 18, 1-5.

Prescott, J.A. (1965) The climatology of the vine (*Vitis vinifera* L.). The cool limits of cultivation. Trans. Roy. Soc. S. Aust. 89, 5-23.

Pszcolkowski, P, Quiroz, M.I. and Salvatierra, A.M. (1985) Effecto de la epoca y numero de chapodas en parronales viniferos, sobre la luminosidad, productividad y calidad del mosto y vino II. temporada. Ciencia e Investigacion Agragaria 12, 37-48.

Smart, R.E. (1977) Climate and grapegrowing in Australia. 3rd Aust. Wine Ind. Tech. Conf.; Aust. Wine Res. Inst., Adelaide, 12-18.

Smart, R.E. and Dry, P.R. (1980) A climatic classification for Australian viticultural regions. Aust. Grapegrower and Winemaker No. 196, 8-16.

Smart, R.E., Robinson, J.B., Due, G.R. and Brien, C.J. (1985a) Canopy microclimate modification for the cultivar Shiraz. I. Definition of canopy microclimate. Vitis 24, 17-31.

Smart, R.E., Robinson, J.B., Due, G.R. and Brien, C.J. (1985b) Canopy microclimate manipulation for the cultivar Shiraz. II. Effects on must and wine composition. Vitis 24, 119-28.

Tukey, R.B. and Clore, W.J. (1972) Grapes — their characteristics and suitability for production in Washington. Coop. Ext. Serv., College Agric. Washington State Univ. Pullman E.B. 635. pp. 12.

Wendland, W.M. (1983) A fast method to calculate monthly degree days. Amer. Meteorological Soc. Trans. 64, 279-81.

Winkler, A.J., Cook, J.A., Kliewer, W.M. and Lider, L.A. (1974) General Viticulture. 2nd edition. University of California Press, Berkeley.

Woodham, R.C. and Alexander, D. McE. (1966) The effect of root temperature on development of small fruiting Sultana vines. Vitis 5, 345-50.

Zelleke, A. and Kliewer, W.M. (1980) Effect of root temperature, rootstock and fertilization on bud-break, shoot growth and composition of Cabernet Sauvignon grape vines. Sci. Hortic. 13, 339-47.

CHAPTER FIVE

Taxonomy — The Grapevine as a Member of the Plant Kingdom

A. J. ANTCLIFF

Scientists dealing with animals and plants have developed a system of naming and classifying them intended to reveal their inter-relationships and to allow each to be referred to without ambiguity. The basic unit is the species; related species are grouped into genera, related genera into families and related families into orders. To refer to a species the name of the genus is given first, followed by the name of the species. As an example, the domestic cat is *Felis domestica;* lion and tiger are other species of the genus *Felis,* lynx and cheetah belong to other genera in the family Felidae, and dogs, bears and seals belong to other families in the order Carnivora. Sometimes the same species has been described under different names by different people, or the same name has been given to different species. When essential for accuracy the authority is given after the name of the species.

5.1 The Order Rhamnales

Grapes belong to the order Rhamnales, which comprises three families, Rhamnaceae, Leeaceae and Vitaceae. The order will be described in Volume 24 of the Flora of Australia (not yet issued).

5.1.1 Rhamnaceae

The relationship of this family to the grapevine is not apparent to the casual observer. Most members are shrubs or trees with dry fruit. A few have fleshy fruit, including *Ziziphus mauritiana,* the jujube, and *Ziziphus lotus,* thought to be the lotus of ancient Greece. There are a number of genera in Australia, ranging from small trees in the coastal forests to desert shrubs. In the extreme north there are two native species of *Ziziphus,* the specific name of one, *Z. oenoplia,* suggesting that it might be possible to use it for making wine. This species is a spiny, sprawling shrub with small, black, acid, edible fruit.

5.1.2 Leeaceae

Leea, the only genus in the family, is more readily recognizable as related to the grapevine and has sometimes been included in the grape family. The plants are shrubs with terminal flower clusters. The Australian species, *Leea rubra* (Figure 5.1), formerly *L. brunoniana,* is common in the northern monsoonal areas. The soft woody shoots grow from a large woody underground organ to which they may die back under unfavourable conditions. However, in monsoonal rainforest it maintains a permanent bushy structure, interweaving through adjacent trees, and can reach a height of 5 m. Although different in

Figure 5.1. Leea rubra, *a species of the family Leeaceae, which is related to Vitaceae, grows in the monsoonal areas of Australia. Note its compound leaves and terminal clusters.*

anatomical detail the black berries are reminiscent of grapes and have grape-like seeds. The fruit is quite tasty and perhaps with selection and breeding a useful fruiting plant could be obtained.

5.1.3 Vitaceae

This family, which has been variously known as Vitidaceae, Ampelidaceae or Ampelidae, is at present considered to have 12 genera with about 700 species. This would be a conservative estimate as it is thought, for example, that up to a third of the northern Australian species have not as yet been described and similar situations no doubt exist elsewhere. It is a very widely spread family represented throughout the tropical and temperate zones around the world. Characteristically the plants are climbers with leaf-opposed tendrils, the grapevine being a typical member in this respect.

5.2 The Family Vitaceae

The genus of importance to viticulture, *Vitis*, is a member of this family and is detailed below in sections 5.3, 5.4 and 5.5. There are five other genera

which feature in the flora of the Australia continent: *Cissus, Cayratia, Clematicissus, Tetrastigma* and *Ampelocissus.*

5.2.1 Cissus

By far the largest genus is *Cissus*, with about 350 species. It includes what are thought to be the most primitive members of the family, some with terminal inflorescences like *Leea.* However, the pattern of two nodes with a tendril followed by one without, characteristic of cultivated grapes, is already evident in some species. There is a wide range of plant types, from succulent species resembling cacti to lianas in tropical jungles.

Ten species are known in Australia. Some are perennial vines of the rain forests; one of these, *C. antarctica*, with attractive simple leaves, has been adopted internationally as an ornamental subject. Being adapted to deep shade it can be used as an indoor plant. Other species develop a rhizome from which new shoots are produced in each growth cycle. The shoots are in some cases small and upright, in others long and trailing over trees. Species in areas with well defined wet and dry seasons are

Figure 5.2 Cayratia saponaria, *an Australian member of the family Vitaceae, is a rhizomatous plant with deciduous shoots. Leaf structure varies from simple to trifoliate.*

very regular in their timing. Shoots appear shortly before the start of the wet season and complete their growth and fruiting before dying back in the next dry season. Others, such as *C. opaca* of the brigalow regions, are more erratic. The rhizomes can be quite large, perhaps up to 50 cm in length and 20 cm in diameter.

All Australian species have purple-black berries, ranging from about 1 to 2 cm in diameter, but the fruit is rather dry and unattractive, often with an unpleasant pungent taste and irritating crystals in the flesh. The tubers of those species which possess them seem to be more attractive as food. The aborigines ate them either raw or roasted and pigs like them well enough to dig for them. One species, *C. repens*, with succulent young stems and heart-shaped leaves, is said to have been a source of edible leaves, used perhaps in the way that vine leaves are used in Mediterranean countries.

5.2.2 Cayratia

Members of this genus were formerly included in *Cissus* but usually have five rather than four petals, compound rather than simple leaves, and more than one seed per berry. Of the 45 species described, eight are found in Australia and all of these have underground rhizomes with ephemeral shoots. Figure 5.2 shows a shoot of *C. saponaria* with a simple, an unequally-trifoliate, and an equally-trifoliate leaf. This sort of variability is very common in Australian Vitaceae and makes for difficulties in distinguishing between them. The berries of the *Cayratia* species, although small, seem to be somewhat juicier and more palatable than those of the *Cissus* species but again irritating crystals are present.

5.2.3 Clematicissus and Tetrastigma

These two genera are each represented by a single species in Australia. *Clematicissus* has only one species, *C. angustissima*, confined to the Murchison area of Western Australia. It is another plant which grows from a rhizome each year, and its rhizomes are also attractive to pigs. *Tetrastigma* is a genus of about 90 species, extending from S.E. Asia to Australia. The only Australian species, *T. nitens*, is a vigorous climber with trifoliate leaves found in the rain forests of Eastern Australia. Its fruit is said to be easily the most palatable of the native grapes, approaching the cultivated grape in flavour.

5.2.4 Ampelocissus

The other genus represented in Australia is *Ampelocissus*, which has 95 species altogether extending throughout the tropics. It is thought to be the most closely related to the true grapes. The Australian plants are mostly referred to as *A. acetosa* but may compose several species. They occur in the northern tropical areas and have rather soft, herbaceous shoots which grow in the wet season each year from rhizomes. These rhizomes also were roasted and eaten by the aborigines.

5.2.5 Other genera

Two genera, *Pterisanthes* with 20 species in south east Asia and *Rhoicissus* with 12 species in tropical and southern Africa, are thought to be closely related to *Ampelocissus* and *Vitis*. *Pterisanthes* is unusual in having its flowers borne on curious leaf-like structures. *Ampelopsis* (20 species) and *Parthenocissus* (15 species) are closely related to each other and include the virginia creepers. They are found in the temperate regions of North America and Eastern Asia and some *Ampelopsis* extend into sub-tropical areas. Finally, there are two genera with a single species each; *Acareosperma* in Laos, related to *Cissus*, and *Pterosperma* in Haiti.

5.3 The Genus *Vitis*

The cultivated grapes all belong to the genus *Vitis*. This genus is distinguished from the other genera of the family Vitaceae by having petals which remain joined at the top and separate at the base to fall as a calyptra or 'cap'. With rare exceptions the other genera have flowers which open out in the usual way. This distinction may be somewhat artificial and in some ways part of the genus *Vitis* seems to be more closely related to *Ampelocissus* than to the rest of *Vitis*. The exact number of species in the genus *Vitis* is not certain, the species in Asia in particular being poorly defined. There would seem to be at least 40, mostly in the temperate regions of the northern hemisphere with a few in the tropics. The genus is divided into two clearly distinct sections, *Muscadinia* and *Euvitis*, which differ in chromosome number and therefore cannot readily be crossed to give fertile hybrids. *Muscadinia*, like *Ampelocissus*, *Parthenocissus* and *Ampelopsis* has 40 chromosomes, while *Euvitis* has only 38.

5.3.1 *Muscadinia*

This section is characterized by vines with smooth, persistent bark, small bunches, and berries which have very thick, tough skins and drop as they ripen. Many of these features are also found in *Ampelocissus*.

There are only three species in *Vitis* sect. *Muscadinia*. The best known is *Vitis rotundifolia*, native to the south eastern United States. It was domesticated by the European settlers when they found that European grapes were too susceptible to disease to be grown in the region and the fruiting varieties are known as muscadines. All species of *Vitis* in the wild normally are dioecious i.e. they have separate male and female plants with flowers all of one sex (Figure 5.3). This requires a proportion of unproductive male vines in a planting to pollinate the fruiting vines. However under domestication a sport of *V. rotundifolia* with perfect flowers was ultimately found and by crossing and selection a range of varieties with perfect flowers and large berries is now available. The very thick skins and musky flavour are sometimes unattractive to those used to eating European grapes. *V. munsoniana*, found in Florida and the Bahamas, has more slender canes and is more nearly evergreen than *V. rotundifolia*. Its bunches are made up of a larger number of smaller berries that are not so thick skinned and have a less musky flavour. The third muscadine species, *V. popenoe*, is a little known vine found in Mexico.

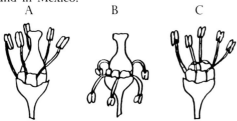

A   B   C

Figure 5.3. Types of grape flowers: A. Hermaphrodite; B. Functionally female, due to the reflexed stamens; C. Male, due to the lack of an ovary. (From Galet 1979)

5.3.2 Euvitis

The species of Section *Euvitis* have proved closely enough related to interbreed easily whenever this has been attempted, even though they occur in widely different areas and show a great diversity of form. Apart from the cultivated grape, *Vitis vinifera*, which also occurred naturally in Europe, the species from Asia have been little studied. They seem to show an interesting parallelism with the American species—e.g. *V. coignetii* resembles *V. labrusca*, *V. lanata* resembles *V. caribaea* and *V. vinifera* itself resembles *V. californica*. Some species have been used occasionally as ornamentals but the only species to attract viticultural attention is *V. amurensis*. This is the most northerly species and it has been used in cross breeding, apparently with some success, to introduce resistance to winter cold into cultivated grapes.

Much more attention has been paid to the North American species (Bailey 1935). The early European settlers tried to domesticate them, as with *V. rotundifolia*, when the vines brought from Europe failed. They were not satisfactory, because of such characteristics as very small berries, extreme seediness, and overpowering or pungent flavours. The first really successful varieties were natural hybrids with *V. vinifera* and deliberate crossing has produced many more. The hybrid nature of varieties like Delaware and Catawba is indicated by their bisexual flowers. While this character might arise on very rare occasions by mutation it would be more easily inherited from vinifera ancestors and the improved fruit quality would come from the same source.

Some of these hybrids were taken to Europe as curiosities and unfortunately carried with them diseases and pests which were to prove very damaging to European vines. As a result the wild American species were then more closely studied in search of sources of resistance. The names used for the species by viticulturists are sometimes different from those used by botanists but are preferred here to avoid confusion. The following are some of the better known species.

V. labrusca

This species has the largest but also the most highly, and to many people unpleasantly, flavoured berries. It is native to a rather limited area of the north-eastern United States and is involved in the parentage of most American hybrid varieties. It is a strongly growing vine with large, thick, almost entire leaves, dull green above, with the lower surface densely covered with white to brownish or reddish hairs. It differs from the other species of *Vitis* in having tendrils at all nodes beyond the base of the shoot, instead of every third node being without a tendril. The fruit is most often black, but vines with red or white fruit can also be found. The bunches are usually short, with no more than about 20 berries. The berries fall easily when ripe and the flesh can readily be squeezed out of the skin without being crushed. The juice is likely to be lower in both sugar and acid than that of other North American species.

V. aestivalis

Native to the south-eastern United States, *V. aestivalis*

is another strongly growing species which by natural and deliberate crossing forms part of the make-up of many American hybrid varieties. Its leaves resemble those of *V. labrusca* except that the hairs on the lower surface tend to be in tufts and are rusty or red-brown in colour. The fruit is always black, does not have the intense flavour of *V. labrusca*, and can be quite juicy and sweet. The bunches are longer but the berries are smaller.

V. riparia (syn. *V. vulpina*)

This is the commonest species in the northern United States west of New England and it extends north into Canada and south almost to the Gulf of Mexico. It appears to hybridize naturally with *V. labrusca* and has found its way into the parentage of some American varieties. It is a vigorous, tall-growing vine usually occurring along streams. The leaves are generally long and 3-lobed, of a brighter green and thinner than those of the two preceding species and hairless on the lower surface. The fruit is black and acid but free of objectionable flavours. The berries are very small with rather small seeds.

V. rupestris

This species is unusual in being a small, much-branched shrub which only sometimes, under favourable conditions, becomes slightly climbing. The tendrils are small and usually do not persist. It occurs in a rather narrow band running north-east from south-west Texas, preferring the gravelly banks of mountain streams or the rocky beds of dry watercourses. The roots tend to penetrate vertically instead of spreading laterally as in other species. The leaves are rather small, of a characteristic kidney shape, wider than they are long, light silvery-green, smooth and glossy above and below. The bunches are small with small black berries a little larger than those of *V. riparia* and again free of disagreeable flavours.

V. berlandieri

A stocky, moderately climbing vine, *V. berlandieri* is found on the limestone soils of south-west Texas and adjacent areas of Mexico. It has medium to large, slightly 3-lobed leaves, glossy above and becoming hairless below as they expand to full size. The bunches are more branched than those of the species previously mentioned and carry numerous small black berries. The fruit ripens very late, is high in both sugar and acid, and is juicy with a pleasant taste. The species is notorious for being extremely difficult to root from cuttings.

V. cinerea

This is a somewhat similar species which extends further north than *V. berlandieri* and grows in wetter situations. Its leaves are similar, but duller on the upper surface and remaining hairy below when fully expanded. The bunches are larger and looser, again with numerous small black berries. The fruit ripens late, becoming sweet and pleasant after frost.

V. cordifolia

One of the most vigorous species, *V. cordifolia* can climb to the top of very tall trees and develop a trunk up to 50 cm in diameter. It is found over a wide area of the eastern United States. It has medium to large, entire, heart-shaped leaves, bright green and glossy above and with at most only a few hairs on the lower surface. Bunches are medium to large and loose with numerous small black berries. The berries have thick skins and little pulp and are often sour and astringent.

V. candicans

This species is a vigorous, climbing vine, notable for the disagreeable, pungent flavour of the fruit. It occurs on limestone soils in a rather limited area of the south central United States. It has leaves which are dull green above but covered with dense white hairs below and on the petiole, deeply 5- to 7-lobed on strong shoots, but more nearly entire on normal growth. It has short bunches of about 12 to 20 berries. The berries, which remain firmly attached to the bunches after they are fully ripe, can be up to 2 cm in diameter and range from purple to black in colour.

V. longii

The name is sometimes given as *V. solonis*, apparently from a misreading of the label on one lot of cuttings sent to Europe. It is a rather variable species, which has led to the suggestion that it may have arisen by hybridization among some of the preceding species. However, it is so well established in its own area, north west of the area of *V. candicans*, and grows so far from its supposed parents that it is best kept as a distinct species. It is vigorous, resembling *V. riparia*, but with rounder leaves, often hairy on the lower surface.

V. champini

It has also been suggested that *V. champini* may be a hybrid. It is intermediate in character between *V. rupestris* and *V. candicans* and occurs in the area in which these two species overlap. On the other hand it is not as variable as *V. longii*. Its berries are fairly large and adhere very firmly, as do those of *V. candicans*, but they are always black and do not show the fiery pungency of *V. candicans*.

V. monticola
A slender, trailing or climbing vine from the limestone hills of south west Texas, *V. monticola* does not show any clear affinities with other species. It has rather small, thin leaves which are dark green and glossy above and greyish green below. The bunches are short and broad with black or light-coloured, sweet berries 1 cm or more in diameter.

V. caribaea (syn. *V. tiliaefolia*)
This species is widespread in tropical America around the Caribbean Sea including the West Indies. It is a slender, climbing vine which does not thrive in temperate climates. It has entire, heart-shaped leaves with very shallow teeth, slightly rough on the upper surface and with dense white or rusty hairs on the lower. The bunches are rather long with a long stalk but the berries are small and intensely acid until very ripe.

Other species
Also of interest to viticulturists have been *V. lincecumii*, similar to and sometimes regarded as a sub-species of *V. aestivalis*, and *V. rufotomentosa*, a species from Florida and west along the Gulf of Mexico, at one time included in *V. caribaea*. Two species names have been proposed for cultivated American grapes; *V. labruscana* for the types of predominantly labrusca-vinifera parentage (e.g. Concord) and *V. bourquiniana* for those of predominantly aestivalis-vinifera parentage. *V. californica* and *V. girdiana*, native to California, are of less practical interest; having developed in the absence of the pests and diseases found east of the Rocky Mountains, they show little resistance to them.

5.4 The Species *Vitis vinifera*

The European grape is *Vitis vinifera* and, apart from rootstocks, this species comprises the majority of the genetic material used for viticulture in Australia, as in many grape countries.

5.4.1 Wild vines
In Europe and Western Asia, where *V. vinifera* has been cultivated for many centuries, wild vines also occur. One school of thought has seen the wild vines

as related to, and possibly ancestors of, the cultivated vines but now distinct from them. At the beginning of the nineteenth century Gmelin (quoted by Levadoux 1956) described the wild vines of the middle Rhine as a separate species, *V. silvestris*. This name has been extended to the wild vines in general, although sometimes the distinction has been seen as only sub-specific—*V. vinifera silvestris* as distinct from *V. vinifera sativa*, the cultivated grape. The opposing view is that the wild vines are simply the spontaneous form of *V. vinifera*, the differences between the wild and cultivated vines being merely the effect of domestication.

In practice it is difficult to distinguish wild vines arising from cuttings or seeds of cultivated vines from primordial wild vines which apparently have not been through a cycle of domestication. There are no obvious differences in general appearance such as allow the American species to be readily recognized as distinct from one another or from *V. vinifera*. The differences thought to distinguish the primordial wild vines from cultivated vines mostly tend to disappear when both are grown under the same conditions. Indeed, in leaf, fruit and seed characters they are not as great as the differences among the cultivated varieties themselves.

One such difference was that the wild vines appeared to have smaller, looser bunches of small, sour and in most cases black berries. However trials in several countries have shown that when looked after in the same way the best of the wild vines of the region have fruit comparable in size and composition with some cultivated varieties. Conversely it is common experience that when vines are more lightly pruned the bunches are smaller and looser. A variety such as Pinot Noir, allowed to run wild, would be no better than the primordial wild vines. Breeding with cultivated varieties has shown that black fruit colour is dominant over white and the inheritance of colour in the wild vines has been found to be the same as in cultivated varieties.

However, the wild vines survive in nature without any protective treatments, suggesting that they have some resistance to pests and diseases. This has raised hopes that they could be used in breeding to impart such resistance to cultivated varieties. In fact, however, wild vines have disappeared from large areas of Europe since powdery mildew, phylloxera and downy mildew arrived from America. Those that remain owe their survival to situations which do not favour the diseases and pests and a sufficient dispersion to prevent major outbreaks. They may show more resistance than the average cultivated varieties but no more than varieties such as Tannat, Baroque and Petit Manseng grown in the high rainfall and humidity of the foothills of the Pyrenees in south west France. They are in no way comparable with the American species.

A more fundamental difference would appear to be that the primordial wild vines are dioecious, that is they have distinct male and female flowers borne on separate vines, as in the American species. Most cultivated varieties have perfect flowers, a very desirable character when they are to be grown in pure plantings. However, as already mentioned, a perfect-flowered form of *Vitis rotundifolia* was ultimately found when the species was grown under domestication. This is a single gene mutation, probably involving a simple hormonal change, since it has been found experimentally that the application of certain growth regulators will promote the development of male flowers into perfect flowers. There can be little doubt that perfect-flowered forms of wild *Vitis vinifera* would also arise. These would not be favoured in the wild because their own seed would mostly be self-fertilized and produce weak offspring and the amount of pollen they would provide would be small compared to that available from male vines for fertilizing female flowers. On the other hand, under domestication they would stand out by their better fruitset and, once the possibilities of vegetative propagation were realized, they would be multiplied.

Thus there does not seem to be a case for separating the primordial wild vines as a distinct species or subspecies of *Vitis*. They can be regarded simply as the spontaneous form of *V. vinifera* to which cultivated varieties would revert if allowed to run wild. For some of the more primitive varieties very few generations would be required.

5.4.2 Cultivated vines

Vitis vinifera in its cultivated varieties (see Chapter 6) shows a much greater range of variation than any of the wild species of *Vitis*. There are large differences in the size and shape of leaves, berries and seeds and in other characters such as the degree of hairiness. Although the position has been somewhat confused by the widespread movement and deliberate crossing of varieties it is possible to recognize various groups that are characteristic of particular regions. The differences between these groups may be not entirely a matter of response to environment but partly due to human selection.

Thus in Western Europe the selection would have been mainly for grapes for winemaking while in the Middle East it would have been for fruit for eating fresh. The most favoured scheme of classification recognizes three major groups, called proles. Some differences in the shoots of proles are illustrated in Plate 5.

a. Proles pontica
This group comprises varieties native to the countries around the Aegean and Black Seas. They are characterized by a dense white hairiness on the growing shoot tips and the lower surface of mature leaves. Bunches are medium to compact, berries are usually round, medium to small, and juicy. There is a fairly high proportion of fruitful shoots, with more than one bunch per fruitful shoot. The greatest resistance to cold in winter is found in this group. Varieties grown in Australia include Zante Currant, Clairette, Chaouch and Furmint.

b. Proles occidentalis
These are the varieties native to Western Europe. The development of hairs on the shoot tips and leaves is less dense than in the proles pontica and the leaves often tend to turn or fold back to give a convex upper surface. The bunches are usually small and compact, and the berries usually round, small and juicy. The proportion of fruitful shoots is high with two or more bunches per fruitful shoot. The varieties are adapted to long days and a short growing and ripening season, and are fairly resistant to cold. Many of the winegrape varieties of high quality belong here, some well known examples being Riesling, Cabernet Sauvignon, Traminer, Chardonnay, Semillon and Mataro.

c. Proles orientalis
The varieties of this group are native to the Middle East, Iran, Afghanistan and nearby areas. Their young shoot tips are hairless and shining and the leaves have at most a few bristly hairs on the lower surface. Leaves tend to fold inwards to give a concave upper surface. Bunches are large, often loose and branching. Berries are usually oval to elliptical and large unless seedless. There is a strong tendency to seedlessness in many varieties so that bunches may have both large berries with seeds and smaller seedless berries. The flesh of the berries is usually firm, often crisp, and the juice tends to be lower in both sugar and acid than it is in the other two proles. The proportion of fruitful shoots is lower and there is often only one bunch per fruitful shoot. A long growing season

is generally needed and there is very little resistance to cold.

This group provides most of the table and raisin varieties. It accounts for more than half of the area of vines in Australia with varieties such as Sultana, Muscat Gordo Blanco, Waltham Cross, Cinsaut and Ohanez.

The differences between the proles are not as clear cut as the above descriptions might suggest and exceptions in particular features are not hard to find. In the Murray Valley, Sultana retains more acid at maturity than many of the varieties of the proles occidentalis and Muscat Gordo Blanco shows a high proportion of fruitful shoots. It is doubtful whether the further division of proles into sub-proles serves any practical purpose. At the other end of the scale it is possible to find small groups of very closely related varieties such as those shown in the following:

Cabernet:	Malbec:	Folle:
Cabernet Sauvignon	Malbec	Folle blanc
Cabernet Franc	Valdiguié	Ondenc
Merlot	Mérille	Jurançon
Petit Verdot	Tannat	
Fer	Négrette	

The close resemblance in these cases is in the characteristics of the vine. It does not follow that the varieties will produce comparable wines. The study of such relationships may help in tracing where a variety originated and techniques are now available to aid this work.

5.4.3 Vinifera breeding program

Until the early nineteenth century all cultivated varieties appear to have come from naturally occurring vines. New varieties arose by bud mutation or as natural seedlings. In 1824 Louis Bouschet became interested in varieties with red juice as a possible means of improving the colour of the red wines of the Midi of France. When none of the varieties available proved to yield well enough he crossed the most highly coloured, Teinturier du Cher, with the local varieties Aramon, Carignan and Grenache to try to combine colour with yield. His selection Petit Bouschet (Aramon × Teinturier) was widely planted by 1865. His son, Henri Bouschet, used Petit Bouschet as a parent in further crosses and obtained Grand Noir de la Calmette with Aramon, Alicante Bouschet with Grenache, and Morrastel Bouschet with Morrastel. Although Petit Bouschet has almost disappeared from France, Henri Bouschet's varieties occupied more than 50,000 ha in 1968 and they have also been grown in other countries.

Most major viticultural countries now look to breeding programs as a source of improved varieties. The extra variation introduced is likely to be useful in extending the climatic range for successful viticulture. Thus in Germany the variety Mueller-Thurgau, raised from a cross in 1882, has become the leading variety because of its reliable maturation in the short growing season, and other new varieties such as Kerner and Morio-Muskat are also becoming established. At the other extreme, breeding may provide better winegrapes for the inland areas of California and Australia where temperatures are much higher than those natural to the proles occidentalis. Ruby Cabernet, bred in California and released in 1948, occupied more than 7,300 ha by 1976. Tarrango, released in 1975, is designed to suit Australian conditions through its later maturity and higher natural acidity.

5.5 *Vitis* hybrids

Hybrids of the species of *Vitis* have not so far been very important in Australian viticulture, in contrast to the situation in other parts of the world. The first commercially important hybrids were those which enabled the growing of grapes in the difficult conditions of the eastern United States. Later, with the spread of diseases and pests from North America to Europe, the use of hybrids became important in Europe also. The main use of hybrids is as rootstocks for vinifera varieties, but some are used directly as fruiting varieties.

As mentioned earlier, the species of section *Euvitis* will interbreed quite readily and after repeated crossings hybrids were produced with up to eight species in their ancestry. Incorporation of section *Muscadinia* species into hybrids is more difficult; because of the difference in chromosome number the first generation hybrids are almost completely sterile. However, after many attempts, fertile backcrosses to *Euvitis* were finally obtained, some of which will cross successfully with either subgenus. In effect, *V. rotundifolia* and more tropical Euvitis species have been added to the complex synthesis of species already obtained.

5.5.1 American hybrids

This term is generally reserved for the hybrids developed in the eastern United States (Hedrick

1908) in which the species *V. labrusca* and/or *V. aestivalis* are the most important components other than *V. vinifera*. They are used to some extent for wine and as table grapes but principally for unfermented grape juice. Many varieties have highly flavoured fruit reminiscent of raspberries, strawberries, passionfruit or pineapples, and make a more attractive juice than the sweet and rather insipid juices from vinifera varieties.

By far the most important variety is Concord, a black labrusca type, with over 20 000 ha in the United States. Other well known varieties grown on a smaller scale include Ives (black), Catawba and Delaware (red), and Niagara (white). Another black labrusca type, Isabella, discarded in favour of Concord in the United States, is grown in Colombia, apparently being more satisfactory near the Equator; Bangalore Blue of India is very similar. Delaware is an important table grape in Japan. In Australia there are very limited areas of Jacquez (black aestivalis type), Isabella, and Ferdinand de Lesseps and Canada Muscat (white labrusca types). Many other varieties have been introduced for testing.

5.5.2 French hybrids

When the French vineyards began to succumb to phylloxera around 1870 some of the early American hybrids were tried as replacements. Varieties such as Jacquez and Noah (riparia-labrusca) can still be found in parts of Europe. They gave wines of very poor quality and since 1934 it has been illegal to plant them in France. Nevertheless the ideal of producing hybrids that would combine good fruit quality with adequate disease and pest resistance persisted. French breeders such as Couderc and Seibel and, more recently, Seyve-Villard and Joannes Seyve spent many years crossing and recrossing towards this ideal. They concentrated on the more productive vinifera varieties, made some use of

American hybrids, and as well brought in species such as rupestris, riparia and berlandieri with excellent disease and pest resistance. The fruit of these species was not attractive enough to have suggested domesticating them but it was free of the strong flavour of *V. labrusca*.

Considerable success was achieved (Galet 1956) and by 1958 an area of just over 400 000 ha, or nearly one third of the French vineyards, was planted to French hybrid varieties. Wine quality, particularly for some of the earlier releases, was often below standard, although in some cases the wines could be described as unusual rather than unpleasant.

New planting regulations brought into force from 1955 onwards aimed to eliminate or discourage the planting of inferior varieties, both vinifera and hybrid; by 1968 the area of hybrids had declined to about 300 000 and less than 80 000 ha in 1980. However the area of a few of the better hybrids actually increased during this period. The pedigree of two of these, Villard blanc and Villard noir, is shown in Figure 5.4, which gives some idea of the effort that went into producing them. It is interesting to note that the Californian varieties Rubired and Royalty are much less complex, differing from S.2510 only in having Tinta Cao and Bastardo respectively as the vinifera parents instead of Piquepoul. For many years the French hybrids were known only by their breeder's numbers, but those which may still be planted have been given names.

Many French hybrids have been tested in the eastern United States, Canada and New Zealand, and some are now grown commercially. As well, a new generation of hybrids is appearing from crosses of American and French hybrids, e.g. Cayuga White, a cross of Seyval (French) × Schuyler (American) from New York Agricultural Experiment Station. Details, based on European experience, of some of the French hybrids introduced into Australia

Table 5.1 Details of some French hybrid varieties which have been introduced into Australia (from Boubals 1956, 1961 and 1966; Galet 1956, 1979)

Variety	Breeder's Number	Fruit		Resistance to:			
		Colour	Maturity	Phylloxera on roots	Phylloxera leaf galling	Oidium	Plasmopara
Chambourcin	JS 26-205	black	early	excellent	very good	very good	very good
Garonnet	SV 18-283	black	very early	fair	excellent	very good	good
Seyval	SV 5-276	white	very early	good	fair	excellent	good
Varousset	SV 23-657	black	early	fair	fair	very good	good
Villard blanc	SV 12-375	white	mid-season	fair	very good	excellent	good
Villard noir	SV 18-315	black	early	poor	excellent	excellent	good

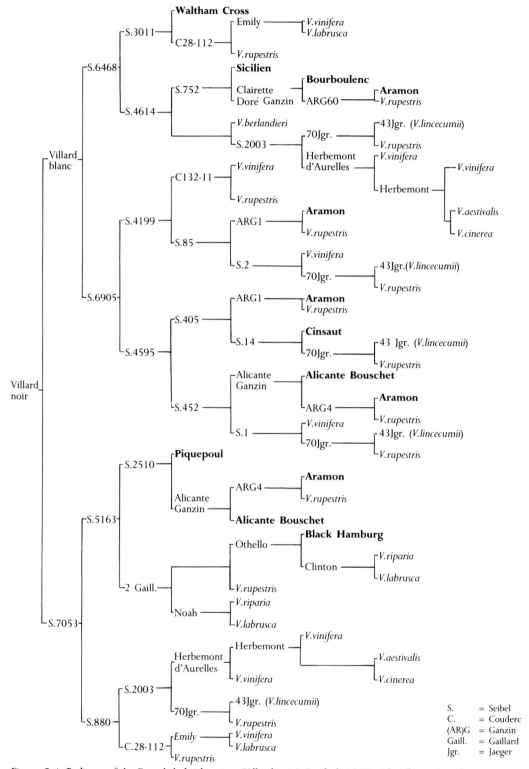

Figure 5.4. Pedigree of the French hybrid variety 'Villard noir' (Boubals 1956). The above gives the majority opinion; there is a minority view that Villard noir may be a cross between S.6905 and S.7053. Varieties in bold type are V.vinifera.

116

are given in Table 5.1. Villard blanc, the first of these to be established in Australia, has proved to be healthy and productive, and there could be a place for such varieties in situations where disease control is a problem. A table grape imported at the same time, Carolina Blackrose, descended from Villard blanc by successive back crosses to Chaouch and Blackrose, also performs well and should be a good backyard variety. This variety was one of the parents of the recently released table grape Marroo Seedless, bred at CSIRO, Merbein (Clingeleffer and Possingham 1988).

5.5.3 Rootstocks

The use of rootstocks was the second and ultimately the preferred method of dealing with the phylloxera problem in France (see Chapter 8). Most French vines, including the French hybrids, are grafted onto rootstocks. The first varieties used, apart from some of the American hybrids which gave some protection when used as rootstocks, were varieties of a single species e.g. *V. rupestris* var. du Lot (syn. St. George in California) and *V. riparia* vars. Gloire de Montpellier and Grand Glabre. It was soon found advantageous to use hybrids of the American species to combine their desirable features—tolerance of moist conditions (*V. riparia*), of dry conditions (*V. rupestris*) and of calcareous soil (*V. berlandieri*). Hybridization was particularly important in the case of *V. berlandieri,* which could not be used as the pure species because of the difficulty of rooting its cuttings.

Notable early successes in France were 3309 and 101-14 (riparia × rupestris), 161-49 and 420 A (riparia × berlandieri) and 99R and 110R (rupestris × berlandieri). Other species have been incorporated into rootstocks but the three species mentioned above have proved to be the most important. As phylloxera spread to other European countries local hybrid rootstocks were produced, such as the rupestris-berlandieri 140 Ru and 1103 P in Italy and the riparia-berlandieri selections of Teleki in Hungary.

Under European conditions hybrids of *V. vinifera* with any one of the above American species do not generally give enough protection against phylloxera. Even 41B (vinifera × berlandieri), which has been used for many years in the Cognac area, sometimes fails and a replacement is being sought. In north eastern Victoria where vinifera vines can survive in the presence of phylloxera for a long time on their own roots it is possible to use rootstocks such as

ARG1 (vinifera × rupestris) which would succumb after only a few years in Europe. The risk in using such stocks is similar to, although perhaps not so severe as, growing vinifera vines on their own roots. An interesting finding in Europe has been that it is possible to obtain a stock giving good protection by selecting varieties from crosses of two vinifera × American species.

Another root pest which can debilitate vinifera vines is rootknot nematode. This is a problem in sandy soils, in contrast to phylloxera, which is most serious in clayey soils. As it happens, many of the phylloxera resistant rootstocks will also give protection against rootknot, but the American species which appears to be most effective in both respects is *V. champini.*

5.5.4 Glory vines

The red juice character in varieties such as those with which the Bouschets worked is accompanied by a brilliant red coloration of the foliage in autumn which makes it a very attractive ornamental plant. The so-called glory vines are selected with this in mind.

The foliage character is expressed even if there is little or no fruit to show the juice character, so male vines or fruiting vines with very small bunches giving very small berries if pollinated are used. This allows vigorous vegetative development capable of covering large structures and avoids the mess which fruit can cause.

The use of hybrids with American species ensures healthy foliage without the need for protective sprays. One of the most popular varieties of glory vine in Australia would appear to be ARG9, another selection from the same population as the rootstock ARG1 mentioned above, and which is also a male variety. This might well be named Ganzin Glory in recognition of the breeder, Ganzin, who was the first to make the cross of *V. vinifera* and *V. rupestris* (Antcliff 1980).

Further reading

Bailey, L.H. (1944) Standard Cyclopedia of Horticulture. Popular Edition 1941-1944 MacMillan, New York.

Clingeleffer, P.R. and Possingham, J.V. (1988) Marroo Seedless. A new table grape variety. Agricultural Science. Feb/March 18-19.

Cribb, A.B. and Cribb, J.W. (1975) Wild Food in Australia. Collins, Sydney.

Galet, P. (1979) A Practical Ampelography. Grapevine Identification. Comstock Publishing Assoc., Ithaca, N.Y.

Hedrick, U.P. (1908) The Grapes of New York. J.B. Lyon Co., Albany, N.Y.

Levadoux, L., Boubals, D. and Rives, M. (1962) Le genre Vitis et ses espèces. Ann. Amélior. Plantes 12, 19-44.

Olmo, H.P. (1976) Grapes. In: 'Evolution of Crop Plants'. N.W. Simmonds (Ed.). Longman, London, pp 294-8.

Other references

Antcliff, A.J. (1980) The glory vine in South Australia. J. Adelaide Botanic Garden 2, 353-4.

Boubals, D. (1956). Amelioration de la resistance de la vigne au mildiou (*Plasmopara viticola* (B. et C.) Berlese et de Toni). Recherche de géniteurs de résistance. Ann. Amelior. Plantes 6, 481-525.

Boubals, D. (1961) Etude des causes de la resistance des Vitacées a l'oidium de la vigne — Uncinula necator (Schw.) Burr. — et de leur mode de transmission héréditaire. Ann. Amélior. Plantes 11, 401-500.

Boubals, D. (1966) Étude de la distribution et des causes de la resistance au *Phylloxera* radicicole chez les Vitacees. Ann. Amelior. Plantes 16, 145-184.

Galet, P. (1956) Cepages et vignobles de France. I. Les vignes americaines. Ecole Nat. Sup. Agric., Montpellier.

Levadoux, L. (1956) Les populations sauvages et cultivées de *Vitis vinifera* L. Ann. Amélior. Plantes 6, 59-118.

CHAPTER SIX

Grapevine Varieties

P. R. DRY and G. R. GREGORY

Almost all commercial grapevines grown in Australia are varieties of *Vitis vinifera* which originated in Asia Minor (see Chapter 5). The reliance on *V. vinifera* contrasts with the situation in some viticultural countries of importance, notably France, where about 20 per cent of the vineyard area consists of hybrids of *V. vinifera* and American species of *Vitis*.

Apart from its susceptibility to phylloxera and downy mildew, *V. vinifera* will not survive in very cold climates where freezing temperatures can kill vines. Here it is necessary to rely on native grapes and hybrids which are far more tolerant of cold injury. Winter conditions of this kind are rare in Australia.

Although about 24,000 varieties of *V. vinifera* have been named (Viala and Vermorel 1909) it is likely that only 5,000 or so are genuinely different varieties (Truel *et al.* 1980) and only a small proportion of these are used commercially. In France, the official statistics list 216 varieties of 10 ha or more, of which 179 are *V. vinifera* and 37 are hybrids. The number of varieties of commercial importance in Australia is much smaller. Until the early 1960s, the total number of known varieties in Australia was less than 100; the early emphasis on fortified wines did not create a demand for a wide array of table wine

varieties. Even now there are probably only 60 to 70 varieties with 10 ha or more, which is a small number considering that there are no planting restrictions in Australia. Most European countries have restrictions on the varieties which may be planted in each district: for example, Grenache is widely-grown in the south of France but is not permitted in the Bordeaux area. The twenty most important winegrape varieties in the world are listed in Table 6.1. It is interesting that some of these varieties (e.g. Airen, Bobal) are not known at all in Australia and others such as Rkaziteli, Carignan and Barbera have been introduced relatively recently.

Selection of the correct varieties, both for environmental conditions and end-use, is fundamental for the success of any viticultural enterprise. This applies especially for wine as there is such a large number from which to choose. Varieties suitable for drying, on the other hand, are fewer, being limited in Australia to Sultana, Muscat Gordo Blanco, Waltham Cross, Zante Currant and Carina, although some wine varieties such as Shiraz have been dried (Witcomb 1979).

The genetic characteristics of winegrapes, more than any other factor, predetermine the style and quality of a wine. While climate influences the levels of sugar, acid, pigments, tannin and the intensity of fruit flavours, the relative winemaking quality of different varieties is consistent from region to region. Accordingly the performance of a variety in one area can be quite a good guide to its suitability for another.

The 63 varieties described in this text are grouped into three categories based on the 1986/87 planting statistics (Australian Bureau of Statistics): those varieties with a total area (bearing plus non-bearing area) greater than 1,000 ha; those between 100 and 1,000 ha; and those less than 100 ha.

Table 6.1: The top twenty winegrape varieties in the world[1]

Variety	Area ('000 ha)	Countries with the largest plantings (% of global area)
Airen (W)[2]	476	Spain (100)
Grenache (R)	331	Spain (72), France (23)
Rkaziteli (W)	267	USSR (93)
Trebbiano (W)	262	Italy (49), France (49)
Carignan (R)	221	France (94)
Pais/Mission/ Criolla (R)	145	Argentina (72), Chile (27)
Cabernet Sauvignon (R)	135	Chile (19), France (17), USSR (16)
Muscat[3] (W,R)	122	Argentina (20), Spain (19), USSR (16)
Monastrell (R)	113	Spain (100)
Barbera (R)	102	Italy (90)
Bobal (R)	95	Spain (100)
Merlot (R)	90	France (42), Italy (17)
Semillon (W)	75	Chile (47), France (31)
Riesling (W)	66	USSR (38), Germany (29)
Verdicchio (W)	65	Italy (100)
Welschriesling (W)	64	Yugoslavia (33), Hungary (30)
Macabeo (W)	58	Spain (88)
Malbec (R)	43	Argentina (70), Chile (19)
Xarello (W)	43	Spain (100)
Grenache Blanc (W)	41	Spain (61), France (39)

1. Adapted from Robinson (1986)
2. Letters in brackets denote colour of the variety: W = white, R = red
3. Includes Muscat Gordo Blanco, Frontignac

Because many of the varieties are not listed in the published statistics, an estimated area was used to place them in either the second or third category. Within each category the varieties have been divided into 'white' or 'red' and listed alphabetically: white varieties may have ripe berry colours ranging from green to yellow to pink; red varieties may have ripe berry colours ranging from red to purple to black and (if used for winemaking) are usually used for red wine.

Unless otherwise stated in the text, the planting and production statistics are given for 1986/87.

Figure 6.1 shows the changes in tonnages of grapes used for winemaking for the major varieties from 1973 to 1987. The varietal names used are shown in Table 6.2. This list has been modified from one first prepared by Antcliff (1976a). In the text there is reference to the identification of varieties in the 1970s: further details can be found in Antcliff (1976a).

The descriptions attempt to outline the significance of each variety in Australia and elsewhere. This chapter is not intended as an ampelography and for this reason has been cross-referenced with Antcliff (1976b, 1979, 1983). Some morphological characters are summarized in Table 6.3 but the reader should keep in mind that the characters listed in the table may be affected by both cultural and environmental factors.

6.1 Varieties with more than 1,000 ha

6.1.1 White varieties

Chardonnay

Chardonnay was the single most sought-after grape variety in the 1980s in Australia and elsewhere and large areas were planted in many different parts of the world. Chardonnay probably originated in northern France. It is the fourth most important French white variety, with more than 13,000 ha: almost half is grown in the champagne-producing departments of Marne and Aube where it is normally blended with Pinot Noir except in very good years when it is used alone in Blanc-de-Blancs. Most of the remainder is grown in Burgundy where it is the preferred of the two white varieties (the other is Aligote) permitted for white wines. California has more than 10,000 ha, the area having doubled from 1975 to 1985. Chardonnay is not a member of the Pinot group of varieties and therefore the name Pinot Chardonnay, still seen on some Australian wine labels, is best avoided.

In Australia, Chardonnay has been grown since the 1900s, but despite its overseas reputation, plantings remained small. From 1976 to 1986 the planted area increased from 176 ha to 2,625 ha as the demand increased for its high quality table wines. In the 1980s, it has achieved the highest prices of any variety—in the 1988 vintage, prices of $1,500 to $2,000 per tonne were not uncommon, probably double its nearest neighbour. In the mid-1980s, the largest areas were found in the Hunter Valley,

Coonawarra, Padthaway and the Barossa (see Tables 2.3, 2.4).

Chardonnay is a relatively easy variety to grow, with good yields and few problems; it ripens well in all climatic regions in Australia, is not readily damaged by rain before harvest and is easily harvested by machine. Early budburst is its major disadvantage, making it prone to spring frost damage as occurred at Padthaway and Coonawarra in 1987. Although traditionally cane-pruned, many Chardonnay vines in Australia are successfully spur-pruned. Good, well-balanced wines can be produced under a wide range of climatic conditions (Kerridge *et al.* 1987d).

[Antcliff 1976b, p. 39]

Doradillo

Doradillo has been Australia's traditional distillation variety. However, when demand for white table wine base material outstripped supply, the neutral wines of Doradillo were blended with more aromatic varieties, such as Gordo, for the cask market. A decrease in the demand for brandy, fortifying spirit and sherry resulted in a halving of the planted area during the 1970s and 1980s. In 1986, the largest areas were found in the Riverland, Sunraysia and MIA regions, three-quarters of the total area being in SA (see Table 2.3). Although originally imported from Spain, Doradillo 'is not recorded separately in Spanish plantings and may perhaps be included under Jaen, a name said to have been used for more than one variety in Spain' (Antcliff 1979). Doradillo is moderately vigorous with a relatively shallow and weak root system that is sensitive to poor drainage. Yields are high and the fruit ripens late. Pruning is usually to spurs.

[Antcliff 1979, p. 9]

Muscat Gordo Blanco

Muscat Gordo Blanco is Australia's most important winegrape, comprising 20% of the tonnes crushed, almost twice as much as the next variety, Shiraz. Best known internationally as Muscat of Alexandria, it is widely grown throughout the world, with large plantings in Spain, South Africa, Chile, California and Australia. Gordo, as it is most often known in Australia, is a true multipurpose grape: it is used as a tablegrape, dried for raisins, and crushed for unfermented grape juice and wine. In the Australian wine industry, it is used for fortified sweet wines, e.g. cream sherry, and, together with Sultana, makes up the bulk of the white wine used in casks. Almost 50 per cent is planted in South Australia; the largest

areas are found in the Riverland, Sunraysia and MIA regions (see Table 2.3).

Gordo vines lack vigour but, when planted comparatively close, they can produce good yields. In warm areas the fruit can attain a very high sugar content but is then low in acid and has a high pH (Kerridge *et al.* 1987c). The fruit has a strong muscat flavour. The variety is susceptible to erinose and nematodes. Poor berry setting can be a problem impairing its usefulness as a tablegrape. It is best pruned to one-node spurs. [Antcliff 1979, p. 7]

Palomino

Palomino and Pedro Ximenes are grouped together for statistical purposes: they were Australia's sixth most important winegrapes in the 1980s in terms of tonnes crushed and traditionally have been used for fortified wines, particularly sherries. They have also been used for bulk table wine but, during the 1980s, the planted area was halved because of the decreased demand for fortified wine and the need for better table wine varieties. In 1986, about 80 per cent of the plantings were in South Australia, mainly the Riverland and Barossa regions. Palomino is an important variety in Spain, providing almost 90 per cent of the grapes used for sherry, and is the second most important variety in South Africa. Smaller areas are found in California, France (where it is known as Listan) and Argentina. Palomino yields well and when ripe has a high sugar content but low acid and high pH, with neutral flavour. It is better suited to fortified wines than table wines. It is susceptible to sunburn and recovers poorly after frost (Boehm and Tulloch 1967). Although susceptible to oidium and anthracnose (black spot), the bunches stand up well to wet weather near vintage. [Antcliff 1979, p. 11]

Pedro Ximenes (see under *Palomino*)

Pedro Ximenes (also spelt Ximenez) comes from Spain where there are about 35,000 ha: it is a permitted variety in Jerez for sherry production but only a small proportion of the total plantings are in this region. It is the most important white variety in Argentina.

Pedro Ximenes is a productive variety but the berries have a tender skin that is susceptible to rain damage and consequently bunch rot. Lighter pruning of this variety has resulted in more exposed, smaller and less compact bunches that are less susceptible to rain damage. It is also more susceptible to downy mildew and oidium than most varieties, and recovery

Table 6.2: Grape varieties in commercial use in Australia[1]

The format of this table is similar to one given for New Zealand names by Zuur (1988).

Prime name	Valid synonyms[2]	Unacceptable names[3]
Aleatico		
Alicante Bouschet		
Barbera		
Bastardo	Trousseau (B)	Cabernet Gros (D), Touriga (D)
Biancone		White Grenache (D)
Bonvedro		False Carignan (D)
Cabernet Franc		
Cabernet Sauvignon		
Canocazo		False Pedro (D)
Carignan		
Carina		
Chardonnay		Pinot Chardonnay (D)
Chambourcin		
Chasselas		
Chenin Blanc		Albillo, Sherry (C)
Cinsaut		Blue Imperial, Black Prince (C) Oeillade, Ulliade (D)
Clairette		Blanquette (D)
Colombard		French Colombard (C)
Crouchen		Clare Riesling (D)
Dolcetto		Malbec (D)
Doradillo		
Dourado		Rutherglen Pedro (D)
Durif		Petite Sirah (D)
Farana	Planta Pedralba (B)	False Trebbiano (D)
Frontignac		
Brown Frontignac	Brown Muscat (A) Muscat à Petit Grains Rouge (B)	
Red Frontignac	Muscat à Petit Grains Rose (B)	
White Frontignac	Muscat à Petit Grains Blanc (B)	
Goyura		
Graciano	Morrastel (B)	
Grenache		
Grey Grenache		White Grenache (D)
Malbec		
Marroo Seedless		
Marsanne		
Mataro		Morrastel (D)
Melon	Muscadet (B)	Pinot Blanc (D)
Merlot		
Meunier	Pinot Meunier (B)	Millers Burgundy (C)
Mondeuse	Refosco (B)	
Mueller-Thurgau		Riesling Sylvaner (D)
Muscadelle		Tokay (C)
Muscat Gordo Blanco	Gordo (A), Muscat of Alexandria (B)	
Ondenc		Irvine's White (C), Sercial (D)
Palomino	Listan (B)	
Pedro Ximenes	Pedro Ximenez (B)	
Pinot Gris	Rulander (B)	
Pinot Noir		

Table 6.2 (continued)

Prime name	Valid synonyms[2]	Unacceptable names[3]
Riesling	Rhine Riesling(A)	
Rkaziteli		
Rubired		
Ruby Cabernet		
Sangiovese		Canaiolo (D)
Sauvignon Blanc		Fume Blanc (C)
Semillon		Madeira (C), Hunter River Riesling (D)
Shiraz	Syrah (B)	Hermitage (C)
Sultana	Sultanina (B), Thompson Seedless (B)	
Sylvaner		
Taminga		
Tarrango		
Terret Noir		Claret (C)
Tinta Amarella		Portugal (C) Malbec (D)
Tinta Cao		
Tinta Madeira		
Touriga		
Traminer	Gewuerztraminer (B)	
Trebbiano	Ugni Blanc (B)	Saint Emilion (C), White Hermitage (C), White Shiraz (D)
Tullilah		
Valdiguie		Napa Gamay (D)
Verdelho		Madeira (C)
Waltham Cross	Rosaki (B)	Malaga (D)
Zante Currant	Currant (A) Black Corinth (B)	
Zinfandel		

1. Main varieties grown in Australia excluding table grape varieties dealt with in Volume 2, Chapter 12; this list is modified from Antcliff's 1976 list as modified in 1980 by Antcliff - see CSIRO Hort. Res. Div. reprint No. 497.
2. Valid synonyms included are those mainly used in Australia:
   A = Acceptable in Australia.
   B = Used or preferred internationally.
3. Unacceptable names:
   C = Names unacceptable in Australia; rejected for reasons of mis-spelling or local usage.
   D = Misnomers incorrectly applied to a variety or similar to the prime name for another variety.

from spring frost damage is poor. Although most suited to the production of fortified wines, the neutral table wines are suitable for blending.
[Antcliff 1979, p. 13]

Riesling

Riesling is regarded by Robinson (1986) as the world's greatest white table wine variety. It is widely grown throughout the world, with at least 45 synonyms (Robinson 1986) and possesses the ability to produce wines with recognizable varietal character in perhaps all situations. Riesling appears to have originated in Germany where it accounts for about

one-quarter of the vineyard area, second only to Mueller-Thurgau: in the Rheingau and Mosel, it comprises 70 and 95 per cent of the plantings respectively. California and Australia probably have the largest areas outside Germany. Smaller areas are found in north-east France, northern Italy, eastern European countries and Argentina.

In Australia, it is often called Rhine Riesling to avoid confusion with other varieties which have been incorrectly called Riesling in the past, e.g. 'Hunter River Riesling', which is an invalid synonym for Semillon: however, the use of Riesling is preferable to Rhine Riesling. The area of Riesling increased

Table 6.3: Characteristics of grape varieties used in Australia

Variety	End use	Berry				Bunch		Phenology			
		Colour	Size	Shape	Seeded	Size	Compactness	Budburst	Ripening	Yield	Vigour
Barbera	W(t)	B	M	O	+	M	WC	M	L	H	M
Bastardo	W(f)	B	S	R	+	S	C	M	E	M	M
Biancone	W(t,d)	W	M	R	+	ML	W	M	L	H	H
Bonvedro	W(t)	B	M	O	+	M	C	M	M	H	H
Cabernet Franc	W(t)	B	S	R	+	S	LW	E	M	M	M
Cabernet Sauvignon	W(t)	B	S	R	+	S	L	L	M	L	M
Calmeria	T	W	L	E	+	L	L	L	L	M	H
Cannon Hall Muscat	T	W	L	O	+	L	C	L	EM	H	M
Cardinal	T	R	L	O	+	L	L	M	E	M	H
Carignan	W(t)	B	M	R	+	M	C	L	L	H	H
Carina	D	B	S	R	-	L	W	E	E	M	H
Chardonnay	W(t)	W	S	R	+	M	C	E	E	M	M
Chasselas	W(t),T	W	M	R	+	M	C	E	E	M	L
Chenin Blanc	W(t)	W	S	O	+	M	C	E	M	H	H
Cinsaut	W(t,f)	B	M	O	+	M	WC	L	M	M	M
Clairette	W(t)	W	M	O	+	M	W	L	L	M	H
Colombard	W(t)	W	M	R	+	M	W	E	M	H	H
Cornichon	T	B	C	E	+	L	L	M	L	M	H
Crouchen	W(t)	W	S	R	+	SM	C	M	M	H	H
Doradillo	W(t,f,d)	W	L	R	+	L	W	M	L	H	H
Durif	W(t,f)	B	S	R	+	M	C	M	M	M	M
Emperor	T	R	L	E	+	L	W	L	L	H	H
Farana	W(t,f,d)	W	M	R	+	L	W	L	L	H	H
Frontignac	W(t,f)	W,R,B	SM	R	+	M	WC	E	E	M	M
Grenache	W(t,f)	B	M	R	+	M	C	M	L	H	H
Italia	T	W	L	O	+	L	L	M	M	M	H
Malbec	W(t)	B	S	R	+	M	LW	M	M	M	H
Marroo Seedless	T	B	L	O	-	L	L	M	E	MH	H
Marsanne	W(t)	W	S	R	+	M	W	E	M	M	M
Mataro	W(t,f)	B	SM	R	+	M	WC	L	L	M	H
Merlot	W(t)	B	S	R	+	S	L	E	M	M	M
Meunier	W(t)	B	S	R	+	S	C	E	E	M	M
Mueller-Thurgau	W(t)	W	M	O	+	ML	W	M	E	H	H
Muscadelle	W(t,f)	W	S	R	+	ML	W	M	E	H	H
Muscat Gordo Blanco	W,T,D	W	L	O	+	L	L	ML	L	H	L
Muscat Hamburg	T	B	M	O	+	M	W	M	E	M	M
Ohanez	T	W	L	E	+	M	W	ML	L	M	H
Ondenc	W(t)	W	M	O	+	SM	W	M	E	M	M
Palomino	W(t,f)	W	LM	R	+	L	LW	M	M	H	H
Pedro Ximenes	W(t,f)	W	LM	R	+	L	W	M	E	H	H
Perlette	T	W	S	R	-	M	C	E	E	M	M
Pinot Noir	W(t)	B	S	R	+	S	C	E	E	L	M
Red Prince	T	R	L	O	+	L	C	M	M	H	M
Riesling	W(t)	W	S	R	+	S	C	M	M	L	LM
Ribier	T	B	L	R	+	L	L	E	M	H	M
Rubired	W(t,f)	B	S	R	+	M	L	M	M	H	H
Ruby Cabernet	W(t)	B	M	O	+	M	W	L	M	M	H
Sauvignon Blanc	W(t)	W	S	R	+	SW	C	M	M	L	H
Semillon	W(t)	W	S	R	+	M	C	M	M	M	H
Shiraz	W(t,f)	B	S	O	+	M	LW	M	M	M	H
Sultana	W,T,D	W	S	O	-	L	W	M	E	M	H

Table 6.3 (continued)

Variety		Berry				Bunch			Phenology		
	End use	Colour	Size	Shape	Seeded	Size	Compactness	Budburst	Ripening	Yield	Vigour
Sylvaner	W(t)	W	M	R	+	M	C	M	M	H	H
Taminga	W(t)	W	M	R	+	M	W	M	M	H	H
Tarrango	W(t)	B	M	O	+	L	W	M	L	H	M
Tinta Amarella	W(f)	B	M	R	+	L	W	M	M	M	H
Touriga	W(f)	B	S	O	+	SM	W	M	M	M	M
Traminer	W(t)	W	S	R	+	S	C	E	E	M	M
Trebbiano	W(t,f,d)	W	M	R	+	M	W	L	L	M	H
Verdelho	W(t)	W	S	O	+	S	L	E	E	M	M
Waltham Cross	W,T,D	W	L	E	+	L	L	L	M	H	H
Zante Currant	D	B	S	R	-	S	W	E	E	M	M
Zinfandel	W(t)	B	M	R	+	M	C	M	E	M	M

Explanatory notes:
End use: W = winemaking, (t,f,d) = table wines, fortified wines, distillation, respectively; T = tablegrape; D = drying grape
Berry colour: B = black; R = red; W = white
Berry size, bunch size: S = small, M = medium, L = large
Berry shape: R = round, O = slightly oval to oval, E = elongated
Bunch compactness: C = compact; W = well-filled; L = loose
Seeded: + = seeds present; - = seedless
Budburst, ripening: E = early; M = mid-season; L = late
Yield, vigour: L = low, M = moderate, H = high

rapidly in the 1970s and early 1980s, peaking at 4,800 ha in 1982/83. Over-supply resulted in removal of plantings, particularly in hot areas, dropping the area to 3,600 ha in 1987. Nevertheless, it was still Australia's second most important white winegrape (after Gordo) in 1987. Most plantings (77 per cent) are found in South Australia, mainly the Barossa, Coonawarra-Padthaway and Clare regions.

Riesling is only moderately productive and ripens well in all regions in Australia in most seasons. Well-balanced musts can be produced in hot regions (Kerridge *et al.*, 1987d). It is used for dry and sweet table wines that possess a definite varietal character. It is susceptible to bunch rot (due to its compact bunches) and erinose. Traditionally cane-pruned, it has been successfully spur-pruned in Australia.

[Antcliff 1979, p. 21]

Semillon
Semillon is widely used throughout the world for white table wine. It was Australia's fourth most important white wine variety in the 1980s. There has been confusion between Semillon and several other varieties in Australia in the past, particularly Chenin Blanc and Crouchen. It is incorrectly known as Hunter River Riesling in NSW.

Semillon is the second most important white variety in France where it is particularly important

in Bordeaux for both dry and sweet table wines. It is also the leading white variety in Chile and other large areas are found in Argentina and South Africa. The Australian area of Semillon increased during the 1970s to peak at about 3,000 ha in 1980-81. Since that time it has dropped slightly to about 2,600 ha in 1987. Most plantings (72 per cent) are found in NSW: the MIA, Hunter and Barossa have the largest areas.

It is a reasonably vigorous variety with clones showing growth habits varying from spreading to upright. Yields are good (Kerridge *et al.* 1988) but the berries tend to split in wet weather when ripe, leading to bunch rot problems. It is one of the most susceptible varieties to rootknot nematode and is a difficult variety to harvest by machine. Spur-pruning is most common. In Australia it is used for dry white table wines which, although fairly neutral when young, develop distinctive and desirable varietal characters with ageing. [Antcliff 1979, p. 19]

Sultana
Sultana is Australia's most important grape variety, comprising one-third of the planted area. It is primarily a drying grape but in some seasons during the 1970s and 1980s more Sultana grapes were crushed for wine than any other variety (Figure 6.1). In most years in Australia, about three-quarters of

the crop is dried but this can vary from season to season depending on the international trade for dried fruit and domestic demand for bulk white wine. It is the world's most important drying and tablegrape variety. Sultana appears to have originated in Asia Minor or the Middle East, and is grown for dried fruit throughout the entire area from Greece to Afghanistan. California has nearly six times the Australian area; there, Thompson Seedless, as it is known, is used for wine, drying and table. Because of its need for heat almost the entire planted area of Sultana is found in just two regions in Australia: Sunraysia (Vic. and NSW) and the Riverland (SA) with the former having 86 per cent of the total Australian area (see Table 2.3).

Sultana requires cane pruning due to the low fruitfulness of basal nodes. 'Minimal pruning', originally developed for this variety, has been most successful (Clingeleffer 1983). It is very susceptible to the fungal diseases downy mildew, oidium and anthracnose (black spot) and the berries are prone to rain damage when ripe. These factors combine to limit its commercial culture to regions of low summer rainfall. Both fresh and harvest-pruned dried fruit is readily harvested by machine.

Sultana is ideally suited to drying by virtue of its tender skin, capacity to develop high sugar levels and readiness with which the berries shatter from pedicels after drying. The lack of seeds and firm flesh make Sultana attractive as a tablegrape despite its natural small size and tendency to shatter in transit; however, both problems can be overcome by various cultural treatments (see Volume 2, Chapter 12). Sultana musts have moderate acid levels and can produce fresh, neutral table wines, most often used for blending (Kerridge *et al.* 1987d). It is also used for fortifying wine and distillation, thus making it a most versatile grape variety.

[Antcliff 1979, p. 5]

Trebbiano

Trebbiano is the leading white winegrape in Italy (50,000 ha) where it is more specifically known as Trebbiano Toscano to distinguish it from several other varieties also called Trebbiano. It is also the most important white variety in France (130,000 ha), and is mainly planted in Cognac (where it is known as St Emilion), Provence, Bordeaux and Armagnac. The official French name is Ugni Blanc. Elsewhere in the world it is a relatively minor variety, with plantings in South Africa, California and Argentina. Saint Emilion, White Hermitage and White Shiraz are invalid synonyms in Australia.

About 60 per cent of the planted area is found in the MIA (NSW) and most of the rest in the Riverland (SA). The planted area in regions such as the Barossa and Rutherglen declined significantly in the 1980s as demand decreased.

Trebbiano is a productive variety which bursts late. Young shoots are susceptible to wind damage. The thick-skinned berries resist rain damage but it juices badly when machine-harvested. Pruning is normally to spurs. It is very susceptible to rootknot nematodes. In Australia, Trebbiano is mainly used for the production of well-balanced, neutral table wines (Kerridge *et al.* 1988) suitable for blending with more fruity types, and for fortified wines. It is also used for good quality brandy spirit.

[Antcliff 1979, p. 17]

Waltham Cross

Waltham Cross is principally a tablegrape although it is also dried for raisins. It is widely grown throughout the world including the south of France (where it is called Dattier de Beyrouth) the Middle East, South Africa, California and Italy. The preferred international name is Rosaki. It is sometimes incorrectly called Malaga or White Malaga in South Australia. About 60 per cent of production is dried in Australia, 20 per cent is used as tablegrapes and the remainder used for winemaking, mainly distillation. Nearly three-quarters of the planted area is found in the Sunraysia (Vic. and NSW) region and most of the rest in the Riverland. The large, oval berries have a crisp, firm texture with a neutral but pleasant flavour and, although seeded, the seed number per berry is relatively low. The presence of small seedless (shot) berries and the tendency to shatter are disadvantages (see Volume 2, Chapter 12).

6.1.2 Red varieties

Cabernet Sauvignon

Cabernet Sauvignon is widely regarded as the world's premium red winegrape. It comes from the Bordeaux region of France where it is the major variety in the best wines of the Medoc and typically blended with Cabernet Franc, Merlot and several minor varieties. Total French plantings, of which three-quarters are found in Bordeaux, appear to have doubled since the late 1960s. It has always been important in Chile but in countries such as USA (California), Australia and South Africa, the increase in plantings has been more recent. Bulgaria has had the most recent

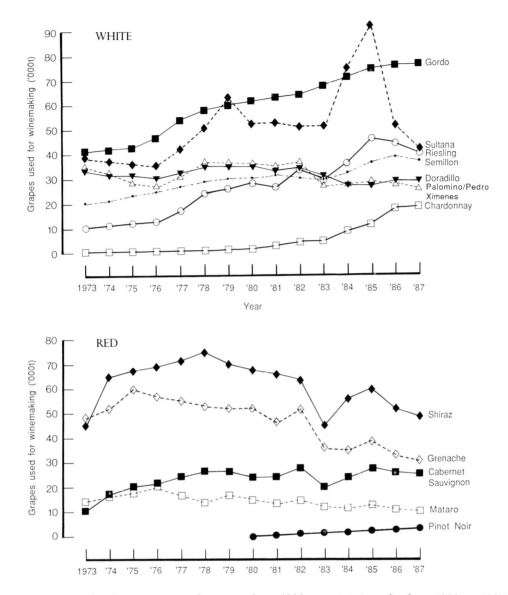

Figure 6.1. White and red grape varieties for winemaking ('000 tonnes) inAustralia from 1973 to 1987.

expansion of Cabernet Sauvignon and now has the largest area of the variety outside of France. In Australia, the planted area increased from 400 ha in the late 1960s to peak at 4,000 ha in the late 1970s. In the 1980s, the area decreased by 500 ha but production has remained steady (Figure 6.1). Sixty per cent of plantings are found in South Australia, with the largest areas in the Riverland, Coonawarra-Padthaway and Barossa regions. Other regions with large areas include Clare, McLaren Vale, MIA and Hunter Valley. The proportion planted in

the cooler areas of Australia increased significantly in the 1970s and· 1980s.

Cabernet Sauvignon has been generally regarded as a low-yielding variety; however, yields have been improved by the use of selected virus-free clones (Whiting and Godden 1988). Traditionally it is cane-pruned, but spur-pruning has been successful in Australia and large areas are mechanically pruned at Coonawarra-Padthaway and elsewhere. Poor set can be a problem, particularly in cool regions in vineyards of high vigour. It is quite susceptible to oidium. The bunches have good tolerance of rain damage and bunch rot. The small, tough berries are readily mechanically-harvested. The wines of Cabernet Sauvignon have a recognizable varietal character in all climatic regions but this is usually most intense when vines are grown under cool conditions. Under hot conditions, musts may have a high pH (Kerridge *et al.* 1987a).

[Antcliff 1979, p. 49]

Grenache

Grenache is a very important variety in southern Europe. In Spain, where it is known as Garnacha, it is the most important red winegrape, covering about 15 per cent of the planted area (more than 200,000 ha). The area in France tripled in the 1960s and 1970s, mainly at the expense of the poor-quality variety Aramon, so that it is now the second most widely planted red variety after Carignan. Grenache is concentrated in the south of France, where it is often blended with other varieties such as Carignan and Mataro. Some of the most prized wines of the Rhone Valley are blends of Grenache and Shiraz, a traditional but currently unfashionable combination in Australia. It is also found in Corsica, Sardinia and the south of Italy. Outside of Europe, the largest areas are found in California and Australia.

In Australia the area of Grenache increased during the 1960s to reach a peak of nearly 7,000 ha in the early 1970s. Since that time the area has declined by two-thirds. This situation has arisen in response to changes in the demand for red table wine in Australia during the 1970s and 1980s. It is likely that Grenache will be replaced by Cabernet Sauvignon as Australia's second most important red winegrape in the 1990s. More than 80 per cent of the plantings are found in South Australia, mainly the Riverland, Barossa and Southern Vales (see Tables 2.3, 2.4).

Grenache yields well but both the amount of shoot growth and fruit colour are more sensitive to crop level than in most red varieties. Experience in South Australia and Europe has shown that it is one of the best varieties in hot, windy conditions. It is susceptible to poor set, bunch rot, downy mildew and oidium. Pruning is generally to spurs. Most of the Grenache vines throughout the world are not trellised ('bush vines'); the erect growth habit facilitates this method of training. The wines of Grenache are often low in colour, by Australian standards, and age rapidly (Kerridge *et al.* 1987a). It is the principal rosé variety and is also used for tawny port. For red table wines it is usually combined with other varieties such as Shiraz and Mataro.

[Antcliff 1979, p. 43]

Shiraz

Shiraz is Australia's principal variety for the production of fortified and non-fortified red wines. This is in contrast to the situation in other wine-producing countries where the variety is comparatively unimportant. In France, where it represents less than 2 per cent of all red winegrape plantings, it is highly regarded: the red wines of the Hermitage area of the Rhone Valley are made totally from Shiraz. Recently, the area in France (where it is known as Syrah) has greatly increased, particularly in the Midi where it is used to add character to wines based mainly on Carignan and Grenache. Robinson (1986) suggests that there may be as many as 20,000 ha in France in the mid-1980s, compared with just 3,000 ha 20 years before. A little is also grown in Argentina, South Africa and Italy. The Petite Sirah of California is a different variety, Durif.

The area of Shiraz in Australia increased greatly during the 1960s and 1970s, reaching a peak of about 10,000 ha in the mid- to late-1970s. Over the next 10 years the area halved but production decreased by only 40 per cent (Figure 6.1) because many of the vines removed were old and low-yielding. More than 50 per cent of Shiraz plantings are found in South Australia, particularly the Barossa (see Tables 2.2, 2.3), Riverland and Coonawarra-Padthaway. NSW has large areas in the MIA and Hunter regions where it has been incorrectly called Hermitage. The largest recent decreases in planted area have been in the Barossa and Hunter Valley.

Shiraz has become Australia's most important red winegrape because it yields well under a range of climatic conditions with relatively few problems. The bunches stand up to wet weather near harvest better than most varieties (this accounts for its popularity in the Hunter Valley), but the berries tend to wilt when ripe and become more difficult to harvest mechanically. Shiraz wines are of good colour, contain moderate amounts of acid and tannin and possess a positive though mild fruit flavour (Kerridge *et al.* 1987a). The role of canopy management in determining wine quality seems to be more important in Shiraz than many other varieties; this may be a consequence of its spreading growth habit and vigorous shoot growth.

[Antcliff 1979, p. 41]

Zante Currant (Currant)

Zante Currant is essentially a drying variety. However, being very early ripening, small quantities are sold as tablegrapes. It is an important variety in the Mediterranean region: Greece produces most of the world's dried currants followed by Australia, California (where it is known as Black Corinth) and South Africa. About half of Australia's plantings are found in the Sunraysia (Vic. and NSW) region with most of the rest in the Riverland (SA) and Swan Valley (WA) (see Tables 2.3, 2.4). The planted area halved in the 1970s and 1980s. Currant has very small, seedless berries and ripening is very early. Set is unsatisfactory without girdling or use of growth regulators. It is susceptible to oidium and berries split readily after rain.

6.2 Varieties with 100 to 1000 ha

6.2.1 White varieties

Calmeria

Calmeria is a very late ripening, white, seeded tablegrape. It was selected from a seedling of Ohanez (Almeria) in California in 1939. Mainly grown in the Sunraysia (Vic. and NSW) and Swan Hill-Kerang (Vic.) regions, it is suitable for export (see Volume 2, Chapter 12).

Chenin Blanc

Chenin Blanc is the main variety in the Loire Valley of France where it is used for both still and sparkling wines. The largest area (30,000 ha) of this variety is found in South Africa (where it has been known as Steen or Stein), occupying about one-third of total vineyard area. California has the next largest area; there, plantings have more than doubled since the early 1970s. Chenin Blanc appears to have been grown in Australia for a long time but under different names — in the 1970s, much of the Semillon in Western Australia and all of the Albillo (Sherry) in South Australia was found to be Chenin Blanc. The planted area has increased little since the mid-1970s: nearly 60 per cent is in South Australia, principally the Riverland and Barossa regions. The Swan Valley also has a large area.

Chenin Blanc is a vigorous variety with early budburst making it prone to spring frost damage. Shoots adhere firmly and are not readily blown off by strong winds in spring. Yields are high but it is susceptible to fungal diseases; there is clonal variation in bunch compactness and time of ripening and at least some clones are susceptible to splitting by rain and bunch rot at harvest. Pruning is mainly to spurs. Chenin Blanc has good acidity and hence is used for well-balanced table wines in hot regions in Australia, California and South Africa (Kerridge *et al.* 1988). It also provides good material for sparkling wines.   [Antcliff 1979, p. 25]

Colombard

Colombard is a comparatively recent introduction from California; there its area increased from 9,600 ha in 1973 to 29,000 ha in 1983, mainly in the hot Central Valley. Colombard comes from the southwest and west of France; it is one of the varieties used for Cognac but the largest plantings are found to the east of the Gironde in the Bordeaux area where it is used as an accessory variety in white table wines. The total area in France decreased from 13,000 ha in 1958 to 6,000 ha in 1979. In Australia, the area has doubled since 1980: the 550 ha in 1987 were almost entirely restricted to the Sunraysia, Riverland and MIA regions (see Table 2.2).

Colombard is very vigorous and high-yielding. Young shoots are liable to be damaged by strong winds in spring. It is very susceptible to oidium but moderately tolerant of downy mildew and bunch rot. Fruit hangs well on the vine after it is ripe. The main feature of the variety is its high acid content — because of this, it is considered satisfactory in California and Australia for blending to produce good quality still and sparkling wines. It also has a distinctive varietal character.

[Antcliff 1976b, p. 45]

Crouchen

Crouchen is a variety from the south-west of France. It has now almost disappeared from that country because of its susceptibility to foliar fungal diseases and bunch rot. The variety now appears to be grown only in South Africa (about 2,000 ha) and Australia (620 ha). In South Africa it was previously known as Riesling and appears to have been introduced under that name to South Australia. Until correctly identified, Crouchen was known as Clare Riesling (Antcliff 1975a). Also, because of morphological similarity, some Crouchen was mistakenly known as Semillon in the Barossa.

The area of Crouchen in Australia has more than halved since the late 1970s as it has fallen out of favour with winemakers. Most of the plantings (90 per cent) are in South Australia, mainly the Riverland and Barossa regions. Crouchen is a high-yielding variety used for dry white table wines. It is very susceptible to fungal diseases and rootknot nematode. In cool areas it may not ripen adequately.

[Antcliff 1979, p. 23]

Frontignac - see 6.2.2.

Muscadelle

Muscadelle was formerly known as Tokay in Australia and hence assumed to have originated from the Tokay-Hegyalja district of Hungary. However in 1976 it was identified as Muscadelle (Antcliff 1976a), a variety of the Bordeaux region where it forms a minor component in the dry and sweet white table wines of Graves, Barsac, Sauternes, etc. There are also small plantings in California (where it is incorrectly known as Sauvignon Vert) and eastern Europe. The Muskadel of South Africa is really Frontignac (Orffer 1979). Three-quarters of the Australian area (394 ha) is in South Australia, mainly the Barossa and Riverland regions. Small areas also exist in the Swan Valley (WA) and at Rutherglen (Vic.).

Muscadelle is a fairly vigorous and productive variety. The fruit ripens early and can attain a very high sugar content: for this reason it has traditionally been used for sweet fortified wines, some of high quality. More recently it has been used for dry white table wines which possess a full, rich flavour, somewhat reminiscent of muscat.

[Antcliff 1979, p. 31]

Ohanez

Ohanez is a late-maturing, white tablegrape suitable for cold-storage and export. Also known as Almeria, it has male-sterile flowers and adequate pollination is necessary to produce a crop. Spain produces and exports large quantities of Ohanez but it appears to be of minor importance elsewhere. Almost 70 per cent of Australia's 250 ha are grown at Swan Hill-Kerang: smaller plantings are found in other tablegrape producing regions.

It is a vigorous variety, often grown on an overhead (pergola) trellis. Cropping is more reliable when cane-pruned.

Sauvignon Blanc

Sauvignon Blanc increased in popularity in Australia, California and New Zealand in the 1980s. By comparison, the area in France has decreased since the early 1970s. The main plantings have traditionally been near Bordeaux where it is used as a minor but important partner of Semillon, however, at the present time it is likely that the largest area is found in the Loire Valley, where it is used on its own. After France, California probably has the largest area with about 5,000 ha (in the late 1970s there were only 1,500 ha). There are also modest plantings in northern Italy, eastern Europe and Argentina. The so-called Sauvignon in Chile is a closely-related variety known as Sauvignonasse in France and Tocai Friulano in Italy. In Australia, the area increased from about 100 ha in 1977 to 700 ha in 1987: it is widely planted in the Southern Vales-Adelaide Plains, Barossa, Riverland and MIA regions (Table 2.3). Twenty-two per cent of the planted area was non-bearing in 1987.

Sauvignon Blanc is a vigorous variety with a large leaf area to fruit weight ratio. Although classed as unproductive in France, yields from locally-selected clones have been good. It has responded well to minimal pruning in the south-east of South Australia. In cooler climates, Sauvignon Blanc gives wines with a strong varietal character. This character is less developed in warmer areas where fresh, well-balanced table wines can be produced (Kerridge *et al.* 1987c).

[Antcliff 1979, p. 27]

Traminer

Traminer produces table wines with a distinctive varietal character. The best-known Traminer wines are probably from the Alsace region of France where there are about 2,500 ha, making it the most important variety in that region. Germany and Austria each have less than 1,000 ha. In California, the area has doubled in the last decade to about 1,800 ha. Traminer has been grown in Australia for some time, mainly in NSW; however, the area increased from less than 100 ha in the early 1970s to about 750 ha in 1987. Nearly half is found in NSW (Hunter Valley and MIA); the south-east of South Australia and the Barossa also have significant areas (see Table 2.3).

Traminer is not a very vigorous variety and yield is usually low although good yields have been reported from the Sunraysia area (Kerridge *et al.* 1987c). The small bunches have short bunchstems and are borne close to the base of the shoot, making hand-harvest difficult. There is marked clonal variation within the variety with respect to aromatic character and berry colour, which ranges from white to red. The pink and red clones tend to be more aromatic and, in Alsace, were originally distinguished as Gewuerztraminer ('gewuerz' being the German word for spice): today, Gewuerztraminer is more commonly used as a synonym for Traminer, irrespective of clone.   [Antcliff 1976b, p. 35]

Verdelho

Verdelho is a Portuguese variety, grown on the island of Madeira and in the Douro Valley, where it is known as Gouveio: in both regions it is used for fortified wines. In Australia, there are about 100 ha divided almost equally between Western Australia, South Australia and NSW. The name Madeira has been incorrectly used for this variety in NSW. Budburst, flowering and ripening are early. It is very susceptible to oidium. Verdelho is generally used for table wine in Australia.

[Antcliff 1979, p. 33]

6.2.2 Red varieties

Cardinal

Cardinal is a tablegrape from California. A hybrid of Flame Tokay and Ribier, it is important in California and France. Forty per cent of the Australian area (278 ha) is found in Queensland, the bulk of the remainder in Swan Hill-Kerang and Sunraysia (Vic.) and the Swan Valley (WA). It is the earliest coloured tablegrape (see Volume 2, Chapter 12).

Frontignac

Frontignac has at least 34 synonyms in commercial use throughout the world (Robinson 1986). 'Muscat á petit grains' is the official name for this variety and means Muscat with small berries. Both Frontignan and Frontignac have been widely used in Australia and while the former is unacceptable to the Office International de la Vigne et du Vin, the latter is not; hence we recommend the use of the name Frontignac for Australia. There are three colour variants of the variety; white, rose and red (brown). The coloured forms mutate readily from one to the other and there seems to be two types of white — one which is stable and one which mutates readily to the coloured forms (Antcliff 1979).

The stable white form appears to predominate in Europe. France and Italy have about the same amount (3,000 ha): in France, it is grown in the south (Frontignan, Banyuls, etc.) where it is used for sweet fortified wine, and in Alsace for table wine; in Italy, as Moscato Bianco, it is widespread and is used for the popular Asti spumante. It is also grown in other European countries. Most of the Muskadel, as the variety is known in South Africa, is the red form (Orffer 1979) but only the white form seems to be grown in California and Argentina. More than 60 per cent of the 514 ha grown in Australia is found in South Australia, particularly the Barossa and Riverland regions. North-east Victoria has a high reputation for fortified wines from Brown Muscat, as the variety is known there, but the plantings are quite small (see Table 2.3).

Frontignac has moderate vigour and yield. Spur pruning is most common. It is very susceptible to oidium. If left on the vine, the fruit wilts to give a very high sugar concentration: this is no doubt one of the reasons for its use for sweet fortified wines, known as muscats. In spite of the excellent quality of these wines, demand has fallen and most fruit is used for white table wine with a distinctive muscat flavour.   [Antcliff 1979, p. 39]

Cornichon

Cornichon is more correctly known as Olivette Noire. In the tablegrape trade in Australia it is more commonly called Purple Cornichon or Black Lady's Fingers. It is grown in the hottest areas of France and is the last black tablegrape on the market. Half of the plantings are found in Queensland and most of the remainder at Swan Hill-Kerang (Vic) and in NSW. The bunches are very attractive with deep purple berries with thick tough skins. While the berries stand up well to transport they are predisposed to shattering. It is very susceptible to downy mildew. All known clones in Australia are infected with leafroll (see Volume 2, Chapter 12).

Emperor

Emperor is a late-ripening red tablegrape suitable for cold storage and export. Although not particularly important in Europe, it is a major tablegrape in California where 90 per cent of production comes from the San Joaquin Valley. Sometimes known as Red Emperor in Australia, almost half of the planted area is found at Swan Hill-Kerang (Vic.) the rest being in Sunraysia (Vic.), NSW and WA. The berries are light red to reddish-purple with firm texture and tough skins. It is the main storage variety in California, being kept in cold storage for up to six months (see Volume 2, Chapter 12).

Malbec

Malbec comes from the west of France where it is known as Cot. The area in France has decreased since the early 1960s from 10,000 ha to less than

5,000 ha, mainly because of low productivity. It is grown near and to the east of Bordeaux, and in the Loire Valley. Malbec is the most important red variety in Argentina with about 30,000 ha and Chile has 5,000 ha.

It is estimated that the Australian area is about 200 ha of which three-quarters are found in South Australia, particularly the Riverland and south-east regions. The situation in Australia has been confused because at least two other varieties, Dolcetto and Tinta Amarella, have sometimes been incorrectly called Malbec. Malbec is notorious for its irregular cropping due to poor set; however, this problem has been partly overcome by the use of improved clones. It is easily harvested by machine. The limited quantities of Malbec wines in Australia are of good quality, rich in colour and tannin (Kerridge *et al.* 1987a), and often blended with Cabernet Sauvignon and/or Shiraz.   [Antcliff 1979, p. 51]

Mataro

Mataro was the fourth most important red wine variety in Australia in the 1980s. Although widely distributed throughout the world it is not an important variety, except in Spain where there are 110,000 ha (it is also known as Monastrell or Morastell). The area in France increased from 2,000 to 8,000 ha during the 1970s, mainly in Provence where it is known as Mouvedre. Three-quarters of the 700 ha grown in Australia are found in South Australia, mainly the Riverland and Barossa regions. The area has more than halved since the mid-1970s and it is likely to continue to decline even more in the future.

Mataro has a late budburst and recovers well after frost; for this reason it was originally planted in frost-prone sites in South Australia instead of Shiraz or Grenache. Growth habit is erect and yields are high. It is a hardy variety requiring warmer sites than Grenache in order to ripen fruit adequately. The wines of Mataro are neutral (Kerridge *et al.* 1987b) and often very astringent, usually blended with Shiraz and/or Grenache for table or fortified wine.
                  [Antcliff 1979, p. 45]

Merlot

Merlot is the principal red variety of Bordeaux. The area of Merlot in France has doubled since the early 1960s: 85 per cent is found near Bordeaux. It is also grown throughout Italy and the area in eastern Europe is expanding. There is less than 800 ha in California. The area in Australia increased from just

a few hectares in the 1970s to 260 ha by 1987; 37 per cent of the planted area was non-bearing in 1987. The largest plantings are found in the south-east of SA, Southern Vales, Clare, Barossa (SA) and Victoria (see Table 2.3).

Merlot is more productive than Cabernet Sauvignon or Cabernet Franc in Bordeaux but this has not always been the experience in Australia because it is susceptible to poor set. It is particularly sensitive to salinity. Merlot, Cabernet Franc and Cabernet Sauvignon all ripen at about the same time and the harvested fruit of the three varieties is very similar in appearance. In France it is said to be very susceptible to bunch rot. The wine of Merlot is similar to that of Cabernet Sauvignon but is softer and ages more rapidly. It is often blended with Cabernet Sauvignon and/or Cabernet Franc.
                  [Antcliff 1976b, p. 5]

Muscat Hamburg

Muscat Hamburg is a specialist tablegrape with a strong muscat flavour. Grown widely throughout southern Europe, it is the second most popular tablegrape in France. Very little is found in California. It is Australia's second most important tablegrape after Sultana. Sixty-five per cent of plantings are found in Queensland, and much of the remainder in the tablegrape-producing regions of NSW, e.g. Mudgee, Sydney. It is popular with growers in these areas because it is resistant to rain damage. Not a particularly good shipping variety, it is mostly grown fairly close to the principal market outlets (see Volume 2, Chapter 12).

Pinot Noir

Pinot Noir is the variety used for the red wines of Burgundy and one of the principal varieties for the white sparkling wines of Champagne. France has the world's largest plantings of Pinot Noir: 17,000 ha in 1979 as opposed to 12,000 in 1968. It is one of the few red varieties ripening early enough for Germany (4,000 ha as Spaetburgunder) and Switzerland. It is grown in Italy and most eastern European countries but not extensively. There are 5,000 ha in the coolest parts of California and although Oregon has just one-tenth of that area, the wines of that state have an enviable reputation. The area in Australia has increased from less than 50 ha in 1974 to 669 ha in 1987. Half of the planted area is found in South Australia, particularly the south-east and Barossa regions. The Hunter Valley (NSW) and southern Victoria also have significant areas (see Table 2.3). Thirty-three per cent of the planted area was non-bearing in 1987.

Pinot Noir is an old and variable variety; some authors claim the existence of more than 1,000 different clones (Robinson 1986). Amongst the 20 or so different clones in Australia there are recognizable differences in growth habit, berry size, bunch compactness and leaf shape. The results from clonal comparisons suggest that some clones are better adapted to particular areas than others (Dry and Smart 1986, Ewart and Sitters 1987). Budburst is early, thus predisposing the vines to spring frost damage. The compact bunches are very susceptible to bunch rot but clones with less compact bunches are now available in Australia. The colour of Pinot Noir wines is not intense and fruit from hot areas may make uninteresting wines lacking in colour and flavour (Kerridge *et al.* 1987b). However, in cool areas, the wines can be of excellent quality with a distinctive varietal flavour. [Antcliff 1976b, p. 15].

6.3 Varieties with less than 100 ha

6.3.1 White varieties

Biancone
Biancone is a high yielding variety from Corsica mainly grown in the Riverland (SA). Previously known as White Grenache, it was correctly identified in the 1970s. Apart from its high yield, it has no great merit even though some winemakers claim it is useful for dry white wine.

[Antcliff 1979, p.37]

Cannon Hall Muscat
Cannon Hall Muscat - is grown almost exclusively in the Swan Valley (WA). Originally an English hothouse variety (Antcliff *et al.* 1976) it is mostly used as a tablegrape for both the local and export markets. The Australian area decreased from about 100 ha to 30 ha in the 1980s. It is a seeded, early- to mid-season grape, with a distinctive muscat character (see Volume 2, Chapter 12).

Canocazo
Canocazo was known for many years as False Pedro in South Australia and Common Palomino in the Sunraysia region before being identified as Canocazo. A minor Spanish variety, it is no longer authorized for planting in that country. It produces neutral wine and has mainly been used in Australia for fortified wines and distillation. [Antcliff 1979, p. 15]

Chasselas
Chasselas is the principal variety in Switzerland where it is mainly used for white table wine. It is also an important tablegrape in Europe with about 15,000 ha planted for this purpose in France and widespread plantings in Italy. Chasselas is grown in Alsace (France), Germany, Austria and in eastern Europe for winemaking. The Australian area is small. In Victoria it is used for white table wine and in NSW and WA as a tablegrape. Although its quality as a tablegrape is not high, it matures early and thereby attracts reasonable prices. In cooler areas, Chasselas is used to produce table wine without pronounced varietal character. In hot areas yields are low and the fruit is too low in both sugar and acid to be satisfactory for winemaking (Kerridge *et al.* 1987d).

[Antcliff 1983, p. 27]

Clairette
Clairette is an important variety in the south of France where much of the white table wine is a blend of this variety and Trebbiano. It is also grown in South Africa. In France it is sometimes known as Blanquette and this name has been used in NSW. In Australia, most plantings are found in the Hunter Valley (NSW) and in north-east Victoria. Clairette is a vigorous variety with the young shoots susceptible to wind damage in spring. Although prone to poor set, it is tolerant of oidium and bunchrot. The wines of Clairette tend to oxidize readily; in the absence of oxidation, wines have a distinctive though rather assertive fruity aroma and bouquet.

[Antcliff 1983, p. 29]

Farana
Farana is a variety of Mediterranean origin, known as Planta Pedralba in Spain, Mayorquin in France, Damaschino in Sicily and Farana in Algeria. In Australia, a little is grown in the Barossa Valley where it was formerly known as False Trebbiano. Yield is very high. It is used for both table and fortified wine.

[Antcliff 1983, p. 33]

Italia
Italia is a tablegrape variety derived from a cross between Bicane and Muscat Hamburg. It has been planted widely in southern Europe and California. In Australia the largest plantings are in the Swan Valley (WA) and in Queensland. The berries are large, attractive, yellow-white with a pleasant muscat flavour. It is very susceptible to downy mildew, oidium and bunchrot (see Volume 2, Chapter 12).

Marsanne

Marsanne is a minor French variety from the Rhone Valley. The Australian area is small, mainly found in the Goulburn Valley and north-east of Victoria. Marsanne is vigorous and productive with a spreading growth habit. Table wines from Marsanne have little varietal character and tend to age rapidly. Viognier has similarities.   [Antcliff 1979, p. 35]

Mueller-Thurgau

Mueller-Thurgau is the leading winegrape of Germany with 26,000 ha. Although grown elsewhere in Europe (Hungary 8,000 ha; Austria 6,000 ha; Czechoslovakia 5,000 ha), it is not important in France, there being only a small area in Alsace. It has become the major winegrape in New Zealand with nearly 50 per cent of the crush, in spite of its susceptibility to bunchrot. Mueller-Thurgau was developed as a hybrid of Riesling and Sylvaner (hence the use of the synonym Riesling Sylvaner in New Zealand) but it is now suspected that it may be a seedling of Riesling. It is well suited to cool regions because it ripens very early, and recovers well after frost (the secondary buds are fruitful). However, it is very susceptible to fungal diseases. The table wines of Mueller-Thurgau are pleasant and fruity.

[Antcliff 1976b, p. 31]

Ondenc

Ondenc is a minor French variety grown in different areas of the south west of France under different names which were not recognized as belonging to the same variety until relatively recently, e.g. Piquepout de Moissac in Armagnac and Blanquette in Bordeaux. The situation in Australia has been similarly confused because, until recently, it was known as Irvine's White in Victoria and Sercial in South Australia (Antcliff 1976a). In the mid 1970s there were about 250 ha planted but today the area is probably less than 100 ha because many Ondenc vines were removed at Drumborg and Great Western (Vic.) in the 1980s. In France Ondenc is used for brandy and white table wines. It has been used successfully for sparkling wine in Australia.

[Antcliff 1979, p. 29]

Perlette

Perlette is an early, white, seedless tablegrape. It is a hybrid of Muscat Reine des Vignes and Thompson Seedless (Sultana) from California where it is grown on a large-scale. Most of the Australian plantings are

found in NSW. Cane pruning is usually required to obtain satisfactory yields (see Volume 2, Chapter 12).

Sylvaner

Sylvaner is widely-grown throughout central and eastern Europe. Until recently it was the leading winegrape in Germany but has lost this position and now ranks third to Mueller-Thurgau and Riesling. There are numerous small plantings in Australia but the variety has not been accepted to any extent because of the indifferent quality of its wines here. Sylvaner is capable of producing distinctive wines but they are often neutral in flavour (Kerridge *et al.* 1988). It is high-yielding but susceptible to fungal diseases.   [Antcliff 1979, p. 33]

Taminga

Taminga is a new Australian variety bred by the CSIRO at Merbein (Antcliff 1982). A cross of (Planta Pedralba × Sultana) × Traminer, it is a high-yielding, aromatic white wine grape, particularly suited to hot climatic regions (Kerridge *et al.* 1987c). More than 600 tonnes were produced in 1988, mainly in the Riverland and Sunraysia regions (G.H. Kerridge, pers. comm.). Goyura, Merbein Seedless and Tullilah are other white grapes bred by CSIRO.

6.3.2 Red varieties

Barbera

Barbera is one of the world's most widely-planted grape varieties. It is the most important red winegrape in Italy, with production centred in Piedmont where it accounts for about 50 per cent of the planted area. It is also important in California, particularly in the hot San Joaquin Valley, and in Argentina. The Australian area is small, with the largest plantings in the MIA (NSW) and Riverland (SA). It is particularly suited to mechanical harvesting. The fruit hangs well on the vine, retaining a high acidity even in hot conditions (Kerridge *et al.* 1987a). Barbera wines from moderately cropped vines are usually intensely coloured and astringent.

[Antcliff 1976b, p. 23]

Bastardo

Bastardo is considered one of the better port varieties in Portugal, although it is not as widely-grown as Touriga or Tinta Amarella. It is also grown in a small way in the east of France under the name Trousseau. The area in Australia is small: some in South

Australia where it was previously called Cabernet Gros and a little in north-east Victoria and in NSW. The fruit attains a high sugar concentration which increases even further as berries wilt. It is susceptible to rain damage. Although Bastardo has been used in Australia for red tablewine (as Cabernet Gros) it is best suited for fortified wines.

[Antcliff 1979, p. 57]

Bonvedro

Bonvedro was incorrectly called Carignan in Australia until the 1970s. It is a Portuguese variety also grown in north-east Spain as Cuatendra. In Australia, all but a few hectares are located in South Australia, mostly in the Barossa Valley. The area has declined since the 1970s. It is more susceptible to disease, frost and drought than comparable varieties such as Mataro. Table wines from Bonvedro are low in colour and tannin, and are often used for blending.

[Antcliff 1979, p. 53]

Cabernet Franc

Cabernet Franc is an important variety in the Bordeaux area and in the Loire Valley. The planted areas of Cabernet Franc and Cabernet Sauvignon in France are very similar, but Cabernet Franc is more widely planted in the cooler north. In Italy, it is more highly regarded than Cabernet Sauvignon and planted in more provinces. It is also important in eastern Europe. In Australia, Cabernet Franc is mostly found as odd vines in blocks of Cabernet Sauvignon, a situation which is especially common in north-eastern Victoria. New plantings of Cabernet Franc can now be found in regions such as Coonawarra, Padthaway, Clare, Barossa (SA) and in southern Victoria.

Cabernet Franc is better suited to cool climates than Cabernet Sauvignon: budburst and ripening are earlier. Also, Cabernet Franc may produce better wine than Cabernet Sauvignon in hot climates (Kerridge *et al.* 1987a). Cabernet Franc is more productive than Cabernet Sauvignon, but does not always attain the yields of Merlot, to which it bears a strong resemblance. The wines of Cabernet Franc are of high quality with a distinct varietal character and are softer than Cabernet Sauvignon, with which it is often blended. [Antcliff 1976b, p. 7]

Carignan

Carignan is probably the most important winegrape in the world. In France, it occupies about 16 per cent of the planted area. Like Aramon it is planted entirely in the south and, although less productive, Carignan produces better wines of good colour and average quality. It is said in France that the wines benefit from blending with those of Grenache or Cinsaut to reduce the time required for ageing. It is also an important variety in Spain (where it is known as Mazuela), but not in other European countries. In California it is the most important red winegrape and mainly used for bulk red wines. The Australian area is small.

It has an erect growth habit and is often grown without trellising in France and Spain (see Grenache). Carignan is more susceptible to fungal diseases, particularly oidium, than most varieties, and does best in a hot, sunny, dry climate where high yields are possible. It has some nematode tolerance and the fruit hangs well on the vine after ripening. Carignan gives wines of moderate colour, good tannin and no pronounced varietal character.

[Antcliff 1976b, p. 3]

Carina

Carina is a new variety bred in Australia by the CSIRO and released for commercial use in 1975. It is a small black seedless grape, suitable for drying into currants. It has the distinct advantage over Zante Currant in being resistant to rain damage when the fruit is ripening. It requires treatment with fruit-setting sprays to produce reliable crops (Antcliff 1975b). Carina has also shown promise as a winegrape (Kerridge *et al.* 1987b).

Cinsaut

Cinsaut is a variety from the south of France. Sometimes spelt Cinsault, it is often confused with another distinct variety Oeillade. Occasionally used as a tablegrape, it is regarded as a good winegrape in the south where it is recommended for blending with Carignan. It is the principal red wine variety of South Africa where it was previously called Hermitage. Cinsaut has declined in importance in Australia — most of the remaining vines are located in the Barossa Valley, Rutherglen and MIA regions. It is well-adapted to hot dry conditions. Although susceptible to fungal diseases, the fruit is not easily split by rain when ripe. It is readily harvested mechanically. In Australia it is used for red table wine and port of average quality, often blended with more tannic varieties. [Antcliff 1979, p. 47]

Durif

Durif originates from the Rhone Valley of France and may be a seedling or sport of Peloursin. In fact, the commercial plantings of Durif in north eastern Victoria are a mixture of Durif and Peloursin, as is the so-called Petite Sirah of California. Durif produces wines of intense colour and high tannin requiring long ageing. In Australia it is used for red table wine and port.   [Antcliff 1983, p. 13]

Marroo Seedless

Marroo Seedless is a black, seedless tablegrape bred by the CSIRO. A cross of Carolina Blackrose and Ruby Seedless, it was released for commercial evaluation in the early 1980s. It has medium berries (produced without the use of gibberellic acid; see Volume 2, Chapter 12) and is resistant to downy mildew (Clingeleffer and Possingham 1988).

Meunier

Meunier appears to be a simple sport of Pinot Noir with tetraploid dermal tissue. Commercial plantings in Australia are often a mix of the two varieties. The greatest area of the variety is in France, and mainly in the Champagne region where it makes up 44 per cent of the planted area. It is one of the few red winegrapes grown in Germany. In Australia, where it is often known as Pinot Meunier, plantings are small (less than 20 ha) and mainly located in southern Victoria. It is preferred to Pinot Noir in frost-prone sites because it has later budburst. It also has better set and higher yields than Pinot Noir and ripens slightly later. In France Meunier is blended with Pinot Noir and Chardonnay for champagne. In Australia it is being increasingly used for sparkling wine in the same way, but traditionally has been used for attractive, light, dry red wines.
[Antcliff 1983, p. 21]

Red Prince

Red Prince is a table variety, mainly grown in Western Australia. The berries are large, red and firm-fleshed. Berry thinning is necessary to produce an export-quality product (see Volume 2, Chapter 12).

Ribier

Ribier is a table variety grown in most of the tablegrape-producing regions of Australia. It performs well in Queensland. The berries are large and black (see Volume 2, Chapter 12).

Rubired

Rubired is a hybrid of Tinta Cao and Alicante Ganzin. It was bred in California and released in 1958. Intended as a port wine type, and having red juice, it produces wines of intense colour. This has prompted its use as colouring material for table wines. Three-quarters of the Australian area (38 ha) is planted in the Sunraysia and Kerang-Swan Hill regions of Victoria. The *Vitis rupestris* ancestry of Alicante Ganzin has resulted in Rubired possessing some resistance to fungal diseases.
[Antcliff 1976b, p. 13]

Ruby Cabernet

Ruby Cabernet is a cross between Carignan and Cabernet Sauvignon, bred in California and released in 1948. It has achieved significance in California with a planted area similar to that of Cabernet Sauvignon. It was designed for producing quality red wines in hot areas and shows considerable promise in Australia (Kerridge *et al.* 1987a) although the area planted so far is small. It is susceptible to fungal diseases and unfavourable soil conditions but has performed well on nematode-resistant rootstocks in the Riverland and elsewhere (Nicholas 1985). It is readily harvested mechanically.
[Antcliff 1976b, p. 11]

Tarrango

Tarrango was bred in Australia by the CSIRO and released in 1975. A cross of Touriga and Sultana, it is designed for light, fast-maturing red table wines. The fruit ripens late with good acidity and low pH (Kerridge et al. 1987b). Cane pruning is recommended (Antcliff 1975b).

Tinta Amarella

Tinta Amarella is widely grown in the Douro Valley of Portugal where it is regarded as a good variety for port. There is a small area in South Australia, mainly the Barossa, where it has been known as Portugal in the past. Tinta Amarella has no special attributes as a winegrape and is usually blended with other varieties for port production.
[Antcliff 1979, p. 55]

Touriga

Touriga is the most widely-planted of the best port varieties in the Douro Valley of Portugal. There are small areas in Australia, principally north-east Victoria and the Barossa Valley. It produces fortified wines of excellent colour and flavour and shows promise as a table wine variety (Kerridge *et al.* 1987a).
(Antcliff 1979, p. 59)

Zinfandel

Zinfandel is the most widely-planted red winegrape in California, where it is grown in all regions. It is thought to be the same as Primitivo of Italy and Mali Plavac of Yugoslavia. It is very susceptible to rain damage and bunchrot, hence its usefulness in Australia is likely to be limited to the low autumn rainfall areas such as the Swan Valley (WA) and Riverland (SA). Although yields are good, it ripens unevenly and is difficult to harvest by machine. It is prone to second-cropping and the exposed fruit is liable to sunburn. Zinfandel can produce good quality red wines with a distinct varietal character reminiscent of raspberries. [Antcliff 1976b, p. 27]

6.4 **Concluding remarks**

For the first 150 years Australia's viticulture was primarily based on initial introductions of varieties from southern France and Spain. These suited the predominant use of grapes during this time, that is, fortified wine production and dried fruit. The advent of phylloxera forced the introduction of resistant rootstocks at the end of the nineteenth century, but no significant change was made to the range of vinifera varieties.

The big shift in demand to table wines during the 1960s led to the diversion of some varieties from their former use and the planting of available table wine varieties, often unsuited for this purpose. Further introduction of many varieties during this period led to the evaluation and adoption of a significant number which have proved well-suited to Australian conditions, both for table wine and as tablegrapes; it is likely that this trend will continue for the remainder of this century.

A significant grape breeding program by the CSIRO Division of Horticultural Research has produced several new varieties especially suited to hot regions. There is a need for similar work directed to other regions and for genetic engineering to incorporate single useful genes into present varieties.

Further Reading

Ballantyne, I. and Macrae, I., eds. (1984) Gordo: rootstocks and management. Agric. Note Series No. 143, Dept. Agric. Vic.

Galet, P. (1979) A Practical Ampelography. (Translated by L.T. Morton). Comstock Publishing Assoc., Ithaca, NY.

Geyle, A., ed. (1986) Proc. 2nd. National Table Grape Ind. Tech. Conf., July, 1986; Stanthorpe, Qld.: Qld. Dept. Primary Ind., Agdex No. 243-10.

Gregory, G.R. (1984) Grape Varieties. In: Len Evans Complete Book of Australian Wine, Lansdowne, Sydney, pp. 354-383.

Leamon, K., ed. (1984) Proc. 1st Table Grape Ind. Tech. Conf., 1984; Mildura, Vic.: Agric. Note Series 147, Dept. Agric., Vic.

Other References

Antcliff, A.J. (1975a) A probable identification of Clare Riesling. Aust. Grapegrower & Winemaker No. 141, 16-17.

Antcliff, A.J. (1975b) Four new grape varieties released for testing. J. Aust Inst. Agric. Sci. 41, 262-4.

Antcliff, A.J. (1976a) Variety identification in Australia. A French expert looks at our vines. Aust. Grapegrower & Winemaker No. 153, 10-11.

Antcliff, A.J. (1976b) Some Wine Grape Varieties for Australia (Melbourne: CSIRO), 62 pp.

Antcliff, A.J. (1979) Major Wine Grape Varieties of Australia (Melbourne: CSIRO), 62 pp.

Antcliff, A.J. (1982) Taminga: a new white winegrape with varietal character J. Aust. Inst. Agric. Sci. 48, 161-2.

Antcliff, A.J. (1983) Minor Wine Grape Varieties. (Melbourne: CSIRO), 64 pp.

Antcliff, A.J., Skene, K.G. and Possingham, J.V. (1976) The Cannon Hall Muscat Grape. Vitis 15, 1-4.

Australian Bureau of Statistics (1988) Viticulture Australia, 1986-87. Catalogue No. 7310.0, Canberra.

Boehm, E.W. and Tulloch, H.W. (1967) Grape varieties of South Australia. S.A. Dept. of Agric., Adelaide.

Clingeleffer, P.R. (1983) Sultana vine management. Aust. Grapegrower Winemaker No. 232, 7-17.

Clingeleffer, P.R. and Possingham, J.V. (1988) Marroo Seedless: a new tablegrape variety. Agric. Science, N.S. 1(2), 18-19.

Dry, P.R., and Smart, R.E. (1986) Clonal variability of Pinot Noir. Aust. Grapegrower & Winemaker No. 272, 14.

Ewart, A.J.W. and Sitters, J.H. (1987) Oenological parameters for the selection of Pinot Noir and Chardonnay. In: Lee, T.H., (ed.) Aspects of grapevine improvement in Australia: proceedings of a seminar; 20 November; Canberra, A.C.T.: Australian Society of Viticulture and Oenology; Adelaide, S.A.; pp. 77-84.

Kerridge, G.H., Clingeleffer, P.R. and Possingham, J.V. (1987a) Varieties and varietal wines from the Merbein grape germplasm collection. I. Varieties producing full-bodied red wines. Aust. Grapegrower & Winemaker No. 277, 14-18.

Kerridge, G.H., Clingeleffer, P.R. and Possingham, J.V. (1987b) Varieties and varietal wines from the Merbein grape germplasm collection. II. Varieties producing light-bodied red wines. Aust. Grapegrower & Winemaker No. 279, 14-19.

Kerridge, G.H., Clingeleffer, P.R. and Possingham, J.V. (1987c) Varieties and varietal wines from the Merbein grape germplasm collection. III. Varieties producing aromatic white wines. Aust. Grapegrower & Winemaker No. 280, 29-34.

Kerridge, G.H., Clingeleffer, P.R. and Possingham, J.V. (1987d) Varieties and varietal wines from the Merbein grape germplasm collection. IV. Varieties producing delicate white wines. Aust. Grapegrower & Winemaker No. 283, 17-23.

Kerridge, G.H., Clingeleffer, P.R. and Possingham, J.V. (1988) Varieties and varietal wines from the Merbein grape germplasm collection. V. Varieties producing full-bodied white wines. Aust. Grapegrower & Winemaker No. 292, 31-35.

Nicholas, P.R. (1985) Selection of varieties and rootstocks for quality cask wine production in the Riverland. In: Lester, D.C. and Lee, T.D. eds. Irrigation, Salinity and Grape Quality: proceedings of a seminar; 2 November, 1984; Loxton, S.A.: Australian Society of Viticulture and Oenology, Adelaide, pp. 51-60.

Orrfer, C.J. (ed.) (1979) Wine Grape Cultivars in South Africa. Human and Rousseau, Cape Town and Pretoria.

Robinson, J. (1986) Vines, Grapes and Wines; Mitchell Beazley.

Truel, P., Rennes, C. and Domergue, P. (1980) Identifications in collections of grapevines. Proc. 3rd Int. Symp. on Grape Breeding, June 15-18, Davis, Calif., USA: Dept. of Vitic. and Enol., Univ. Calif., Davis, pp. 78-86.

Viala, P. and Vermorel, V. (1909) Ampelographie. 7 volumes. Masson, Paris.

Whiting, J. and Godden, G. (1988) Grapevine clonal assessment in Victoria: Cabernet Sauvignon, Riesling and Chardonnay. Aust. Grapegrower & Winemaker No. 292, 18-20.

Witcombe, R. (1979) Is there money in drying Shiraz? Aust. Grapegrower & Winemaker No. 182, 15-16.

Zuur, D. (1988) Ampelographic problems in New Zealand. Proc. 2nd. Int. Symp. for Cool Climate Viticulture and Oenology, Auckland, NZ, pp. 30-33.

CHAPTER SEVEN

Grape Phenology

B. G. COOMBE

Phenology is the study of natural phenomena that recur periodically in plants and animals, and of the relationship of these phenomena to climate and changes in season. It aims to describe the causes of variation in timing by seeking correlations between weather indices and the dates of particular growth events and the intervals between them. Such information helps in the understanding of how living things react to the weather and in predicting their behaviour in new environments. For perennial plants like the grapevine most emphasis is given to its growth and development during each annual cycle.

Phenological data are essential for making good decisions during many phases of grapegrowing, for example: selecting a vineyard site, designing the plantings, planning of labour, equipment and cash requirements throughout each year, and determining the best timing of vineyard operations such as soil management, irrigation, pest and disease control, canopy management, harvesting, etc. Such data also provide a basis for correlative studies with factors of weather and climate to gauge the behaviour of individual varieties and for predicting their behaviour in new grape regions (see Chapter 10 on Site Selection).

7.1 Annual growth cycles of the grapevine

Most of the cultivated species of *Vitis* originated in parts of North America, Europe and Western Asia and developed the characteristics of deciduous, temperate, woody perennials (Chapter 5). Seedlings of these plants display extensive genetic variation which, with deliberate hybridization, is used for the genetic improvement of grape varieties. However, the grape has been adapted for cultivation by the simple process of vegetative propagation using rooted cuttings, or by the budding or grafting of scions on to rooted cuttings of rootstock varieties (Chapters 8 and 9). The root systems of cultivated grapes are not derived from seeds but from the adventitious roots formed at the base of cuttings; thus, unlike many other cultivated fruits, variation between individual vines and vineyards cannot be attributed to genetic variation in roots.

The events in the vegetative and reproductive cycles of the grapevine are shown in a generalized timetable in Figure 7.1 (and some are illustrated in Kasimatis 1981). Following an initially slow growth of shoots after budburst there is a massive growth of vegetative tissues during late spring which has been termed the *grand period of growth*. Lateral shoots form readily on vigorous shoots adding to the general leafiness. Unless the pruning is light and the training expansive, the vine can be dense and heavily-shaded inside with undesirable consequences for initiation, setting, ripening and the occurrence of pests and diseases. Shoot lengthening slows in mid-summer but without the terminal bud formation that is common with many deciduous trees; instead the shoot tip abscises.

Grapevines differ from deciduous trees in that the spring flush of root growth occurs some weeks after budburst, rather than before. Additionally, the reproductive cycle of growth shows distinctive features: initiation of inflorescences and flowering

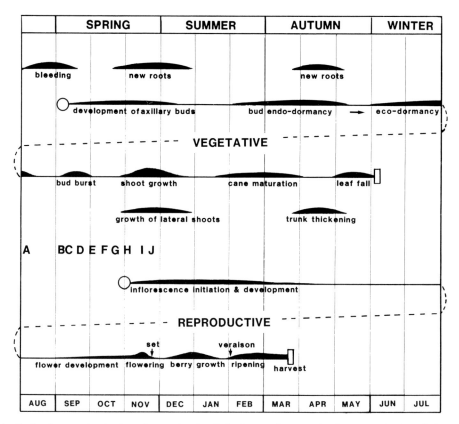

Figure 7.1. Cycle of vegetative (top) and reproductive (below) growth events in the grapevine in relation to months of the year (southern hemisphere). Each cycle begins at the circle and ends at the rectangle. The letters A to J refer to the developmental stages described in Figure 7.3.

and fruit setting occur in late spring, in the middle of the grand period of growth. The fact that these two events, initiation and flowering, occur at about the same time means that the interval between them occupies one full year i.e. flowering culminates a long and slow development of the inflorescences and flowers beginning at the initiation of the inflorescence primordium one year before. Berry setting, which is usually the only abscission episode of flowers and berries, begins the fruit development period occupying 10-20 weeks. Fruit development has two distinct cycles: the first, coinciding with the latter part of the shoot growth flush, takes the berries to the hard, green, slow-growing phase; during the second cycle, beginning at veraison, berry ripening processes occur. While berries ripen, the shoot stems lignify and become canes, the buds become dormant, and some basal leaves abscise. Then the woody tissues, trunks and roots expand in girth, and a second flush of root growth occurs. Finally, leaves fall as winter approaches.

These growth cycles bring about large mass changes in the vine during the course of each year, a fact which must be accounted for in the training of the vineyard. The nature of fresh weight changes are illustrated in Figure 7.2; Conradie (1980) has published a similar figure based on measured values of dry mass. The range of quantities of different grapevine organs found per square metre of commercial vineyard is given in Table 7.1.

Over and above the annual changes, there are long-term ageing changes in the structural roots and tops which have not been recorded in Australia; there is a need for an analysis of grapevine ageing similar to that done for peach trees by Chalmers and van den Ende (1975).

7.2 Timing and duration of grapevine developmental events

All of the developmental events mentioned above are subject to variations in timing according to

**Table 7.1 Quantities of different grapevine parts in commercial vineyards.
Expressed per square metre of total land surface***

Part	Units	Range of commercial values		
		Low	Median	High
Pruning weight	kg per m²	0.03	0.3	1.0
Nodes retained at pruning	nodes per m²	3	10	30
Number of shoots	shoots per m²	2.5	8	25
Total leaf area	m² per m²	0.5	2	5
Number of bunches	bunches per m²	5	25	50
Crop weight	kg per m²	0.2	1.3	5
Equivalent volume of table wine	L per m²	0.12	0.8	3

* Multiplication factors to convert from amount per m²:
(a) × (space per vine in m²) gives *amount per vine* e.g. × 7 gives amount per vine in a vineyard spaced 2 ×3.5 m.
(b) × 4047 gives *amount per acre.*
(c) × 10,000 gives *amount per hectare.*

Some approximate conversion factors:

kg per m²	× 4	gives tonnes per acre	
	× 10	gives tonnes per hectare	
	× 100	gives quintals per hectare (used in Italy).	
L per m²	× 4	gives kilolitres per acre	
	× 10	gives kilolitres per hectare	
	× 100	gives hectolitres per hectare (used in France).	
hL per ha	÷ 6	gives tonnes per hectare	

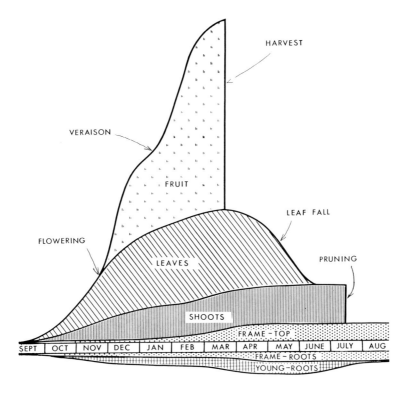

Figure 7.2. Yearly cycle of accumulation and loss of fresh matter on one mature grapevine.

141

Table 7.2. Dates of budburst, flowering and harvest of 11 grape varieties in 12 districts of Australia. *

	Sultana	Riesling	Semillon	Shiraz	Palomino	Cabernet Sauvignon	Grenache	Muscat Gordo	Waltham Cross	Trebbiano	Doradillo	Median Dates
Budburst date (days after 31 August)												
Cessnock NSW		16	12	15		19				15	18	15 Sept
Swan Valley WA	9	6	1	8		16	12	18	16			12 Sept
Griffith NSW	9	16	20	19	18	20	21	26	25	27	23	20 Sept
Mildura Vic.	1	11	7	12	14		10	8	14		16	10 Sept
Loxton SA	3		16	8	13	13	8	18	23	18	17	15 Sept
Adelaide SA		5	14	5	4	21	5			5	7	9 Sept
Rutherglen Vic.		24		25	29	28	31		33	32		30 Sept
Nuriootpa SA		7	21	8	16	20	13	24		25	14	16 Sept
Swan Hill Vic.	12			17	16		10	20	28		19	18 Sept
Eden Valley SA	6	18		20							19	19 Sept
Coonawarra SA		26	24	16	20	31	26				31	21 Sept
Tabilk Vic.		11		28		16				17		17 Sept
Median Dates (Sept)	8	12	14	14	15	20	14	20	22	19	18	16 Sept
Flowering date (days after 31 October)												
Cessnock NSW		4	6	6		8				12		7 Nov
Swan Valley WA	15	10	8	9		12	14	16	19			13 Nov
Griffith NSW	8	10	10	13	11	18	11	18	8	21	13	13 Nov
Mildura Vic.	8		4	5	11		7	13	11		11	9 Nov
Loxton SA	11	1	8	3	14	6	5	12	14	19	12	10 Nov
Adelaide SA		18	20	21	21	20	20			21	20	20 Nov
Rutherglen Vic.		28		23	28	24	26		35	32		29 Nov
Nuriootpa SA		20	20	20	23	21	21	24		27	20	22 Nov
Swan Hill Vic.	18			16	19		15	20	24		20	19 Nov
Eden Valley SA		26		35								2 Dec
Coonawarra SA		26	28	30	28	33	29				30	30 Nov
Tabilk Vic.		34		31		30					33	2 Dec
Median Dates (Nov)	14	13	14	15	17	16	15	19	20	22	17	17 Nov
Harvest date (days after 31 January)												
Cessnock NSW		18	16	26						57		28 Feb
Swan Valley WA		39	41	51		56		31	29			10 Mar
Griffith NSW	17		22	32	36	55	51	58	38	49	66	15 Mar
Mildura Vic.	24			30	55		45	50	62		85	20 Mar
Loxton SA	36		42		47		52	71	76	66	88	21 Mar
Adelaide SA		30	46	38	33	33	62			46	67	20 Mar
Rutherglen Vic.		48	49	44	63	31	55					21 Mar
Nuriootpa SA		61	55	36	52	51	52	63		74	53	27 Mar
Swan Hill Vic.	24			38				50	74	85	89	29 Mar
Eden Valley SA		65		68								5 Apr
Coonawarra SA		50	63	71	59	54	89					6 Apr
Tabilk VIC		65		65		81					83	11 Apr
Median dates (Mar)	2	17	18	19	21	24	31	(Apr) 1	7	8	18	24 Mar

* Compiled from records collected during 1966 to 1970 by 12 cooperators organized and guided by P. May, CSIRO Division of Horticultural Research. The values in the body of the tables are medians of the year values and those at the base and right-hand side are medians of medians (calculated by O. Mayo, Biometry Section, Waite Agricultural Research Institute); they are arranged within each of the three tables in the order shown by the median harvest dates of varieties and districts.

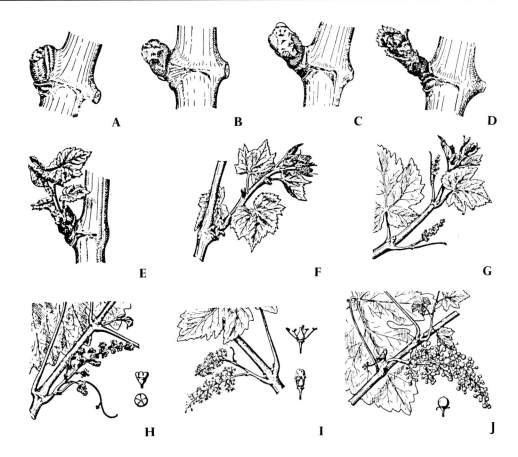

Figure 7.3. Developmental stages of the grapevine described by Baggiolini (1952) and copied from Eggenberger et al. (1975). The stages are:

A Winter bud: Main bud in the winter dormant state covered with two brown protective scales.

B Budswell or woolly bud: The scales are separating as the bud swells revealing brown woolly hairs.

C Green tip: The bud swells further showing the tip of the young green shoot.

D Leaf emergence: A rosette of young leaves appears. The scales and wool are still obvious.

E Leaf unfolding: The shoot becomes clear and the first leaf blades are completely free. Varietal characteristics are evident.

F Inflorescence visible: The inflorescence primordia become visible at the shoot tip. Four to six leaves are unfolded.

G Inflorescences separated: The inflorescences grow and enlarge but the flowers are still clumped.

H Flowers separated: The inflorescence attains its typical form and individual unopened flowers separate. The drawing shows single flowers from the top and side.

I Flowering: Calyptras (caps) fall and expose the ovary and five stamens.

J Setting: Ovaries which have set commence growth but dried stamens still adhere. The new berries already display some varietal characteristics.

variety, region and season. Many of them are inter-correlated and a good general time picture of development in any vineyard can be gained from key events such as budburst, flowering, veraison and harvest. However it is a pity that key events in vegetative growth are not also recorded routinely.

There are no extensive and detailed data on grape phenology in Australia and there is an urgent need for them. McIntyre (1982) has reviewed the limited published work, mostly being recordings of budburst, flowering and harvest in specific grape regions. In his discussion of procedures he has made the valuable suggestion that medians are more useful than means since they reduce the undue influence of extreme values.

There is only one set of data that attempts to

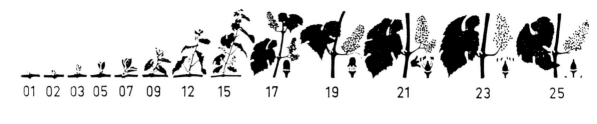

01 02 03 05 07 09 12 15 17 19 21 23 25

27 29 31 33 35 38 41 43 47

Figure 7.4. Phenological stages recommended for German viticulture by Eichhorn and Lorenz (1977). The stage descriptions are as follows:

01. Winter rest, buds 'Romanesque shaped', light to dark-brown and more or less closed, depending on variety.
02. Bud swelling, primordia enlarging inside.
03. Wool stage, brown wool clearly visible.
05. Bud breaking, first green of shoot visible.
07. First leaf unfolded and separating from shoot tip.
09. Two to three leaves unfolded.
12. Five to six leaves unfolded, inflorescence clearly visible.
15. Inflorescence enlarging, single flowers in compact groups.
17. Inflorescence fully developed, single flowers separated.

19. Beginning of flowering, first flower caps loosening from receptacles.
21. Early flowering, 25% of flower caps detached.
23. Full bloom, 50% of flower caps detached.
25. Ending of flowering, 80% of flower caps detached.
27. Fruit set, ovaries enlarging, undeveloped ovaries abscised.
29. Berries buck-shot size, bunches begin to hang down.
31. Berries pea-size, bunches hanging down.
33. Beginning of bunch closure (berries touching).
35. Beginning of ripening, berries start to change colour.
38. Berries ripe (harvest ripe).
41. After harvest, wood maturation complete.
43. Beginning of leaf fall.
47. End of leaf fall.

cover, in one survey, a large number of Australian districts. These results, previously unpublished, are used here despite the fact that they contain some values that appear to be in error, no doubt due to the circumstances under which they were obtained. This survey covered 13 varieties in 14 districts during 5 years; median dates from the 5 years are shown for budburst, flowering and harvest in Table 7.2. Additional data are shown in Tables 7.3–7.5 and Figures 7.5 and 7.6. All of the data refer to normal vineyard conditions; special conditions are considered separately in Section 7.2.5.

7.2.1 Definition of stages

An important contribution to the study of grapevine phenology was the description of ten readily identifiable stages of development, A to J, between budburst and setting, by Baggiolini in 1952 (Figure 7.3). Peterson added five more stages (K, veraison; L, cane hardening; M, harvest; N, leaf colouring and O, leaf fall) as shown in Figure 7.4. A more elaborate

listing of 47 stages between budswell and harvest has been described by Eichhorn and Lorenz (1977); 22 of these stages are illustrated in Figure 7.4.

For the present purposes Baggiolini's system will be followed. The key stages are defined as follows:

(i) budburst (B): woolly bud stage in 60 per cent of buds i.e. buds swollen and scales opened enough to show brown woolly hairs.

(ii) flowering (I): flower caps fallen from 50-75 per cent of flowers on the majority of bunches; turgid stamens prominent.

(iii) veraison (K): change in berry colour from green; berries commence softening and sugar accumulation.

(iv) ripeness (M): when juice from berry samples attains 20° Brix (11.5°Be).

7.2.2 Varieties

In most Australian vineyards budburst occurs during September, flowering during November and December, and harvest from February to May. The

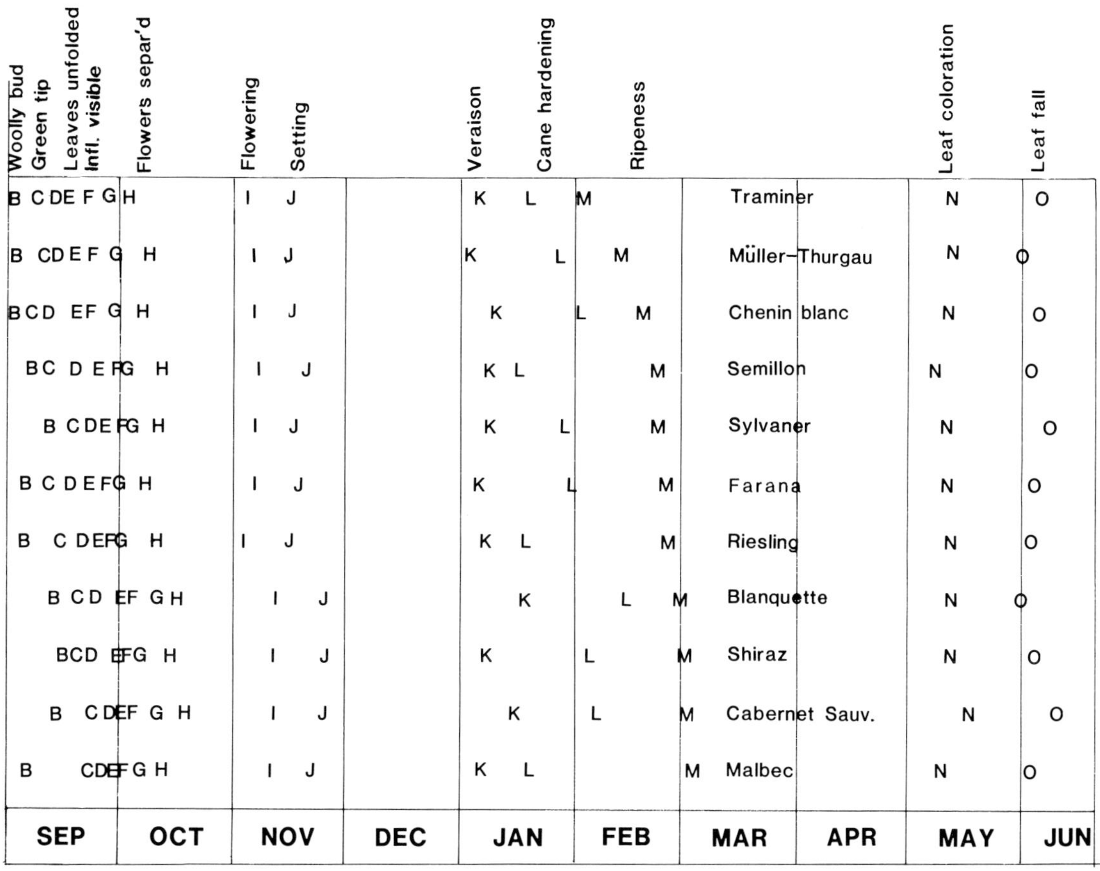

Woolly bud / Green tip / Leaves unfolded / Infl. visible	Flowers separ'd	Flowering	Setting	Veraison	Cane hardening	Ripeness	Variety	Leaf coloration	Leaf fall
B C DE F G H	I	J		K L	M		Traminer	N	O
B CDEF G H	I	J		K	L	M	Müller-Thurgau	N	O
BCD EF G H	I	J		K	L	M	Chenin blanc	N	O
BC D EFG H	I	J		K L		M	Semillon	N	O
B CDEFG H	I	J		K	L	M	Sylvaner	N	O
B C DEFG H	I	J		K	L	M	Farana	N	O
B C DEFG H	I	J		K L		M	Riesling	N	O
B CD EF G H	I	J		K	L	M	Blanquette	N	O
BCD EFG H	I	J		K	L	M	Shiraz	N	O
B C DEF G H	I	J		K	L	M	Cabernet Sauv.	N	O
B CDEF G H	I	J		K L		M	Malbec	N	O
SEP	**OCT**	**NOV**	**DEC**	**JAN**	**FEB**	**MAR**	**APR**	**MAY**	**JUN**

Figure 7.5. Dates of 14 growth stages in each of 11 grape varieties growing at Griffith Viticultural Station, NSW, recorded during three seasons (1970-1, 1972-3 and 1983-4) (J. Peterson, unpublished data).

median dates for the eleven varieties shown in Table 7.2 show a range for varieties within each district of about two weeks for budburst, one week for flowering, but seven weeks for harvest. Flowering dates within a year or district are surprisingly constant between varieties. Because of this, variations in the interval from budburst to flowering are attributable more to varying date of budburst, the shorter periods being years of late budburst.

The phenological data from Griffith shown in Figure 7.5 displays the general timing of other developmental stages of several varieties in relation to budburst, flowering and harvest. This diagram shows that early budburst is a feature of some varieties commonly used in cold regions of Europe. At Pipers Brook, Tas., Chardonnay bursts its buds a month before Riesling and Cabernet Sauvignon (6 September versus 8 October), whereas their flowering and harvest occur within a week of each other (A. Pirie, pers. comm.). Under Australian conditions early budburst can present problems where spring frosts occur.

Figure 7.5 also shows that the most uniform events between the different varieties were flowering, leaf colouration and leaf fall. McIntyre et al. (1982) also report a narrow range for date of flowering between varieties at Davis, California. In addition, their study showed that Semillon had dates of budburst, flowering and harvest that were close to the average of the dates of 114 varieties planted together. However, not all varieties behaved uniformly; Cabernet Sauvignon, for example, had a later-than-average budburst but an earlier harvest while, on the other hand, Almeria (Ohanez) had an earlier-than-average budburst but a later harvest.

Variations in harvest date are due to differences in the interval from flowering to harvest (because of the above-mentioned uniformity of flowering date between varieties within a district): this interval varies hugely between varieties—from 70 to 170 days (10 to 24 weeks)—although for most varieties used in Australia the value is 125 ± 15 days. At Griffith the interval for Traminer is 90 days compared with 110 ± 3 days for eight other varieties (Figure 7.5).

Table 7.3 Harvest dates (± standard error) of six varieties at Merbein, Victoria (from data in Kerridge *et al.* 1987).

Variety	Number of years*	Mean harvest date	S.E. (days)
Traminer	9	6 Feb	± 3
Chardonnay	10	10 Feb	± 3
Pinot Noir	7	13 Feb	± 2
Riesling	12	21 Feb	± 3
Shiraz	11	27 Feb	± 4
Cabernet Sauvignon	14	3 Mar	± 3

* Between 1971 and 1986.

Harvest dates of three long-used winegrape varieties at Merbein cover the 2-week period, 21 February - 3 March, while that of some 'newer' varieties were considerably earlier, viz. 6-13 February (Table 7.3); of 84 varieties from the Merbein grape germplasm collection the earliest harvest period reported was for Morio Muscat (late January) and the latest (early April) for an Argentinian-bred variety, CG 26.879 (Kerridge *et al.* 1987). Viala and Vermorel (1909) report that some varieties have a late veraison but an early harvest.

Relative to each other, varieties may behave differently in different districts. The harvest date of Cabernet Sauvignon is later than that of Shiraz at Griffith and Nuriootpa, but earlier than Shiraz at Coonawarra (Table 7.2). Riesling ripens earlier than Shiraz in warm regions (MJT of 21-23°C) but later than Shiraz in cool regions (MJT of 18-20°C) (Dry 1984). These differences accord with other reports, although more detailed recordings are needed to establish their statistical significance.

7.2.3 Region and district

Despite the uncertainties in the data, Table 7.2 shows that, between districts, averaged over all varieties, budburst occurred during three weeks in September, flowering during the whole of November and into December, and harvest occupied a wide period from late February to late April. This general picture contrasts sharply with that for varietal differences in showing a wide range for flowering date; six weeks between districts compared with one week between varieties within each district.

Other compilations of district differences are shown in Figures 7.6 and 10.2. The former shows the median dates of budburst, flowering and ripeness, and the intervals between them, for a wide array of Australian grape environments. The extreme earliness of harvest in Alice Springs is not due to an early budburst but to the brief intervals from budburst to flowering and flowering to harvest. On the other hand, lateness of harvest has a number of different causes: lateness of budburst (Rutherglen), a long interval between budburst and flowering (Drumborg), and a long interval from flowering to harvest (Hobart). The interval between flowering and harvest does not vary as much between districts as between varieties; the range shown in Figure 7.6 (excluding the earliest and latest) covers 107 to 137 days. In northern parts of Europe, where budburst and flowering are later, this interval is shorter, e.g. 100 days in Bordeaux.

The march of development of grapevines does not follow in strict proportion under all conditions. The order of the median dates of budburst shown in different districts is not the same as the order of flowering dates (see right-hand side of Table 7.2 and also Figure 7.6). Another example is provided by the differences in amount of development of Shiraz shoots in different districts on the same day, compared with the average date of harvest (Table 7.4); although there are general similarities in order, especially in the warmer regions in the top half of the table, there are notable discrepancies: Mudgee and Nuriootpa have earlier harvests than their 1 November shoot growth might indicate while Coonawarra and Drumborg have later harvests. Given the differences between districts in the way the weather unfolds, these variations are not surprising.

7.2.4 Years

In individual vineyards, budburst and flowering dates may vary between years by several weeks (though rarely more than a month); the greatest range is shown by varieties that ripen early or late rather than mid-season (Figure 7.8). However, harvest date displays considerable variation, by up to two months (these data are not seen in the median values in Tables 7.2 and 7.5): large variations in harvest date between years are shown by Riesling, Cabernet Sauvignon and Trebbiano, but those for Semillon and Muscat Gordo were small. Another illustration of this variation is provided by ripeness data of the same Grenache vines : juice samples reached 21°

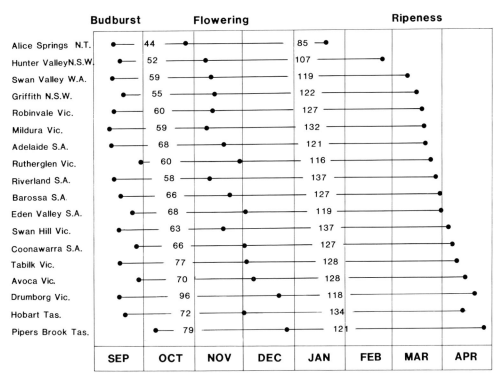

Figure 7.6. Generalized dates of budburst, flowering and ripeness, together with the intervening days, for 18 districts representing a wide array of Australian grape environments. The data include information from the Survey, A.J.G. Pirie pers. comm., and Smart et al. (1980).

Brix on 14 April, 22 February, 15 March and 11 March in the four successive years 1975 to 1978 (Coombe and Iland 1987). They suggested that much of this variation was due to varied date of veraison.

Within any one year the stages do not necessarily vary in the same direction; e.g. in 1967, harvest was early but budburst was late, while in 1969, budburst was early and harvest was late (Table 7.5). The variation between years is about the same whether comparing districts or varieties except for occasional unusual events: for example, several districts had strikingly early budburst and flowering dates in 1969, especially in Tabilk, Vic.; undoubtedly some feature of that season's weather was responsible.

Varieties differ in the stability of their phenology under different conditions. The example already stated of the greater stability of harvest date of Cabernet Sauvignon compared with Shiraz can be quantified as a characteristic of varieties if good records are available over a number of years. Calo *et al.* (1975) have calculated 'stability indices' for a large number of varieties in Conegliano, northern Italy. No such study has yet been done in Australia.

7.2.5 Special growing conditions
The phenology of grapevines may be greatly different when they are grown under special conditions e.g. under different pruning treatments, or when grown under glass or in tropical environments.

Effect of pruning treatments
Late pruning in the spring, after budburst has commenced (as is sometimes done in frost-prone areas), may delay the bursting of the buds left after spur pruning by up to three weeks and flowering by one week compared with normal mid-winter pruning. Double pruning has a very large effect on phenological dates: for instance Shiraz vines repruned on 14 December, when berries were about 8 mm diameter, had budburst, flowering and harvest dates of 21 December, 25 January and 6 May compared with normal dates of 12 September, 6 November and 14 February. Note that double pruning reduced the interval from budburst to flowering from 55 days to 35 days but had no effect on that from flowering to harvest (102 versus 100 days) (Dry 1987).

Table 7.4 Number of visible internodes[1] on shoots of Shiraz grapevines on 1 November, 1975, compared with harvest dates[2] (long-term district averages)

District	Number of internodes	Harvest dates
Hunter Valley NSW	19[3]	20 Feb
Griffith NSW		1 Mar
Swan Valley WA	13.5	1 Mar
Mildura Vic.		1 Mar
Robinvale Vic.		3 Mar
Swan Hill Vic.	13	9 Mar
Adelaide SA		9 Mar
McLaren Vale SA	11.5	12 Mar
Barooga NSW		18 Mar
Cowaramup WA	11	2 Apr
Mudgee NSW		9 Mar
Coonawarra SA	10.5	8 Apr
Milawa Vic.		20 Mar
Frankland River WA		-
Drumborg Vic.	10	24 Apr
Nuriootpa SA		12 Mar
Tabilk Vic.	9.5	5 Apr
Great Western Vic.		1 Apr
Clare SA	9	1 Apr

1. Numbers of internodes longer than 7 mm (pencil thickness) on the majority of shoots of winter-pruned vines.
2. Data collected by the author plus some harvest dates from P.R. Dry, R.E. Smart and A.J.G. Pirie.
3. These vines were flowering.

Table 7.5 Dates of budburst, flowering and harvest of grapevines during five successive years. Values are medians of medians from the same data from 11 varieties in 12 districts shown in Table 7.2.

	1966	1967	1968	1969	1970
Budburst date in Sep	17	18	18	11	14
Flowering date in Nov	20	12	18	14	20
Harvest date in Mar	25	17	25	31	18

Glasshouse grapes
The culture of some early table grape varieties in glasshouses with early pruning and cyanamide treatment may bring about budburst in June, flowering in September and harvest in November in contrast with 'outside' vines where the corresponding dates are September, November and

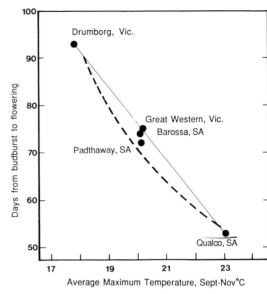

Figure 7.7. Relationship between days from budburst to flowering and average daily maximum temperatures (°C) during September, October and November in five grape regions calculated from data in Heinze (1977). The dashed line represented the plot which would follow a temperature summation value of 625 degree days using a base temperature of 11.2°C.

February. Similar behaviour is being found in hot, northerly regions in Queensland and Northern Territory.

Tropical grapes
In tropical environments, with an absence of cold temperatures, plants like the grapevine behave as evergreens with a continuous but desultory emergence of shoots and production of fruit throughout the year. If such vines are defoliated or pruned there is a synchronization of budburst, flowering and cropping with a timing predetermined by the date of the initial treatment. In this way, two or more crops can be obtained each 12 months. In an Australian example (Anon. 1987), table grapes near Townsville, Qld, are being harvested in September.

7.3 Correlations with weather factors

In view of the many examples that point to a relationship between the weather and grapevine development it is understandable that attempts have been made to seek correlations between them. Correlations can be made between dates and

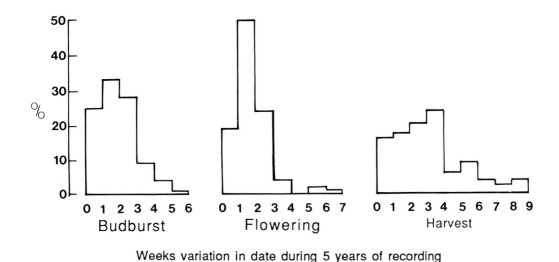

Figure 7.8. *Distribution histograms, in week intervals, of the amount of variation between years (1966-70) in the dates of budburst, flowering and harvest. Calculated from the five years of data of the records summarized in Table 7.2.*

durations, on the one hand, and selected climatic or weather factors on the other. Significant correlations, even excellent ones, do not prove anything; they only indicate associations.

It should always be borne in mind that the particular growth event being measured may itself be correlated with another event which may be the one being influenced by the weather factor. For example, the formation of new nodes on shoots is closely correlated with the development of flowers such that anthesis (full bloom) occurs when the shoot has 17 to 18 visible internodes (Pratt and Coombe 1978). Does a correlation between, say, flowering date and a temperature index indicate that temperature influences flowering, or is it node formation that is being influenced?

The reverse problem also occurs, namely that the particular weather factor being quantified may be correlated with another factor that may in fact be the more realistic controller. Nevertheless, correlations are worth seeking since they lead to ideas that may be investigated by other methods, and because they may help in predicting vine behaviour in different seasons and regions.

Most of the work correlating grape phenology with weather has dealt with the timing of the major growth events—budburst, flowering, veraison and harvest. Often this is done for one region or site using weather variations between years as one of the correlates; however, the general value of a

correlation depends on its applicability to a wide array of environments. Similarly the data may be more meaningful if the weather records are taken adjacent to the vines being measured (McIntyre 1982).

There is a large body of literature which discusses differences in quality of wine made from grapes grown in different regions. The popular view is that highest quality table wines derive from cool regions while table wines from hot regions have, in general, poorer aroma, taste and balance. These differences are attributed to the effects of temperature. A statement by Becker (1977) embodying these thoughts is quoted in Chapter 4, section 4.2.2.

In commenting on the scientific validity of such conclusions Coombe (1987) has pointed to the possibility that correlations with other climatic factors may be equally valid and that general conclusions between regions may be confounded with factors unrelated to the weather in the vineyard during the growing season, such as differences in stage of harvesting and in vinification conditions. Also, the quality of some winegrapes is clearly favoured by warmer temperatures. From present information, caution is necessary in drawing conclusions about the role of temperature *per se* in determining the composition and quality of winegrapes. Nevertheless temperature is clearly a key environmental factor for viticulture and most of the correlative work done has been with various forms of temperature index; these, and some non-temperature indices, are discussed below.

7.3.1 Heat degree days

The heat-unit concept was developed to calculate the interval between planting and harvest of annual crops. When applied to winegrapes in California, heat degree days gave a useful correlation with wine styles (Amerine and Winkler 1944) and the system has since become widely adopted in many countries for the classification of regions (see Chapters 2 and 4 and note the suggestion that MJT is a possible alternative). Its use for the calculation of correlations with grapevine phenological development has not been as extensive.

The best example has been the finding that, under Californian conditions, specific varieties in different seasons and regions have a constant number of heat units (mean temperature $> 10^{\circ}C$) accumulated during the days between flowering and harvest (Winkler *et al.* 1974) : $900^{\circ}C$ units for early varieties and 1650 for late. However McIntyre *et al.* (1987) dispute this result for Californian conditions and claim that number of days is as accurate a measure of this interval as heat days. Workers in other countries, including Australia, have also found that heat units are not constant for this interval (Coombe 1987). Some improvement has been found when units are calculated with different base temperatures, or by discounting temperatures above an upper threshold (as is done in calculating 'corn heat units').

Heat degree days have been calculated for the interval from budburst to flowering: Boehm (1970) found that summations were more nearly constant if the units were calculated with a base of $8^{\circ}C$ rather than $10^{\circ}C$. It is now considered that numbers of days or other functions of temperature over this period are often less variable as indicators than degree days (McIntyre 1982, McIntyre *et al.* 1987).

7.3.2 Other temperature functions

The most commonly used functions of temperature are calculated from daily maxima and minima, often the average of the two. The results below are discussed in three parts relating to the work on budburst, flowering and harvest. Reference is made to some as yet unpublished work (G.R. Due, M.M. Morris and B.G. Coombe, pers. comm.) wherein the survey data summarized in Table 7.2 has been compared by regression analysis with weather data from neighbouring meteorological stations. In this,

temperatures were expressed as averages of daily maxima, daily minima, daily means and daily range (maximum—minimum). The averages were calculated for a long period (of about two months) and a short period (the last 10 days) before the events of budburst, flowering and harvest; regressions were also done for the two intervals between these events. In the last of the four years of data, 9 am readings of dry and wet bulb temperatures were also analysed. This work is referred to here as the Survey.

Budburst

There is ample evidence that budburst date is hastened by higher temperatures during the latter part of winter, with temperatures calculated either as daily max. (Antcliff and Webster 1955, Baldwin 1966, McIntyre 1982) or as daily means (Alleweldt and Hofäcker 1975, Pouget 1967). Similarly, in the Survey most variance was accounted for, during four years in all districts and varieties, by mean temperatures after 1 August and, to a lesser extent, maximum temperatures during the last 10 days. The importance of long-term warmth is supported by the finding that budburst is earlier when soil at 20 cm depth is warmer (Alleweldt and Hofäcker 1975). Comparing four Australian districts, Heinze (1977) considers that altitude and proximity to the sea are more influential than latitude. Varieties which burst early are considered by Pouget (1968) to be those with a low temperature threshold.

Flowering

The fact that flowering of most varieties is quite uniform within a region, although it varies between regions and years (7.2.2 and 7.2.3), is probably attributable to the unifying effect of the onset of spring heat in each region/year.

Winkler *et al.* (1974) state that flowering in California happens when mean daily temperature rises to $20^{\circ}C$; but this is not the case in Australia where mean temperature at flowering was found to range from $15.5^{\circ}C$ at Drumborg, Vic. to $18.5^{\circ}C$ at Qualco, SA (Heinze 1977). Note that temperature averages depend on the epoch involved in their calculation.

The close link between the rate of node formation at the shoot tip and of the development of flowers, referred to above, suggests that it is likely that both growth processes are influenced together over a long period. This is borne out by the Survey results: most of the variation in flowering date was accounted for by temperatures after 1 September but none over the last 10 days before flowering; of all the functions, averaged maximum temperature accounted for most of the variation while mean temperature, minimum temperature and temperature range over the same period did not. This agrees with the findings of McIntyre *et al.* (1982). Heinze (1977) also pointed to the dominant effect of maximum temperature during spring on the interval from budburst to flowering; see Figure 7.7. The Survey, however, showed that correlations were better with temperatures from a specific date (1 September) rather than from budburst.

Harvest

The large variation found in harvest date has led to many attempts to draw correlations with temperature functions. The results are confusing. Some are mentioned above in Section 7.3.1; others (cited in Coombe 1987) may be summarized as follows:

(i) mean January (southern) temperature correlated with the harvest date of four varieties

(ii) mean November-December (southern) temperatures predicted veraison date and hence harvest date of Grenache in four years.

(iii) temperature predicted harvest date for late varieties but not early varieties

(iv) temperature predicted harvest date of var. 'Riesling' but not var. 'Pollux'.

The Survey showed several different significant correlations: in two of the four years most variation was accounted for by mean temperature after 1 January, in another, by temperature range after 1 January and in the fourth year, by temperature range from flowering to harvest; when all years were analysed together maximum temperature during the last 10 days was the most important factor. Clearly the important contributors to variation have not been found, or alternatively, the event of ripening is complexly controlled by several independent factors. Differentiation into two sections—flowering to veraison and veraison to ripeness—will help clarify this matter.

The temperature range factor deserves further investigation, especially since Gladstones (1977) points to the value of low temperature variability during the last month of ripening in favouring quality in grapes for table wines. He notes the inverse relationship between air humidity and the size of the temperature range.

Attention is drawn to the large body of literature on the relationship between temperature and grape composition. Reference is made to this in section 4.2.2 and in Figure 4.1. Probably the largest effect

is that of high temperature in lowering malate concentration; an interesting extension of this is the finding of an inverse correlation between grape acidity and temperature of the soil at 50 cm depth (Hofäcker *et al.* 1976).

7.3.3 Water and radiation

Although temperature is the major factor influencing grapevine phenology, additional influences arise from other climatic and growth factors. Water stress, arising from low soil water status and/or high atmospheric deficit, has inhibitory effects on growth and alters phenology (Matthews *et al.* 1983, Smart and Coombe 1983). In his study of grapevine phenology in the Hunter Valley, McIntyre (1982) showed that available soil water became an increasingly important determinant of development as the season progressed. He used the Waite Index $(P/E^{0.75})$ as a long term indicator of available soil water (in the absence of irrigation) and found that the higher the index, i.e. the lower the water stress, the longer the interval from budburst to flowering and from flowering to veraison and harvest.

In the Survey the difference between wet and dry bulb temperatures at 9 am was included as a variable in the last of the four years: the regressions show that this indicator of vapour pressure deficit had a small but significant association with the intervals from 1 July to budburst and budburst to flowering. Relative humidity has been considered as a factor influencing winegrape quality in different grapegrowing regions (Pirie 1978, Gladstones 1977, Dry and Smart Chapters 2 and 10). These studies suggest that the relationship between water and grape phenology deserves more research.

Solar radiation is another key climatic factor determining plant growth. The grapevine is a light-loving plant and it would be expected that lack of radiation incidence would affect grape phenology. In Europe the contribution of daylength is recognized in the use of heliothermic indices to delineate grape areas, but in the present context we are more concerned with radiation intensity. High light favours high bunch numbers, shorter internodes and high content of phenolics, which in turn may inhibit the growth of plant organs (Buttrose 1970, Kliewer 1982, Smart 1987). But from the work thus far it seems that radiation is not a major contributor to the determination of grapevine phenology; however, the matter has yet to be investigated thoroughly. McIntyre (1982) has made the interesting suggestion that an ideal indicator might be one which accommodates shifts in the levels of soil moisture, air temperature and solar radiation.

7.4 Concluding remarks

Phenological records are useful for planning and operating a vineyard. This chapter summarizes the present limited information on grape phenology in Australia. Examination of the association of weather with phenological events suggests that the best correlations are between temperature functions and budburst and flowering; those with harvest are variable and hence give poor predictions. However, much more information is needed before conclusions can be drawn. There is an urgent need for better data on this subject documenting both vegetative and reproductive stages, preferably concurrently in diverse regions. The data are readily obtained if attention is given to recognition of the stages defined in 7.2.1 and if they are noted down methodically. Modern methods of data recording and handling have simplified this job and the main requirement is for an organized, Australia-wide propram of phenological observation. This should be coupled with parallel records of weather factors, preferably with instruments adjacent to the recorded vines.

Further Reading

McIntyre, G.N. (1982) Grapevine phenology. Ph.D. Thesis, Univ. Newcastle, N.S.W. 214 pp.

McIntyre, G.N., Kliewer, W.M. and Lider, L.A. (1987) Some limitations of the day degree system as used in viticulture in California. Amer. J. Enol. Vitic. 38, 128-33.

Coombe, B.G. (1987) Influence of temperature on composition and quality of grapes. Acta Horticulturae 206, 23-35.

Other References

Alleweldt, G. and Hofäcker, W. (1975) Einfluss von Umweltfaktoren auf Austrieb, Blüte, Fruchtbarkeit und Triebwachstum bei der Rebe. Vitis 14, 103-15.

Amerine, M.A. and Winkler, A.J. (1944) Composition and quality of musts and wine of Californian grapes. Hilgardia 15, 493-675.

Anon. (1987) Unique North Queensland vineyard plans major expansion. Aust. Grapegrower & Winemaker No. 284, 16-7.

Antcliff, A.J. and Webster, W.J. (1955) Studies on the Sultana vine: II. The course of bud burst. Aust. J. Agric. Res. 6, 713-24.

Baggiolini, M. (1952) Les stades reperes dans le developpement annuel de la vigne et leur utilisation pratique. Rev. Rom. Agric. Vitic. Arboric. 8, 4-6.

Baldwin, J.G. (1966) Dormancy and time of budburst in the sultana vine. Aust. J. Agric. Res. 17, 55-68.

Becker, N.J. (1977) The influence of geographical and topographical factors on the quality of the grape crop. OIV Symp. Proc. 'Quality of the Vintage'. Oenol. Vitic. Res. Inst., Capetown, Sth. Africa. 169-80.

Boehm, E.W. (1970) Vine development and temperature in the Barossa district, SA. South Aust. Dept. Agric. Experimental Record 4, 16-24.

Buttrose, M.S. (1970) Fruitfulness in grapevines: the response of different cultivars to light, temperature and daylength. Vitis 9, 121-5.

Calo, A., Costacurta, A. and Lorenzoni, C. (1975) Stabilita ambientale di alcune caratteristiche fenologiche in varieta di Vitis vinifera. Estr. Riv. Viticolt. Enol. Conegliano No. 11-12, 3-33.

Chalmers, D.J. and van den Ende, B. (1975) Productivity of peach trees: factors affecting dry-weight distribution during tree growth. Ann. Bot. (London) 39, 423-32.

Conradie, W.J. (1980) Seasonal uptake of nutrients by Chenin Blanc in sand culture: I. Nitrogen. S. Afr. J. Enol. Vitic. 1, 59-65.

Coombe, B.G. and Iland, P.G. (1987) Grape berry development. In: T.H. Lee (ed.) Proc. 6th Aust. Wine Industry Tech. Conf., Aust. Industrial Publ. pp. 50-4.

Dry, P.R. (1984) Recent advances in Australian viticulture. In: T.H. Lee and T.C. Somers (eds) Proc. 5th Aust. Wine Industry Tech. Conf., Aust. Wine Res. Inst., Glen Osmond, SA. pp. 9-21.

Dry, P.R. (1987) How to grow 'cool climate' grapes in hot regions. Aust. Grapegrower & Winemaker No. 283, 25-6.

Eggenberger, W., Koblet, W., Mischler, M., Schwarzenbach, H. and Simon, J-L. (1975) Weinbau. Verlag Huber, Frauenfeld, Switz.

Eichorn, K.W. and Lorenz, D.H. (1977) Phaenologische Entwicklungsstadien der Rebe. Nachrichtenbl. Deut. Pflanzenschutzd. (Braunschweig) 29, 119-20.

Gladstones, J.S. (1977) Temperature and wine grape quality in European vineyards. Proc. 3rd Aust. Wine Industry Tech. Conf., Aust. Wine Res. Inst., Glen Osmond, SA, pp. 7-11.

Heinze, R.A. (1977) Regional effects on vine development and must composition. Proc. 3rd Aust. Wine Industry Tech. Conf., Aust. Wine Res. Inst., Glen Osmond, SA, pp. 18-25.

Hofäcker, W., Alleweldt, G. and Khader, S. (1976) Einfluss von Umweltfaktoren auf Beerenwachstum und Mostqualität bei der Rebe. Vitis 15, 96-112.

Kasimatis, A.N. (1981) Annual growth cycle of the vine. In: D.L. Flaherty (ed.) Grape Pest Management. Univ. Calif. Div. Agric. Sci. Publ. No. 4105, Berkeley, Calif. 12-18.

Kerridge, G.H., Clingeleffer, P.R. and Possingham, J.V. (1987) Varieties and varietal wines from the Merbein grape germplasm collection. Aust. Grapegrower & Winemaker Nos. 277, 14-8; 279, 14-9; 280, 29-34; 283, 17-23.

Kliewer, W.M. (1982) Vineyard canopy management—a review. Proc. Int. Symp. on Grapes and Wine, Davis, California, June 1980, pp. 132-6.

Matthews, M.A., Anderson, M.M. and Schultz, H.R. (1987) Phenologic and growth responses to early and late season water deficits in Cabernet Franc. Vitis 26, 147-60.

McIntyre, G.N., Lider, L.A. and Ferrari, N.L. (1982) The chronological classification of grapevine phenology. Amer. J. Enol. Vitic. 33, 80-5.

Pirie, A.J.G. (1978). Comparison of the climates of selected Australian, French and Californian wine producing areas. Aust. Grapegrower & Winemaker 15(172), 74-8.

Pouget, R. (1967) Methode d'appreciation de l'evolution physiologique des bourgeons pendant la phase de pre-debourrement: Application a l'etude comparee du debourrement de la vigne. Vitis 6, 294-302.

Pouget, R. (1968) Nouvelle conception du seuil de croissance chez la vigne. Vitis 7, 201-5.

Pratt, C. and Coombe, B.G. (1978) Shoot growth and anthesis in *Vitis*. Vitis 17, 125-33.

Smart, R.E. (1987) Influence of light on composition and quality of grapes. Acta Horticulturae 206, 37-47.

Smart, R.E., Alcorso, C. and Hornsby, D.A. (1980) A comparison of winegrape performance at the present limits of Australian viticultural climates - Alice Springs and Hobart. Aust. Grapegrower & Winemaker No. 196, 28-30.

Smart, R.E. and Coombe, B.G. (1983) Water relations of grapevines. In: Water Deficit and Plant Growth: T.T. Kozlowski, ed. Vol. VII, 138-96. Academic Press, New York.

Viala, P. and Vermorel, V. (1909) Ampelographie. 7 volumes. Masson, Paris.

Winkler, A.J., Cook, J.A., Kliewer, W.M. and Lider, L.N. (1974) General Viticulture. Univ. Calif. Press, Berkeley.

CHAPTER EIGHT

Grapevine Rootstocks

W. J. HARDIE and R. M. CIRAMI

Viticulture in Australia is based on varieties of the European vine, *Vitis vinifera* L., the predominant species of commercial grape production throughout the world. This species is particularly prone to attack by two soil-borne pests, the grape phylloxera and plant parasitic nematodes. It has been found that the European vine can be protected from these pests by grafting to rootstock varieties derived from other vine species and hybrids that are resistant. Many of the rootstocks used for this purpose are well adapted to particular soil types and some may also be used to overcome vineyard problems such as drought and salinity.

8.1   Resistance

Nematodes and phylloxera attack the vine by quite different and distinct mechanisms. No vines are immune to either pest. However, the rootstocks used to protect against them possess heritable characteristics that permit relatively less retardation of total growth compared to other varieties at the same level of infestation. A stock that displays such traits is termed resistant, in a relative sense. Resistance to insects or nematodes may involve any of the following properties (Painter 1951):

(i) Non-preference: when the rootstock possesses characteristics that are unattractive to soil-borne pests for reproduction, feeding or shelter.

(ii) Antibiosis: when the rootstock adversely affects the growth and reproduction of the pest.

(iii) Tolerance: when the rootstock can live and thrive, suffering little permanent damage, despite supporting a pest population capable of severely damaging more susceptible varieties. Tolerant varieties may even be more conducive to the build-up of a pest population than susceptible varieties.

The advantage of this concept of resistance is that it distinguishes between the total growth of the plant and the inherent protective properties that contribute to this growth. It is the *effectiveness* of the protective properties rather than their mere presence that is of practical importance. It follows that resistance is properly measured as *the fractional reduction in total growth, in a specified period of time, in the presence of a pest, disease or debilitating condition.*

Figure 8.1. Effects of phylloxera on a Cabernet Sauvignon vineyard. Own-rooted vines in the foreground, vines on rootstocks in the background.

Such an expression of resistance on a fractional basis with respect to the healthy condition of that particular stock would standardize the differences in absolute growth that exist between different stocks.

Existing measures of resistance are usually based either on evidence of the protective properties alone (e.g. evidence of root damage and differences in the size of the population), or, alternatively, on the growth of the stock in the presence of the pest compared to that of some standard type (e.g. *V. vinifera*) under the same conditions. The shortcoming of the former approach has already been mentioned; the latter allows no distinction between the benefits due to resistance and those due to other physiological characteristics of the stock.

While it seems that existing measures of resistance have served their purpose in a general sense, it is also apparent that the lack of clear distinction between resistance and other physiological characteristics such as absolute growth or rate of growth has clouded the assessment of rootstock performance and recommendations based thereon.

The situation in the vineyard is even more complex. As this chapter unfolds it will become apparent that vineyard performance of a grafted vine depends not only on resistance and other inherent properties of the stock but also on factors such as stock—scion relationships, cultural conditions and activity of specific pests.

8.1.1 Resistance to phylloxera

The life cycle of phylloxera is described in Volume 2, Chapter 10. Under Australian conditions, phylloxera is frequently found on both leaves and roots of some of the most popular rootstocks. However, the occurrence and extent of leaf galling and root symptoms has been shown to be closely related to the species origin of the rootstock (Boubals 1966, Buchanan and Hardie 1978). Economic losses are caused only when the soil-inhabiting form of the insect feeds upon the root tissue of non-resistant vines (Figure 8.1).

The lesions caused by the feeding are of two kinds; *nodosities*, characteristic hook-shaped galls which develop on young roots, and *tuberosities*, rounded swellings which occur on older tissue giving the root a 'warty' appearance. The damage to grapevine roots, especially abnormal growth and disturbance of metabolism in the affected tissues, is primarily due to the activity of phylloxera itself (Rilling 1975). Decay of the root lesions caused by soil-borne micro-organisms is considered to be largely responsible for the subsequent decline of the vine.

Anatomical differences between the roots of *V. vinifera* and the American species have been used to account for differences in the root damage caused by phylloxera (Pratt 1974). However, according to Boubals (1966), it is only susceptibility to the formation of tuberosities that has practical significance as to whether or not a rootstock will succumb to phylloxera. Certain resistant rootstock species form numerous nodosities without showing marked diminution in growth. Boubals studied the behaviour of phylloxera on the roots of numerous representatives of *Vitaceae* and found two types of resistance:

(i) *resistance by tolerance,* brought about by the formation of a layer of cork tissue (periderm) around the root lesion, which is the type found in all resistant *Vitis* species; the periderm limits the spread of decay into the root or may cause abscission of all or part of the lesion (Niklowitz 1955).

(ii) *Resistance by repulsion* of the insect by the root, which is found in *V. rotundifolia* and to a lesser extent in *V. berlandieri, V. rupestris* and *V. riparia.* Boubals regarded this as evidence of *antibiosis,* however *non-preference* may have been involved. The same type of resistance was also found in several other vine genera not exploited commercially, such as *Cissus* and *Leea.*

Several attempts have been made to rank the phylloxera rootstocks according to numerical ratings of resistance, e.g. Viala and Ravaz 1896, Boubals 1966. These ratings are generally subject to the aforementioned limitations associated with existing measures of resistance. Thus they provide only a cursory guide to the resistance of rootstocks. As noted previously, vine performance in the vineyard is also governed by factors that influence the activity of the insect or the growth of the vine. For example, in coarse textured soils where phylloxera activity is low, infested vines, even on their own roots, can survive for longer than in soils of finer texture (Nougaret and Lapham 1928). Similarly, under conditions that favour vine growth, such as moist, deep, soils of high fertility, own-rooted vines are able to survive far longer in the presence of phylloxera than under less favourable conditions.

It is apparent that this principle applies equally to the performance of rootstocks. Hence ARG1, a rootstock with only moderate phylloxera resistance, has been used satisfactorily for many years in north-eastern Victoria. It is also recommended for phylloxera control in fertile, moist soils in California (Lider *et al.* 1978). Conversely, this stock failed to resist when used in South Africa and Sicily (Perold 1927). Perold (1927) did introduce a further factor to explain the decline of vines grafted to this stock in South Africa, namely, the possible evolution of a new biological race of phylloxera. This concept has been developed further with the description of two biotypes of phylloxera, types A and B, and the finding that some rootstocks with *V. vinifera* in their parentage show susceptibility to biotype B, e.g. ARG1 (Granett *et al.* 1987). These experiences show the importance of field evaluation to determine rootstock performance under specific viticultural conditions and concurrent examination of the biology of the phylloxera aphid under the same conditions.

8.1.2 Resistance to nematodes

The nature of rootstock resistance to nematodes is not well understood; however, no rootstock is immune. Rootknot nematodes have been found associated with some of the most resistant stocks (Lider 1960, Sauer 1972). This suggests that resistance is achieved by tolerance, although other properties cannot be discounted.

It is also clear that the resistance of a particular stock is generally, though not necessarily, specific, in that it is confined to one nematode species or a group of closely related species. Thus Kunde *et al.* (1968) found that Ramsey (tested under the incorrect name Salt Creek, see 8.3.1) and Dog Ridge, stocks that are highly resistant to rootknot nematodes (*Meloidogyne* spp.), were susceptible to dagger nematode (*Xiphinema index*).

Little is known of the resistance of rootstocks to nematodes of other genera. Sauer (1977) monitored the relationships of citrus nematode (*Tylenchulus semipenetrans*) and rootlesion nematode (*Pratylenchus* spp.) to a number of rootstocks in a field study lasting five years. Population size of both nematode species appeared to be related to rootstock host. This may reflect differences in stock resistance. However, in the trials associated with these observations, there was no indication that either nematode species had any effect on crop productivity (Sauer 1974). Rootlesion nematode has been shown to cause extensive root damage to 1613 and Harmony in experiments conducted in pots (Sauer

1977). While there is no evidence of yield loss in the vineyard, the use of these stocks on sites infested with this species may create unnecessary risks.

8.2 Phylloxera-resistant rootstocks

8.2.1 Development of phylloxera-resistant rootstocks

The grape phylloxera is indigenous to North America where its native habitat is the region to the east of the Rocky Mountains. Many of the wild vine species of this region have acquired inherent resistance to this aphid-like pest. In 1863, phylloxera, undoubtedly introduced with American vines, appeared in France. The subsequent spread of the insect through Europe and other grape areas is recounted in Volume 2, Chapter 10.

In the early 1880s rootstocks derived from resistant American species were developed. These and their successors have been adopted as the principal long-term counter to phylloxera in the vineyards of the world. A well-documented account of the impact of phylloxera on European viticulture and the subsequent development of resistant rootstocks is presented by Ordish (1972). Alternative methods of control have been less satisfactory.

The principal species used in the development of phylloxera-resistant rootstocks were *V. aestivalis*, *V. berlandieri*, *V. cordifolia*, *V. monticola*, *V. riparia* and *V. rupestris*.

Two species, *V. rotundifolia* and *V. munsoniana*, which belong to the *Muscadinia* section, are highly resistant to phylloxera. Unfortunately morphological and botanical differences between these species and vines of the *Euvitis* or true vine section, to which most other species belong, prevent satisfactory grafting and make hybridization difficult (see Chapter 5). However, Jelenkovic and Olmo (1968) reported successful hybridization between *V. vinifera* and *V. rotundifolia* which suggests that, in future, it may be possible to exploit the muscadine species as a breeding source of rootstock varieties. Other attempts to combine the resistance of the American vine species with the desirable fruit characteristics of the *V. vinifera* varieties through hybridization have met with considerable success. The culture of varieties of this nature, the so-called American and French-American hybrids, is considerable, with over 400,000 hectares grown in France and large areas grown in eastern Europe.

8.2.2 Phylloxera-resistant rootstocks in Australia

Phylloxera was first identified in Victoria in 1877 and in New South Wales in 1884. Resistant rootstocks have been used extensively in the infested areas of both states. Experience with rootstocks in Victorian vineyards commenced in 1900 when over 100,000 resistant vines and cuttings, mainly selections and hybrids of *V. rupestris* and *V. riparia*, were distributed to growers and nurseries throughout the state. These stocks comprised some imported directly from France and others previously imported into New South Wales (Despeissis 1894, Dubois 1902). Prior to this date attempts to control phylloxera had relied upon eradication based on fumigation with carbon bisulfide and the removal of infested vines. The rootstock solution to the phylloxera problem was prompted by the failure of these eradication methods and the successful reconstitution of the vineyards of Europe. Experiments were established to investigate the adaptation of the stocks to local conditions and the compatibility of stocks with popular grape varieties.

In 1908 the Victorian Government commenced the distribution of bench-grafted rootlings from a nursery at Wahgunyah. During the period 1909-12, following further outbreaks of phylloxera in north-eastern Victoria, the supply of rootstocks was supplemented by the importation of grafted rootlings from France. In 1909 alone, 168,000 imported rootlings were distributed through the Melbourne agency of Richter's nursery in Montpellier. Planting material from these sources allowed the phylloxera-infested vineyards of the proclaimed North-Central Vine Disease District to be almost fully reconstituted by 1920. The stocks upon which this reconstitution was based were Rupestris du Lot, 1202, 3306, 3309 and ARG1 (de Castella 1920). In 1924 Richter's *V. berlandieri* × *V. rupestris* hybrids 99 R and 110 R were imported by the Victorian Department of Agriculture. 99 R subsequently performed very favourably in comparison with other stocks popular at that time (see 8.5.3). The rootstock imported in 1964 from California as 99 R (Australian Accession Code I.V.64.2083) is, in fact, 110 R (Hardie *et al.* 1981). Vein necrosis disease has been found in some vines of this selection. It seems likely that much of the Californian experience purportedly with 99R has actually been with 110 R. (see 'Letter to the Editor' American Journal of Enology and Viticulture, by C.J. Alley and H.P. Olmo, Vol. 32, issue 1, 1981.)

The vineyards of the Geelong Vine Disease District, where phylloxera was originally found, were not re-established. Plantings made in that district since 1967 have generally been with ungrafted vines.

In New South Wales, phylloxera outbreaks were confined to two separate regions; the Counties of Camden and Cumberland near Sydney and a small area near Corowa. Rootstocks were adopted in that state in 1900 (Blunno 1901). Those that were popular in Victoria were also used in New South Wales. In addition, Riparia Gloire and 106.8 were used successfully to promote early ripening of Muscat Hamburg table grapes in the areas close to Sydney. The 101-14 rootstock also performed satisfactorily in these areas (de Castella 1935).

Phylloxera was found in Queensland, in the Brisbane suburb of Enoggera in 1910 and reappeared at Myrtletown, another Brisbane suburb, in 1932. The insect has not been recorded elsewhere in the state.

At the time of the second phylloxera outbreak the Brisbane district was an important area of early tablegrape production. The varieties cultivated included European (e.g. Brown Frontignac and Muscat Hamburg) and American types (e.g. Isabella and Iona). The American varieties remained comparatively healthy while the European varieties rapidly declined. From the rootstock experiments which followed, 1202 and ARG1 gained most widespread acceptance, not only to combat phylloxera but also to improve the growth of vines planted in infertile soils (Smith 1938, Prest 1957). Tablegrape growers at Stanthorpe commenced using rootstocks in 1910 in preparation for the possible appearance of phylloxera. Despite the absence of the pest, rootstocks such as Rupestris du Lot, 3309 and ARG1 have been used to improve vine growth and productivity in infertile soils (Taylor and Bowen 1955). More recently, Rupestris du Lot, 3306 and to a lesser extent Isabella have been recommended for this purpose.

It is probable that the vineyards of South Australia, Western Australia, Tasmania, the Victorian and New South Wales Sunraysia districts, the mid-Murray horticultural areas around Robinvale and Swan Hill and the Murrumbidgee Irrigation Areas have been protected from phylloxera by regulations that control the introduction of grapevines into those areas, thus avoiding the possibility of the pest entering on infested material. Additional safeguards exist in the form of laws in New South Wales, Victoria and Queensland which isolate affected localities and prohibit the transfer of vines from within them (Proclaimed Vine Disease Districts).

According to Coombe (1963) the introduction of resistant rootstocks into South Australia was also opposed on the grounds that, if phylloxera was inadvertently introduced, rootstocks might assist in its spread. The reasons were twofold. The winged form of phylloxera initiates a sexual cycle that results in the formation of leaf galls. The establishment of viable leaf galls occurs only on certain American vines and their hybrids. Hence the use of American rootstocks provides a potential for spread of phylloxera by means of the winged form. The other possibility was that the roots of American vines, whether in a grafted vineyard or a mother vine planting, could harbour the root-living form of phylloxera without showing symptoms and so provide a source for the unwitting infestation of clean areas.

It is now generally considered that the benefit of having rootstocks that are readily available and that can also be used for other purposes overrides the risk of phylloxera infestation by either of these means. In recent years therefore, South Australia and Western Australia, along with most other states, have established source plantings of important, virus-tested, rootstock varieties.

8.3 Nematode-resistant rootstocks

8.3.1 Development of nematode-resistant rootstocks

Rootstocks that resist rootknot nematode
Nematode resistance in *Vitis* species was first recognized in Florida, USA by Neal (1889) who was also the first to suggest that rootstocks might be used for this purpose in commercial vineyards.

Snyder (1936) reported the first comprehensive study of the commercial application of nematode-resistant grapevines in the San Joaquin Valley, California. A large number (154) of varieties of *V. vinifera* as well as other grape species selections and hybrid rootstocks were examined in soils infested with rootknot nematodes. In these studies all *V. vinifera* varieties were heavily infested. Most of the American species selections and hybrids were likewise infested; a few, however, exhibited moderate-to-high resistance. Among the latter were 1613, 1616 and three *V. champini* varieties: Dog Ridge, Barnes and de Grasset. Similar resistance was also found in a variety tested under the name *V. doaniana* Salt Creek; however it now seems probable that this was actually a fourth *V. champini* variety, Ramsey, the error apparently having been made before this study commenced. The wrong name was used in studies subsequent to Snyder's in both California and Australia but Loomis and Lider (1971) re-established its correct identity. The name Ramsey will be used for the variety in this chapter. The grape species considered by Snyder to have the most potential were *V. champini*, *V. longii* and *V. cinerea*. This work laid the foundation for future nematode rootstock investigations. The succeeding studies which took place in California and which ultimately aroused world-wide interest in rootstocks as a means of combating the nematode problem have been reviewed by Lider (1960).

The two rootstocks of particular importance with respect to rootknot nematode control are both vigorously growing selections of *V. champini*, namely Ramsey and Dog Ridge. Both possess a high degree of resistance to rootknot nematode and are capable of producing high-yielding, vigorously growing scions in sandy, relatively infertile vineyards. In California, the less vigorous 1613 performed satisfactorily on fertile soils infested with rootknot nematode, although some instances of susceptibility were recorded.

In an attempt to combine the high nematode resistance of Dog Ridge with the more easily controlled vigour of 1613, Weinberger and Harmon (1966) at Fresno, California produced Harmony, a stock derived from the hybridization of open-pollinated seedlings selected from each of these stocks. Harmony seems well-suited to all but the most severely rootknot nematode-infested and infertile soils in California (Winkler *et al.* 1974).

Several other rootstock varieties resist rootknot nematodes. These include 99 R, 34 EM and Schwarzmann (Galet 1956, Goss and Cameron 1977a.). In general, none of these provides the resistance of the *V. champini* hybrids, but it is likely that some could be suited to particular vineyard conditions where other factors such as soil type or stock-scion interaction necessitate some compromise in this property.

Rootstocks that resist dagger nematode
In preliminary trials in which resistance of some commonly used rootstocks was rated on visible root damage and changes in the population of the nematode, Kunde *et al.* (1968) found that 1613 and Riparia Gloire were moderately resistant. *V. vinifera* and 25 other rootstocks out of a total of 35 tested were quite susceptible. The important aspect of these trials was an indication of resistance in several American vine species also tested, namely *V. candicans*, *V. longii*, *V. arizonica*, *V. rufotomentosa* and

V. smalliana. Several hybrids of these species developed at the University of California, Davis are currently undergoing tests in California.

8.3.2 Nematode-resistant rootstocks in Australia
One of the earliest reports of plant-parasitic nematode attack on vines in Australia was that of Quinn (1947) who noted an occurrence in a sandy vineyard at Geelong, Victoria. Although this report did not specify the particular type of nematode encountered, there are two species of nematode that are cause for particular concern in the vineyards of this country; rootknot nematode (*Meloidogyne* spp.) and dagger nematode (*Xiphinema index*). The biological characteristics of these and other nematode species which occur in Australian vineyards are discussed in Volume 2, Chapter 11.

Rootstocks that resist rootknot nematode
Rootknot nematodes occur in most vineyard areas in Australia. However, serious infestation is confined to soils of coarse texture. Rootknot nematode seldom causes serious problems in fine-textured soils.

The testing of rootstocks as a control measure commenced in the 1950s. Early research was based on readily-available phylloxera-resistant rootstocks. In Western Australia the rootstocks Schwarzmann (erroneously known then as 'Teleki') and 34 EM (erroneously thought to be 161-49) achieved early popularity. In Victoria, Sauer (1967) demonstrated that 101-14 and Rupestris du Lot could be used to improve the yield of Sultana vines grown in nematode-infested replant vineyards in the Sunraysia district. However, it has been the studies that commenced with the introduction in the early 1960s of Ramsey, Dog Ridge and 1613 from the University of California, Davis that have produced the most progress in this field.

In 1966, the CSIRO Division of Horticultural Research included these stocks in a series of trials designed specifically to solve the rootknot nematode problem for Sultana growers. These trials, which were confined to sand and sandy loam soils, showed conclusively that Ramsey was the best available rootstock for Sultana under these conditions. Worthwhile yield increases were achieved whether nematode infestation of these soils was severe, moderate or absent (Sauer 1972, May *et al.* 1973, Sauer 1974). In the Sunraysia district, other varieties which have shown a similar response when grafted to this stock, even on sites where nematodes cause no obvious damage, include Palomino, Cabernet

Sauvignon and Shiraz (P. May pers. comm.), and Colombard, Chenin Blanc, Barbera and Carignan.

Trials on coarse-textured soils infested with rootknot nematode in New South Wales, Victoria, South Australia and Western Australia all show similar responses, with both Ramsey and Dog Ridge commonly inducing superior productivity (Stannard 1976, Goss and Cameron 1977b, Cirami *et al.* 1984). Both stocks are recommended for nematode-infested soils in Queensland.

Rootstocks that resist dagger nematode
In Australia, the dagger nematode appears to be confined to a few vineyards within a small area close to Rutherglen in north-eastern Victoria (Meagher *et al.* 1976). This nematode not only damages vine roots, causing replant failure and decline of mature vines, but is also the vector of grape fanleaf virus. The effects of fanleaf virus are discussed in Volume 2, Chapter 11. Rootstocks being developed in California to combat the effects of this nematode are being tested in Victoria.

8.4 Rootstock adaptation

Some of the American species from which modern rootstocks are derived have their origins in quite distinct geographical regions of North America (Bailey 1934). Rootstocks derived from these species often display the traits of their parents in terms of adaptation to certain soil types. The corollary of this feature is that some rootstocks tolerate adverse soil conditions more readily than others. The examples which follow illustrate the importance of adaptation with respect to the choice of rootstock.

8.4.1 Limestone soils
Unlike *Vitis vinifera*, many American vine species are particularly intolerant of lime; in soils rich in this constituent they suffer from chlorosis. This trait is present in many rootstocks and may cause chlorosis of the scion. The tolerance of rootstocks to such conditions has been ranked by Viala and Ravaz (1896) and Galet (1956). *V. cordifolia* and *V. riparia* have a low tolerance while *V. berlandieri* has a high tolerance; this is apparent also in the rootstocks derived from the species, for example, 420 A, 99 R and the Teleki selection 5 BB Kober.

Thus far in Australia, tolerance to lime has not been an important criterion for the choice of rootstock because the use of rootstocks has been mainly confined to phylloxera or rootknot nematode

control; phylloxera is presently confined to regions with non-calcareous soils and rootknot nematode is a serious problem only on sandy soils. However, if it becomes necessary to use rootstocks on calcareous soils, lime tolerance is likely to be an important consideration.

There have been indications of chlorosis associated with the use of certain rootstocks on the finer textured loam or clay loam soils of the Sunraysia district. Limestone occurs in these soils usually as a loosely aggregated sub-stratum (see 3.2.5) and the calcium carbonate content of the topsoils range from 0.0 per cent to 21.6 per cent (Penman *et al.* 1940). In two successive seasons, Colombard vines grafted to Ramsey in an experiment established on sandy loam at the Sunraysia Horticultural Research Centre, showed 62 per cent and 29 per cent incidence of chlorosis symptoms respectively, while ungrafted Colombard vines, randomly interplanted, displayed no symptoms. Similar observations have been made in young, grafted Muscat Gordo Blanco vines grown on moderate-to-heavy textured soils in the same district (Figure 8.2). Vines grafted to Harmony, Dog Ridge and Schwarzmann have all shown these symptoms. Own-rooted vines of Muscat Gordo Blanco were unaffected on two sites where it was possible to make this comparison. The effect on vine growth and productivity has not been assessed in any of these situations, but observation suggests that this condition is likely to appear with excessively high soil moisture during spring and that growth made later in the season is usually unaffected.

8.4.2. Compact clay soils
Hybrids of *V. cordifolia* are particularly well-suited to fine-textured clay soils. Australian experience with these stocks has been limited. The only *V. cordifolia* hybrid grown in commercial vineyards in this country is 106.8. Muscat Hamburg grafted to this rootstock was superior to own-rooted vines and those on other phylloxera-resistant stocks in a trial established on heavy volcanic clay loam at Orchard Hills, NSW (G.R. Gregory pers. comm.). This stock warrants further testing.

8.4.3 Poorly-drained soils and phytophthora disease
Some rootstocks, particularly those derived from *V. berlandieri*, will not tolerate the waterlogged conditions that are frequently encountered in poorly-drained soils. This is likely to be, at least partly, a consequence of poor root aeration, but root rot

Figure 8.2 Chlorosis symptoms in the leaves of young vines of Muscat Gordo Blanco grafted to Harmony rootstock. Soil type: Irymple clay loam. Left: Whole vine Right: Individual shoots. (See Colour Plate 6).

caused by *Phytophthora cinnamomi* (a fungal organism which thrives in waterlogged soils) has been isolated as the cause of decline of vines grafted to *V. berlandieri*-derived stocks in South Africa.

The rootstock 3306 is quite tolerant of faulty drainage and has been used for this purpose in some vineyards in north-eastern Victoria. It should be noted, however, that rootstocks are a necessity in this district and that there is no indication that any rootstock is more tolerant of waterlogged soils than own-rooted *V. vinifera* varieties.

8.4.4 Saline soils

V. vinifera varieties are moderately tolerant of salinity (i.e. high total salts). However, injury may result from excessive intake of chloride. Certain rootstocks reduce the accumulation of chloride in the scion variety (Sauer 1968, Bernstein *et al.* 1969). For example, Sauer (1968) reported that the level of chloride in the leaf petioles of Sultana vines grafted to Ramsey and 101-14 was about 75% lower than that of own-rooted vines (even those that had been grafted to Sultana to determine whether the graft itself affected chloride status). Dog Ridge and 1613 induced reductions of about 50%. Evidence also

suggested that Rupestris du Lot and 99 R were probably even better than Ramsey in limiting chloride, although the differences were relatively small.

Downton (1977), working with Ramsey, Harmony and Schwarzmann, reported similar effects. He also found that the magnitude of the chloride reduction depended on the scion variety. Vines grafted on to any of these rootstocks should tolerate conditions of high chloride in the field more readily than ungrafted vines. However, the practical advantage of rootstocks used for this purpose remains to be demonstrated. Francois and Clark (1979) have noted that stocks which reduce chloride uptake by the roots would be of little benefit with sprinkler irrigation because chloride is readily absorbed directly by the leaves.

8.4.5 Acidic soils

In highly acidic soils vines become susceptible to toxic effects of excesses of aluminium and/or manganese. Rootstocks derived from species, such as *V. riparia*, *V. cordifolia* and *V. labrusca*, which are native to regions with acid soils seem likely to best tolerate such conditions. This may explain why Branas (1974) found the *V. berlandieri* × *V. rupestris* hybrid 99R and Rupestris du Lot to be unsuited to acidic soils. However, in a study of the growth responses of potted Chenin Blanc grafted to a range of rootstocks (Conradie 1983) those on the *V. berlandieri* × *V. rupestris* hybrids 140 Ru and 99 R were least affected by acidic conditions. In accord with the finding of Branas (1974), the vines grafted to Rupestris du Lot were greatly affected.

8.4.6 Drought

The ability to withstand drought varies among *Vitis* species and reflects their adaptation to the water regimes of their natural habitats. Variation can be observed in traits associated with water uptake, e.g. the size, density and distribution of the root system, and those associated with water use, e.g. leaf size and indument, and the structure and density of the stomata.

Rootstocks generally retain these traits in accordance with their origin. For example, those derived from *V. riparia* are, in common with this species, notably poor in regard to drought tolerance. It was largely for this reason that de Castella (1935) recommended against the use of Riparia Gloire and 101-14 in north-eastern Victoria. Goss and Cameron (1977a) reached a similar conclusion regarding the use of Schwarzmann and 34 EM in non-irrigated vineyards in Western Australia.

However, the ability of the grafted vine to withstand dry conditions will depend on the specific soil, climate and physiological interaction between the rootstock and scion variety. An example is that of vines grafted to Rupestris du Lot which tolerate drought well, but only when grown on deep penetrable soils which allow the development of the characteristically plunging root system capable of fully utilizing soil moisture (de Castella 1921b).

Factors which influence water-use through effects on the size and structure of the foliar canopy, such as scion/rootstock interaction (see 8.5.2) and cultural practices, are likely to exert a major influence on the drought tolerance of specific graft combinations.

The drought tolerance of some rootstocks of interest in Australia is presented in Table 8.1. The ratings are based on the water-use of potted, grafted Cabernet Sauvignon vines (Carbonneau 1985) and correspond well to vineyard observations. All the

Table 8.1 Grapevine tolerance of drought

Rating	Rootstock
Highly tolerant	110 Richter, 140 Ruggeri
Tolerant	1103 Paulsen, 5 C, 99 Richter
Less tolerant	3309 Couderc, 420 A Millardet and de Grasset 5 BB Kober, Rupestris du Lot 101-14 Millardet and de Grasset
Susceptible	Riparia Gloire

Source: Carbonneau (1985)

rootstocks listed are primarily used for phylloxera resistance. In the absence of further information regarding the efficiency of water-use for growth and/or grape production it is not yet clear if the inherent differences between rootstocks are great enough to provide practical advantages in the vineyard or whether any would provide a significant advantage over ungrafted *V. vinifera* varieties on the basis of drought tolerance alone.

8.5 Stock-scion relationships

8.5.1 Compatibility

Successful grafting depends on the formation of a sound union between rootstock and scion variety. The inability of parts of two different plants, when grafted together, to produce such a union, and of the resulting single plant to develop satisfactorily, is termed incompatibility (Hartmann and Kester 1968).

The compatibility of *V. vinifera* varieties grafted onto resistant rootstocks has been studied extensively in California, e.g. Snyder and Harmon (1948), Harmon (1949), and in Australia, e.g. Anon (1928), Manuel (1948). Incompatibility was not a serious problem in any of these experiments.

In Australian experience, most varieties can be matched with suitable stocks, but for some, such as Muscat Gordo Blanco, Muscadelle (incorrectly known as Tokay), Muscat Rouge (syn. Brown Muscat, Brown Frontignac), Zante Currant, Cardinal, Barlinka and Ohanez, care in the choice of stock is required.

Sarooshi and Bevington (1976) reported that the combination of Muscat Gordo Blanco and Ramsey was incompatible, the symptoms being die-back of shoot tips, stunted growth, poor fruitset and eventual death of the vine. Similar effects (Figure 8.3) have been encountered in an experiment at the Sunraysia Horticultural Research Institute.

The cause of this condition is unknown, but Sarooshi and Bevington reported symptoms of legno riccio virus (apparently transmitted from the scion) on Rupestris du Lot vines included in their experiment.

A selection of the tablegrape variety Barlinka that is grown in Western Australia is incompatible with Ramsey. Decline of the scion occurs one to four years after grafting (W.R. Jamieson, pers. comm.). In Western Australia, vines of Cardinal grafted to Schwarzmann have declined with weak growth following the production of the first crop (Goss and

Figure 8.3 Decline of Muscat Gordo Blanco grafted to Ramsey. Above left: Retarded shoot growth, mid-November; Above right: Wilted leaf canopy; Bottom left: Longitudinal trunk cracks at the graft union; Bottom right: Left: dead vine, five years old; right: unaffected vine.

Cameron 1977a). Leaf roll disease of the scion is suspected as the cause (I.J. Cameron, pers. comm.). Muscat Gordo Blanco was also incompatible with 34EM in rootstock experiments conducted in the Swan Valley, WA, from 1965 to 1977.

Bioletti *et al.* (1921) suggested that growth abnormalities of the graft union, either overgrowth of the stock by the scion or the size of the swelling, could be used as measures of an incompatible condition. The former characteristic, expressed as the percentage ratio of the diameter of the stock to that of the scion, was favoured as it was less dependent on other factors such as cultural conditions or vine age. Percentages greater than 100 or less than 75 were associated with weak vines. Ratios of 80 to 100 were considered excellent and normal. This relationship has been considered to apply in a general sense, for example, severe overgrowth of stock by scion was a factor correlated with the abandonment of *V. riparia* stocks in Victora (de Castella 1921a). However, Wilkinson and Burney (1921) cite a European example of 40-year-old vines grafted to Riparia Gloire which displayed no signs of deterioration despite very marked scion overgrowth.

The percentage does seem to fail as a sensitive method for predicting yield performance. In a compatibility study of Muscat Gordo Blanco on nine rootstocks, yield of any given stock-scion combination was not correlated with the relative diameters of stock and scion at the graft union. In Western Australia there is significant scion overgrowth with Schwarzmann, but there is no apparent ill-effect on vines at least 20 years old.

8.5.2 Affinity

In early studies the terms *compatibility* and *affinity* were often used interchangeably to indicate the harmony existing between stock and scion after grafting. However, Rives (1971) has made a distinction between these terms. He showed that the potential vegetative vigour (measured as the weight of prunings) of grafted vines depends on three factors, namely, the vigour of the rootstock, the vigour of the scion variety and the complex interaction or combining ability of the stock and scion. It is the effect of the interaction between the stock and scion in a particular graft combination that Rives calls *affinity*.

8.5.3 Longevity

Grafted vineyards are sometimes considered to have a shorter life than ungrafted vineyards. This has been attributed to weaknesses arising from the graft union and/or infestation of the union by insects or decay organisms. It has been suggested that failure of grafted vines may occur from the time of vineyard establishment.

However, Husmann *et al.* (1939) reported the results of trials involving 311 vinifera grape varieties grafted to 105 nematode and phylloxera resistant rootstocks. It was ascertained that 1,903 vinifera stock combinations comprising 6,966 vines maintained an average growth rating considered as satisfactory or excellent for a 20-year period or more. Some were still growing satisfactorily after 32 years. Although the tests had not run long enough to determine the longevity of grafted vines, they indicated that lack of compatibility or affinity was not an important factor. de Castella (1920) estimated that the useful life of a grafted vineyard under Australian conditions could range from 30-40 years. Experience supports this claim.

8.5.4 Rootstock effects on yield

Rootstocks influence the total vegetative and reproductive growth of the grapevine. The primary function of rootstocks in problem soils or where nematodes or phylloxera are present is to maintain, if not increase, the total growth of the vine. In some cases, crop production effects can be attributed to the direct influence of rootstocks on bud fruitfulness, fruitset or berry size. For example, de Castella (1920) noted that grafting often improved fruitset, particularly in varieties poor in this respect. He suggested that this improvement was due to the graft union behaving like a cincture. Any increase in

Figure 8.4 Influence of rootstock on vegetative growth: Top: Ungrafted Sultana vines planted 1971; Bottom: Sultana vines in adjacent rows, same as above, on Ramsey rootstock planted 1973 and grafted in following season; Soil: Benetook loam. Courtesy of R.B. Johnstone, Irymple, Victoria.

vegetative growth (e.g. Figure 8.4) if adequately managed may also contribute directly to improved productivity by allowing the retention of more fruiting units at pruning. Thus, even in the absence of specific soil problems, grafted vines may be more productive than ungrafted vines. Examples of this have been previously discussed (see 8.2.2 and 8.3.2).

The long term influence of rootstocks on productivity was demonstrated by an experiment conducted at Wahgunyah, in north-eastern Victoria, in which the yield of eight scion varieties, each grafted to eight rootstocks, was compared for 35 years. The outstanding stock from this experiment was 99 R. All scion varieties grafted to this stock significantly outyielded those grafted to ARG1, currently the most widely-used stock in north-eastern Victoria (Figure 8.5). Sampling at the trial site indicated the presence of dagger nematode, rootknot

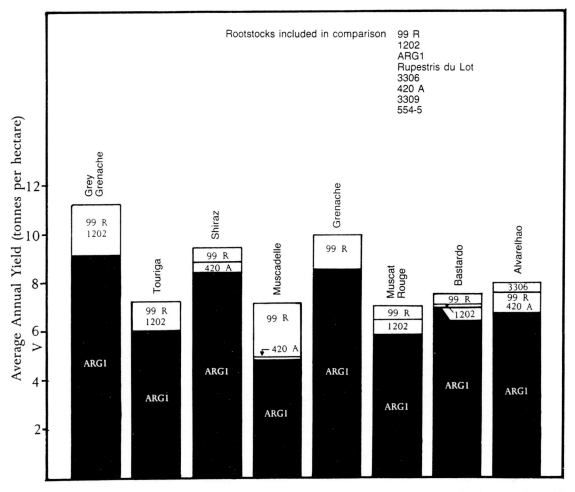

Figure 8.5: Average annual yield of eight scion varieties grafted to different rootstocks. Results shown as the yield increment (white area), compared with ARGI (black area), of the highest- and second highest-yielding stocks. Location: Wahgunyah, Victoria. Source: W.J. Hardie (unpublished data).

nematode, rootlesion nematode and stubbyroot nematode (*Paratrichodorus* spp.), and phylloxera. The soil was a deep loam overlain with silty alluvium deposited by successive flooding of the adjacent Murray River.

Low yields may be encountered when rootstocks induce excessive vegetative growth. This problem occasionally occurs in the Sunraysia district when Dog Ridge or Ramsey are planted in deep and/or fertile soil. Typically, fruitset is poor and the number of bunches is low. This condition is likely if shoot growth is rapid during the periods of fruitset and inflorescence initiation. Dense foliage during the latter period may aggravate the condition by preventing adequate light penetration for optimum initiation of fruitful buds. Cultural practices aimed at slowing shoot growth during these critical periods,

such as application of growth retardants or pruning to induce relatively higher cropping levels, offer scope for alleviating this problem.

Poor fruitset has also been associated with excessive levels of nitrate in leaf petioles at flowering (Cook and Kishaba 1956). Cook and Lider (1964) found that scions grafted to Rupestris St George (syn. Rupestris du Lot) consistently accumulated high levels of nitrate in the petioles. In north-eastern Victoria the use of this stock has been associated with poor set, particularly in the scion variety Malbec, a variety notorious in this respect (de Castella 1921a).

Consideration of the problem induced by excessive shoot growth and that associated with high levels of nitrate leads us to conclude that nitrogenous fertilizer should only be applied sparingly, if at all, in vineyards established with vigorous rootstocks.

8.5.5 Rootstock effects on fruit composition

The effect of rootstock on fruit composition has been the subject of much speculation since the practice of grafting commenced. Early experience revealed that European varieties did not acquire the distinctive flavour characteristics of the American species to which they were grafted.

However, as early as 1904, it was reported that rootstocks modified the weight and colour of berries and their content of sugar, acid and minerals (Curtel 1904). Benard *et al.* (1963) found that rootstocks could influence the mineral composition of grapes but concluded that other variables such as climate, soil and fertilizer should have more influence than rootstocks on wine composition. Nevertheless recent investigations suggest a more critical role of rootstocks in modifying grape composition, and greater emphasis should be given to this feature in the selection of rootstocks, particularly those used in winegrape production.

For example, in California, Ough *et al.* (1968a) compared the quality and composition of fruit of ten varieties grown on two different rootstocks, Rupestris St George (syn Rupestris du Lot) and 99 R (8.2.2), and found large and easily-detected differences. Most scion varieties grafted to the more vigorous Rupestris St George rootstock yielded fruit with higher concentrations of total nitrogen, titratable acid, tannin, potassium, phosphorous, ammonia, biotin and a higher pH. The changes in the mineral composition of the fruit were closely related to the influence of rootstock on the ratio of leaf area to crop load. These authors also showed that the composition and quality of wine produced differed significantly according to rootstock (Ough *et al.* 1968b).

In Australia, Hale (1977) and Hale and Brien (1978) found that grapes produced in experimental plots in the Sunraysia district on vines grafted to Ramsey and Dog Ridge had higher concentrations of potassium and malic acid, higher pH and less colour (in red varieties) than grapes produced on ungrafted vines. Wine produced from fruit of the ungrafted vines was preferred to that of the grafted vines. These results and those of Downton (1977) also suggest that the extent of the effect depends upon scion variety.

From extensive co-operative experiments in South Australia and Victoria (Ruhl *et al.* 1988), four rootstocks were found to give high juice pH, associated with high K content and low tartrate/malate ratio (Harmony, Dog Ridge, Freedom and Rupestris du Lot), and five rootstocks gave low juice pH (140 R, 1202, 5 A, 5 C and 101-14).

The effects of rootstock on grape composition may thus be considered a result of a physiological interaction between soil, roots and scion which affects crop load, vegetative growth and the nutritional status of the vine. Ough *et al.* (1968a) suggested that such influence may be detected only under conditions that allow full expression of the growth differences due to different rootstocks. Some of the effects on fruit composition attributed to rootstocks—such as high pH, low titratable acid and low colour—may even be encountered in own-rooted vines when the ratio of crop to leaf area is low and/or the fruit develops in shade (Jackson 1986, Smart 1980).

Rootstocks may also influence the ripening date of the scion. Ripening date is particularly important to tablegrape producers seeking economic benefits associated with early markets. The continued popularity of the stock Riparia Gloire in the Cumberland region of New South Wales is due primarily to the early ripening and desirable colouration which it imparts to Muscat Hamburg, a popular tablegrape variety. Conversely, stocks that induce profuse growth, e.g. Ramsey, Dog Ridge and Rupestris du Lot, have been associated with delayed ripening and poor colouration. These stocks should be avoided for tablegrapes, particularly red types.

8.6 Problems with rootstocks

8.6.1 Susceptibility to disease

Crown gall (Agrobacterium tumefaciens)
This bacterial disease occurs worldwide and can cause severe damage on *Vitis vinifera,* especially in cool climate regions (see Chapter 2). The incidence of crown gall in the field in Australia is quite low, but has increased in recent years with some nurseries reporting very high incidence of galls. This has been correlated with the increased use of rootstocks (Ophel *et al.* 1988).

These authors surveyed a range of rootstock and scion propagation material and found that the bacterium survives systemically in grapevines. Levels of contamination in two of the most useful rootstocks in South Australia (Ramsey and K51-40) were very high (50 to 100% of cuttings infested), low or undetectable in other rootstocks and moderate (10 to 40% of cuttings infested) in almost all scions tested. Recent studies (Burr *et al.* 1988)

Table 8.2 Grapevine susceptibility to
Phytophthora cinnamomi

Susceptibility	Rootstock
High	Rupestris du Lot, 99 Richter 1103 Paulsen
Moderate	140 Ruggeri, 101-14 Millardet and de Grasset, 110 Richter
Low	Ramsey

Source: Marais (1979)

indicate that hot water dipping (50°C for 30 minutes) can eradicate the bacterium or reduce it to below the level of detection.

Phytophthora cinnamomi
This fungal organism can cause root rot and sudden decline of grapevines (Volume 2, Chapter 11). The first record of this disease in grapevines was from a planting of Rupestris du Lot rootlings in New South Wales in 1964 (McGechan 1966). Resistance to *P. cinnamomi* has been investigated by Marais (1979). *Vitis vinifera* varieties appeared strongly resistant; however, there were notable differences among rootstocks. The results pertaining to rootstocks of interest in Australia are summarized in Table 8.2. The use of rootstocks with high susceptibility should be avoided in vineyards where *P. cinnamomi* is present.

Fanleaf virus
In a recent study (A.C. Goheen pers. comm.), the severity of fanleaf virus symptoms on Chenin Blanc vines, grafted on ARG1, 1613, Harmony and Ramsey and established as replants in a vineyard infested with the dagger nematode *(X. index)*, was strongly correlated with the rootstock type. The vines grafted on ARG1, 1613 and Harmony showed slight leaf-deforming symptoms but those on Ramsey were severe. Yields of vines on Ramsey were significantly less than those from the other three stocks. Goheen attributes this response to a difference in susceptibility of the rootstocks to the virus rather than to nematode resistance.

8.6.2 Spread of virus-like diseases
Many rootstocks are symptomless carriers of virus-like diseases. The use of rootstocks thus infested has undoubtedly contributed greatly to the spread of such diseases throughout the world. Luhn and Goheen (1970) noted that vines in an old vineyard established in California prior to the introduction of rootstocks were relatively free of virus-like diseases. This is in contrast to the subsequent widespread occurrence of virus-like diseases in grafted vines and those propagated therefrom. There seems little doubt that rootstocks were a primary source of virus-like disease in Australian vineyards also. It is imperative that only virus-tested rootstocks be used in future plantings. The extent to which infection with virus-like diseases has influenced the evaluation of rootstocks in the past is not clear. However this is a factor that warrants consideration (see also Volume 2, Chapter 11).

8.7   Choice of rootstock

In Australia, rootstocks are most commonly used to avoid the problems of rootknot nematodes or phylloxera. Situations have been described where rootstocks provide benefits even in the absence of these pests. In general, however, economics determine that rootstocks are used only as a matter of necessity. The successful choice of a stock requires careful consideration of the purpose for which it is required and conditions under which it is to be grown. Obviously, stocks to be used to control nematodes or phylloxera must have adequate *resistance*.

In Australia, the soils which favour phylloxera are generally unfavourable to rootknot nematode, the most common nematode problem, and the choice of rootstock can be straightforward. There are, however, a number of soils where both occur and fortunately there are a number of rootstocks which have a high level of resistance to both. Some examples are Ramsey, 5 C, 5 BB Kober and 99 R. The coincidence of phylloxera and the dagger nematode in the soils of north-eastern Victoria is cause for concern; rootstocks that will resist both are required in this region.

Consideration must also be given to the other factors that influence the performance of the grafted vine, viz. *adaptation* to location and soil type, and *compatibility* and *affinity* between stock and scion. It is apparent that yield and fruit composition are directly influenced by each of these factors. A summary of the important characteristics of rootstocks currently used in Australia is presented in Table 8.3.

Table 8.3. Characteristics of important grape rootstocks[1] for Australian vineyards.

Rootstock	Species origin	Scion vigour	Nematode resistance			Phylloxera resistance
			Rootknot	Dagger[2]	Root Lesion[2]	
Ramsey (incorrectly known as Salt Creek)	V. champini	high	high	low	high	high
Dog Ridge	V. champini	very high	high	low	high	moderate
K51-32	V. champini × V. riparia	high	high	moderate	—	unknown
K51-40	V. champini × V. riparia	high	high	—	—	unknown
Freedom	V. champini × 1613	moderate	high	high	—	high
1616 Couderc abbr. 1616	V. longii × V. riparia	moderate	high	—	—	very high
1613 Couderc abbr. 1613	V. longii × [V. vinifera × (V. riparia × V. labrusca)]	moderate to high	moderate	moderate	low	moderate
Harmony	A hybrid of open-pollinated seedlings selected from V. champini and 1613.	moderate to high	moderate	high	low	low[3]
Rupestris du Lot syn. Rupestris St George	V. rupestris	moderate to high	none to low	low	moderate	high
Aramon × Rupestris Ganzin No. 1 abbr. ARG1,	V. vinifera × V. rupestris	moderate	none	low	low	low to moderate

These rootstock varieties are illustrated in Colour Plate 4.

Lime tolerance	Root strike	General comments
moderate	poor	**Ramsey** is well suited to coarse-textured soils of low fertility. It has performed well with Zante Currant in the Swan Valley, Western Australia, with a wide range of scion varieties in South Australia, and is recommended for Sultana on sandy soils in the Murray Irrigation districts. Susceptible to zinc deficiency. Muscat Gordo Blanco and Barlinka are incompatible with this stock.
moderate	poor	**Dog Ridge** is suited only to very coarse-textured, infertile soils. Excessive vigour and low productivity result from its use on more fertile soils. Ramsey usually provides greater yields and is more easily managed. Susceptible to zinc deficiency. May be suited to scion varieties of low vigour such as Muscat Gordo Blanco and Riesling.
unknown	excellent	**K51-32** was developed for resistance to rootknot nematode at the University of California, Davis. It has similar vigour to Ramsey, but is more readily propagated. It does not appear to be as productive as K51-40. There are indications that it is susceptible to citrus nematode.
unknown	excellent	**K51-40** was developed for resistance to rootknot nematode at the University of California, Davis. In South Australia it appears to be about as productive as Schwarzmann in nematode-infested situations.
unknown	excellent	**Freedom** has similar characteristics to Harmony but has out-yielded Harmony in California. Relatively untested in Australia, it shows promise in dryland vineyards in South Australia.
low to moderate	excellent	**1616** grows poorly in infertile and light sandy soils. On better soil it produces scions of moderate vigour, with good crops of high quality fruit. It does tolerate wet soil conditions and saline soils.
low	excellent	**1613** is best suited to moist, fertile sandy/sandy loam soils. It has been outperformed by both Ramsey and Dog Ridge wherever these rootstocks have been compared on sandy soils.
moderate	excellent	**Harmony** is well suited to all but the most coarse soils. It appears well-suited to Muscat Gordo Blanco and most table grape varieties but further testing is warranted.
moderate	excellent	**du Lot**, syn. St George, when planted on deep, well-drained soils which allow unrestricted root development imparts drought resistance to its scions. Only a moderate performer in trials. Shy-bearing varieties grafted to it often show symptoms of excessive vigour, poor set and reduced yield e.g. Muscat Gordo Blanco. Suckering may be a problem.
moderate	excellent	**ARG1** is not a rootstock for dry, infertile, shallow soils. Used successfully for many years in north-eastern Victoria for a wide range of scion varieties. Its phylloxera resistance appears adequate for that region, but other rootstocks with nematode resistance as well are likely to do better. It was outyielded by 99 R in a long term experiment at Wahgunyah.

Rootstock	Species origin	Scion vigour	Nematode resistance			Phylloxera resistance
			Rootknot	Dagger[2]	Root Lesion[2]	
1202 Couderc abbr. 1202	*V. vinifera* × *V. rupestris*	moderate	none	low	—	moderate
Riparia Gloire de Montpellier syn. Riparia Gloire	*V. riparia*	moderate to high	none to low	moderate	—	very high
Schwarzmann (incorrectly known as Teleki in Western Australia)	*V. riparia* × *V. rupestris*	moderate	high	high	—	high
101-14 Millardet and de Grasset abbr. 101.14	*V. riparia* × *V. rupestris*	low to moderate	moderate	moderate	moderate	high
3309 Couderc abbr. 3309	*V. riparia* × *V. rupestris*	moderate	low to moderate	high	high	high
3306 Couderc abbr. 3306	*V. riparia* × *V. rupestris*	moderate	low	low	low	high
106-8 Millardet and de Grasset abb. 106-8	*V. riparia* × *V. cordifolia*: *V. rupestris*	moderate	moderate	—	—	very high
99 Richter abbr. 99 R	*V. berlandieri* × *V. rupestris*	moderate	high	moderate	moderate	high
110 Richter abbr. 110 R	*V. berlandieri* × *V. rupestris*	moderate	moderate	low	low	high
140 Ruggeri abbr. 140 Ru	*V. berlandieri* × *V. rupestris*	high	moderate	low	—	high

Lime tolerance	Root strike	General comments
moderate	excellent	**1202** is best suited to deep, fertile soils, but performs satisfactorily on heavier types. It is used extensively in north-eastern Victoria for Brown Frontignac. It was once used widely in the Cumberland region of NSW for Muscat Hamburg and Purple Cornichon but it lost favour due to poor fruit colour development, particularly in wet years. It may cause excessive vigour.
low	excellent	**Riparia Gloire** is the only pure *Riparia* selection still in commercial use in Australia. It is suited only to deep, moist, and fertile loams with good drainage. In the Camden and Cumberland regions of NSW this rootstock has been used successfully to promote early ripening of Muscat Hamburg table grapes. Varieties grafted to this have often declined through a tendency to overbear.
moderate	excellent	**Schwarzmann** has been used for most table, dried fruit and wine varieties in Western Australia. Results have been good, but it appears to be incompatible with the tablegrape variety Cardinal. It does best on moist, deep soils and should not be used where summer drought is common.
moderate	excellent	**101-14** assumes much of the character of riparia. It has a shallow root system and requires moist deep soils. It performed satisfactorily with Sultana under irrigation at Merbein, Victoria but has been outclassed by Ramsey in more recent trials.
moderate	excellent	**3309** has been used quite widely in north-eastern Victoria, particularly for Shiraz grown on heavy loams. Experience in California and Australia suggests that other rootstocks are usually better. It does not tolerate saline soils well.
moderate	excellent	**3306** has been used quite widely in north-eastern Victoria. It is better suited to wetter, fine-textured soils than 3309. It is recommended in Queensland for replanting on well-drained shallow soils or where low fertility is a problem on such soils. It does not tolerate saline soils well.
low	excellent	**106-8** is the only cordifolia hybrid used in Australian vineyards. It is well suited to lime-free, stiff, compact soils. It has been used in the Camden and Cumberland regions of NSW for Muscat Hamburg table grapes and some wine varieties.
moderate	fair	**99 R** is well suited to a wide range of soil types, but wet, poorly-drained situations should be avoided. It is drought tolerant. Scion varieties grafted to this stock typically develop slowly but after several seasons consistently bear large crops of excellent quality. This was the outstanding rootstock in the long term rootstock trial at Wahgunyah, Victoria.
moderate	fair	**110 R** is similar in many respects to 99 R. It is considered to impart greater drought tolerance than 99 R. It is preferred to 99 R in France, Spain, Greece and Turkey.
high	fair	**140 Ru** imparts considerable drought resistance to scions. It has not been widely tested in Australia.

Rootstock	Species origin	Scion vigour	Nematode resistance			Phylloxera resistance
			Rootknot	Dagger[2]	Root Lesion[2]	
1103 Paulsen abbr. 1103 P	*V. berlandieri* × *V. rupestris*	moderate	moderate to high	moderate	—	high
34 E.M. Foex abbr. 34 EM	*V. berlandieri* × *V. riparia*	moderate	moderate	moderate	—	very high
5 C Teleki abbr. 5 C*	*V. berlandieri* × *V. riparia*	moderate	moderate	moderate	—	very high
5 BB Kober syn. 5 BB Teleki	*V. berlandieri* × *V. riparia*	low to moderate	moderate	moderate	—	very high
420 A Millardet and de Grasset abbr. 420 A	*V. berlandieri* × *V. riparia*	low to moderate	moderate	low	low	high
5 A Teleki (abbr. 5 A)	*V. berlandieri* × *V. riparia*	moderate	moderate	—	—	high

1. Information has been drawn from the following sources: Galet (1956), Kunde *et al.* (1968), Lider (1960), Kasimatis and Lider (1975), King *et al.* (1982) Goss and Cameron (1977ab), Sauer (1977), Snyder (1936), Boubals (1966), Boubals (1978 Boubals (1979), Harris (1983), Stirling and Cirami (1984), Whiting *et al* (1987).
2. Further evidence of field performance required.
3. Cirami, McCarthy and Glenn (1984).
*Incorrectly named SO 4 in earlier printings. This name change has also been made in Plate 4 and on pages 162, 166, 167, 173 and 208.

Lime tolerance	Root strike	General comments
moderate	fair	**1103 P** imparts drought resistance to scions. It is moderately tolerant of salt. It has not been widely tested in Australia.
moderate	poor	**34 EM** has been used with considerable success in Western Australia where it has been mistakenly considered to be the rootstock 161-49. It appears to be the best rootstock for Muscat Gordo Blanco and Cardinal under those conditions. It is not recommended for use where summer drought is a major problem.
moderate	excellent	**5 C** is a cool region rootstock widely used in Germany. Tried at Irymple, Victoria for Muscat Gordo Blanco; other rootstocks are better.
moderate	excellent	**5 BB** is best suited to moist, compact soils. It is widely used in Europe and warrants further investigation under Australian conditions as a dual purpose phylloxera/nematode resistant rootstock.
moderate	fair	**420 A** seems well suited to poorer, heavy textured soils. It tolerates dry conditions well, but does not withstand waterlogging. Overcropping may be a problem in early years of vine development. Other rootstocks have performed better in trials in California and Victoria.
high	excellent	**5 A** has not been sufficiently tested in Australia. In California its performance has been erratic with best results being obtained under irrigated conditions in the interior valleys. Along with other *V. berlandieri* × *V. riparia* hybrids it has performed well in NE Victoria with Brown Frontignac.

8.8 Concluding remarks

Rootstocks derived from American vine species have been used in grape culture since the early 1880s when they were introduced into Europe to counter the effects of phylloxera. The subsequent discovery of nematode resistance, also possessed by certain American vine species, has led to the increasing use of rootstocks for this purpose. Historically, the use of rootstocks has been confined primarily to these two aspects of pest control.

The other attributes of rootstocks described herein, e.g. drought tolerance and lime tolerance, have been regarded as secondary factors which aid in the selection of a stock to suit a particular soil type or vineyard condition. However, it is becoming increasingly apparent that rootstocks may be used to improve productivity in situations free of phylloxera or parasitic nematodes. The extent of the range of conditions under which these advantages occur and the extent to which economics will allow the establishment of grafted vineyards under such conditions remain to be determined.

Further Reading

de Castella, F. (1935) Phylloxera-resistant vine stocks. J. Dept. Agric. Vic. 33, 281-88, 303.

Galet, P.G. (1979) A Practical Ampelography. Cornell University Press, Ithaca. 248 pp.

Goss, O.M., and Cameron, I.J. (1977b) Rootstocks for Currants. Aust. Dried Fruits News N.S. 4(4), 9-10.

Lider, L.A. (1960) Vineyard trials in California with nematode-resistant grape rootstocks. Hilgardia 30(4), 123-52.

Ordish, G. (1972) The Great Wine Blight. Dent London, Dent. 237 pp.

Painter, R.H. (1951) Insect Resistance in Crop Plants. Macmillan, New York. 520 pp.

Pongracz, D.P. (1983) Rootstocks for Grapevines. David Philip, Capetown. 150pp.

Sauer, M.R. (1972) Rootstock trials for Sultana grapes on light textured soils. Aust. J. Exp. Agric. Anim. Husb. 12, 107-11.

Other References

Anon. (1928) Guide, Field Day, Viticultural Station, Rutherglen. Dept. Agric. Victoria. 27 pp.

Bailey, L.H. (1934) The species of grape peculiar to North America. Gentes Herbarum, 3, 151-244.

Benard, P., Jouret, C., and Flanzy, M. (1963) Influence des porte-greffes sur la composition mineral des vins. Ann. Technol. Agric. 12, 277-85.

Bernstein, L., Ehlig, C.F. and Clark, R.A. (1969) Effect of grape rootstocks on chloride accumulation in leaves. J. Am. Soc. Hortic. Sci. 94, 584-90.

Bioletti, F.T., Flossfeder, F.C.H. and Way, A.E. (1921) Phylloxera resistant stocks. Calif. Agric. Exp. Stn Bull. No. 331.

Blunno, M. (1901) Report of the Viticulturist. Agric. Gaz. N.S.W. 12, 944-49.

Boubals, D. (1966) Etude de la distribution et des causes de la résistance au phylloxera radicole chez les vitacées. Ann. Amelior Plant. 16, 145-84.

Boubals, D. (1978) Résultats de tests de résistance effectués sur les porte-greffes Harmony et Fercal. Progres Agricole et Viticole, 95, 12-4.

Boubals, D. (1979) Situation des porte-greffes résistant aux nematodes ravageurs directs. Bull. O.I.V. 52, (578) 265-271.

Branas, J. (1974) Viticulture. Dehan, Montpellier, 990pp.

Buchanan, G.A., and Hardie, W.J. (1978) Phylloxera: the implications of D.C. Swan's observations to viticulture in Victoria. J. Aust. Inst. Agric. Sci. 44, 77-81.

Burr, T.J., Ophel, K. and Kerr, A. (1988) Eradication of *Agrobacterium tumefaciens* biovar 3 from dormant grapevine cuttings using a hot water treatment. Plant Disease (in press).

Carbonneau, A. (1985) The early selection of grapevine rootstocks for resistance to drought conditions. Amer. J. Enol. Vitic. 36, 195-8.

Cirami, R.M., McCarthy, M.G. and Glenn, T. (1984) Comparison of the effects of rootstock on crop, juice and wine composition in a replanted, nematode-infested Barossa Valley vineyard. Aust. J. Exp. Agric. Anim. Husb. 24, 283-9.

Conradie, W.J. (1983) Liming and choice of rootstocks as cultural techniques for vines in acid soils. S. Afr. J. Enol. Vitic. 4, 39-44.

Cook, J.A., and Kishaba, T. (1956) Petiole nitrate analysis as a criterion of nitrogen needs in California vineyards. Proc. Am. Soc. Hortic. Sci. 68, 131-40.

Cook, J.A., and Lider, L.A. (1964) Mineral composition of bloomtime grape petiole in relation to rootstock and scion variety behavior. Proc. Am. Soc. Hortic. Sci. 84, 243-54.

Coombe, B.G. (1963) Phylloxera and its relation to South Australian viticulture. Dept. Agric. South Australia. Tech. Bull. No. 31.

Curtel, M.G. (1904) De l'influence de la greffe sur la composition du raison. C.R. Seances Acad. Agric. Fr. 139, 491.

de Castella, F. (1920) Twenty years of reconstitution. J. Dept. Agric. Vic. 18, 481-92.

de Castella, F. (1921a) Resistant stocks. J. Dept. Agric. Vic. 19, 278-89.

de Castella, F. (1921b) Resistant stocks. J. Dept. Agric. Vic. 19, 490-9.

de Castella, F. (1935) Phylloxera-resistant vine stocks. J. Dept. Agric. Vic. 33, 281-8, 303.

Despeissis, J.A. (1894) Phylloxera-resisting vines. Agric. Gaz. N.S.W. 5, 226-8, 284.

Downton, W.J.S. (1977) Influence of rootstocks on the accumulation of chloride, sodium and potassium in grapevines. Aust. J. Agric. Res. 28, 879-89.

Dubois, R. (1902) Annual report of the Director of the Viticultural Experiment Station, Rutherglen. Dep. Agric. Victoria. Annual Report 1900-1. pp. 83-112.

Francois, L.A., and Clark, R.A. (1979) Accumulation of sodium and chloride in leaves of sprinkler-irrigated grapes. J. Am. Soc. Hort. Sci. 104, 11-13.

Galet, P. (1956). Cépages et Vignobles de France. Vol. 1. Les Vignes Americaines. Montpellier. 670 pp.

Goss, O.M., and Cameron, I.J. (1977a) Grapevine rootstocks for use in Western Australia. Dept. Agric. Western Australia. Bull. 4008.

Granett, J., Goheen, A.C., Lider, L.A., and White, J.J. (1987) Evaluation of grape rootstocks for resistance to type A and type B grape phylloxera. Amer. J. Enol. Vitic. 38, 298-300.

Hale, C.R. (1977) Relation between potassium and the malate and tartrate contents of grape berries. Vitis 16, 9-19.

Hale, C.R., and Brien, C.J. (1978) Influence of Salt Creek rootstock on composition and quality of Shiraz grapes and wine. Vitis 17, 139-46.

Hardie, W.J., Whiting, J.R. and Fletcher, G.C. (1981) The identity of an imported selection of 99R rootstock. Aust. Grapegrower and Winemaker (210), 6-10.

Harmon, F.N. (1949) Comparative value of thirteen rootstocks for ten vinifera grape varieties in the Napa Valley in California. Proc. Am. Soc. Hortic. Sci. 54, 157-62.

Harris, A.R. (1983) Resistance of some Vitis rootstocks to Xiphinema index. J. Nematol. 15, 405-9.

Hartmann, H.T., and Kester, D.E. (1968) Plant Propagation; Principles and Practice 2nd Ed. Prentice-Hall, Englewood Cliffs, N.J. 702.pp.

Husmann, G.C., Snyder, E. and Husmann, F.L. (1939) Testing vinifera grape varieties grafted on phylloxera-resistant rootstocks in California. U.S. Dept. Agric. Tech. Bull. No. 697.

Jackson, D.I. (1986) Factors affecting soluble solids, acid, pH and color in grapes. Am. J. Enol. Vitic. 37, 179-83.

Jelenkovic, G. and Olmo, H.P. (1968) Cytogenetics of Vitis III. Partially fertile F1 diploid hybrids between V. vinifera L × V. rotundifolia Michx. Vitis 7, 281-93.

Kasimatis, A.N., and Lider, L.A. (1975) Grape rootstock varieties. Division of Agricultural Sciences, Univ. Calif. Leaflet 2780. 16 pp.

King, P.D., Meekings, J.S. and Smith, S.M. (1982) Studies of the resistance of grapes (vitis spp.) to phylloxera (Daktulosphaira vitifoliae) N.Z.J. Exp. Agric. 10, 337-44.

Kunde, R.M., Lider, L.A., and Schmitt, R.V. (1968) A test of Vitis resistance to Xiphinema index. Amer. J. Enol. Vitic. 19, 30-6.

Lider, L.A., Ferrari, N.L., and Bowers, K.W. (1978) A study of longevity of graft combinations in California vineyards with special interest in the vinifera × rupestris hybrids. Amer. J. Enol. Vitic. 29, 18-24.

Loomis, N.H., and Lider, L.A. (1971) Nomenclature of the 'Salt Creek' grape. Fruit Var. Hortic. Dig. 25, 41-3.

Luhn, C.F., and Goheen, A.C. (1970) Viruses in early California grapevines. Plant Dis. Rep. 54, 1055-6.

Manuel, H.L. (1948) Phylloxera resistant grapevine stocks—experiments at Griffith Viticultural Nursery, 1929-47. Govt. Printer : Sydney.

Marais, P.G. (1979) Situation des porte-greffes résistants a Phytophthora cinnamomi. Bull. O.I.V. 52, 357-76.

May, P., Sauer, M.R., and Scholefield, P.B. (1973) Effect of various combinations of trellis, pruning and rootstock on vigorous Sultana vines. Vitis 12, 192-206.

McGechan, J.K. (1966) Phytophthora cinnamomi responsible for a root rot of grapevines. Aust. J. Sci. 28(9), 354.

Meagher, J.W., Brown, R.H., Taylor, R.H. and Harris, A.R. (1976) The distribution of Xiphinema index and other parasitic nematodes associated with grapevines in north-eastern Victoria. Aust. J. Exp. Agric. Anim. Husb. 16, 932-6.

Neal, J.C. (1889) The root-knot disease of the peach, orange and other plants in Florida, due to the work of Anguillula. Division of Entomology, U.S. Dept Agric. Bull. No. 20, 1-31.

Niklowitz, W. (1955) Histologische Studien an Reblausgallen und Reblaus abwehrnekrosen (Viteus vulpinae C.B. auf Vitis vinifera und Vitis riparia). Phytopathol. Z. 24, 299-340.

Nougaret, R.L., and Lapham, M.H. (1928) A study of phylloxera infestation in California as related to types of soils. U.S. Dept. Agric. Tech. Bull. No. 20, 1-38.

Ophel, K. Burr, T.J. Magarey, P.A. and Kerr, A. (1988). Detection of Agrobacterium tumefaciens biovar 3 in South Australian grapevine propagation material. Australasian Plant Pathol. (in press).

Ough, C.S., Lider, L.A. and Cook, J.A. (1968a) Rootstock-scion Interactions concerning wine making. 1. Juice composition changes and effects on fermentation rate with St. George and 99-R rootstocks are two nitrogen fertilizer levels. Amer. J. Enol. Vitic. 19, 213-37.

Ough, C.S., Cook, J.A. and Lider, L.A. (1968b). Rootstock-scion interactions concerning wine making. 11. Wine compositional and sensory changes attributed to rootstock and fertilizer level differences. Amer. J. Enol. Vitic. 19, 254-65.

Penman, F. Hubble, G.D., Taylor, J.K. and Hooper, P.D. (1940). A soil survey of the Mildura Irrigation Settlement, Victoria. CSIRO. Bull. No. 133.

Perold, A.I. (1927) A Treatise on Viticulture. Macmillan, London. 696pp.

Pratt, Charlotte (1974) Vegetative anatomy of cultivated grapes—a review. Amer. J. Enol. Vitic. 25, 131-50.

Prest, R.L. (1957) Grapes in southern coastal Queensland. Queensl. Agric. J. 83, 381-4.

Quinn, D.G. (1947) Current news of vine stocks—report to Federal Viticultural Congress (Melbourne), November 1947.

Rilling, G. (1975) Zur Frage der direkten oder inderekten Schädigung von Rebenwurzeln bei Befall durch die Reblaus (Dactylosphaera vitifolii Shimer). Vitis 14, 40-2.

Rives, M. (1971) Statistical analysis of rootstock experiments as providing a definition of the terms vigour and affinity in grapes. Vitis 9, 280-90.

Ruhl, E.H. Clingeleffer, P.R. Nicholas, P.R., Cirami, R.M., McCarthy, M.G. and Whiting, J.R. (1988). Effect of rootstocks on berry weight and pH, mineral content and organic acid concentrations of grape juice of some wine varieties. Aust. J. Exp. Agric. 28, 119-25.

Sarooshi, R.A., and Bevington, K.B. (1976). Graft incompatibility in a Gordo Blanco rootstock trial. Aust. Grapegrower Winemaker, 13(148), 11-2.

Sauer, M.R. (1967) Rootknot tolerance in some grapevine rootstocks. Aust. J. Exp. Agric. Anim. Husb. 7, 580-3.

Sauer, M.R. (1968) Effects of vine rootstocks on chloride concentration in Sultana scions. Vitis 7, 223-6.

Sauer, M.R. (1974) Yield of Sultanas on rootstocks. J. Aust. Inst. Agric. Sci. 40, 84-5.

Sauer, M.R. (1977) Nematode resistant grape rootstocks. Aust. Dried Fruit News N.S. 5(1), 10-4.

Smart, R.E. (1980) Vine manipulation to improve wine grape quality. Proc. Int. Symp. Grapes Wine. pp.362-75. University of California, Davis.

Smith, J.H. (1938) Pests of the grapevine. Queensl. Agric. J. 50, 700-7.

Snyder, E. (1936) Susceptibility of grape rootstocks to root-knot nematode. U.S. Dept. Agric. Circ. No. 405, 1-15.

Snyder, E., and Harmon, F.N. (1948) Comparative value of nine rootstocks for ten Vinifera grape varieties. Proc. Am. Soc. Hortic. Sci. 51, 237-94.

Stannard, M.C. (1976) Research for the fruit industries—viticulture. Dept. Agric. New South Wales 61pp.

Stirling, G.R. and Cirami, R.M. (1984) Resistance and tolerance of grape rootstocks to South Australian populations of root-knot nematode. Aust. J. Exp. Agric. Anim. Husb. 24, 277-82.

Taylor D., and Bowen, T.J. (1955) Resistant stocks for grapes at Stanthorpe. Queensl. Agric. J. 81, 15-8.

Viala, P., and Ravaz, L. (1896) American Vines. (Trans. by R. Dubois and W.P. Wilkinson (1901)). Government Printer, Melbourne. 390pp.

Weinberger, H.J., and Harmon, F.N. (1966) Harmony, a new nematode and phylloxera resistant rootstock for vinifera grapes. Fruit Var. Hortic. Dig. 20, 63-5.

Whiting, J.R., Buchanan, G.A. and Edwards, M.E. (1987) Assessment of rootstocks for wine grape production. In: Lee, T.H. (ed) Proc. Sixth Aust. Wine Ind. Tech. Conf., pp.184-90 Australian Industrial Publishers, Adelaide, 280pp.

Wilkinson, H.H., and Burney, M. d'A. (1921). Affinity. Aust. Brewers J. 39, 379-87.

Winkler, A.J., Cook, J.A., Kliewer, W.M., and Lider, L.A. (1974). General Viticulture. University of California Press, Berkeley. 710pp.

CHAPTER NINE

Grape Planting Material

M. G. McCARTHY

The ease with which grapes are propagated from cuttings, and low establishment costs, were important factors contributing to the early development of viticulture in Australia. Even when rootstocks became necessary following the advent of phylloxera, the price of propagation material was kept low by the provision of grafted rootlings at subsidized prices. The passing of the era of low costs has brought major change in the cost-benefit analysis of the planting material for vineyards.

In primary industries based on annual crops it has long been accepted that planting material should be disease-free, genetically-uniform and high-yielding, and such is the practice. The same needs are even more cogent in an industry such as viticulture where the crop is perennial and is expected to be productive for 30 or more years and where costs of establishment are now so high. In Australia, little emphasis was given to the provision of improved planting material before the 1960s, but since that time, as in most grapegrowing countries, there have been many developments in the provision of scion and rootstock material. Due to a readiness to accept

new concepts Australia is in a fortunate position to make use of new material.

It is anticipated that nearly all plantings will be with improved material within the next few decades. The ready acceptance of improved planting material can also be seen in California where, since the first certified grapevine was offered to the grape industry in 1960, approximately 65 million certified vines were sold in the ensuing 16 years (Goheen 1977).

The process of selection and improvement of grapevine material is largely a matter of organization and an account of several schemes is given below.

9.1 The need for improvement of planting material

9.1.1 Mixed and misnamed plantings
The primary reason for selection is to ensure that the variety planted is true-to-type; this is difficult to determine in a vineyard at pruning. One off-type in a patch can result in a large number of off-types in the vines derived from it. A positive identification of the variety is necessary to ensure that similar varieties do not become mixed or misnamed. Confusion has existed in Australia in the identification of some varieties; misnaming of varieties may lead to serious disappointments or misuse. For example, the variety wrongly named Albillo in South Australia, and called Sherry in the Barossa, made only an average quality fortified wine; now that it has been correctly identified as Chenin Blanc, winemakers are treating it differently and successfully using it for quality table wines.

9.1.2 Clonal differences
A clone is defined as 'genetically uniform material derived from a single individual and propagated exclusively by vegetative means such as cuttings,

divisions or grafts' (Hartmann and Kester 1975). The existence of clonal differences in grapes and the value of selection was first documented by Sartorius (1926). Conflicting results from clonal selection trials were reported by Bioletti (1926); he found that mass selection of vine cuttings on the basis of yield of the parent vines was of no value in improving or maintaining production. Rives (1961) has pointed out that the failure in Bioletti's experiment to detect differences may have been due in part to the fact that European varieties were probably introduced into the New World from quite a small number of cuttings. The results of clonal selection in France (Huglin and Julliard 1962) and Australia (Woodham and Alexander 1966) provide ample evidence of clonal differences within a variety and of the opportunity for the improvement of planting stock. It is now appreciated that differences in vine performance can be caused by gene changes or by infection with virus or mycoplasma.

Differences due to genotype
Rives (1965) stated: 'The multiplication of possible sites of stable genetic variations, (i.e. vegetative propagation), also provides a fine opportunity for the diversification of an originally homogeneous clone into numerous clonal types'. This is the basis of the German 'Clone of a clone' whereby it is claimed to be possible to reselect clones giving a further yield improvement from an existing clone as a result of genetic variation even when vegetative propagation is used (Becker and Sievers 1978). Mutations are common in grapevines. Most that have been recorded are of a conspicuous nature (e.g. colour change) but it is probable that less conspicuous mutations occur frequently. These less obvious differences may be in growth habit, leaf morphology, vigour, sugar content, or other characteristics (e.g. Todorov and Dimitrov 1980). By careful observation it is possible to select for these differences. The largest percentage of mutations involving growth habit, bunch type, berry colour etc. are detrimental and therefore discarded. However, there are some instances where mutations have proved to be an improvement over the parent vine.

Differences caused by infections
Viruses and mycoplasmas are submicroscopic parasitic organisms that infect and damage plants (and animals). Leafroll virus, for example, reduces yield, vigour, sugar content and berry skin pigmentation in red varieties and delays maturity. Ricksettia-like organisms (modified parasitic bacteria) have also been found to be associated with certain plant diseases (e.g. Pierce's Disease of grape). These organisms multiply rapidly, utilizing the plant's metabolites for their own growth. They may also disrupt translocation of metabolites in the phloem causing the plant to wilt or grow poorly. Diseases of this type are transmitted by vegetative propagation. Their effects are made more serious as a result of virus complexing, as for example when infected scions are grafted onto infected rootstock.

9.2 Method for improvement of planting material

There are five generally recognized methods used for the improvement of planting material:
— taking cuttings from good plantings
— negative selection
— positive selection
— clonal comparison and selection
— heat therapy
The first three are mass selection techniques and require only a small number of observations. Clonal selection and heat therapy are specialist methods used by viticultural research organizations; they are labour-intensive, long-term selection methods requiring many measurements and hence are unsuitable for growers or nurseries.

9.2.1 Mass selection methods

Cuttings from good plantings
This is the simplest method. It achieves no improvement in the standard of the propagation material compared with the source block, although there may be improvement compared with the district average for the variety. A 'good' block may be one that has a history of consistent yields and an absence of off-types and disease symptoms. However, it is possible that satisfactory yields may be due to management or environmental factors and not a reflection of the standard of the planting material of the block.

Negative selection
An improvement on mass cutting from good plantings is to mark the undesirable vines in a block. This method has been widely advocated and is quite useful. As long ago as 1882 Sutherland wrote in his book *The South Australian Winegrowers Manual*, 'indifferent or poor vines giving but little fruit are

prone to propagate poor or sterile vines from their cuttings'. Undesirable vines would include off-types, low-yielding vines, virus-infected vines as indicated by autumn leaf colours of red varieties, tetraploid vines and various other symptoms. The method avoids the trap of taking cuttings from vines from which a large number of cuttings would be obtained as a result of improved vigour brought about by poor cropping.

Positive selection

A further refinement on negative selection is to mark the above-average vines in a vineyard, i.e. to positively select the desirable vines. Positive selection is done by marking the vines in the vineyard at harvest that have above-average crops due either to more bunches, bigger bunches, better set, heavier berries or a combination of these factors. Assessments are best checked throughout the season, especially in autumn when visual symptoms of virus-like diseases may be apparent; suspect vines should be discarded. If this procedure is repeated for several years the selected planting material is likely to have less or even nil virus and a desirable cropping performance.

In effect, this method was the basis for the original selection of cultivated varieties; through positive selection over many centuries from among the wild *Vitis vinifera* of the Near East with their small bunches and few large-seeded berries, selections of promising plants were obtained with larger bunches of small-seeded berries. Environmental pressures aided further in this selection process by eliminating varieties and genetic mutations that were poorly adapted; many however survived and from these has come the now wide range of varieties in existence today (see Chapters 5 and 7).

9.2.2 Specialist selection methods

Clonal comparison and selection

The vines marked by positive selection can be further examined and subjected to clonal comparison. The procedure used is designed to distinguish whether the better-than-average performance of an individual grapevine is due to its genetic superiority or whether it is simply favoured by different environmental conditions, different methods of pruning, different rootstocks, etc. Clonal comparison and selection consists of the establishment and comparison of selected clones on a uniform soil type in a trial designed to allow statistical analysis of the results with observations made over a number of years, e.g. up to a decade. As Basler (1976) stated, the aim of clonal selection is to maintain high, regular yields of good quality fruit. He divided the selection program into three phases:
(i) the selection of clones
(ii) comparison of the initial selections in clonal trials, and
(iii) testing of an advanced selection of clones in different areas.
Clonal selection in Germany normally involves four phases with up to five stages of multiplication (Schöffling and Rouday 1978). The important features of clonal selection in Germany are:
(i) the results of nine annual productions are recorded before the completion of the main selection program in order to determine which clones are of highest potential.
(ii) the clones under test are grafted onto virus-tested rootstocks.
(iii) at least two locations and several rootstocks are used for the intermediate selection, and,
(iv) the smaller the performance differences, the more important it is to include wine characteristics. Fortunately, for the majority of the grapegrowing areas in Australia, the added complication of testing selected clones on rootstocks is not yet necessary, although in time it will be.

All State Departments of Agriculture involved in viticultural research have active clonal selection programs and all have similarities. The selection program used by the South Australian Department of Agriculture can be used as an illustration; it is broadly divided into two major stages. Stage I involves the selection of candidate clones in each of the major grapegrowing districts and assessing their performance in selection trials under their local environment. Top-performing selections from each trial are concurrently virus-indexed allowing for possible early release of 'clean' material into the Vine Improvement Scheme. At the termination of Stage I (usually 4-7 years of cropping data) the top few clones, assessed from cumulative yield, are chosen for further comparison against selections from other districts. In this Stage II of the program more detailed assessments are made of the components of yield and maturity. Small-lot winemaking and sensory evaluation of wines is done on selected trials. As shown in Figure 9.1 the number of selections under test in Stage II is much reduced thus permitting more detailed testing.

Based on data obtained from Stage II some selections may be multiplied into sufficient numbers (two hectare units) for assessment of yield and winemaking attributes by industry.

Heat therapy

The inferior performance of a grape clone is frequently due to virus infection. The significantly lower yield of one of the six clones of Muscat Gordo Blanco in a trial reported in Table 9.1 is associated with leafroll infection and it is believed this infection is the cause of the inferior performance. Working at Merbein, R.E. Woodham (unpublished data) demonstrated the detrimental effect of two levels of virus infection on yield and pruning weights of Sultana clone H5 compared with clean material (Table 9.2).

Removing leafroll virus by heat therapy from a high yielding Muscadelle selection resulted in a significant increase in fruit yield and vegetative growth (Table 9.3) in each of three consecutive years (McCarthy *et al.* 1989). However, it is not certain that all viruses detected in grapevines are harmful, as some high-yielding clones have identifiable virus infections. Australia is fortunate that a number of virus diseases found overseas are not present and others are not widespread. This makes selection easier since most of the clones selected from trials are also free of known viruses; it also emphasizes

Table 9.1 The influence of leafroll infection on performance of Muscat Gordo Blanco clones at Loxton Research Centre for the years 1972-1978.

Clone number	Cumulative Yield kg/vine	Status
131 A.S.70.2268	237	clean
173 A.S.70.2266	229	clean
19 A.S.70.2270	227	clean
15 A.S.70.2269	222	clean
138 A.S.70.2267	218	clean
103 —	103	infected
LSD 5%	17	

the need for continual quarantine surveillance on imported grapevine material to ensure that only 'clean' material is introduced.

If clean material is not available the technique of heat therapy can be used. The technique (Goheen *et al.* 1965) consists of growing potted vines for 2-4 months in a growth cabinet held at a temperature too high (38 °C) for the development

Variety under test: Cabernet Sauvignon

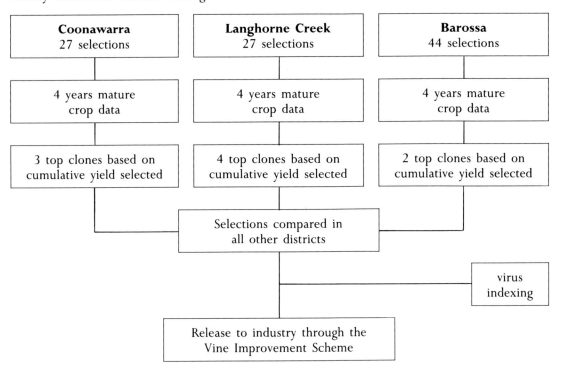

Figure 9.1 An example of the clonal selection and evaluation program used by the S.A. Department of Agriculture.

Table 9.2 Yield and pruning weight of Sultana H5 (A.C.70.8160) with degrees of leafroll infection (data supplied by R.C. Woodham, CSIRO Merbein)

Degree of leafroll Infection	Pruning Wt. kg/vine		Fresh yield kg/vine	
	1971	1972	1971	1972
Nil	6	4	16	31
Mild	5	4	12	29
Severe	4	3	8	23

Table 9.3 Influence of leafroll infection on the performance of a Muscadelle selection for years 1985-87.

Selection	Leafroll status	Fresh yield, kg per vine		
		1985	1986	1987
32	infected	5.7	9.6	9.9
Heat treated 32	clean	8.0	13.3	11.9
LSD 5%		1.2	1.3	0.8

of virus in the growing shoot tips. The shoot tips that grow during this time are removed and rooted under mist culture. Vines subsequently propagated from these tips are frequently lower in virus infection than the mother vine and often the new material is 'clean'. Heat therapy treatment of potted vines is, however, time consuming and expensive with no certainty that shoot tips will be freed from virus.

Extended periods of heat treatment can have adverse effects on the performance of subsequent material and re-indexing is necessary to determine its virus status. Barlass *et al.* (1982) developed a quicker method of virus elimination using short periods of heat treatment during tissue culture. By changing the temperature at which the explants are propagated it is possible to eliminate the major graft-transmissable virus diseases.

9.2.3 Introduced material

The use of selected planting material from other viticultural regions of Australia or from overseas is a further, often important, method of increasing the range of material available from which selections can be made.

On arrival in Australia all imported material, regardless of origin, is treated with methyl bromide to kill arthropod and other pests and hot-water-dipped to inactivate Pierce's Disease. Vines are grown for a minimum of two years in an official quarantine glasshouse during which time they are visually screened for disease. The time spent in post-entry quarantine is often longer if virus indexing is necessary.

In an attempt to avoid long post-entry quarantine times several overseas pathologists are recognised as sources of vines with superior health status; material originating from them does not have to be re-indexed upon arrival in Australia. The Australian Quarantine and Inspection Service (AQIS) currently (1988) recognizes only two overseas suppliers viz. the University of California, Davis and the Canadian Department of Agriculture, Post Entry Quarantine Station, Sidney, British Columbia, Canada. AQIS will consider material from other sources provided there is documentation that the stock was indexed to prescribed standards for the diseases listed in Table 9.4, and certain other requirements such as how the tested material was held after indexing (e.g. grown in the field or in a glasshouse).

Prior to 1984 the introduction of grapevines from overseas was restricted to official agencies such as the CSIRO and Departments of Agriculture. Private individuals could only import new material through the official agencies and had to agree to make such material available to others following its release from quarantine. Multiple entries of the same material were discouraged.

In 1984 several changes were made to the Commonwealth Quarantine Act, the most important being the abolition of the need for official sponsorship of the import and general distribution after release from post-entry quarantine. While all imported material still undergoes mandatory quarantine (for which there is a fee), individuals or commercial groups can now import propagation material and retain the sole right to its use after release. This change in policy has allowed the importation of patented varieties into Australia by individuals or groups provided they meet the breeder's requirements regarding royalties, etc. An identification code has been adopted for both imported and locally-collected virus-tested material (Table 9.5).

Although imported selections are in the majority of cases the best available in the country of origin they need to be tested again for yield and performance when grown in a new region where both growing conditions and production requirements differ. For example, selection programs in Northern Europe may place more emphasis on earliness of ripening than is the case in Australian selection programs.

Table 9.4 Quarantinable graft-transmitted diseases of grapevine stocks and scions (Australian Quarantine and Inspection Service 1988)

Scion material

Flavesence doree (only in France)

Nepoviruses (Grapevine fanleaf, tomato ringspot, arabis mosaic, Joannes seyve virus, grapevine chrome mosaic and grapevine Bulgarian latent.)

Stem Pitting

Legno riccio

Asteroid mosaic

Bratislava mosaic virus (only in Europe)

Corky bark

Leafroll

Stock material

The following diseases, additional to those for scion material, are indexed:

Vein mosaic

Yellow speckle

Vein necrosis

Absence is desirable for the following viruses of unknown importance:

Tobacco necrosis virus

Tomato bushy stunt virus

Alfalfa mosaic virus

Broad bean mosaic virus

Sowbane mosaic virus

Tobacco mosaic virus

Absence is required for the following diseases:

Guignardia bidwellii (Black rot)

Xanthomonas ampelina (Bacterial necrosis)

Table 9.5 Identification code adopted for the Commonwealth Accession List of Virus-Tested Fruit Varieties in Australia (approved by Australian Agricultural Council in 1971).
Once allocated, the code is retained at all times for each clone irrespective of transfers; transfers to other places are coded by years and State letter.

Code group			Code
I	Source:	Imported or introduced	I.
		Australian or local	A.
II	Place:	Western Australia	W.
		New South Wales	N.
		Victoria	V.
		Queensland	Q.
		South Australia	S.
		Tasmania	T.
		Commonwealth (CSIRO: Department of Health)	C.
III	Year of introduction or establishment as virus free in Australia		e.g. 70
IV	Serial numbers of accessions:		
	New South Wales		0001-1999
	Victoria		2001-3999
	Queensland		4001-4999
	South Australia		5001-5999
	Western Australia		6001-6999
	Tasmania		7001-7999
	CSIRO		8001-8999
	Commonwealth (other departments including Health)		9001-9999
V	Name of variety:		Arranged alphabetically

9.3 Performance of improved planting material

The higher costs in using selected planting material need to be compared objectively with its advantages. Antcliff (1965) reported yield differences of up to 92 per cent between low- and high-yielding clones in a Sultana trial. Woodham and Alexander (1966) found increases of 30 to 100 per cent between selected low and high-yielding Sultana vines; they further demonstrated that these differences were reproducible in propagules from the source mother vines. H.R. Tulloch (unpublished data), working with variety blocks each with 180 vines at the Barossa Viticultural Research Centre, found large yield differences between individual vines. For example, in the years 1958-1962 the mean yield of the top Cabernet Sauvignon selection was 9.7 kg per vine, while the lowest averaged 1.5. Other varieties showed similar variation in yield. From these sources Tulloch created the first clones distributed through the South Australian Vine Improvement Scheme to industry; some have become well known, for example Cabernet Sauvignon SA 125 (A.S.70.2351) and Shiraz SA 1654 (A.S.70.2271).

The Tulloch selections were made from a small population, thus reducing the probability of finding improved material. Later selections were made from amongst a large population involving many vineyards. When the Barossa Vine Selection Society planted their local selections in a clonal trial in 1970 SA 125 was included for comparison: the cumulative yields for the years 1973 to 1976 inclusive revealed 22 selections that yielded more fruit than SA 125

Table 9.6 Comparison of total weight for 4 years of crop (1977-1980) of some 30 Cabernet Sauvignon selections at Langhorne Creek, SA (McCarthy 1986)

Numerical ranking based on yield		Clone number	Total fruit weight (kg)
1st		10 ⎞ Local	39.0
2nd		9 ⎬ clone	38.7
3rd		6 ⎠ identification	38.2
28th	SA	159	29.0
29th	SA	95	28.7
30th	SA	125(A.S.70.2351)	27.0
LSD (5%)			3.2

(the author, unpublished data). In the Langhorne Creek district south of Adelaide, S.A. Cabernet Sauvignon SA 125 has been compared with 27 local selections; based on the total weight of fruit picked over 4 years all of the Langhorne Creek selections were better than SA 125 (Table 9.6). On the other hand, SA 125 compared favourably with selections from the Coonawarra district of South Australia when tested in that region. Cumulative yields after 4 years of cropping (1977-1980) revealed that the selection with the greatest yield had produced a total of 36.7 kg fruit per vine; SA 125 was placed third with 35.6 kg fruit per vine (not significantly less) while the poorest producer had a significantly lower 23.6 kg per vine. The different performance of SA 125 at Langhorne Creek and Coonawarra indicates the necessity to compare selections in their intended region.

Whiting and Hardie (1981) reported consistent and significant differences in the fruit yield, fruit composition and vegetative growth as assessed by the weight of prunings over a five-year period of eight Cabernet Sauvignon selections from Australia, France and U.S.A. The cumulative yield of the Californian selection I.V.69.2217 was approximately three times the cumulative yield of the poorest clone I.C.70.8158 and consistently outyielded the popular Australian selections A.S.70.2259 and A.S.70.2351 (Table 9.7). Significant differences were reported between selections in the concentration of soluble solids and pH of the juice in every year although these differences were not related to yield. The concentration of titratable acid was only significantly different between selections in two years.

Until the 1980s yield was often the sole selection criterion used in Australian selection programs, although analytical measures of Brix, pH, titratable acid and colour were used to discriminate clonal differences. While it was recognized that wine quality should also be assessed, the large number of clones, rootstocks and combinations under test in Australia made wine evaluation impracticable. As the number was reduced through elimination of poor yielders, small-lot winemaking and sensory evaluation was integrated into many Australian selection programs. The need for wine evaluation increased as it became obvious that high yielding clones could not be separated on yield alone. Developments in small-lot winemaking such as yeast technology and control of oxidation, combined with computer analysis of sensory data, have increased the plausibility of the determination of differences in wine quality between experimental lots.

Table 9.7 A comparison of selections of Cabernet Sauvignon at Mildura (Whiting and Hardie 1981)

Clone	Country of origin	Cumulative fresh yield (kg/vine) 1975/1979 inclusive
I.V.69.2217	California	79.9
R3V19E	Australia	79.5
A.V.70.2351	Australia	67.8
R2V1W	Australia	67.2
A.V.70.2259	Australia	66.9
IC.70.8157	France	57.9
IC.70.8159	France	52.7
IC.70.8158	France	26.6
LSD 5%		8.6

9.4 Vine improvement schemes

In many grapegrowing areas of the world, government or other authorities have initiated 'Vine Improvement Schemes'. The aims of such schemes are to provide industry with sufficient numbers of cuttings of the best planting material available to meet demand and to ensure that the material is free of known viruses and is true-to-label. The selection and testing procedures used by viticultural research organizations for obtaining improved clones have been outlined above.

Once it has been established that a clone is pathogen-free, high-yielding and true-to-type it needs to be maintained and multiplied for distribution to the viticultural industry. Distribution schemes are devised to provide large quantities of vine cuttings that meet a minimum standard of cleanliness (e.g. freedom from harmful viruses) and genetic uniformity. While such schemes usually increase the cost of the planting material, the expense can be justified by improved production and/or quality.

9.4.1 Overseas schemes

France

After the phylloxera invasion of Europe in the latter part of the nineteenth century it became necessary for most growers to graft phylloxera-susceptible vinifera varieties on to phylloxera-resistant American species (Chapter 8). Before 1944 French nurserymen were unrestricted in the quality or quantity of propagation material sold and, as in other countries, this led to serious problems with virus.

In 1944 the 'Section de Controle des Bois et Plantes de Vigne' was formed to regulate rootstock propagation and hence reduce the spread of virus. In 1954 this job was taken over by the Institut des Vins de Consommation Courante (IVCC), the official French Certification Bureau; strict regulations applying to propagation and distribution of rootstock and scion material were enforced. Since 1976 the work of the IVCC has been taken over by the Office National Interprofessional des Vins de Table (ONIVIT). Clonal selection in France is in three stages, each controlled by officially recognized organizations. The first stage, that of testing the selected clones, is carried out by research establishments approved by the Minister of Agriculture. In 1977 two such selection stations were the National Institute of Agronomic Research (INRA) and the National Technical Association for Improvement in Viticulture (ANTAV): the latter is a professional organization whose members belong to winemakers or vinegrafters unions as well as to agricultural service centres.

The objectives of ANTAV are; 'To undertake all activities and provide collaboration with all organizations promoting the selection, premultiplication, multiplication and the clonal propagation of healthy and environmentally adapted vines with a view to improving viticultural production'. Clones selected must be approved by a technical committee for the selection of improved plants. Approval for the release of clones is not granted until they have been freed of identifiable virus diseases. Only certified clones are allowed to be propagated. Pre-propagation is carried out at propagation centres that have been awarded permits from the Minister of Agriculture.

These centres produce basic material for the planting of mother plantations and the supply of certified vine material. This stage of propagation of vines is supervised by IVCC. In 1975, 471 clones had been certified, consisting of 192 rootstocks, 249 winegrape varieties and 50 table grape varieties. If any clone of a scion variety shows sign of any virus-like disease, all of the propagation material from it (as far back as the original mother vine) may be destroyed; thus it is necessary that other clones be available. As can be seen, exacting rules, laid down by the Minister of Agriculture, apply at each stage of propagation, thus helping to ensure that only good material is distributed.

Germany and the European Economic Community
The production and certification of grapevine planting material in Germany is strictly controlled. Certification was first introduced voluntarily in Germany, through the Deutsche Landwirtschafts-Gesellschaft immediately after the First World War. This voluntary scheme later became law. Competence for certification of material rested with regional authorities using uniformly-agreed principles.

The German producers of grafted vines amalgamated in 1968 to form a national organization; this is affiliated with the German winegrowers association (Deutscher Weinbauverband) and belongs to the International Committee and Co-ordinating Group of the producers of the European Economic Community (E.E.C.). A directive from the Council of the E.C.C. to the member countries in 1968 endeavoured to standardize regulations on the commercial vegetative propagation of the grapevine. The directive was a further step in restricting the release to industry of only propagation material produced under the control of an officially recognized organization. The directive specified three grades of propagation material (base, certified and standard) including conditions covering length and diameter of cuttings and rootlings, label size, number per bundle, etc. Member countries may impose supplementary or more rigorous conditions.

California
The Californian Vine Improvement and Distribution scheme is supervised by the Nursery and Seed Services Division of the Californian Department of Food and Agriculture. The State of California enforces strict regulations over the nursery trade. It is illegal to sell any nursery stock, including grapevines, without a licence. All nurseries have to meet minimum requirements in the following areas: pest control, stock shipment, grades and standards, labelling and sanitation.

The Californian grape improvement and distribution scheme had its origin in 1952 as the California Grape Certification Association. It was an organization formed to develop and maintain grape stock free from known grape virus diseases and varieties that were true to name. In 1955 the first planting was made in the Foundation vineyard. New procedures for virus indexing were developed and by 1960 the Foundation vineyard was re-established with many varieties. To date all of the important grape varieties and rootstocks in use in California,

and many of the lesser varieties, are planted in the Foundation vineyard.

When the program first started, it was completely subsidized by industry and governmental grants but by 1968 the scheme had become self-supporting through the payment of royalties for certified stock. The Californian grape registration and certification scheme is a good example of a successful program. In 1976, 95 per cent of all grape planting material sold was from certified stock (Goheen 1977).

9.4.2 Australian schemes
The establishment and maintenance of multiplication and distribution schemes for horticultural crops in Australia is the responsibility of the individual states with the Commonwealth Government being responsible for horticultural crop repositories. Repositories are the ultimate source of propagation material but are not a direct source. The National Grapevine Foundation Planting was established at Mildura, Victoria in 1974 and contains two vines of the best clones of important grape varieties. Preservation of the material in the repository as pathogen-free, true-to-type stock involves:

(i) Sanitation to eliminate the spread of disease by unclean equipment, soil mixes etc.

(ii) Inspection and testing to ensure that the plants conform to their original standards.

(iii) Isolation which ensures that the plants do not become recontaminated with virus by insects or nematodes as vectors. Fortunately this is not a widespread problem in Australia because most of the more serious insect/virus combinations do not occur, apart from the *Xiphenema index*/fan leaf complex in Rutherglen and, also, the suspicion that the disorder known as Australian Vine Yellows may be insect-spread (P. Magarey, personal communication)

The South Australian scheme
The South Australian improvement scheme commenced in 1974 and is represented diagrammatically in Figure 9.2. Much of the history of clonal selection and the vine improvement scheme in South Australia, including the important contributions of H.R. Tulloch, M.A. Loder and R.T.J. Webber, has been described by Cirami (1984) and McCarthy (1986).

Vine Foundation Blocks are located at the Nuriootpa Research and Advisory Centre; these consist of three vines each of the best available clone of commercially grown and introduced varieties. The virus status of all vines in the block is known and

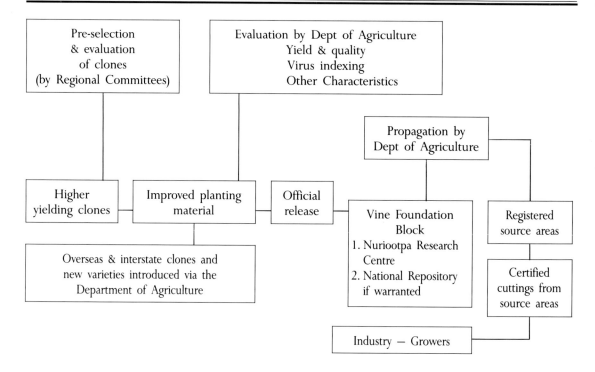

Administration of Vine Improvement and Distribution Scheme
State Vine Improvement Committee

- Representatives from Department of Agriculture; Regional Vine Improvement Committees; South Australian Phylloxera Board.
- *Role* — To co-ordinate activities of Regional Committees

South Australian Phylloxera Board

- Approve vine introduction
- Fund & receive monies (Vine Improvement Trust Fund)

Regional Vine Improvement Committee

- Barossa, Riverland, Clare, Southern Vales, South East and Langhorne Creek.
- Representatives — Department of Agriculture, Grapegrower, winery interests, Phylloxera Board and nurserymen.
- Role:
  1. Pre-selection of clones from established vineyards.
  2. Select sites for Registered Source Areas and determine areas and varieties required.
  3. Arrange collection, distribution and sale of cuttings from Registered Source Areas.
  4. Promote use of improved planting material.
  5. Assist in evaluation of new clones.
  6. Foster relations with nurserymen.
  7. Inspect registered source areas for trueness-to-type etc.

Figure 9.2 Vine Improvement and Distribution Scheme operating since 1974 in South Australia.

where possible the vines are virus-free. The Foundation Block is the basic source of best planting material in the State.

Vines in the Foundation Block are regularly inspected for the presence of bud mutations and visible virus symptoms. Registered Source Areas are established to supply the vine industry with cuttings of the best available clone or clones of each variety. The variety and area required in a district are determined by the Regional Vine Improvement Committee. The vines for the registered source areas are propagated under contract by the Department of Agriculture and rootlings sold to owners of source areas.

The registered source areas are located on growers' properties and are managed in the normal manner. The areas are marked with coloured metal plates at the end of each row to help ensure that cuttings are collected correctly. An officer of the Department of Agriculture has the responsibility of collecting cuttings from the Research Centre that are required for new source areas, organizing the field nursery, lifting the rootlings for source areas, allocating rootlings and, when the source area is planted, of defining and mapping the location. This officer also assists the Regional Vine Improvement Committee in the inspection of the source areas for off-types ensuring that a satisfactory level of management is maintained and, with the assistance of horticultural advisers, keeps a record of all registered source areas.

Cuttings from registered source areas are distributed in bundles of fifty. To each bundle is attached a Certification label. The Regional Committees in each area have the task of taking orders for cuttings and grafting budwood, cutting the required number of cuttings (in co-operation with the owner of the block), labelling, bundling and then distributing the cuttings to growers and nurserymen.

Rootstocks for benchgrafting or field budding are supplied from a rootstock mother vine planting established in the S.A. Riverland by the State Vine Improvement Committee. Proceeds from the sale of rootstocks meet the cost of leasing the land and development and operating expenses.

The New South Wales scheme
The NSW scheme is supervised by the NSW Horticultural Propagation Co-operative Society. The Department of Agriculture publishes approved sources of supply of horticultural propagation material from which cuttings can be taken. Approved sources of supply of grapevine varieties are plantings of important grape varieties grown on private vineyards or the Department of Agriculture Research Centre.

By 1983 it was apparent the Co-operative Society could not meet the demand for vine propagation material. The NSW Vine Improvement Committee was established to initiate a vine improvement scheme to operate as an autonomous unit of the Co-operative Society. The Committee co-ordinates the regional committees established in each of the four main grapegrowing regions in the state, viz. MIA, Sunraysia, Central Tablelands and Coastal. Members of these regional committees are drawn from all sectors of the grape industry. The NSW Department of Agriculture is responsible for the selection and introduction of new varieties or clones, their assessment and multiplication for the establishment of registered mother vine plantings. The scheme distributed over one million cuttings annually from 1984 to 1986.

The Victorian scheme
A vine improvement scheme for scion varieties was started in Victoria in 1978. This scheme was established under the control of the Fruit Variety Improvement Committee (Vines) (FVIC). The committee included representatives of the Department of Agriculture, commercial nurserymen and grape industry representatives from the producing areas of the state as well as the Australian Dried Fruits Association (ADFA). Between 1978 and 1986 the Victorian Department of Agriculture and Rural Affairs provided the impetus to expand the vine improvement scheme. In 1986 the Victorian and Murray Valley Vine Improvement Association Inc. was formed with statewide responsibilities. The Association is financially self-supporting.

The Department of Agriculture and Rural Affairs provides planting material and replacements for registered mother vine plantings and inspects them for trueness to type and pest and disease freedom and, like NSW and SA, is responsible for clonal selection and evaluation and virus testing. New South Wales and Victoria have agreements covering the supply of cuttings from near-border source areas in each State.

Other states and the Australian scheme
Other states of Australia, while having only small grape industries compared with SA, Vic and NSW, have recognized the need for selected planting material to supply their expansion. Western Australia, for example, has a clonal selection program covering

winegrapes, dried fruit and table grape varieties, and a nucleus of planting material is being established for all virus-tested grapevine material under the Western Australian Fruit Variety Improvement Scheme. Two vines are to be maintained of each clone/variety of commercial significance. The multiplication of the improved grapevine material is carried out at the Swan Research Station for release to the industry. Where quarantine controls allow there is movement of cuttings across regional and state boundaries. The South Australian scheme for example has provided large numbers of vinifera and rootstock cuttings to other states and has established several overseas markets for cuttings.

The Australian Vine Improvement Association (AVIA), founded in 1988, co-ordinates vine improvement nationally and has representatives from each state and observers from CSIRO, State Departments of Agriculture and the Grape and Wine Research Council. The objectives of AVIA are:

1. To co-ordinate vine improvement activities throughout Australia.
2. To recommend vine improvement research priorities to the Grape and Wine Research Council.
3. To negotiate and enter into agreements for the entry of new vine material into Australia by acting, where necessary, as a primary licensee for overseas vine breeders.
4. To facilitate the equitable distribution of high quality propagation material throughout Australia.

9.4.3 Plant variety protection

Plant variety protection is a patenting system which gives the breeder of a new variety legislated rights in the propagation and sale of a variety for defined periods. For this period the patentee can collect royalties from licences required for the variety's use by others. To be awarded varietal protection a variety must be adjudged new, distinct, uniform and stable.

Californian grape breeders are given protection under the USA Plant Patent Act of 1930 which covers vegetatively propagated crops. Breeders in Europe are protected by the International Union for the Protection of New Varieties of Plants, which is an agreement between member countries to offer legal safeguards in their territories for the rights of breeders of new plant varieties. The signatories (1981) were Denmark, Federal Republic of Germany, France, the Netherlands, Sweden, United Kingdom, Belgium, Italy, Switzerland, Austria, Spain, Hungary,

and, Romania, Russia, Argentina, South Africa, New Zealand, Israel, Japan and Czechoslovakia.

Australia has recently (1987) enacted plant variety rights (PVR) legislation and regulations are being promulgated. The introduction of PVR followed a long and often emotive public debate on the merits of such legislation: protagonists referred to the advantages to the Australian grapegrowing industry if access was gained to overseas material such as that recently bred in California and Europe, especially some table-grape varieties; antagonists argued that higher costs and monopolistic controls could result.

Under the enacted Australian scheme the onus rests on the breeder of protected varieties to promote the material, to arrange for the collection of royalties, and to police the rights. There is no provision for an official system for testing the merit of patented varieties. For grapes the impact of this legislation is therefore likely to be tied to material whose merit can be readily established; this is easiest with table and drying grapes but is difficult with winegrapes because of the long lead time required for proving variety merit. It would appear that the role of the Australian Vine Improvement Association and State Vine Improvement Schemes will not be greatly affected by the introduction of PVR and they may even play a role in distributing patented material.

9.5 Concluding remarks

The benefits to be gained by using selected and tested planting material have been shown to be considerable for the grapegrower. In this chapter, the source, testing and distribution of selected propagation material for grapegrowers has been described. Australian grapegrowers have clearly demonstrated their acceptance of the benefits to be gained through the use of improved planting material as indicated by the ever-increasing sale of cuttings and rootstocks by the various State organizations. The acceptance of Australian schemes is in part due to their voluntary nature and, perhaps, the lack of bureaucratic control.

Further Reading

Lee, T.H. (Ed.) (1986) Aspects of grapevine improvement in Australia. Proceedings of a seminar organized by the Australian Society of Viticulture and Oenology, Inc.

Becker, H. (1980) Clonal selection of grapevines in Germany. Eastern Grape Grower and Winery News 4 (2) and (3).

Becker, H. (1981) Geisenheimer Rebsorten und Klone. Bull Inst. für Rebenzuechtung and Rebenverderlung der Forschungsanstalt, Geisenheim. 18 pp.

Cirami, R.M. and Furkaliev, D.G. (1981) Report of a viticultural study tour to Yugoslavia and West Germany. Sth. Aust. Dept. Agric. Adelaide, 49 pp.

Pongrácz, D.P. (1978) Practical Viticulture. David Philip, Capetown, South Africa)

Other References

Antcliff, A.J. (1965) A comparison of cropping levels in the sultana. Vitis 5, 1-9.

Barlass, M., Skene, K.G.M., Woodham, R.C. and Krake, L.R. (1982) Regeneration of virus free grapevines using *in vitro* apical culture. Ann. Appl. Biol. 101, 291-5.

Basler, P. (1976) Klone and Klonselektion in Ostschweizer Weinbau. Wo stehen wir heute? Deutsche Weinbau 112, 252-6.

Becker, H. and Sievers, E. (1978) Leistungssteigerung durch Kloneselektion. Deutsche Weinbau 25.

Bioletti, F.T. (1926) Selection of planting stock for vineyards. Hilgardia 2, 1-23.

Cirami, R.M. (1984) The South Australian Vine Improvement Scheme. The South Australian Vine Improvement Committee Inc. & The South Australian Department of Agriculture.

Goheen, A.C. (1977) Virus and virus-like diseases of grapes. HortScience 12, 465-9.

Goheen, A.C., Luhn, C.F. and Hewitt, W.B. (1965) Inactivation of grapevine viruses 'in vitro'. Proceedings of the international conference on virus and vector on perennial hosts. Davis, California, pp. 255-65.

Hartmann, H.T. and Kester D.E. (1975) Plant Propagation Principles and Practices. Third Edition. Prentice-Hall, Inc; Englewood Cliffs, New Jersey.

Huglin, P. and Julliard, B. (1962) Résultats de la sélection clonale de la vigne en Alsace. Ann. Ameleor. Plantes 12, 123-50.

McCarthy, M.G., (1986) Vine clonal selection trials 1958-1985. Nuriootpa Research and Advisory Centre. Department of Agriculture. South Australia. Technical report No. 100.

McCarthy, M.G., Cirami, R.M. and Van Velsen, R.J. (1989) Virus thermotherapy effects on the performance of a 'Muscadelle' selection. Vitis, in press.

Rives, M. (1961) Bases génétique de la sélection clonale chez la vigne Ann. Ameleor. Plantes 337-48.

Rives, M. (1965) In. Proceedings International Conference on Virus and Vector on Perennial Hosts, with Special Reference to Vitis. University of California. September 1965, pp 1-9.

Sartorius, O. (1926) Zur Rebenselektion unter besonderer Berücksichtigung der Methodik und der Ziele aufgrund von 6-bis 14 jährigen Beobachtungen an einem Klon. Z. f. Pflanzenz. 11, 31-74.

Schöffling, H. and Rouday, L. (1978) Les principaux aspects de la sélection clonale dans la viticulture allemande. Revue suisse Vitic. Arboric. Hortic. 10, 135-42.

Todorov, I. and Dimitrov, B. (1980) Studies on chimeric plants of the grapevine (Vitis vinifera L., cultivar Bolgar) Vitis 19, 317-20.

Whiting, J.R. and Hardie, W.J. (1981) Yield and compositional differences between selections of grapevine cv. Cabernet Sauvignon. Amer. J. Enol. Vitic. 32, 212-8.

Woodham, R.C. and Alexander, D. McE (1966) Reproducible differences in yield between Sultana vines. Vitis 5, 257-64.

CHAPTER TEN

Vineyard Site Selection

P. R. DRY and R. E. SMART

European viticulture has long recognized the importance of site selection, having gone through centuries of trial and error evaluation. Since early Roman times viticulturists have been interested in the proper location of vineyards for producing the best grapes; the proverb *Bacchus amat colles* (Bacchus loves the hills) was the result of their experience. Sites prone to freezing or frost injury were avoided, as were those giving inadequate ripening in cold regions.

Since the first European settlement in Australia, most vineyard regions, and indeed vineyards, have been selected almost by chance. It is only since 1960 that scientific site selection has been employed; examples of this will follow relating mainly to winegrapes although many of the principles relate equally to table and drying grapes.

This chapter has drawn heavily on the booklet produced for the Vineyard Site Selection short course held at Roseworthy Agricultural College in December 1979 (Smart and Dry 1979).

10.1 Definitions

10.1.1 Macroclimate, mesoclimate and microclimate
The three levels of climate were defined by Smart (1984):

1. Macroclimate (or regional climate) describes the general climate pattern as may be determined from a central recording station. The appropriate scale is from tens to hundreds of kilometres.
2. Mesoclimate (or topoclimate or site climate) can vary from the general macroclimate due to differences in elevation, slope, aspect or distance from large bodies of water (tens of metres up to kilometres).
3. Microclimate (or canopy climate) is the climate within and immediately surrounding a plant canopy (millimetres to metres).

10.1.2 What is site selection?
Site selection is simply the choice of a vineyard site to optimize some aspect of vineyard performance. Typically this is in terms of projected yield, wine quality or costs of production, but there are many

important non-viticultural factors affecting the appropriateness of a vineyard site, e.g. reputation of the region, previous land-use, proximity to markets, labour and services. In Australia, where the majority of regions are not used for grapegrowing, site selection involves selection of 'new' regions and is thus macroclimate selection. In regions where vineyards are already established, site selection may also involve mesoclimatic evaluation.

The suitability of soils and macroclimate for grapegrowing has been discussed in detail in Chapters 3 and 4 respectively; this chapter will emphasize the importance of mesoclimatic factors in site selection.

10.1.3 Sources of mesoclimatic variation

Elevation
Mean temperature decreases by 0.5 to 0.6°C for every 100 metre increase in elevation; the so-called lapse rate. Also exposure to wind generally increases with elevation, especially on escarpments. Vineyards in the Barossa Hills experience lower growing season temperatures (approximately 1.5°C) than those on the valley floor and consequently ripen about three weeks later (Boehm 1970)—this is associated with an elevation difference of 200 m or more. Similarly, Shiraz vineyards in central Victoria with an elevation difference of 250 m are harvested 17 days apart (Dry 1984).

Proximity to large bodies of water
Large bodies of water store heat and reduce both diurnal and seasonal temperature range. For maximum effect the water body must be large. The vineyards near Australia's coastline experience this moderating influence, as also do those near Lake George (ACT) and the Tamar estuary (Tas.).

Slope and aspect
Vineyards on slopes have many advantages over those on flat land, particularly in cool climates. In the coolest regions of Europe grapegrowing may sometimes be successful only on sloping land. A slope facing the sun will intercept more solar radiation than flat land. Aspect is also important: a slope facing the sunny part of the sky will be warmer than one on the opposite side of the hill.

Generally, slopes are important only as far as radiation interception is concerned at high latitudes,

47° and higher, when temperatures are limiting and when the sky is mostly cloud-free. Most Australian regions do not satisfy the first two criteria.

Therefore, in Australia, slope and aspect are mainly important from the point-of-view of protection from frost and wind. Slopes can be warmer and have a longer frost-free period than flat land due to the downward flow of cold air. Differences in minimum temperature can be large: a gradient of 10°C was recorded by Spurling and Jennings (1956) over a horizontal distance of 1,500 m during frost conditions in the relatively flat Loxton Irrigation Area. Because of the lower energy gain from the morning sun, the intense night cooling in the lower terrains produces an after-effect which extends well into the late morning.

Aspect and adjacent topography affect the degree of exposure to wind. Wind not only affects grapevine physiology (Chapter 4) but also affects the heat budget of a site (10.4.2). This is particularly important in cool areas where cold winds may occur during sunny weather. Examples of areas in Australia where selection of the appropriate aspect for shelter from cold winds has been an important consideration include Pipers Brook (Tas.), Geelong, Macedon, Mornington Peninsula (Vic.) and Adelaide/Barossa Hills (SA).

Rainfall can also be affected by aspect and is generally higher on the windward side of hills. Where high rainfall during the growing season promotes fungal disease problems, rain-shadows may be deliberately chosen as a method of disease 'escape'.

Figure 10.1 shows the different temperature zones (mesoclimates) in a hypothetical location in the southern hemisphere. Becker (1977) studied the performance of Pinot Gris grapevines in southern Germany, planted on sites corresponding to (a) and (g) in Figure 10.1. The former had 14 per cent more heat days from March to October and 57 per cent more during the ripening period: flowering and ripening commenced nine and six days earlier respectively, the fruit had higher sugar and lower acidity, and the wine was better.

10.2 History of site selection in Australia

10.2.1 The first vineyards
Table 10.1 shows the decade of first plantings in major Australian viticultural regions (Smart and Dry 1979). Their location in most instances was historical accident—vineyards were usually planted to provide

Figure 10.1. Association of mesoclimates with topography in the southern hemisphere (from Jackson and Schuster 1987).

(a) *A warm site catching more sun owing to the lie of the land—it misses late spring and early autumn frosts, since the cold air will drain to low-lying areas.*

(b) *The advantages of (a) will be counteracted by the cold which comes with altitude.*

(c) *A cold site: although it may miss frosts in spring and autumn, it will accumulate much less heat in summer due to exposure to wind and a poor angle to sun.*

(d) *Very cold and the area most susceptible to frost—cold air from surrounding districts will drain into this area.*

(e) *Still frosty but less than (d). Some shelter from wind may be obtained by the hill behind.*

(f) *The trees densely planted at the base of the hill prevent cold air draining away and a potentially frost-free site has been lost.*

(g) *Less from than (e), but a prevailing cold wind and altitude may prevent the accumulation of warm air in summer.*

(h) *Cold, like (c) above.*

wine and fresh fruit for the local population. Gold mining, in particular, provided the stimulus for vineyard development in many cases, e.g. Mudgee (NSW), Avoca, Bendigo, Great Western, Ballarat and Rutherglen (Vic.).

There were few, if any, weather records available at that time, so what factors guided these early vignerons in their site selection? A study of the early accounts of Australian viticulture by Busby (1825), Kelly (1861), Belperroud (1859), Ward (1862) and de Castella (1891) reveals a good understanding of the important roles that soil type, aspect and topography play in European viticulture. However, the summer drought in most Australian regions required an essential change in their European-influenced attitudes. Whereas Busby (1825) recommended calcareous soils for winegrapes in preference to fertile clay soils, just a few years later Kelly (1861) wrote:

The vine in our drier climate requires soils more retentive

of moisture than in Europe . . . from ignorance of the great difference between climates of the northern and southern hemisphere, many vineyards planted according to the general practice of France or Germany on the sunny slopes of calcareous hills have proved failures, while many damp situations where there is a subsoil permeated by water from higher ground which would be considered unfit for the vine in Europe have proved excellent vineyard sites in Australia.

Hence the predominance of vineyards on the deep alluvial soils of the valleys (Swan, Clare, Barossa, Hunter, Yarra) and plains. Vineyards on more elevated sites on shallow soils were tried but abandoned due to a combination of water stress and wind, but Sutherland (1892) clearly recognized their potential for producing quality wines.

The importance of shelter from hot northerly and cold southerly winds was recognized at an early stage; another reason for the tendency to plant in the more sheltered valleys. Where natural shelter

Table 10.1. Decade of first plantings in major Australian regions in the 1800s[1]

			Decade			
1820s	1830s	1840s	1850s	1860s	1870s	1890s
Hunter Valley (NSW)	Southern Vales (SA)	Yarra Valley (Vic)	Rutherglen (Vic)	Great Western (Vic)	Corowa (NSW)	Mildura (Vic)
	Swan Valley (WA)	Geelong (Vic)		Langhorne Creek (SA)		Renmark (SA)
		Barossa Valley (SA)		Milawa (Vic)		Coonawarra (SA)
		Clare (SA)		Roma (Qld)		

[1] Adapted from Smart and Dry (1979)

was not provided, most early vineyards were protected by windbreaks planted at the time of vineyard establishment. In many parts of South Australia, the windbreaks of olives still remain even though the vineyards have long since gone.

10.2.2 Irrigation settlements

The first vineyards to be irrigated from the River Murray were planted in the 1890s; however, the major expansion in the Riverland (SA), Sunraysia (Vic., NSW) and Murrumbidgee (NSW) regions did not take place until after the world wars when the government instituted a policy of settling repatriated soldiers on the land (see Chapter 1). Site selection was governed more by the proximity of towns and water reticulation than any other factors. Most soil types were planted indiscriminately prior to the advent of CSIR (later the CSIRO) soil surveys (see Chapters 2 and 3).

Frost is a major problem, but more so for the evergreen citrus orchards than the winter-dormant vineyards. Spurling and Jennings (1956) delineated sites at Loxton with least frost risk.

Today the dried fruit industry is centred in the Sunraysia (Vic., NSW) and Riverland (SA) regions, due to a combination of high yields and good drying conditions in late summer and autumn. By comparison, grape drying was tried in the equally productive MIA (NSW), but later abandoned because the drying season was found to be shorter and less reliable. In the past, dried fruit has been an important product in dryland areas with dry, sunny autumns, e.g. Swan Valley (WA), Clare, Barossa, Southern Vales and Adelaide (SA). The variety Zante Currant was particularly popular because it ripens early (ensuring a long drying season) and the small berries dry easily without pre-treatment. However, low productivity and poor returns have caused the demise of this industry in these districts.

10.2.3 The 1960s to the 1980s

Consumption of wine per head of population in Australia almost doubled in the 1960s. Most of this increase comprised table wines rather than the more traditional fortified wines. To satisfy this increased demand new vineyards were planted, generally in regions with a long-established wine industry. Others however were planted in regions which had supported a thriving wine industry in the past but were virtually vine-free in the early 1960s (e.g. Yarra Valley); some were planted in regions with no previous history of commercial viticulture. With few

exceptions, it is likely that factors such as proximity to markets and reputation were more important in site selection than assessment of climate, soils and water resources.

In the rush to plant new vineyards the experience of the previous 150 years was often ignored: the Hunter Valley is just one of many examples. The early vineyards in the lower Hunter (and most of those vineyards that had survived to the 1960s) were generally planted on fertile sandy-loams and red loams of volcanic origin (see Chapters 2 and 3): these soils have good depth and drainage. Many of the vineyards established after 1960 were planted on shallow, acidic, poorly-drained clay soils with no provision for irrigation to counter the occasional summer drought. Most of these vineyards with an average yield of 1 to 3 tonnes/ha have since been removed. It is possible, however, that new developments in subsoil amelioration, e.g. soil slotting (Blackwell pers. comm.) may improve yields in such soil types.

In many cases there was an attempt to maximize water availability to new vineyards to improve yields and profitability. To this end, vineyards were established beyond what were regarded as the traditional boundaries for grapegrowing in regions such as the Barossa, Clare, Riverland (SA) and Hunter Valley (NSW). For example, new vineyards were established in the Barossa Hills: previous attempts here had usually failed due to lack of water, but modern developments in dam construction and drip irrigation systems allowed commercially viable grapegrowing, even on relatively shallow soils. Many of the new sites in the Hunter Valley (mainly the Upper Hunter) were chosen so that the vineyards could be irrigated from the Hunter River and its tributaries: a stark contrast to the non-irrigated vineyards of the traditional base in the lower Hunter.

The initial impetus for new vineyard development was fuelled by a demand for table wine, including bulk wine; hence the diversion of large quantities of Sultana and Gordo from drying to winemaking and the establishment of large plantings of traditional winegrapes in the Riverland, SA (near Waikerie, Morgan and Renmark) and Sunraysia (Vic., NSW). Subsequently, there was recognition that the best table wines from 'noble' varieties such as Cabernet Sauvignon and Riesling would be produced from sites that were cooler than the traditional hot areas. Such sites could be found at higher elevations, e.g. the Barossa Hills, Adelaide Hills (SA), the slopes of the Great Dividing Range in Victoria and NSW, or in more southerly locations, e.g. south-west of WA, Padthaway (SA), Drumborg, Mornington, Gippsland (Vic.), and Tasmania. At the same time, pressure of urban development was decreasing the availability of fruit from traditional areas, e.g. Swan Valley (WA), Southern Vales (SA). Similarly, suitable land was in short supply at Coonawarra (SA) and Great Western (Vic.). These factors also promoted the search for new vineyard sites (Smart 1977, Gladstones 1977, Smart and Dry 1979).

For many of these new areas, grapegrowing has been successful where it would have failed miserably a century ago; modern irrigation technology, land preparation and disease and pest control have made this possible. Nevertheless, some of the current problems of these new areas, e.g. wind, excess vigour and acid soils, were not foreseen when they were originally selected.

The following examples are representative of some of the developments in Australian viticulture since the early 1960s where there appears to have been a deliberate attempt to assess macro- and mesoclimatic suitability, soils, water resources and other factors. Other examples, not covered in this discussion, include Pipers Brook (Tas.), the environs of Canberra (ACT), the Mornington Peninsula and other areas close to Melbourne (Vic.).

South-west of Western Australia

Viticulture in WA has traditionally been centred on the Swan Valley because of its close proximity to Perth and suitability for the production of grapes for fortified wine and for table and drying. Olmo (1956) concluded that the cooler southern parts of the state were better suited to table wine production than the Swan Valley; in particular, he selected the Mt Barker—Frankland region.

Gladstones (1965, 1966) later extended Olmo's work, using a temperature basis modified to allow for the lower latitude of south-western Australia compared with Europe and California and also taking into account frost risk, ripening period, rain and hail risk, sunshine hours and susceptibility to high temperature extremes in middle and late summer. He suggested that the slightly warmer and sunnier Busselton—Margaret River area could have advantages over Mt Barker—Frankland for table wine production.

More recently, Gladstones (1987) has recommended further locations in the south-west including Manjimup-Pemberton, Nannup, Albany and Denmark, and also particular mesoclimates

within the established regions, e.g. the northern slopes of the Porongurup ranges near Mt Barker.

Padthaway-Keppoch (SA)

In the early 1960s, the Seppelt wine company was looking for new areas suitable for Riesling and Cabernet Sauvignon. Using Coonawarra as a standard, a search was conducted in the south-east of SA. The Padthaway—Keppoch area was found to have well-drained soils and plentiful supplies of underground water. The frost liability of the region was determined using temperature records from nearby meteorological stations (M.B. Spurling, pers. comm.); despite limitations, the frost risk was predicted to be lower than that for Coonawarra and this has subsequently proved correct. Experience has also shown that the early predictions of good yields and good wine quality were justified.

Drumborg

A lack of suitable land and inadequate water resources at Great Western (Vic.) led the Seppelt wine company to search for alternative sites suitable for early-maturing winegrapes. An area of well-drained fertile, volcanic soil (see Chapters 2 and 3) near the southern coast was planted in 1964. The low temperatures (Chapter 2; Heinze 1977) and low radiation during the growing season result in delayed flowering and ripening (Table 10.2), with inadequate ripening for all but the earliest varieties. The high number of raindays (almost one day in two from budburst to harvest) causes fungal disease problems. Although vine growth is slow for the first three to four years, subsequent excessive vegetative growth creates problems. Cold weather during flowering causes poor set (Heinze 1977).

Barossa Hills and Adelaide Hills (SA)

For the purposes of this discussion, the boundary between the Barossa Hills and the Adelaide Hills is a line between Springton and Mt Pleasant, even though Irvine (1986) has recently suggested that the Adelaide Hills should include the area historically known as the Barossa Hills.

Until the 1960s the vineyard area in the Barossa Hills was small compared to that on the valley floor and lower slopes. Recognition of the relationship between elevation and temperature and consequent effects on fruit composition and wine quality led to the establishment of vineyards comprising premium table wine varieties such as Riesling and Cabernet Sauvignon initially and Chardonnay and Pinot Noir later. Modern technology of dam construction,

Table 10.2. Phenology and composition of Riesling at Drumborg (Vic), Padthaway, Barossa, Riverland (SA) — average of five seasons[1]

Location	Budburst[2]	Date of: Flowering[3]	Harvest	Juice composition Sugar (°Be)	Acid (g/L)	pH
Drumborg	18 Sept	21 Dec	11 Apr	11.8	9.4	3.20
Padthaway	9 Sept	23 Nov	29 Mar	12.0	8.0	3.38
Barossa	9 Sept	23 Nov	12 Mar	11.5	8.0	3.38
Riverland	9 Sept	3 Nov	20 Feb	11.3	7.9	3.48

[1] 1971/72 to 1975/76   [2] 75% woolly bud   [3] 75% flowering   Adapted from Heinze (1977)

contour banking, water reticulation and drip irrigation made possible the establishment of vineyards on shallow soils susceptible to summer drought; such sites had been tried in the past but abandoned because of low yields.

The first vineyard was planted in 1961 at Pewsey Vale and further development has continued up to the mid-1980s. Many vineyards are found at 450 m elevation or higher. The grapevines were slow to establish on these sites due to a combination of water stress (not all vineyards were irrigated at first), wind and soil problems (acid soils are common: Dundon *et al.* 1984 reported surface soil pH ranging from 4.2 to 4.7). The importance of wind as a factor limiting productivity on these elevated and generally exposed sites has been recognized only recently (Ewart *et al.* 1987, Hamilton 1988, Dry *et al.* 1988).

Until the late 1970s there were few vineyards in the Adelaide Hills. Planting in the Piccadilly—Summerton area commenced in the late 1970s and this was followed by vineyard development at Mt Pleasant (550 m), Lenswood (550 to 580 m) and Gumeracha in the 1980s. Steep slopes have been planted for frost avoidance and the recent tendency to run rows up and down the slope (rather than following the contour as practised in the earlier vineyards) requires the use of sod culture to decrease erosion. In turn vines must be irrigated to avoid water stress, the risk being exacerbated by the presence of actively-growing herbage during the growing season. Winds from the south and south-east appear to significantly reduce fruitset.

10.3 Vineyard site selection in other countries

The three examples described below have delineated optimal areas for grapegrowing by mapping climatic

or soil indices and using an overlay approach (for further discussion of the overlay technique see Smart 1977). For each region it is necessary to use a limited number of critical yet quantifiable criteria.

10.3.1 British Columbia, Canada

An atlas based on climate and soil characteristics has been developed in British Columbia to assist in the identification of suitable sites for economical grape production in the Okanagan and Similkameen valleys (Anon. 1984, Vielvoye 1988a). Solar radiation, degree days (base 10°C) over the growing season and autumn freeze risk data were each grouped into four classes for the purpose of mapping. Similarly, 87 soil classifications were reduced to 14 groupings of soils with similar parent material: these 14 groupings were further reduced to four suitability classes based on limitations for viticulture. The final suitability maps were developed by overlaying all of the climatic and soil themes: five suitability classes were derived.

Land areas in Class I are the most desirable and the least restrictive for grape production: they have the highest number of growing season heat units (1390 degree days (base 10°C) or higher), a long frost-free season (0 to 10% autumn freeze risk), high solar radiation (4000 MJ/m² or higher from 1 April to 31 October) and desirable soil characteristics (well-drained, moderate to high available water-holding capacity, no restrictions to root growth, non-saline, etc.) and are capable of growing the widest range of grape varieties. Large areas of land as yet unplanted to vineyards or orchards were found in Class I.

10.3.2 Oregon, USA

Optimal areas in Oregon for *Vitis vinifera* varieties were delineated by the mapping and overlaying of four climatic indices: expected 20-year minimum temperatures, heat summation, Thornthwaite's potential evapotranspiration index and length of growing season (Aney 1974).

10.3.3 Rheingau, West Germany

A viticultural atlas for site selection in the Rheingau region was first published in 1967 and was followed by more detailed maps (Zakosek *et al.* 1972-1985, 1979). The maps include information on soil type with recommendations on rootstocks and soil amendments. In addition, three climatic zones are mapped: the warmest zones have a long vegetation period suitable for Riesling and similar varieties (Becker 1988).

10.4 Components of site selection

Some of the following aspects concerning vineyard sites are illustrated in Figures 10.2 to 10.5.

10.4.1 Water supply

The overriding importance of water supply in vineyard site selection in Australia has already been emphasized in this chapter. In the more arid regions, the need for an assured supply of water for irrigation is obvious. But it is also vital in many of the high rainfall districts. With few exceptions, Australian grapegrowing is practised in regions with low summer rainfall (Table 2.1) and Australian grapegrowing soils are generally unable to store enough of the winter rainfall for the full growing-season requirements; therefore water-stress occurs. In many instances this problem is exacerbated by shallow root zones; subsoils are not conducive to root growth because of poor aeration, acidity, physical strength, etc. (see Chapter 3). Even sites with an annual rainfall of 1,000 mm or more may require irrigation from mid-summer onwards, e.g. Adelaide Hills (SA), Margaret River (WA). Moreover, rainfall is often unreliable and reliance on average data in site selection is dangerous; for example, although the Hunter Valley (NSW) has a small surplus rainfall over estimated vineyard water use based on long-term averages (Table 2.1), the reality is that this region has experienced summer drought one year in three since the mid-1970s.

A reliable supply of water is so crucial to success that many would be unwilling to plant a vineyard in southern Australia without providing some form of irrigation. The water may come from rivers and streams, bores, wells or springs, dams or public supply. The amount of rainfall required for assured vine growth in most seasons varies from 150 mm per season in cool humid districts to 700 mm in hot arid districts. If rainfall and evaporation records are available the requirements can be roughly estimated by the difference between half of Class A Pan evaporation (an estimate of vineyard evapotranspiration) and rainfall during the growing season. A more precise water budget can be calculated by taking soil water storage capacity and run-off factors into consideration.

10.4.2 Climate

The macroclimatic requirements for grapegrowing are described in detail in Chapter 4. Once the desired macroclimate has been selected (often using the 'homoclime' approach—see 10.5), the climatic factors important in site selection may be modified by topography, aspect and elevation (10.1.3).

If a site has misty, foggy mornings, a westerly aspect may be chosen to increase radiation interception; on the other hand, in regions where afternoon cloud is common, an easterly aspect may be best.

The flow of cold air during radiation frost conditions is influenced by topography and there is a close correlation between frost hazard and contour height. Any obstruction of air-flow by fences, windbreaks, etc. will raise the frost hazard above them. It is often possible to avoid or remove obstructions on slopes, but hollows and closed valleys present a permanent hazard demanding special management practices or frost-prevention measures. In narrow valleys, vineyards must be kept at higher elevations above the valley floor than in broad valleys. Frost is particularly hazardous for a young vineyard because the developing shoots are closer to the ground where temperatures may be two or three degrees Celsius lower than at trellis height.

Lower night temperatures in valleys also lead to higher relative humidities. Since vineyards on valley floors are often vigorous and poorly ventilated, the risk of fungal diseases is greater.

Wind not only affects grapevine physiology directly (see Chapter 4) but also affects the heat budget of a site. For example, in northern Tasmania, a northerly aspect has the highest energy gain; however, strong cold winds from the north-west are frequent during sunny weather and consequently the more protected north-east to east-facing slopes are preferred for grapegrowing (N. Marquis, pers. comm.). Wind can limit the yield on coastal sites, e.g. Margaret River (WA), southern Victoria (Drumborg, Geelong, Mornington Peninsula,

Figure 10.2. A contour-planted vineyard on sloping ground at Great Western, Victoria. Vineyards on the flats in this region are prone to frost damage. (See Plate 8)

Figure 10.3. Excessive vegetative growth on a deep, fertile soil (Mornington Peninsula, Vic.)

Gippsland) and Tasmania, and those inland at higher elevations, e.g. Barossa Hills, Adelaide Hills (SA), Macedon (Vic.). In the latter region, the frequency of moderate to strong winds during the growing season is high; it is estimated that the stomates are at least partially closed (and thus photosynthesis is impaired) for an average of two to five days per week during the whole of the growing season (Dry and Smart 1986). It is ironic that both Kelly (1861) and Ward (1864) emphasized the importance of choosing vineyard sites in southern Victoria with protection from cold southerly winds, and that this advice is just being heeded 120 years later.

10.4.3 Soil
The potential of soils for grapegrowing, including site selection, and the criteria for good soils are described in detail in Section 3.5.

In hot, dry areas, the criteria for evaluating soils may be different to those in cool, wet areas. For example, in the former areas, good soil depth with a moderately high clay content may be important for water storage capacity. In cool, wet areas good drainage may be more important to avoid water-logging and to increase soil temperature, particularly in early spring.

Problems with acid soils, on the one hand, and excessive vigour, on the other, have been encountered in many new vineyards in high rainfall areas. The latter problem is often a consequence of vineyard establishment on deep, fertile, moist soils, e.g. the volcanic soils of Mornington Peninsula, south-west Victoria and north-east Tasmania. In a few cases, there has been a deliberate attempt to choose sites with less luxurious soils to decrease the vigour problem; an example is a Mornington Peninsula (Vic.)

vineyard that has been established on a duplex soil with a sandy loam A horizon (Anon. 1987).

Corrective measures on problem soils can be initially expensive (e.g. addition of gypsum, lime and other ameliorants, installation of drains, deep-ripping through calcrete and removal of stones) so judicious site selection is an important economic decision. However, soil amelioration before planting may be more cost-effective than installing and operating an irrigation system.

10.4.4 Disease and pests
Certain pests and diseases obviously can be avoided by planting grapevines in regions without those problems. For example, downy mildew (*Plasmopora viticola*) appears to be absent from Western Australia (McLean *et al.* 1984) and phylloxera is absent from most regions in Australia (Chapter 8). However, there is no guarantee that this situation will last indefinitely.

Regions with high growing season rainfall have been less preferred for grapegrowing in the past due to problems with fungal diseases, notably downy mildew. Some exceptions such as the Hunter Valley (NSW) were established prior to the introduction of downy mildew to Australia; downy mildew was first recorded in the Hunter Valley in 1921 (1.1.3).

The advent of systemic, eradicant fungicides, modern spray application technology and improved, resistant varieties has diminished this problem, and new vineyards have been established at Port Macquarie, Nowra (NSW) and Townsville (Qld). The likely incidence of downy mildew and botrytis bunch rot in new areas can be predicted from long-term climatic data (Dry 1979).

Figure 10.4. Sod culture is generally used in new vineyards in the Adelaide Hills, SA to decrease erosion. The row spacing in this case is 2.0 m.

Figure 10.5. Retention of native forest around vineyards at Margaret River, WA may provide protection from wind and an alternative food source for bird pests.

Downy mildew
A moderate to high incidence of downy mildew is expected where:

Rainfall (October to March) exceeds 200 mm
Rainfall (November) exceeds 40 mm
Raindays (October to March) exceed 40
Relative humidity (9 am, November) exceeds 60%

Botrytis bunch rot
A moderate to high incidence of botrytis bunch rot is expected where, in the harvest month:

Rainfall exceeds 60 mm
Raindays exceed 8
Relative humidity (9 am) exceeds 60%

Table 10.3 lists rainfall, raindays and relative humidity for a range of viticultural regions in Australia. Note the high potential disease risk in new regions such as Macedon, Heywood (Vic.), Launceston (Tas.) and Adelaide Hills (SA). Although the incidence of downy mildew in the Barossa Valley (SA) is generally low, epidemics can occur in some seasons, e.g. 1973/74.

10.4.5 Vegetation analysis
The local vegetation has been used as an indicator of site quality since the early days of Australian viticulture when particular *Eucalyptus* species were found to be associated with deep well-drained soils. Vegetation, whether native or introduced, reflects the integral effect of all of the physical, chemical and biotic factors of the environment (see 3.5.2).

Indicators of good sites for grapegrowing in eastern Australia include *Eucalpytus macrorhynca* (red stringy bark), *Eucalyptus obliqua* (messmate stringy bark), *Eucalyptus rubida* (candlebark) and *Eucalpytus viminalis* (manna gum); sites to be avoided have *Eucalyptus fasciculosa* (pink gum), *Eucalyptus leucoxylon*, *Eucalyptus ovata* (swamp gum) and *Eucalpytus sideroxylon* (red ironbark) (Due 1979). The performance of improved pastures of perennial grasses and other woody perennials—e.g. *Pinus radiata*, apple—can also provide useful information.

10.4.6 Other factors
The choice of a particular site may be determined as much by the following factors as those mentioned so far.

a. Cost of land

b. Proximity to skilled labour and services. In new regions there will often be a lack of skilled or available labour for vineyard establishment and operation, supplies (chemicals, spare parts, etc.) and technical expertise.

c. Proximity to markets

d. A demonstrated performance of grapevines in the area. If you buy a piece of Coonawarra, you buy a lot of prior advertising. In a completely new area, you have to start from scratch. Sometimes the reputation of the new area grows to such an extent that nearby 'old-fashioned' established areas may wish to take advantage of its newly acquired status. The recent 'growth' of the Adelaide Hills viticultural region is one example.

e. Community co-operation in such matters as irrigation, drainage, control of herbicide use on neighbouring land (particularly hormone herbicides) etc.

f. Birds. Birds can devastate isolated vineyards. In larger areas the problem is shared. Control of a bird problem is expensive.

Table 10.3. Rainfall, raindays and relative humidity data for some Australian regions[1]

Region	Station	Rainfall (mm)			Raindays		Relative Humidity(%)	
		Oct to Mar	Nov	Harvest month[2]	Oct to Mar	Harvest month	Nov	Harvest month
Hunter Valley	061260	479	72	101 (Feb)	70	12	53	66
Granite Belt	041175	482	60	66 (Mar)	71	10	58	71
Yarra Valley	086104	423	83	76 (Apr)	67	10	60	70
Macedon	088123	407	64	93 (Apr)	53	10	71	77
				83 (May)		16		88
Heywood	090048	297	62	76 (Apr)	73	12	72	80
Launceston	091104	305	53	62 (Apr)	59	11	63	79
				63 (May)		13		85
Barossa Valley	023321	164	27	20 (Mar)	38	5	47	55
1973/74		343	29	—	48	—	—	—
Adelaide Hills	023801	320	47	128 (Apr)	57	14	59	66
Margaret River	009574	198	40	34 (Mar)	42	6	60	70
				76 (Apr)		10		77

[1] Australian Bureau of Meteorology (1975)
[2] Harvest month indicated only for rainfall; also applies to raindays and relative humidity

10.5 The homoclime approach

Wines from European regions have been used as standards for the development of similar styles in Australia since the early 1800s, in particular Bordeaux, Burgundy, Champagne, Sherry and Port. In the absence of long-term climatic data the early settlers instinctively attempted to match the varieties from these regions with similar environments in Australia; for example, Kelly (1861) recommended Pedro Ximenes and Palomino in recognition of the similarity between areas near Adelaide (SA) and the south of Spain.

Existing Australian viticultural regions were compared with European regions on the basis of mean temperature of the warmest month (Prescott 1969). However, Smart (1977) was one of the first to attempt to find new locations in Australia with climates similar to those of the classic viticultural regions of Europe ('homoclimes') by using more than a single parameter: an overlay technique was employed in which climatic variables were matched in order, e.g. vintage period, maximum and minimum temperatures, spring maximum and minimum temperatures, growing-season solar radiation, rainfall, raindays and relative humidity. Such homoclime studies need to be approached systematically; climatic elements need to be matched in order of importance as it is unlikely that all will be perfectly matched. Also, there needs to be some allowance for climatic variabilities; if, for example, the 'vintage' years of Bordeaux are warmer, sunnier and drier than average in the autumn then values above average may be more appropriate. Further care needs to be taken when using overseas data to ensure that it matches local methods of measurements. For example, evaporation in France is commonly measured with a Piche evaporimeter, whereas a US Class A Pan evaporimeter is used in Australia.

Published studies employing the homoclime approach include Smart and Dry (1979), Pirie (1978), and Dry and Ewart (1986). Figure 10.6 shows the approximate location of homoclimes of the Champagne region of France in Australia. The reverse approach has also been used, i.e. the search for homoclimes of Australian regions in Europe as a guide to variety use, management practices and so on (Dry and Smart 1980, Helm and Cambourne 1987, Kirk 1987).

Table 10.4 presents climatic data for some new viticultural regions in Australia and for those regions in Europe that are often used as the standards in homoclime studies.

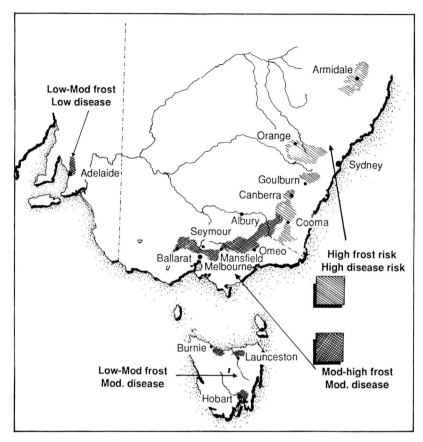

Figure 10.6. Approximate location of homoclimes of Reims, France in Australia and relative risk of frost and fungal disease (from Dry and Ewart 1986). Hatched areas have high frost and high disease risk, crosshatched areas have lower frost and disease risk.

10.6 Choice of grape variety

The choice of grape variety depends on macro- and mesoclimatic factors. For the hot inland regions the choices of varieties for table grapes, raisins and winegrapes are relatively straightforward (see Chapter 6); but for other regions, the matching of varieties to sites, particularly for the production of quality winegrapes, is more difficult. The past success of a particular variety in a macroclimatic zone is not necessarily a guide if the variety is planted away from its traditional sites and/or cultural practices are changed. For example, Shiraz has been successful in the lower Hunter for red table wine when grown on the traditional 'low vigour' sites, i.e. non-irrigated, low fertility soils of moderate depth; however, when grown on the 'high vigour' sites, i.e. irrigated, deep, fertile soils, inadequate ripening, poor wine colour and bunch rot are common in the absence of good canopy management.

The earliest recommendations based on actual performance of varieties on sites in Australia were published in the 1890s (de Castella 1891, Sutherland 1892). For example, Riesling was recommended for '. . .cool high slopes of fairly deep soil and subsoil of schist or decomposed granite' in South Australia (Sutherland 1892). Since that time, recommendations for the established areas have been published at regular intervals in Department of Agriculture journals and elsewhere; in these cases the recommendations have been based as much on market demand as on varietal performance. For example, Grenache ripens well on hot, dryland sites and it was widely planted in the 1930s when the wine export bounty put a premium on sugar concentration (Hankel and Hall 1979).

Choice of variety for new vineyard sites is a more difficult task. The ideal approach is to assess a range of varieties over several seasons; this has been done

Table 10.4. Climatic data for viticultural regions in Australia[1] and Europe[2]

Region	Station	Temperature		Rainfall (mm)		Raindays Oct-Mar	Rel. Humidity %	Bright Sunshine Oct-Mar h/day
		MJT[3] °C	MAR[4] °C	Annual	Oct-Mar			
Australia								
Margaret River	009574	20.4	7.6	1159	198	40	62	8.1
Padthaway	026089	20.4	11.4	526	178	54	65	8.2
Mornington	086079	19.8	9.7	696	316	50	71	(7.3)
Adelaide Hills	023801	19.5	10.9	1134	320	47	56	(8.3)
Yarra Valley	086050	19.4	11.0	911	404	70	63	7.4
Macedon	088036	18.5	12.8	753	294	43	64	(8.0)
Launceston	091123	17.2	10.3	788	305	53	65	7.3
Europe								
Bordeaux	Bordeaux	19.5	14.1	893	384	53	74	7.6
Burgundy	Dijon	19.1	17.7	737	398	68	67	7.8
Alsace	Strasbourg	19.1	18.5	610	390	79	71	6.6
Rheingau	Frankfurt	18.7	18.7	660	370	83	70	6.6
Champagne	Reims	18.3	16.3	596	322	76	73	(6.7)

( ) Denotes estimate
1. Australian Bureau of Meteorology (1975, a, b, 1977, 1981, 1985, 1987)
2. Muller (1982)
3. Mean January temperature and mean July temperature in southern and northern hemisphere respectively
4. Mean annual range — see text of Chapter 2 for explanation

in several Australian locations, e.g. Padthaway, Drumborg; in Washington State, USA (Nagel *et al.* 1972); and in British Columbia, Canada (Vielvoye 1988b). A less precise but more rapid approach is to plant varieties based on their performance in homoclimes in Australia and overseas (Gladstones 1977, Dry and Smart 1980).

Other factors which should be considered in variety choice include:

Recovery after frost
Some varieties recover better after spring frost than others because they have more fruitful secondary buds, e.g. Gamay.

Disease and pest resistance
Varieties with resistance to diseases and pests will be necessary in some locations. For example, Chambourcin has been successful at Port Macquarie (NSW) because it is resistant to downy mildew.

Poor set
Pinot Noir, Riesling, Traminer and Chardonnay set poorly at Margaret River whereas the Bordeaux

varieties, e.g. Cabernet Sauvignon and Sauvignon Blanc, have fewer problems (Gladstones 1987). A similar situation exists for other exposed, coastal sites in Australia.

Ability to ripen
In cool regions, the ability of a variety to reach an adequate sugar level is usually the most important criterion. There have been many attempts to correlate this ability with climatic indices, e.g. Prescott (1969), Gladstones (1977), Dry and Smart (1980), Jackson and Cherry (1988). In hot regions, the optimum conditions might exist in the crop for only a few days (Coombe 1987)—the increase in sugar and decrease in malate are more rapid than in cool regions. Also, once harvested, the fruit is more subject to oxidation. Therefore, the criteria for variety selection in hot regions may be very different from those in cool regions (see Chapter 6 for further discussion).

Overall, it is the market forces of supply and demand that are most likely to determine variety choice (Dry 1988); it has always been this way in Australia and perhaps always will be!

10.7 Concluding remarks

Early viticultural pioneers in Australia had little opportunity for site selection as it is now understood. The country was largely unexplored, climatic records were not available, vegetation and soils were unfamiliar, only a limited range of varieties was available and there were no fungicides, pesticides or herbicides. Over the two centuries of European settlement in Australia, all of these factors have changed for the better. Even the pattern of wine consumption has stabilized since the 1960s to a preference for table wines instead of fortified wines. Now the modern site selector has available well-mapped resources of climate, soils and vegetation.

One problem is now emerging which did not exist 200 years ago and that is the prospect of climatic change due to the so-called 'green-house effect', caused by an increasing concentration of certain gases (principally carbon dioxide) in the atmosphere (Boag *et al.* 1988). Temperature rises of 2-4°C over the next 50 years are suggested. In addition, in southern Australia, summers may be up to 50 per cent wetter and winters 20 per cent drier. This may mean that present sites selected for premium quality table wines may have an economic life measured only in decades.

Further Reading

Becker, N.J. (1985) Site selection for viticulture in cooler climates using local climatic information. Heatherbell, D.A. *et al* (eds.) Proc. Int. Symp. Cool Climate Vitic. Enol., 25-28 June 1984; Eugene, Or.; Oregon State Univ. Tech. Public. 7628, Corvallis, Or.: 20-34.

Smart, R.E. and Dry, P.R. (1979) Vineyard Site Selection. Roseworthy Agric. College, 1979.

Other references

Aney, W.W. (1974) Oregon climates exhibiting adaptive potential for vinifera Amer. J. Enol. Vitic. 25, 212-8.

Anon. (1984) Atlas of suitable grape growing locations in the Okanagan and Similkameen Valleys of British Columbia. Agriculture Canada and Assoc. British Columbia Grapegrowers, Kelowna, B.C., Canada, 141 pp.

Anon. (1987) Mornington Peninsula Regional Report, Aust. N.Z. Wine Industry J., 1, 4, 11-23.

Australian Bureau of Meteorology (1975a) Climatic Averages of Australia. Aust. Government Printing Service, Canberra.

Australian Bureau of Meteorology (1975b) Climatic Atlas of Australia. Map Set 3 (Evaporation), Map Set 4 (Sunshine). Bureau of Meteorology, Melbourne.

Australian Bureau of Meteorology (1977) Rainfall Statistics. Bureau of Meteorology, Melbourne.

Australian Bureau of Meteorology (1981) Climatic Averages (microfiche). Bureau of Meteorology, Melbourne.

Australian Bureau of Meteorology (1985) Evaporation (microfiche). Bureau of Meteorology, Melbourne.

Australian Bureau of Meteorology (1987) Climatic Average (microfiche). Bureau of Meteorology, Melbourne.

Australian Environment Council (1987) The greenhouse effect: current assessment of anticipated climate changes. September 1987. CSIRO Division of Atmospheric Research, Mordiallac, Vic.

Becker, H. (1988) Mapping of soils and climate in the Rheingau. In: Smart, *et al.* (eds). Proc. 2nd Int. Symp. Cool Climate Vitic. Oen., 11-15 January 1988; Auckland, N.Z. Soc. Vitic. Oen., pp.21-22.

Becker, N.J. (1977) Selection of vineyard sites in cool climates. Proc. 3rd Aust. Wine Ind. Tech. Conf., 9-11 August, 1977 Albury, NSW: Aust. Wine Res. Inst., pp. 25-30.

Belperroud, J. (1859) The vine; with instructions for its cultivation, for a period of six years; the treatment of the soil, and how to make wine from Victorian grapes. Geelong, 1859 (Reprinted by Casuarina Press 1979).

Boag, S., Tassie, L. and Hubick, H. (1988) The greenhouse effect: implications for the Australian grape and wine industry, Aust. N.Z. Wine Industry J., 3, 2, 30-36.

Boehm, E.W. (1970) Vine development and temperature in the Barossa, S.A. Experimental Record, South Aust. Dept. Agric. 5, 16-24.

Busby, J.A. (1825) A treatise on the culture of the vine and the art of making wine. Sydney, 1825. (Reprinted by The David Ell Press, 1979).

Coombe, B.G. (1987) Influence of temperature on composition and quality of grapes. Acta Horticulturae 206, 23-35.

de Castella, F. (1891) Handbook on Viticulture for Victoria. Melbourne, 1891.

Dry, P.R. (1979) Prediction of disease, pest and frost incidence. In: Smart, R.E. and Dry, P.R. (eds). Vineyard Site Selection. Roseworthy Agric. College, South Australia, 153 pp.

Dry, P.R. (1984) Recent advances in Australian viticulture. In: Lee, T.H. and Somers, T.C., (eds). Advances in Viticulture and Oenology for Economic Gain. Proc. 5th Aust. Wine Ind. Tech. Conf., 20 Nov - 1 Dec, 1983, Perth, W.A.; Aust. Wine Res. Inst. pp. 9-21.

Dry, P.R. (1988) Wanted: one crystal ball. In: Smart, *et al.* (eds). Proc. 2nd Int. Symp. Cool Climate Vitic. Oen., 11-15 January 1988; Auckland, N.Z. Soc. Vitic. Oen., p. 59.

Dry, P.R. and Ewart, A.J.W. (1986) Sites and variety — selection for premium grapes for Australian sparkling wine. In: Lee, T.H. and Lester, D.C. (eds) Production of sparkling wine by the 'methode champenoise'. Aust. Soc. Vitic. Oen., Adelaide, 25-40.

Dry, P.R., Reed, S. and Potter, G. (1988) The effect of wind on the performance of Cabernet Franc grapevines. Acta Horticulturae (in press).

Dry, P.R. and Smart, R.E. (1980) The need to rationalise winegrape variety use in Australia. Aust. Grapegrower & Winemaker, 196, 55-60.

Dry, P.R. and Smart, R.E. (1986) Wind may be limiting grapevine yield. Aust. Grapegrower & Winemaker 269, 17.

Due, G. (1979) The use of vegetation as a guide to site selection. In: Smart R.E. and Dry, P.R. (eds). Vineyard Site Selection. Roseworthy Agric. College, South Australia, pp.79-89.

Dundon, C.G., Smart, R.E., McCarthy, M.G. (1984) The effect of potassium fertilization on must and wine potassium levels of Shiraz grapevines. Amer. J. Enol. Vitic. 35, 200-5.

Ewart, A.J.W., Iland, P.G. and Sitters, J.H. (1987) The use of shelter in vineyards. Aust. Grapegrower & Winemaker 280, 19-22.

Gibbs, W.J. and Maher, J.V. (1967) Rainfall deciles as drought indicators. Australian Bureau of Meteorology, Bulletin No. 48.

Gladstones, J.S. (1965) The climate and soils of south-western Australia in relation to vine growing. J. Aust. Inst. Agric. Sci. 31, 275-88.

Gladstones, J.S. (1966) Soils and climate of the Margaret River-Busselton area: their suitability for wine grape production. Dept. of Agronomy, Univ. of W.A., Perth. Mimeo, 11 pp.

Gladstones, J.S. (1977) Temperature and Wine grape quality in European vineyards. Proc. 3rd Aust. Wine Ind. Tech. Conf., 9-11 August, 1977 Albury, NSW. Aust. Wine Res. Inst., pp. 7-11.

Gladstones, J.S. (1987) Why Manjimup? In: Winegrapes at Manjimup. Papers from a field day at Manjimup Res. Station, 27 Feb. 1987; W.A. Dept. Agric.

Hankel, V. and Hall, D. (1979) The eager oenographers. Ousback, A. (ed.) The Australian Wine Browser. The David Ell Press, Sydney; 59-71.

Halliday, J. (1985) The Australian Wine Compendium, Angus and Robertson, Sydney, Aust.

Hamilton, R.P. (1988) Wind effects on grapevines. In: Smart, et al. (eds). Proc. 2nd Int. Symp. Cool Climate Vitic. Oen., 11-15 January 1988; Auckland, N.Z. Soc. Vitic. Oen., pp. 65-8.

Heinze, R.A. (1977) Regional effects on vine development and composition. Proc. 3rd Aust. Wine Ind. Tech. Conf., 9-11 August, 1977 Albury, NSW: Aust. Wine Res. Inst., pp. 18-25.

Helm, K.F. and Cambourne, B. (1987) The Canberra district: a multi-climatic wine region. Aust. Grapegrower & Winemaker 280, 109.

Irvine, J. (1986) Move to define Adelaide Hills. Aust. Grapegrower & Winemaker 271, 16-18.

Jackson, D.I. and Cherry, N.J. (1988) Predictions of a district's grape-ripening capacity using a latitude-temperature index. Amer. J. Enol. Vitic. 39, 19-28.

Jackson, D.I. and Schuster, D. (1987) The production of grapes and wine in cool climates. Nelson Publishers, Melbourne.

Kelly, A.C. (1861) The Vine in Australia, Melbourne, 1861. (Reprinted by The David Ell Press, 1980.)

Kirk, J.T.O. (1987) Canberra District, Bordeaux and The Upper Rhine Valley: a climatic comparison. Aust. N.Z. Wine Ind. J. 2, 1, 21-4.

McLean, G.D., Magarey, P.A., Wachtel, M.F. and Dry, P.R. (1984) A climatic evaluation of the question: could grapevine downy mildew develop in Western Australia. In: Lee, T.H. and Somers, T.C., (eds). Advances in Viticulture and Oenology for Economic Gain. Proc. 5th Aust. Wine Ind. Tech. Conf., 29 Nov - 1 Dec, 1983, Perth, W.A.; Aust. Wine Res. Inst. pp. 249-60.

Muller, M.J. (1982) Selected climatic data for a global set of standard stations for vegetation science. Dr. W. Junk Publishers, Netherlands.

Nagel, C.W., Atallah, M., Carter, G.H. and Clore, W.J. (1972) Evaluation of wine grapes grown in Washington. Am. J. Enol. Vitic. 23, 14-7.

Olmo, H.P. (1956) A Survey of the Grape Industry of Western Australia. Vine Trust Resaerch Trust, Perth.

Pirie, A.J.G. (1978) Comparison of climates of selected Australian, French and Californian wine-producing areas. Aust. Grapegrower & Winemaker 172, 74-9.

Prescott (1969) The climatology of the vine (Vitis vinifera) 3. A comparison of France and Australia on the basis of the temperature of the warmest month. Trans. Roy. Soc. South Aust. 93, 7-16.

Smart, R.E. (1977) Climate and grapegrowing in Australia. Proc. 3rd Aust. Wine Ind. Tech. Conf., 9-11 August, 1977 Albury, NSW: Aust. Wine Res. Inst., pp. 12-18.

Smart, R.E. (1984) Canopy microclimates and effects on wine quality. In: Lee, T.H. and Somers, T.C., (eds). Advances in Viticulture and Oenology for Economic Gain. Proc. 5th Aust. Wine Ind. Tech. Conf., 29 Nov - 1 Dec, 1983, Perth, W.A.; Aust. Wine Res. Inst. pp. 113-32.

Spurling, M.B. and Jennings, J.P. (1956) Frost: occurrence, prediction, control. J. Agric. South Aust. Dept. Agric., August, 18-25, 53-54.

Sutherland, G. (1892) The South Australian Vinegrower's Manual; a practical guide to the art of viticulture in South Australia. Government Printer, Adelaide, 1892.

Vielvoye, J. (1988a) Development of a climate and soil atlas for vineyard site selection. In: Smart, et al. (eds). Proc. 2nd Int. Symp. Cool Climate Vitic. Oen., 11-15 January 1988; Auckland, N.Z. Soc. Vitic. Oen., pp. 9-12.

Vielvoye, J. (1988b) Rapid screening of winegrape cultivars. In: Smart, *et al.* (eds). Proc. 2nd Int. Symp. Cool Climate Vitic. Oen., 11-15 January 1988; Auckland, N.Z. Soc. Vitic. Oen., pp. 39-42.

Ward, E. (1862) The Vineyards and Orchards of South Australia — a descriptive tour of Ebenezer Ward in 1862. (Reprinted by Sullivans Cove 1979).

Ward, E. (1864) The Vineyards of Victoria as visited by Ebenezer Ward in 1864. (Reprinted by Sullivans Cove 1980).

Zakosek, H., Becker, H., Hoppmann, D. *et al.* (1972-1985) Weinbaustandortkarte Rheingau, 1:5000. Hess Landesamt fur Bodenforschung.

Zakosek, H. Becker, H. and Brandtner, E. (1979) Einfuhrung in die Weinbaustandortkarte Rheingau i. M. 1:5000; Geol. Jb. Hessen, 261-81.

INDEX

GRAPE VARIETIES